The Employer's Guide to the Law on Health, Safety and Welfare at Work

SAFETY
HEALTH &
WELFARE
at
WORK
Mitchell

EWAN MITCHELL

The Employer's Guide to the Law on Health, Safety and Welfare at Work

SECOND EDITION

Illustrations by Tobi

BUSINESS BOOKS
COMMUNICA - EUROPA

First published 1975
Second impression 1975
Third impression 1975
Fourth impression 1976
Fifth impression 1976
Second edition 1977
Second impression 1978

ISBN 0 220 66341 6

Printed and bound in England by
A. Wheaton & Co. Ltd, Exeter, Devon
for the publishers, Business Books Ltd,
24 Highbury Crescent, London N5.

For
Diane, Caroline, Linda and Jonathan Morris
with love

OTHER BOOKS BY EWAN MITCHELL

The Employer's Guide to the Law on Employment Protection and Sex and Race Discrimination

The Employer's and Personnel Manager's Handbook of Draft Letters of Employment Law

The Director's and Company Secretary's Handbook of Draft Legal Letters

The Director's and Company Secretary's Handbook of Draft Contract Letters

The Caterer's Lawyer and Hotelier's and Restaurateur's Legal Guide

The Business and Professional Man's Lawyer

The Retailer's Lawyer

The Sales Executive's Lawyer and Businessman's Guide to the Laws of Buying and Selling

The Merchandiser's Lawyer

The Lawyer and His World

Farming and the Law

You and the Law

All You Need to Know Anout the Law

Your Property and the Law and Investor's Legal Guide

The Businessman's Guide to Speech-making and to the Laws and Conduct of Meetings

The Director's Lawyer and Company Secretary's Legal Guide

Coping with Crime – the businessman's guide to dealing with stealing, spying, fraud, false trade descriptions and other common commercial crimes.

The Businessman's Guide to Letter-writing and to the Law on Letters

The Businessman's Legal Lexicon

The Business and Professional Man's Lawyer

The Employer's Lawyer

The Businessman's Guide to Travel

Businessman's Guide to Commercial Conduct and the Law

The Transport Manager's Lawyer and Transport Operator's Legal Guide

Contents

Preface

The Health and Safety at Work etc. Act, 1974 (which I shall generally refer to as 'the Act' or as 'the 1974 Act') superimposed a massive new legal structure on existing foundations. Because this book is primarily designed to explain the main features of the Act – and to explain them to executives and managers charged with the heavy burden of putting the Act into full effect – Book 1 is devoted to the new legislation, although frequent references are made to the old. Book 2 summarises existing rules which remain in force.

Precisely because both Books are designed for management in action, legal technicalities have been kept to a minimum. Students should find enough material in these pages to enable them to sail through some of their examinations without difficulty, but while any joy they receive from these pages will be welcome, it is incidental to the main purposes of both Books. Book 1 is a guide to the 1974 Act; Book 2, a condensation of existing law; an appendix provides the text of the Act itself; and the entire work – which now commences – is intended to breathe life and reality into an area of law which is now of supreme importance to everyone from the chairman and members of the board; through top, middle and lower management; and down to the newest and most raw employee. Duties and penalties alike are provided for all.

Preface

Introduction

The Health and Safety at Work etc. Act is the most important statute for industry and commerce. Unlike the Industrial Relations Act, it is here to stay. It affects companies, firms and individuals; employers and employees, from boardroom to shop floor; manufacturers, designers, importers, suppliers . . . occupiers, builders, erectors, installers. . . . Maximum penalties for breach of some of the rules: two years imprisonment and/or a fine, unlimited in amount.

Directors, Company Secretaries, secretaries, officers and managers are personally (and criminally) responsible if a breach of the Act occurs due to their neglect or with their consent or connivance. Any employee who fails to co-operate with safety arrangements is liable to prosecution. This Act provides mighty powers in the hope of reducing the death and carnage caused by industrial and commercial accidents.

Until the 1 April 1975, when the Act came into full force, provided that there was no provable breach of the Factories Act or of the Offices, Shops and Railway Premises Act – or of Regulations made under them – an accident could lead to a civil action for negligence but rarely to a criminal prosecution. Today, there is no need for the prosecution to wait for an accident – even a failure to provide adequate welfare facilities could result in a prosecution. And if the accused wishes to rely on the defence that it would not have been 'reasonably practicable' to make further provision, the burden of proof lies on him.

With such heavy burdens resting on the backs of management and labour alike, it is obviously vital that every level of commerce and industry should know the rules. The higher up the managerial ladder, the greater the responsibility, and the more likely it becomes that a court would say: 'It was your fault. You must personally pay the penalty.' No insurer will stand in the dock in your place.

This book provides a digest of the new Act, set in the context of existing law. The Factories Act; the Occupiers' Liability Act; the Employers' Liability (Defective Equipment) Act; the Offices, Shops and Railway Premises Act – all remain in full force and effect. So do the various Explosives Acts, the Mines and Quarries Act and the Alkali etc. Works Regulations Acts, together with all the common law (judge-made) rules on negligence and the liability of employers and occupiers to third parties. So the book includes an explanation of the old rules as they still apply – and of the court systems which enforce both civil and criminal liability.

Above all, though, the book explains the Act, as it operates in practice. The most important rules – including the overall duty to take such steps as are reasonably practicable for the safety, health and welfare of employees at work – are in Part 1 of the Act. So are the new responsibilities of those who design, manufacture, import or supply 'articles' and 'substances' for use at work.

What, then are *your* personal responsibilities – and what are the liabilities of the company? If you handle, store or transport goods, how far does the Act apply to you?

If you are prosecuted, how can you best defend yourself – personally or on behalf of your company? How can you avoid trouble by preparing for it in advance?

The Act requires every employer to prepare and, where necessary, revise a written statement of his general policy with respect to the health and safety at work of his employees and the organisation and arrangements for carrying out that policy. Have you 'brought the statement and any revision of it to the notice of all your employees'? How should this best be done if you are not to risk trouble with the law?

The Health and Safety Commission and Executive are in lively operation; the Act is enforced by an integrated inspectorate which covers every aspect of commerce and industry. So what precisely does the Act provide? What is the effect of an 'improvement notice' or of a 'prohibition notice' – and what are your rights of appeal?

This book sets out to answer these questions in as forthright and lucid a way as possible. This branch of the law is everyone's business – and no business (and no businessman) can avoid its effect. The Act itself is reproduced as an appendix.

The combination of explanation and text is designed as a permanent handbook – to be read at leisure and if not with pleasure then at least with understanding; and to be consulted in times of need – hence both the text and the Act are fully indexed.

The object of the exercise? To keep you and those over whose health and safety you preside out of trouble with the law; out of the dock; and certainly out of prison. I hope that you will use it in good health and with its help keep as far away as possible from the sort of desperate trouble which ignorance of this new statute would inevitably cause.

My thanks to His Honour Judge Brian Clapham, to Mr D. Sturman and to my wife for their help in the preparation of this book.

The Temple
London EC4
February 1975

Greville Janner, QC, MP
(EWAN MITCHELL)

Introduction to the Second Edition

On 1 October 1978 the new Regulations, Code and Guidance Notes on safety committees and representatives will come into full force. The second edition of this book contains all three – with full explanations and with the answers to most of the questions that employers will need to study and to know in order to comply with the law.

How can you best cope with the Regulations and co-operate with safety representatives? How should you set up or adapt or strengthen your safety committee or committees? Who should chair a committee – and how? This edition explains the practical implications of this vital new area of law.

The Health and Safety at Work Act itself has now been in force for over two years. We can see how it is operating in action – so the advice, guidance and explanations contained in the first edition could be tested . . . expanded in the light of experience . . . and amended where found wanting.

Before long, Magistrates' Courts will probably be able to impose fines of up to £1000 for non-compliance with the rules and the Lord Chancellor has already called for their firmer enforcement. This edition is designed to bring law and practice up to date and to help executives, managers, safety officers, safety representatives and members and chairmen of safety committees to comply with their obligations – and to save life and limb by keeping in line with the law.

The requirement that employers provide written safety statements is becoming increasingly important. These statements must not only set out safety 'policy' (which is simple) and 'organisation' (no problem – if you have one), but also the 'arrangements' designed to protect the individual employee. The main hazards likely to affect the individual must be identified and he must be told how best to guard against them. The Guidance Notes are included in this new edition, in full – so are many comments upon them.

So most of the first half of the book (which deals with the Health and Safety at Work Act) has been either rewritten or heavily amended. And I have taken the opportunity to update and to revise the second half, dealing with the general law on health and safety at work. I am very grateful to Mr Peter Wallington, MA(Cantab), LLB – a Fellow of my old and well-loved College, Trinity Hall, Cambridge – for combing through and amending this Part and my explanations of the new Act with such precise care.

My thanks also to my wife; and to my son, Daniel and to David Ellis (both undergraduates of Trinity Hall), for their help in the preparation and proof reading of this edition.

The Temple,
London EC4
July 1977

Greville Janner
(EWAN MITCHELL)

BOOK 1

THE HEALTH AND SAFETY AT WORK ETC. ACT, 1974

'SAY 'STRIKE'. . . "

Part One

Duties

Chapter 1

Your Guide to the Act

Before digesting a substantial meal, it helps to cast your eye over the menu. To take in a piece of major legislation, it is a great help to know roughly what is coming. So as an introduction to Book One, here is a quick guide to the main rules in the Act. Once you have surveyed the new legal countryside, the exploration can begin in earnest.

The first factory safety laws were introduced in the early 19th century. Since then, there have been plenty of rules and regulations, but the machinery and penalties for their enforcement were clearly defective.

The 1974 Act was devised to give teeth to the law and it does so in six main ways:

1 Increased penalties – up to maximum unlimited fines and two years' imprisonment.
2 Personal responsibility imposed on 'directors, managers and company secretaries'.
3 New administrative set up – Health and Safety Commission and Executive.
4 New enforcement powers (improvement and prohibition notices) given to inspectors.
5 The law extended to cover every employee 'at work' – and not merely those employed in factories, shops, offices, railway premises or mines.

6 Finally, duties imposed on employers to consult and work together with union representatives.

The rules not only cover more employers, but they may also be brought and kept up to date more and more easily through the use of statutory instruments. The Act is an 'enabling statute' and will bite with increasing effort as time goes on.

Penalties

Contravention of the rules may (in theory, at least) lead to the company being fined an unlimited amount. Any executive manager, secretary or other officer with whose *consent* or *connivance* – or due to whose *neglect* – the offence is committed, may also be fined an unlimited sum and/or (in some cases) imprisoned for up to two years – as may any employee who fails to take reasonable care for his own health and safety or for that of 'other persons who may be affected by his acts or omissions at work'; or who fails to co-operate in the carrying out of duties imposed by the Act.

Defences

1 No breach of the rules.
2 Not 'reasonably practicable' to comply – but the burden of proving this defence rests upon the accused.
3 That the offence was due to the fault of another person. A company may successfully place the blame on an executive who failed to carry out his proper instructions. (Tesco's were charged with an offence under the Trade Descriptions Act and were acquitted by the House of Lords by using this approach.)

Where the buck stops

Inevitably, with such massive penalties, there is a greater temptation for anyone charged with an offence to pass the buck down the line. It is vital for every level of management – from the Board to the shop floor – to have at least an outline of its duties, under the Act.

Information

Every employer must prepare a written statement of his safety policy and organisation and of the arrangements for carrying them into effect. These must be 'made available' to all employees – although there is no need to supply copies.

Consultation

Regulations requiring the setting up and operation of safety committees and the appointment of consultation with 'safety watchdogs' (appointed by recognised, independent trade unions), come into force on 1 October 1978. Wise employers are meeting this obligation before it arises – the Regulations, Code and Guidance Notes on safety committees and representatives are included as Appendix 2.

Duties

Section 2 requires every employer to ensure so far as is reasonably practicable, 'the health, safety and welfare at work of all his employees'. This duty includes:

1 Provision and maintenance of safe plant and systems of work.
2 Arrangements for ensuring safety in connection with the use, handling, storage and transport of articles and substances.
3 Provision of all necessary instruction, training and supervision.
4 Provision and maintenance of a safe place of work and working environment. The environment must also be 'adequate as regards facilities and arrangements for employees' welfare at work'.

Note:

1 These duties are very similar to those already imposed by the civil law. If an employee is injured at work and can show (for instance) that his injury was caused by a breach of any of the above duties, the employers may be liable to pay damages. The 1974 Act imposed a criminal liability.
2 The Act is not designed to create any new civil responsi-

bility – but it indirectly does so. If you or your company are convicted of failing to comply with a Section 2 duty, and if as a result of that failure someone has been injured, the prospects of your successfully defending an action for damages for negligence arising out of that failure are virtually nil. Insurers: please note.

3 The above are not absolute duties – if you can show that it was not 'reasonably practicable' to comply with them, you will be acquitted. But (I repeat) proof of this defence rests upon the accused.

4 The word 'welfare' is not defined by the Act – but is potentially very wide. And as the 'working environment' includes any 'place' of work – and 'place' includes, for example, transport – the sting in the tail of (4) above is likely to hurt.

Occupiers' liability

The Occupiers' Liability Act, 1957, requires all occupiers to exercise 'reasonable care' for the safety of all lawful visitors. The Act, in effect, introduces the same responsibility into the the criminal law. Employers are now bound to take proper care for the safety of all persons (including total strangers) who are affected by work carried out on premises under their control. This includes premises, e.g. launderettes, where no employees work.

Danger for suppliers

Anyone who (1) manufactures, (2) designs, (3) imports or (4) supplies any plant, machinery, component or 'substance' for use at work will be liable to the above penalties if he fails to carry out proper inspection, testing or examination or to supply adequate information, so as to avoid risk to the health or safety of those using the article or substance concerned.

Note:

1 As in the case of employers, suppliers etc. may be held liable even if no accident occurs.

2 You do not need to repeat tests, inspection or research carried out by others higher up the line.

3 If you obtain a written undertaking from your customer that he has or will take 'specific steps' sufficient to ensure, so far is reasonably practicable, that the article or substance is safe, then you will have a good defence if it turns out to be unsafe because he fails to comply with that undertaking.

The Commission

Its main tasks: assistance, encouragement, research, information and training; the creation of an advisory service; recommending new regulations to the Government; the setting up of enquiries, when appropriate; and the making of Codes of Practice.

The Executive

The Executive – in collaboration with local authorities – enforces the rules. The Act requires one, unified inspectorate covering the whole country and all industries. The object: to ensure unified standards and control.

The old remains

All the existing industrial safety statues and regulations remain in force, unless and until they are overtaken by new ones. The Factories Act; the Offices, Shops and Railway Premises Act; the Protection of Eyes Regulations; the Abrasive Wheels Regulations; . . . all apply now, as previously. But new rules can be made more swiftly where the old rules get out of date. Watch out for changes. Contravention carries the new penalties and factory inspectors may use the new prohibition and improvement notices in order to enforce the rules, old and new.

All employees 'at work'

While the old statutes and regulations remain confined to

those areas at which they are directed, e.g. factories or offices or shops or as the case may be, the 1974 Act protects all employees 'at work', wherever they may be. About 6 million employees (who work, for example, in hospitals, schools, parks, theatres, research laboratories and other places outside factories, offices, shops or railway premises) are brought under the wing of the law.

No private prosecution

The Factory Inspector decides the crucial question: To prosecute or not to prosecute? A private prosecution under the Act may only be brought with the consent of the Director of Public Prosecutions – which has never been given. The Inspector rules supreme. Do not fall out with him.

* * *

New penalties; new enforcement methods; new structure for supervision and enforcement . . . the codification of industrial safety law and its transfer into the law of crime . . . new personal liabilities on employer and employee . . . new required consultation with trade unions . . . and all this by agreement (in all but comparatively minor respects) between all major political parties. If the death and injury rate at work does not continue to drop with decent rapidity, that will not be the fault of Parliament.

Chapter 2

An Employer's Duties

Section 2: 'It shall be the duty of every employer to ensure, so far as is reasonably practicable, the health, safety and welfare at work of all his employees'. To feel its full impact, try saying: 'Anyone who after 1 April 1975, does not take such steps as are reasonably practicable to ensure the health, safety and welfare at work of each employee may be sentenced to an unlimited fine and/or to two years imprisonment'.

At common law, then, an employer must take reasonable care not to expose his employee to unnecessary risk. If he unnecessarily imperils the health or safety of an employee who suffers personal injury, loss or damage as a result, then the victim may sue for damages. Naturally, these will be paid by the insurers. The Employer's Liability (Compulsory Insurance) Act makes it a criminal offence not properly to insure in such circumstances.

However: the new rule is far more swingeing in effect for three reasons:

1 It imposes a criminal as opposed to a civil liability; the offender may be prosecuted even if no accident occurs. And no insurer will stand in his place in the dock – nor pay his company's fine.

2 As in a case of a breach of the Factories Act, Section 2 may be activated even though no accident has occurred;

but it applies not merely to factories but to every employee, wherever he happens to be working – hospitals, schools, hotels, theatres, parks. . . anywhere.

3 The Section includes: 'Welfare' (see Chapter 3).

The Section then breaks down the general rule into five sub-sections – but 'without prejudice to the generality of an employer's duty' as above. The following are examples of the application of the general principle:

1 An employer's duty extends, first, to: 'Provision and maintenance of plant and of systems of work that are, so far as is reasonably practicable, safe and without risk to health.

This duty almost matches that at common law. Every employer must provide and maintain in operation all necessary plant, materials and appliances – including equipment – if he fails to do so and as a result someone is injured, then he is negligent. 'Plant' includes materials and appliances used at work; it also covers safety equipment and clothing. And the term 'system of work' is extremely broad.

2 Every employer owes a duty to make arrangements 'for ensuring, so far as is reasonably practicable, safety and absence of risk to health in connection with the use, handling, storage and transport of articles and substances'.

Curiously, the word 'article' is not defined by the Act – although 'article for use at work' means plant designed for use or operation by people at work or any article for use as a component in any such plant. 'Substance' means 'any natural or artificial substance, whether in solid or liquid form or in the form of a gas or vapour'. It is not clear whether electricity is included – probably not.

In effect, when you use, handle, store or transport anything – article or substance, liquid or solid – you must do what you reasonably can to avoid risk resulting to health. There is not much difference between this duty and the common law duty to avoid negligence – but the definition is precise and the perils involved in breaking the rules are greater.

3 Next, a duty which exactly matches the law on negligence. An employer must provide 'such information, instruction, training and supervision as is necessary to ensure, in so far as is reasonably practicable, the safety of his employees at work'.

Information, instruction, training and supervision – all are vital to safety at work and required by Common Law. Failure to inform, instruct, train or supervise in safety matters may lead to criminal proceedings.

4 So far as is reasonably practicable, an employer must as regards any place of work under his control maintain it 'in a condition that is safe and without risk to health'.

The civil law requires the maintenance of a safe place of work. But the sub-section continues: The employer's duty extends to 'provision and maintenance of means of access to and egress from' the place of work 'that are safe and without such risks'. Here is a Factory Act rule extended to all other places of work.

The word 'place' is not defined. 'Premises' includes 'any place' and in particular:

1 Any vehicle, vessel, aircraft or hovercraft.
2 Any installation on land (including the foreshore and any other land covered by water); and off-shore installation; and other installation (whether under, over or floating on the sea-bed, or the sub-soil thereafter or resting on any other land covered with water or the sub-soil thereof).
3 Any tent or movable structure.

So 'place' is included in 'premises' – and premises includes vehicles. Now consider:

5 'The provision and maintenance of a working environment for . . . his employees which is so far as is reasonably safe, without risks to health, and adequate as regards facilities and arrangements for their welfare at work.'

Fail to provide a safe working environment and you break the criminal law. But here is a new peril. He who fails to provide 'adequate' facilities for the 'welfare at work' of employees – which, presumably, includes employees in the cabs of their vehicles (which, after all, are 'premises') may be in serious trouble. In the course of time, the Commission will, eventually, provide guidance on the meaning of these provisions. But it will be the courts which provide the definitions. Neither you nor your company should provide the test case.

Chapter 3

'Welfare' at Work – and the 1974 Act

Section 2(2)(e) of the Health and Safety at Work Act imposes a duty on all employers 'to provide and maintain a working environment . . . that is, so far as is reasonably practicable, safe, without risk to health, and adequate as regards facilities and arrangements for . . . welfare at work'. So you could be prosecuted for failing to provide adequate 'welfare' facilities. But what does the word 'welfare' mean?

The Act does not define 'welfare'. So we are thrown back to the ordinary, everyday, English meaning of the word. It covers those aspects of a person's employment that make his work pleasant . . . those amenities which ought to be provided in a normal, modern, decent business outfit.

The Health and Safety Commission have emphasised that 'welfare' in this Act refers to those aspects of industrial amenity covered in Acts like the Offices, Shops and Railway Premises Act: ventilation and sanitation; heat and light; a place to sit and (hopefully) if not a canteen then at least somewhere to eat.

'Welfare' (in this context at least) does not cover financial welfare – pensions and other fringe benefits, for instance. It deals with the conditions in which people are required to spend their working day or night.

As usual, the Act does not lay down any absolute requirements. Do that which is 'reasonably practicable' and you should have no worries on this score. Reasonable practicability, of course, will differ enormously as between different businesses.

Do you carry on your trade in one place . . . one building . . . one centre? Then you should be able to provide facilities which come up to modern standards. The days of the 'dark, Satanic mill' should be gone for ever.

Those whose employees work out of doors or away from base have far less opportunity to care for their bodily comforts.

* * *

We do not yet know (because no one has seen fit to become the test case) whether medical examination and care would qualify as 'welfare'.

Executives are frequently warned that the stress involved in their jobs is likely to cause heart attacks and nervous ailments. Precisely because they shoulder responsibilities in difficult circumstances, their prospects of becoming a burden on the community are considerably increased. Curiously, risk is often higher in lower or middle management than for those who have reached the top and are relaxed in their glory. But we all know people who are ill as a direct result of work situations or the effect of their working environments on their nervous or coronary systems.

In the past, this sort of misery has been accepted as part of the wretched inevitability of modern business life. How far, though, will the 1974 Act be used to extend the employer's duty?

Chapter 4

Medical Examinations – for Employees at Work

Part 2 of the Act, deals with the Employment Medical Advisory Service and, in the main, re-enacts *The Employment Medical Advisory Service Act, 1972.* Bringing together the various categories of doctors employed in industrial medicine; appointing employment medical advisers, with some of the powers of factory inspectors; and causing the medical services division of the Department of Employment to provide the nucleus and focus of the new efforts to develop and co-ordinate occupational medicine and to co-ordinate the work of regional medical consultants and practitioners in Government trainee centres.

The Secretary of State for Employment may delegate to the Health and Safety Commission or to some other body, the responsibility for maintaining the Employment Medical Advisory Service and we shall have to wait and see precisely how the arrangements are carried out, in the course of time and practice. Meanwhile, the greatest interest in the medical field lies in a more general question: As the new Act requires the 'health' of employees at work, will they be able to do so without arranging appropriate medical examinations? Among the powers set out in the third Schedule of the Act which may become the subject matter of health and safety regulations are the following:

Under paragraph 8: 'To require the making of arrangements for securing the health of persons at work or other persons including arrangements for medical examinations and health surveys'. All employers may soon be forced to consider how and when to arrange for medical examinations and tests for both existing and new employees. And any medical practitioner is liable to be consulted – now – by far-sighted employers, expecting the inevitable and in any event wanting to do their best for their employees, existing and future.

* * *

Here, then, is a checklist, covering the problems that medical testing will inevitably set for all employers on every side of industry. When you are considering health examinations, why not check this list with the doctor?

Existing employees

(a) Are all existing employees now medically tested? If not, should testing not be instituted forthwith – from shop floor to (especially) executive level?

(b) If testing is instituted and discloses any disability or defect in health, then:

1 Does employee require treatment? If so, who will provide it?

2 Should employee be transferred to other work – which will not subject (for example) his hearing to noise, his lungs to dust or his constitution to stress? Should alterations be made in his shift?

3 If the employer decides to keep the employee in the same employment, what safety measures should he prudently take in order to prevent any deterioration or (hopefully) to allow recovery? Are, for example, safety clothing, ear muffs or other equipment required?

4 If it is not possible to move the employee to other work, and if no feasible safety measures would be adequate, should the employee be dismissed – for the sake of his own health? Naturally, he would receive his notice or

pay in lieu, and could not claim damages for 'wrongful dismissal'. And the reason for the dismissal would be his health (as specified by the Trade Union and Labour Relations Act) – but would it, in all the circumstances of the case, be reasonable (and hence 'fair') to dismiss him?

5 If it is possible to transfer the employee to other work, would his status or his pay be affected adversely? If so, would he consent to a variation of his contract? If not, then such a move would amount to 'constructive dismissal' – which (under the Trade Union and Labour Relations Act, as amended by the Employment Protection Act) could well give rise to a claim for compensation, or even for reinstatement.

6 If the situation is explained to the employee, would he be prepared to resign – perhaps on receipt of a satisfactory golden handshake?

7 In the event of transfer or dismissal – or, of required further safety measures – will the employer encounter difficulty with trade unions? Are you acting in consultation with them – and if not, then why not?

8 Should the Factory Inspector be consulted or an Advisory Committee, under the aegis of the Health and Safety Commission? Or the Employment Medical Advisory Service?

9 If you have to make a claim under your employer's liability policy – perhaps because the disability arose wholly or in part as a result of the employee's working environment – have you informed your insurers? If not, then you may lose your cover'. And in any event, they should be consulted regarding further action.

10 If complicated questions of unfair dismissal or other litigation arise, have these been discussed with solicitors?

11 Are you under a duty to employ registered disabled people? Has a check been made of all regulations and Codes of Practice applicable – and will any of the (newly discovered) disabilities give rise to possible registration? If so, will the individuals concerned be prepared to register?

12 Once you know that an employee (registered or otherwise) suffers from a disablement or illness, have you

informed (and in the case of certain illnesses, should you inform) the employee's supervisors – including managers and/or foremen – of the disability or illness concerned?

13 What steps are and/or should be taken in respect of employees who return to work after being 'on the sick' or who are known to have been ill or to be undergoing treatment or who bring a doctor's certificate recommending a change of shift or of work? Before making a decision, should you arrange for a re-examination by the company's doctor?

14 What steps should be taken if one or more employees refuse to be medically examined?

15 Should arrangements be made for retesting or reassessment of the health of existing employees – including both those who have been found to be suffering from disablement or illness and those who were previously healthy?

New employees

(a) What steps should be taken to ensure that new employees have safe and healthy placements, having regard to their physical or mental states?

(b) Are you arranging any (or any adequate) medical examinations for new employees – with special reference to jobs known to involve risk – including risk of stress?

The future

Bearing in mind the heavy penalties that may be imposed not only on the company but also on directors, managers, officers and secretaries of the company with whose consent or connivance or as a result of whose neglect employees are submitted to risk to their health and having regard to the answers to the above questions: What changes are required in your system?

In preparing the written statement of the company's arrangements for the health, safety and welfare of employees at work – a copy of which must be 'made available' to all employees – have you included any necessary references to medical examination (or re-examination)? Have you considered inserting a clause in your employees' terms of service, requiring them to submit to medical examination at the management's request? (Always remember that you should explain what you are doing to the union first, if there is a recognised union.)

Chapter 5

Noxious and Offensive Substances

Pollution is a problem – and the Act takes a stab (literally) in the foul air'. One of the objects of the legislation is to 'control substances' from any prescribed premises – and the making of regulations 'prescribing' the premises is the responsibility of the Government.

Section 5: 'It shall be the duty of the person having control' of any prescribed premises 'to use the best practicable means for preventing the emission into the atmosphere from the premises of noxious or offensive substances and for rendering harmless and inoffensive such substances as may be so emitted'.

A 'substance' is defined in Section 53 as meaning 'any natural or artificial substance, whether in solid or liquid form or in the form of gas or vapour'. Electricity seems to be outside the definition.

Nuisance actions can only succeed if the aggrieved neighbours can show that they are suffering disturbance in their enjoyment of their property which goes beyond that which a normal, healthy and not unduly sensitive person would expect to have to endure. It is not enough merely to show that (for example) the smell emanating from the works next door is 'offensive'.

Even if the nuisance action succeeds, the victim will only

obtain an injunction – an order, that is, restraining any continuance of the offensive practice – and damages, probably assessed merely as a form of compensation or financial solace. The offender might be prosecuted under the Public Health Acts, but the penalties are relatively modest.

Section 5 of the 1974 Act imposes a much broader duty than that in any Public Health Act and one which should be easier to enforce. In addition to the old rules, comes a new, wide-ranging, criminal responsibility.

Suppose that it is alleged that you did not 'use the best practicable means' to control harmful emissions. The failure relied upon may include not merely a refusal or omission to provide suitable plant but also 'the manner in which the plant provided is used . . . and the supervision of any operation involving the emission of the substances' concerned. It is not enough to put in the best equipment reasonably practicable – you must also take whatever steps are necessary to ensure its proper use. As usual under the Act, if the prosecution proves that you did not provide equipment or use it properly, then if you wish to show that it was not reasonably practicable for you to have done more, the burden of proving lack of reasonable practicability will rest upon you.

'Any substance or a substance of any description prescribed . . . as noxious or offensive shall be a noxious or, as the case may be, offensive substance' for the purposes of this Section, 'whether or not it would be so apart from this sub-section', says the Act, in a peculiarly clumsy way.

A substance is 'noxious' or 'offensive' if the ordinary person would so describe it. But even if it would not be generally regarded as causing offence or harm – so that, for instance, a nuisance action might not succeed – if it comes within a category prescribed by regulations as being 'noxious' or 'offensive', then it shall be 'deemed to be such' – even if it would otherwise be regarded as harmless and inoffensive. Parliament rules supreme and may take industrial or commercial offence where none is intended.

Any reference in Section 5 'to a person having control of any premises', this Section concludes, 'is a reference to a person having control of the premises in connection with the carrying on by him of a trade, business or other undertaking – whether for profit or not. Any duty imposed on any such person by this Section shall extend only to matters within his control.'

Who has 'control' in your premises? Normally, it will be more than one 'person' – and a corporate person (that is, your company) will come within the definition, along with any human personality charged with the task of actual supervision of the premises, for the company or firm or individual proprietor and on its (or their or his) behalf.

Note: the section does not control pollution through the discharge onto land or into rivers, lakes or sea. It is aimed only at the air we breathe. In practice, it has been rarely invoked.

Chapter 6

Your Duties to Visitors, Contractors and Other Third Parties

Under the Health and Safety at Work Act, everyone 'at work' owes a duty to take care for the health and safety of everyone else. Section 2 imposes duties on employers in respect of their employees. And Section 3 provides: 'It shall be the duty of every employer to conduct his undertaking in such a way as to ensure, so far as is reasonably practicable, that persons not in his employment who may be affected thereby are not thereby exposed to risks to their health or safety'.

Note, first, that this section (like most of the rest in the Act) imposes no absolute obligation. You are not automatically liable if someone other than an employee is injured through your 'undertaking'. Provided that you have taken such steps as are 'reasonably practicable' to avoid risk, you are in the clear. Still – again, as in the case of all other sections – if you rely upon your 'reasonably practicable' steps, you must prove your point – if you can. More of that in a moment.

Second: Note that this Section covers all your visitors: contractors, sub-contractors, sightseers, representatives allowed in to sell or customers welcomed to buy. Neighbours, passers-by, members of the public – you must take reasonably practicable steps to see that your business activities cast no shadow over the lives of any of them.

How, in practice, should you comply with this wide-reaching obligation?

If there are specific dangers which await your visitors, point them out. At best, hand each visitor a paper indicating danger areas. Get a signature, if you can (so that you can prove your innocence, if you must).

If your visitor is a professional, who comes in the exercise of his calling (to quote from the Occupiers' Liability Act – which, of course, deals with your civil and not your criminal liabilities towards your guests), you do not have to teach him his job. You may reasonably expect him to guard against those dangers 'ordinarily incidental to his calling'.

However, you cannot clap your telescope to your blind eye and pretend that your visitors' unsafe practices are not your concern. You must use tact, of course, in trying to get (say) the electrician to tidy up his wiring or the builders to fix their scaffolding. If in doubt, try phoning their boss and saying that you are expecting a visit from your friendly factory inspector. He will thank you for the tip and your intervention may save lives.

(There are special problems about contractors and their employers, and about visitors to your social club, which are more fully covered in Chapter 7.)

You should take special care for children 'affected by your undertaking'. Do youngsters come onto your premises – perhaps with cleaners or on delivery trucks driven by their fathers? If so, are you satisfied that you are taking all reasonable precautions for their safety?

Beware, too, of children (or even of adults) who cross your land without your permission. You may regard them as 'trespassers', but recent court decisions suggest that you owe a 'humanitarian, if not a legal' obligation to take care for their safety. If you know or ought to know that these people are likely to come onto your premises, then you 'owe them a duty of care' – in criminal as well as in civil law.

Happily, the converse also applies. While you must take care for the safety of your visitors and their employees, they must all take reasonable care for your safety and that of your staff. After all, you and yours are affected by their 'undertaking'.

In civil law, each of us is bound to take reasonable care for the safety of his 'neighbour', which means: anyone whom he ought to realise would be likely to be affected by his negligent act, if he applied his mind to the situation. In criminal law, your 'neighbour' is not merely the man next door but also the person 'affected by your undertaking'.

Naturally, your real neighbours retain their original rights. For instance, if they are disturbed by noise, vibration, dust or smoke emanating from your premises, they may seek an injunction, claiming that the nuisance goes beyond that which they ought reasonably to be expected to put up with as 'part of the give and take of neighbourly life'. Wherever there is a question of reasonableness, the Court is left with problems of degree. The outcome of a case depends upon the evidence and the view taken of it by the Judge.

No one can guarantee the results of nuisance actions – except, of course, that these will be expensive for someone and quite possibly for everyone involved. The greater the dispute and the more voluminous and contradictory the evidence, the higher the costs.

Lawyers are bound to win cases, of course. But nuisance actions are especially expensive for anyone else involved, unless he happens to be blessed with legal aid.

Anyway, a nuisance action provides a civil remedy in the County Court or in the High Court. Thanks to the 1974 Act, the unfortunate, disturbed neighbour has a new remedy which he may not even have to use personally in order to get results. He may report the nuisance to the authorities; maintain that his health has been adversely affected; and, if he can, spark off a prosecution.

Prosecutions are much easier to defend where the accused has his documents in proper order. Can you prove not only that your premises were reasonably safe but that you took all reasonably practicable steps to warn your visitors of the dangers?

'In such cases as may be prescribed', Section 3 concludes, 'it shall be the duty of every employer and every self-employed person, in those prescribed circumstances and in the prescribed manner, to give to persons (not being his employees) who may be affected by the way in which he conducts his undertaking, the prescribed information about such aspects of the way in which he conducts his undertaking as might affect their health or safety'.

The Minister has not yet 'prescribed', but one day you may be forced to give information – perhaps to tell visitors or neighbours how to avoid or to minimise or avoid harmful effects of your operations.

Even a self-employed person (or someone who operates as a one-man firm) has a similar obligation to 'conduct his undertaking in such a way as to ensure, so far as is reasonably practicable, that he and other persons (not being his employees) who may be affected thereby are not thereby exposed to risks to their health and safety'. He must also look after himself. You may be convicted under Section 3 even though no one has been hurt as a result of your unlawful behaviour. But if an accident does occur, then you will almost certainly be liable for damages in a court action. Insurers be blessed.

Chapter 7

Your Premises

Under the 1974 Act, it is the duty of 'each person who has, to any extent, control of premises . . . to take such measures as it is reasonable for a person in his position to take to ensure, so far as is reasonably practicable, that the premises . . . and any plant or substance in the premises . . . or provided for use there, is or are safe and without risk to health'.

This provision, and the criminal liability it brings in its train, create interesting and novel problems in two areas which are in other respects unrelated: duties to employees of sub-contractors; and liabilities to employees and their families, on premises which you provide for sports or social activities.

First, sub-contractors. They must look after their own employees. Section 2 requires all employers to ensure, so far as is reasonably practicable, the health and safety at work of all their employees. The capacity or place where the employees are working is irrelevant.

So the primary responsibility for the safety, health and welfare of sub-contractors' servants rests upon their masters, the sub-contractors. They must (for instance) provide and maintain all necessary plant and systems of work; instruct, train and supervise; and accept initial responsibility for a satisfactory working environment.

On the other hand, *you* have twin duties in civil and

criminal law, for the men's safety. Under *The Occupiers' Liability Act, 1957,* you must take reasonable care to see that they are safe. The Act provides (as we have seen) that you are entitled to expect the sub-contractor's men to guard against those risks 'ordinarily incidental to their calling'. You do not have to teach them how to do their job safely or how to make proper use of the plant and equipment which they provide. But you must still see that the place is reasonably safe for them and if and in so far as you provide equipment or materials, you must be careful to ensure that those items are in proper condition.

Second, thanks to Section 4(2) of the Act, as you are in control of the premises and as those premises are non-domestic and are 'made available' to people who are not your employees, you must comply with other duties, imposed by Section 4. You must do whatever is 'reasonably practicable' to see that both the premises and any 'plant or substance in the premises . . . provided for use there . . . are safe and without risk to health'.

So the fact that the sub-contractor's men are not employed by you will free you from your responsibility as an employer but not as the 'controller of premises' where they work. In addition, while you may dispose of your civil liability by making the appropriate contractual arrangements, you cannot dispose of your obligations in criminal law, under the Act.

Equally, the sub-contractors may to some extent at least have control of part of your premises, and your employees may enter that part. Then they must take care under Section 4. And incidentally, if they are erecting or installing machinery or equipment, then they are under a criminal liability thanks to Section 6(3) of the Act, to ensure, so far as is reasonably practicable, 'that nothing about the way in which the article for use at work is erected or installed makes it unsafe or a risk to health when properly used'. They are entitled to presume that you will follow instructions which they have fully and properly given and that you will adequately instruct, train and supervise those of your employees who use the 'article' – but they must take special care with the erection or installation.

So much for sub-contractors. What of those who attend social or sporting functions on your field or in your club-house, or canteen?

The premises concerned are 'controlled' by you. In the case of sports activities, you will certainly provide 'equipment'. The premises are 'non-domestic'. You therefore owe a duty not only to your employees but to others who are not your employees, and that includes husbands, wives, children or other guests, as the case may be.

As occupier, then, of the sports or social premises, you must comply with the 'common duty of care' owed to your guests – and you must bear specially in mind that children will not take as much care of themselves as adults in similar circumstances. You will be liable to prosecution under Section 4 of the new Act if you fail to take adequate and reasonably practicable measures to protect your guests.

Section 4 also imposes duties in relation to non-employees, where non-domestic premises are made available to them as a place of work or as a place where they may use plant or substances provided for their use there. This does not cover the private houses of those who do work for you at home. But it does include premises like launderettes – or even some funfair stalls.

'It shall be the duty of each person who has to any extent, control of such premises . . . or of any plant or substance in such premises to take such measures as it is reasonable to take to ensure – in so far as is reasonably practicable – that the premises, or means of access thereto or egress therefrom available for use by persons using the premises, and any plant or substance in the premises . . . or provided for use there, is or are safe and without risk to health.' Fail to understand this hideous sentence and you may suffer a sentence from the Court. In brief, if you control a launderette or other similar premises, you must take such steps as are 'reasonably practicable' to protect users from harm.

Next: who has 'control'? The section continues: 'Where a person has, by virtue of any contract or tenancy, an obligation of any extent in relation to –

(a) the maintenance or repair of any premises to which this Section applies or any means of access thereto or egress therefrom; or

(b) the safety of or the absence of risks to health arising from plant or substances in any such premises;

that person shall be treated, for the purposes of the above, as being a person who has control over matters to which his obligation extends.'

Landlords, please note. Those who have control of premises 'in connection with the carrying on . . . of a trade, business or any other undertaking (whether for profit or not)' have liabilities in criminal as well as in civil law. And not just landlords. Maintenance engineers, sub-contractors and others whom you employ are – as a result of their civil, contractual liabilities – also under a criminal liability.

Chapter 8

Duties of Designers, Manufacturers, Importers, Suppliers, Erectors and Installers

The Health and Safety at Work Act places for the first time a criminal responsibility on designers, manufacturers, importers, suppliers, erectors and installers for equipment, plant and machinery and on manufacturers, importers and suppliers of 'substances for use at work'. Any person in any of these categories who unnecessarily causes hazards to others as a result of his work is liable to be prosecuted.

Section 6(1) lays down a duty for 'any person who designs, manufactures, imports or supplies any article for use at work'. 'Article' is not defined – but 'article for use at work' means 'any plant designed for use or operation (whether exclusively or not) by persons at work, and any article designed for use as a component in any such plant' (Section 53). Plant, machinery, components . . .

Designers and manufacturers must take care and if they fail to do so, they may be prosecuted within the UK. But where the design or manufacture is carried out abroad, our Courts have no jurisdiction – so the burden is placed on the importer. If you buy from abroad either directly or through an agent then you are covered. If you purchase imported supplies through a 'principal' – even if he happens to call himself an 'import agent' – then he bears the responsibility. Whether the importing is done by the other party on its own behalf or acting for you (and hence is your 'agent') is a question of fact.

The word 'supplier' is widely defined (by Section 53). 'Supply', it reads, 'where the reference is to supplying articles or substances, means supplying them by way of sale, lease, hire or hire purchase, whether as principal or agent for another'. So there is no form of supply which is excluded.

The duty of designers, manufacturers, importers or suppliers falls under three heads. They must:

'(a) Ensure, in so far as is reasonably practicable, that the article is so designed and constructed as to be safe and without risks to health when properly used;

'(b) Carry out or arrange for the carrying out of such testing and examination as may be necessary for the performance of the duty imposed on him by the preceding paragraph; and

'(c) Take such steps as are necessary to secure that there will be available in connection with the use of the article at work adequate information about the use for which it is designed and has been tested, and about any conditions necessary to ensure that, when put to that use, it will be safe and without risk to health.'

So if you design, manufacture, import or supply then you must test, examine, supply information and take ordinary steps to protect those who use your article – at work. If the article is primarily designed for use at home, the fact that it may be used at work is irrelevant. The Section is aimed at the protection of work people.

In addition, designers, manufacturers, importers and suppliers must either carry out 'necessary research' themselves or arrange for it to be carried out so as to 'eliminate or minimize any risks to health or safety to which the design or article may give rise'.

Those who erect or install equipment in work-places must 'in so far as is reasonable practicable' ensure that nothing about the way in which the erection or installation is carried out makes that equipment 'unsafe or a risk to health when properly used'.

Almost identical provisions apply to those who manufacture, import or supply 'any substance for use at work'. 'Substance' is defined as meaning 'any natural or artificial substance, whether in solid or liquid form or in the form of a gas or vapour' – which would appear to include about everything except (apparently) electricity.

How can you avoid your responsibilities?

First, Section 6(6) provides that you do not need to repeat any testing, examination or research which has been carried out by anyone else 'in so far as it is reasonable for you to rely on the results'. If you intend to rely on someone else's testing or examination or research, you should get details onto paper – preferably in the form of an undertaking.

Another form of 'written undertaking' is required where you wish to rely on your customer having taken 'specified steps sufficient to ensure, in so far as is reasonably practicable, that the article will be safe and without risk to health when properly used'. If you manufacture or design to someone else's specification, get your documentation right.

As usual, then, the law lays down a heavy burden which careful documentation can ease. But Section 6 makes life exceedingly perilous for those who provide articles or substances which others will use at work.

Chapter 9

When an Employee Breaks the Safety Rules

You must supply your employees with all necessary plant, materials and appliances – including safety equipment. Where appropriate, you must ensure that your equipment and machinery is properly guarded and that the employee is not exposed to unnecessary risk.

If your employee fails to take precautions required by you, then he may be prosecuted under the Health and Safety at Work Act, for failing to take such steps as are 'reasonably practicable' to ensure his own safety. But even so, you may be responsible for his breach of the rules – unless you can prove that you have (to use an expression frequent in civil cases) 'used all reasonable persuasion and propaganda' to induce your employee to follow the safety rules.

In addition to your civil liability if the employee is injured, the Act has laid a criminal responsibility on you to avoid 'consent', 'connivance' or 'neglect', which causes a breach of the Act. So – for the safety of your company, its employees and yourself – you must 'persuade and propagandise' your employees to take proper care for themselves.

A man may prefer not to use guards or equipment because these slow down his work or reduce his earnings; because he finds the equipment uncomfortable or the guard clumsy; or out of sheer laziness. Whatever the reason, here is a suggested procedure, designed to put the maximum, fair pressure on your employees to look after their own safety and so to avoid civil or even criminal liability which may otherwise fall on the company, on you or on him.

1 Include a term in all employees' contracts of service (confirmed and set out in the written particulars required by *The Contracts of Employment Act, 1972,* as amended) that he will comply with the company's health and safety rules. You may add: 'Failure to do so may lead to dismissal'. This term is implied into contracts in any event, but making the term express avoids trouble; enables you to point to it; and may stand you in good stead if eventually you decide to dismiss for breach of the rules (see later).

2 Check that your system of working, the equipment and machinery concerned and all safety clothing etc. are adequate and in satisfactory condition.

3 Train, instruct and supervise the employee and all who work with him in the use of the system and/or of the equipment.

4 Consult employees, their safety representatives, their safety committees or other organisations, to ensure that you obtain their opinions; involve them in any safety decision making process; and ensure that they fully understand the arrangements made for their safety and that they approve of those arrangements. Seek their help in the enforcement of the rules and in remonstrating with non-complying employees.

If a breach of rules occurs:

1 Speak personally to the erring employee; emphasise the importance of compliance with the rules, for his own sake; if danger may be caused to others, say so; and warn him of the consequences of any repetition, both in terms of safety and discipline.

2 Refer the employee to Section 7 of the Act, which requires the employee to take proper care for his own safety and that

of his colleagues – and (if appropriate) to Section 8, which forbids interference with safety equipment and the like. Warn him of the potential criminal penalties. But avoid threatening that action is likely, when it is not.

3 If the initial warning fails, discuss the breach with the employee's shop steward or other representative. Ask him to lean on his colleagues. Trade unions should be harnessed on your side of the safety wheel.

4 Either at this stage or (certainly) if there is another repetition, deliver a written warning. If possible, get the employee to sign a carbon, a receipt or other acknowledgement. If he refuses to do so, make a note on the file. Ensure that the employee's records carry notes of warnings so far – and in the future.

5 If danger (actual or potential) is caused to fellow employees, emphasise the unfairness to others of the conduct complained of.

6 If dangerous behaviour persists, consider dismissal. Factors to be taken into account include:

a the nature and extent of the danger, to the employee himself and to others;

b the effect of dismissal on good industrial relations;

c the employee's length of service, degree of responsibility and general conduct;

d whether the conduct is common – so that picking on the employee for dismissal might be regarded as victimisation; and

e all the other circumstances of the case which might make dismissal 'unfair', so as to give the employee a claim which could reach up to five figures.

7 Collate documentation – including records and efforts to persuade employee to take care; and discussions with safety representatives, trade unions and/or fellow workers.

8 Deliver second written warning, stating:

(i) if applicable, that further non-compliance will leave you with no alternative other than to dismiss. Remember: the Code of Industrial Relations Practice

requires you to give at least one written warning of intended dismissal, where reasonably practicable. In any event

(ii) drawing attention to previous warnings; to the Act and rules thereunder; stating that no responsibility can be accepted by the company in the event of the risk giving rise to injury, loss or damage to the employee. (This disclaimer may be of help in a civil action, but it will not necessarily free you from liability under the Act. It will, in any event, clearly show the employee the importance you place on his compliance with the law.)

9 Consider whether equipment or system of work requires redesign, either to remove employee's objections to following the rules or to make it impossible for the machine or equipment to be used in the dangerous manner concerned.

* * *

You will not necessarily wish to use all the above steps or to do so in the order suggested. Adapt them as best suited to your business and circumstances. But follow those rules and it can hardly be said that you did not take 'reasonable steps' to influence your employee.

In the event of an accident, you will probably avoid liability – the employee's case for his own responsibility would be 100 per cent. He knew the dangers; you can prove your case; and the responsibility would be his.

Equally; if you are prosecuted, your defences would be well prepared.

Even more important, by bringing in union representatives at an early stage, and by doing so on your side, your approach will be in accordance with the best industrial relations practice. You will be bringing the unions onto your side of the bargaining table, for the protection of their members. And that which you can successfully achieve in relation to safety should stand you in good stead in other respects, as well.

If your shop stewards are not prepared to join you in the business of saving the lives and limbs of their members, then your lines of communication have gone sadly astray. And your training programme needs urgent overhaul.

Chapter 10

Statements of Policy, Organisation and Arrangements

By now, most employers have put out what they choose to call 'policy statements' on health and safety. In so far as they go, these statements are usually as worthy as they are worthless. They set out 'policy' and (in most cases) 'organisation' – but they do not detail the arrangements for putting that policy and organisation into useful effect. Employers who do not supply details of 'arrangements' are themselves liable to prosecution.

Section 2(3) of the Health and Safety at Work Act reads: 'Except in such cases as may be prescribed' – tiny firms with less than five employees – 'it shall be the duty of every employer to prepare and as often as may be necessary to revise a written statement'. This must be a statement 'of his general policy with respect to the health and safety at work of his employees and of the organisation and arrangements for the time being in force for carrying out that policy'.

'Policy', 'organisation' and 'arrangements'.

'Policy' is easy – 'the company gives paramount importance to the health and safety of employees at work' – or (as one great retail outfit puts it, with typical skill): 'We are pleased to have this opportunity of restating what has always been the company's policy – of giving paramount importance to the health and safety of employees at work. . .'.

*The Guidance Note is set out in full, as Appendix 3.

'Organisation' is no problem – assuming that you have one. Who is in charge of safety co-ordination? Do you have a safety officer, safety representatives, safety committees? Work out your organisation and put it onto paper.

'Arrangements' are more complicated. According to the Guidance Notes (which, of course, do not have the legal force of a Regulation nor the weight of a Code), you should identify the main hazards applicable to a particular job and explain how the employee can avoid injury or accident resulting from those hazards. This means applying your mind to the specific risks involved in each job and explaining how those risks may be minimised or avoided. And that is a process which few employers have carried out. If you are a defaulter, now is the time to act.

Naturally, the safety statement is not intended to achieve book length. Like the proverbial woman's dress, it should be long enough to cover the essential points but short enough to be interesting.

The Section provides that the employer must 'bring the statement and any revision of it to the notice of all his employees'. You are not required to supply a copy to each person – but it is certainly wise to do so. You may, if you wish, put the statement on notice boards – but you are better off to give each employee a copy and to obtain a receipt, so as to prove that he really did get it.

The statement may be contained in several documents. For instance, you may find that one statement of policy and organisation is adequate for all employees. Alternatively, a variety of job functions within your set up requires the provision of separate statements of 'arrangements' for each group or place or job within your establishment or undertaking. There is no reason why you should not divide up the information and supply it in whatever way seems most sensible – and most likely to be noted and absorbed by the recipients.

When you next receive a visit from your factory inspector, do not be surprised if he immediately asks for your health and safety statement. If you have none, you are in breach of the Act. If the statement is defective, you are equally liable to prosecution. And if your statement is full and adequate and lays down safety arrangements, you had better adhere to them – otherwise you will be condemned on the fact of your own document.

Section 2(3) has so far been gingerly enforced. But do not expect this kindly attitude to continue – there are still far too many accidents for that.

Chapter 11

Codes, Regulations and Guidance

Parliament rules directly through statutes – such as the Health and Safety at Work Act, the Factories Act, the Trade Union and Labour Relations Act and the Employment Protection Act. But each of these is typical of an 'enabling statute' – it enables the Government or its appointees (such as the Health and Safety Commission or the Advisory, Conciliation and Arbitration Service) to produce related rules which 'regulate' the activities of the people concerned. Parliament, then, delegates subsidiary legislation to others because Parliament laid down the ground rules and the overall policies but will leave to others the more detailed regulation of industrial, commercial and general society.

It is vital, though, to understand the effective difference in law between statutes and the regulations made under them – and mere 'Codes' or 'Guidance', both of which are achieving new popularity under the latest employment legislation.

* * *

The difference

Statutes and regulations are binding and have equal effect in law, e.g. the penalties are the same for a breach of the 1974

Act itself as they are for a breach of the Protection of Eyes Regulations, the Abrasive Wheels Regulations or any other Regulations made pursuant to powers contained in that Act. It is no answer, then, to say: 'It was *only* in the Regulations . . . and not in the Act. . .'.

Codes

Failure to comply with the terms of a Code is neither a breach of the civil law (which can lead to a claim for damages) nor of the criminal law (causing a prosecution). But – and this applies to every Code – a breach may (and inevitably, will) be used in evidence in any proceedings, civil or criminal, to which it is relevant.

For instance:

1 *The Highway Code* came first. Ignore its terms and you may be prosecuted under the Road Traffic Acts and/or sued for damages by any person who has suffered loss as a result of an accident caused (or contributed to) by that breach.

2 *The Code of Industrial Relations Practice* (slowly being overtaken by later Codes put out by ACAS), an employer must, where reasonably practicable, give at least one written warning of intended dismissal. Fail to do so (especially for good reason) and you may still win your case – but no warning usually means poor prospects before the Tribunal. Conversely, any number of written warnings may be given unfairly – you may have an excellent procedure, unreasonably used – but follow the Code and you will probably win.

3 *ACAS Codes* – in draft or in prospect – under the Employment Protection Act include those on: Disclosure of information to independent trade unions during the course of collective bargaining; time off for trade union officials for industrial relations duties; recognition; disciplinary procedures; and collective bargaining. None will have the force of law – but in several cases, e.g. disclosure and trade union time off, the law will not operate until the Codes are approved.

Health and Safety – Committees and Representatives

The Health and Safety Commission has prepared regulations, Code and Guidance Notes, dealing with safety committees and representatives. They will come into force on 1 October 1978. Regulations (when implemented) will have the power of law; the Code will explain how the Code is to be applied in practice; and the Guidance Notes provide further help to those charged with implementation of the rules. Part 3 of this book, and Part B of the Questions and Answers, explain in detail how the new rules work in practice.

In addition, current Health and Safety Codes (noise; lead; and vinyl chloride) are likely before long to be incorporated into Regulations, i.e. pressed upwards in the scale of enforceability and power.

* * *

So remember: treat Regulations as if they were laws – they have the same power in effect. Do not regard a Code as mere guidance – it will be brought into play. And as for 'Guidance' – well, good advice should always be welcome and followed where sensibly possible.

Finally: By the time you read this chapter, the ACAS Code of Practice on Time Off for Trade Union Duties may already be in force – which will bring this area of new law into effect. Employees will still be entitled to unpaid time off for union activities – but we shall then know the basis upon which they are entitled to time off on a paid basis for industrial relations reasons.

Chapter 12

Ignorance of the New Law – Is it an Excuse?

There is all the difference in the legal world between deliberately reckless or dangerous driving and mere carelessness, brought on, perhaps, through fatigue or overwork. Equally, the employer who causes an accident through his failure to comply with regulations of which he was in ignorance may be in deep trouble with the law – whether that accident occurred in a shop or office, on a coach or ship or in an airport – but it is the employer who deliberately ignores the rules who is in the greatest legal danger.

Normally, it is no excuse for the accused to show that he knew nothing of the law. But he may be able to prove the reason for his ignorance was that someone else did not provide him with information. Or he may be able to blame the 'mistake or default' on someone else.

The business man cannot know the lot – especially about the 1974 Act. But at least he must know where to find the information that he requires – from printed or from human sources. And he must (personally or otherwise) make the appropriate consultations or risk personal as well as corporate liability.

Suppose, for instance, that you are charged with an offence under the Act. You say (truthfully): 'I did not know that I was breaking the law'. You will not be acquitted because of that reason. But your lack of knowledge will be a source of mitigation. You (or, preferably, your defending Counsel or solicitor) will say: 'Guilty of the offence – but please impose a light penalty'. With luck, you may get an absolute or conditional discharge, a bind-over or a light fine.

It may be, of course, that you can blame your lawyers. While neither solicitors nor Counsel may be successfully sued for negligence in the course of litigation, there are plenty of cases in which lawyers who have failed to notice changes in statute or common law have been made personally responsible for failing to give adequate, up-to-date advice to their clients or (more likely) for failing to take required steps within appropriate periods.

Suppose, for instance, that your solicitor forgets to issue a notice or to start legal proceedings within the prescribed time. The axe of the law chops down and the claim or right concerned dies. The lawyer is liable.

Or suppose that the lease of your premises is about to expire. You are protected by *The Landlord and Tenant Act, 1954* (as amended). Wisely, you let your solicitor do the haggling for you and leave it to him to serve the appropriate notices – first saying that you do not intend to leave your premises and second (where no agreement is reached with the landlord), applying to the court for a new lease.

Unfortunately, either because he leaves the matter to someone who does not know the legal time limits, or, more likely, through inadvertance, the appropriate notices go unserved. The time limit passes and your rights against your landlord die. But you acquire a new one against your lawyer. You can claim damages for negligence.

Or suppose that you are injured in an accident. The period of limitation for the bringing of claims for damages for personal injuries is three years – normally from the date of the accident. You put your lawyer on the trail and he haggles and is on the brink of an agreement – so he fails to issue a writ within the prescribed period. The claim then becomes 'statute-barred'. The lawyer has been negligent and you may substitute a claim against him for the one which is lost against the employer or driver or other person who caused the accident.

Naturally, the claim against the lawyer can succeed only to the extent that the original claim would have survived. There is a long legal road between bringing your claim and winning it. But the principles are clear.

It follows that if you are in doubt about your duties under the 1974 Act, then it is up to you to instruct your solicitors in good time to take any necessary steps in order to protect your interests. You should yourself undergo any necessary training; you should take any necessary medical or other advice; if in doubt about safety procedures, speak to the local inspector – and prepare yourself to protect the lives and limbs of others affected by your work.

"ONE DAY, SON – ALL THESE SUMMONSES WILL BE YOURS!"

Part Two

Enforcement, Liabilities and Penalties

Chapter 13

Enforcement and Penalties

The new penalties and enforcement procedures provided for in the Act have applied to existing statutes and regulations since 1 January 1975. The Act does not dispose of the old legislation. The Tenth Schedule sets out repeals. Look in vain there for the Factories Act or the Offices, Shops and Railway Premises Act. You will find neither. Both those Acts and all the regulations made under them remain – at present unaltered except for a new code of fire safety regulations – along with the Mines and Quarries Act, the Explosive Acts, the Alkali etc. Works Regulation Acts and the rest.

Changes in the regulations are likely (as we shall shortly see). More codes of industrial safety will probably appear before long. But the Act does not of itself replace any existing rule of any industrial importance. It simply adds a superstructure to the foundations created by previous Parliaments. It consolidates the law on health and safety into a criminal code; it provides new responsibilities, duties and standards of care, and it creates new supervisory and enforcement arrangements – it is these which, in the main, were brought into play first, in respect of existing legislation.

Take the Health and Safety Commission, for a start. In the past, supervision and the like was spread over a series of Ministries. The Act brought it together under one umbrella.

In brief, the Commission is given the following powers, mainly by Section 11:

1. To assist and encourage safety measures.
2. To make all necessary arrangements for research, publication and results of research, and the provision and encouragement of training, information and research, under their own aegis and carried out by others.
3. The making of arrangements for an information and advisory service.
4. The recommendation of new regulations.
5. The direction of investigations and enquiries.

Remember: The Act applies whether or not there has been an accident. But once disaster has struck, the Commission will have its attention forcibly drawn to arrangements which might otherwise have been approved or, more likely, which had previously escaped the appropriate inspector's eagle eye.

As to health and safety regulations, these may repeal or modify any existing statutory provision – without Parliamentary intervention. Watch out carefully for this sort of delegated legislation and if you find it coming your way and regard it as unreasonable, then protest loudly, personally and through your MP.

Again, the Commission will 'approve and issue such codes of practice (whether prepared by it or not)' as it regards as suitable and necessary. As we saw in Chapter 11, a Code of Practice has no statutory force, but you dare not ignore it. Once you are shown to have acted in breach of the Code, you will normally be found guilty of an offence under the Act.

Anyway, it is the Executive which must make 'adequate arrangements' for the enforcement of the rules. The Secretary of State may make regulations, requiring local authorities or others to accept responsibility for the enforcement of the provisions.

Under the Act, a unified Inspectorate was set up for the first time, covering the entire country. The Factory Inspectorate . . . the Mines and Quarries Inspectorate . . . the Alkali Inspectorate . . . and all the rest, including now the Agricultural Inspectorate (which originally remained under the Department of Agriculture) have been brought together under the wing of the Executive. Apart from convenience of administration, every effort is now being made to avoid the uncertainties which previously existed due to differing standards applied by different inspectors in various parts of the country. If, for instance, you are able to convince an inspector in the North of England that a particular machine or system of work is either safe or as safe as reasonably practicable, then you should have the same good fortune in the South. Or, for that matter, anywhere else in the United Kingdom.

Inspectors, in the main, have the same powers as before – and you must provide them with all necessary facilities to carry out their work. Otherwise you offend against the Act. And (as usual) you face a maximum penalty of two years imprisonment or a fine of unlimited amount, in most cases, plus often a further fine at the rate of £50 per day from the date of conviction.

How, then, may an inspector deal with what he regards as an infringement?

Section 21: 'If an inspector is of the opinion that a person

(a) is contravening one or more of the relevant statutory provisions, or

(b) has contravened one or more of those provisions in circumstances that make it likely that the contravention will continue or be repeated,

he may serve on him . . . an improvement notice . . . stating that he is of that opinion'. The notice will specify the alleged breaches; it will give particulars of the reason why the inspector considers that a breach has occurred; and the alleged offender will be required to put matters right within the period stated.

In cases of serious risk, expect a prohibition notice under Section 22.

If an inspector 'is of the opinion that . . . activities . . . as carried on or about to be carried on by or under the control of the person in question . . . involve or . . . will involve risk of serious personal injury, the inspector may serve on that person a . . . prohibition notice'.

A prohibition notice has an enormous impact. It will state the reason why the inspector considers that the activity is unsafe or unhealthy and will give his reasons. Once you have been served with that notice, you will have to cease carrying on the practice, no matter how much loss you may suffer as a result. We shall take a rather closer look at the way inspectors use their powers in practice in Chapter 14.

You may appeal, though, against both an improvement and a prohibition notice. Your appeal will go to the Industrial Tribunal.

The Tribunal – with its legally qualified chairman and two lay members – will not necessarily be qualified in specialist matters. You will have to present your case, preferably with the help of experts. You will explain why (for instance) you regard the present practice as safe – or as safe as is reasonably practicable in all the circumstances. And you will back your view by the strongest evidence you can muster. After all, if you lose, you will have to call a halt to the practice – permanently.

As with all litigation, appeals to Industrial Tribunals are likely to be risky and their outcome uncertain. So what happens in the meantime to the practice complained of? Here there is a vast difference between the two forms of notice.

Where you appeal against an improvement notice, the bringing of the appeal has the immediate effect of suspending the operation of the notice until the appeal is either heard or withdrawn. Until the Industrial Tribunal is out of the legal picture, you may carry on with the practice or activity concerned or continue to use the equipment.

However: 'In the case of a prohibition notice, the bringing of the appeal shall' have the effect of suspending the operation of the notice 'only if, on the application of the appellant, the Tribunal so directs (and then only from the giving of a direction)'.

You receive your prohibition notice? Then you must call a halt to the prohibited activity. You will rush to the Tribunal and, no doubt, be allowed to jump the queue. You will ask the Tribunal to direct that the order shall be suspended.

The Tribunal will immediately require to be satisfied that the inspector is wrong in believing that there is a risk of serious personal injury if the practice continues. You will have to collect your evidence, as swiftly and powerfully as possible. And the Tribunal may (in this case and that of all other appeals) appoint 'assessors' – probably qualified experts – to go into the matter on its behalf.

From the Industrial Tribunal, you have a right of appeal to the Court of Appeal. This will apply not only against the substantive decision of the Tribunal – its decision, that is, on whether or not the practice concerned shall be allowed to continue in the long run – but you may also appeal against any refusal of the Tribunal to order a suspension of a prohibition. Once again, speed will be essential.

Obviously, you should do everything reasonably practicable

(to use the phrase frequently repeated in the Act) to avoid having a notice served upon you. What is or is not 'reasonable' depends (here as throughout our law) upon all the circumstances of the particular case. To estimate your prospects of success in the litigation, you have to consult experts and preferably let a lawyer call the odds on the basis of the evidence which will be available.

In practice, only a handful of recipients of prohibition or improvement notices have exercised their right to appeal. In almost every one of these cases, no complaint was made against the notice as such, but the appellant sought time to carry out the inspector's orders.

Inspectors are issuing far more of these notices than anyone expected, but they are doing so with good sense and discretion. Theoretically, if an inspector closes down your works by serving a prohibition notice and he does so negligently, you might have a claim for damages against him – a point yet to be decided by the courts. He would no doubt be indemnified by his employers (the Executive), but his own job prospects would not improve. Conversely, if he misjudges the situation and serves no notice when one was justified and an accident occurs which would have been avoided had the process or operation been stopped in its tracks by the service of a prohibition notice, then he bears heavy responsibility.

So the inspector's job has not become any easier. The framework within which they work has altered radically and some have adapted easier than others.

Not only have the inspector's responsibilities increased and his muscle extended by his power to serve the new notices, but he may also remove from your premises any article or substance which he regards as unsafe. To do so, he may enter not only your office, works, site or garage but also your transport. He may then remove the article or substance which he considers to be a 'cause of imminent danger of serious personal injury' and 'cause it to be rendered harmless, whether by destruction or otherwise'.

So inspectors have become even more important people than they were in the past. Their powers have been extended – and so have their numbers. Several hundred more have been appointed. Their job is to prevent industrial and commercial accidents. Unfortunately, past efforts have left too many killed, maimed or absent employees. If the rate of injury and death remains unabated, the inspectorate is likely to be in political trouble. Therefore you should expect a continuation of the now more vigorous enforcement of the rules, both old and new.

Naturally, the Inspectorate still cannot conceivably cope with its enormous potential workload. Dangerous sites get visited often; and those where the hazard is small, rarely indeed.

For the Act to work, industry must be self-policing. Safety representatives and safety committees spark off action. Safety officers (appointed by the thousand) chivvy and monitor. Managers who recognise their personal liabilities take a new and vivid interest in the health and safety of their employees.

A phone call to the local Inspectorate will generally bring results – and often lead to the issuing of a prohibition notice. 'Stop work – until the scaffolding is safe. . . .'

On its own, the Inspectorate is weak. Buttressed by vigilant management and men, it is powerful indeed.

Chapter 14

Inspectorates – and How to Cope with Them

The owner of a large factory once asked his favourite Factory Inspector whether it was wise to call in the Inspectorate if in doubt about whether or not a particular practice was safe. The Inspector replied by quoting an ancient proverb: 'Love work; hate tyranny; live righteously; and do not let your name get too well known to the authorities. . . .'

If the inspector keeps away, you should be lucky. Still, if disaster strikes and someone is hurt, you may regret your silence.

An inspector will try to help you but is not bound to provide solutions to your problems. Equally (and despite the proverb) you may decide to call in the inspector knowing that if he makes suggestions, you will no doubt have to comply with them.

Anyway, you may call in the inspector as and when you see fit and – time permitting – he will soon call on you. How often, though, will he call without an invitation?

There are not enough inspectors to go round (physically as well as metaphorically). Units in the construction or engineering businesses, with a high level of risk, may expect frequent visits from inspectors. Other outfits with low accident risks and good safety records may see their inspectors only every few years.

If an inspector does turn up – whether on his own initiative or because he has been called in – he may request a change. You may think his proposals costly and unjustified, but if he is determined that change there must be, you are likely to receive a prohibition or an improvement notice.

A prohibition notice will specify the change required and forbid you to carry on the way complained of. You will probably be required to cease using the machine or the method – forthwith. As we have seen in Chapter 13, you may appeal to an Industrial Tribunal against the prohibition notice but the notice will remain in full force and effect, unless and until the Tribunal decides otherwise – or, of course, unless and until you have complied with the notice.

An improvement notice will require you to improve a situation which the inspector regards as hazardous. Whereas a prohibition notice is likely to be peremptory and immediate (although it may give time for compliance), an improvement notice is likely to give time (although it may require immediate change). You may appeal against an improvement notice and once your appeal is lodged the improvement notice will be suspended until the Tribunal has laid down the law.

A prohibition notice may shut down the business and prove quite catastrophic to your output. So the Tribunal may call in additional assessors and will try to deal with any appeal as swiftly as possible.

The Factory Inspectorate, the Alkali Inspectorate and the Explosives Inspectorate under the Department of Employment; the security aspects of explosives under the Home Office; thanks to the tragedy of Flixborough, a Major Hazards Co-ordinating Unit . . . and regulations to decide which authority does what. But in the end, enforcement depends mainly on the individual inspector.

The inspector himself is under new pressures. Suppose, for instance, that he considers that a particular operation involves risk of serious injury to health. Is he to bang in a prohibition notice at once, forcing you to change your ways forthwith – or even to close down the process? If he does this, then he will clear himself of worry because the process cannot start again unless and until an Industrial Tribunal overturns his ruling or gives an interim order, allowing the work to go on, when you have lodged your appeal.

On the other hand, the inspector will normally request a change and provide a reasonable time for you to mend your ways. But if in that interim period an accident occurs, there will be a heavy weight of responsibility on his shoulders.

Or suppose that you, in your senior position, spot a safety hazard. You jump on the offender and get matters put right as soon as possible. The top manager leaps on the middle manager who, knowing that he will be personally responsible under the Act and liable to the new and fierce penalties, will bear down on the line manager – the Act places responsibility on all.

Or maybe safety problems are now in the realm of a safety officer or advisor? The Act has led to important changes in safety organisation.

A 'competent person' must put matters right. The term 'competent person' is not defined by the Act, but clearly the inspector will wish to know that someone who is properly trained, skilled, experienced and authorised will be doing the particular job and that another such person will supervise. Normal good management requires not only information and understanding but delegation.

The inspector may have to take the decision: Whom do I prosecute? You must ask yourself the question: If our procedures are queried by the inspector, will I be able to satisfy him that both man and manager are 'competent'?

The inspector will certainly co-operate with the personnel manager or safety officer in charge of your arrangements, new and old. But the mere fact that you appoint a person to do the job will not free higher management from its responsibility. If, for instance, he places pressure on you to provide new equipment or alter methods, then he is doing his job and, within the limits of what is 'reasonably practicable' (a question of fact, in each case), you will have to give way to that pressure. Assuming that he has the necessary technical knowledge and know-how and is duly qualified, then you must heed his advice. If he lacks the necessary expertise, then you should not have appointed him. If you have not given him the necessary independence, then you will be to blame; but if you make him independent and fail to supply sufficient muscle to his arm, then, once again, the responsibility will remain yours.

On the other hand, if you operate a substantial business and fail to have a safety officer or manager or other delegate, deputed to ensure that the provisions of the Act are complied with, then you lose a valuable protection. While the safety officer will be expected to be independent of mind and objective in approach, by appointing him you protect yourself.

Inspectors have enormous discretion. Not only do they retain their previous powers: to enter and inspect; to collect information for evidence; to require you to co-operate with them. Not only can they now serve 'improvement' and 'prohibition' notice But (as we have seen) they also have authority to seize any artic or substance which they consider to be an imminent source of danger or of serious personal injury, and, if necessary, forthwith to destroy such article or substance.

An inspector may also require you to disclose information – which may include important trade secrets. Still, thanks to Section 28, he is forbidden to divulge your secrets except in so far as he needs to in order to do his job; or for the purpose of his report or enquiry or investigation; or for legal proceedings; or with your permission. Naturally, he must also comply with the Official Secrets Act.

In practice, the Inspectorate continues to carry on its duties with care and discretion. For instance, an inspector is very unlikely to use his powers under Section 25 to seize or destroy an article or substance belonging to you, unless the situation is one of grave emergency. If 'practicable', he must take a sample and provide a marked portion of it to some appropriate person at your premises before he takes any action. And in any event, he must provide details of his action in a written report and you are entitled to a copy of that report. As a final protection, if he was not justified in taking his action, then you would be entitled to sue him for damages in a civil court.

Chapter 15

Health, Safety – and the Shop Steward

Dividing the number of work places in the United Kingdom by the number of inspectors available to visit them, you find that each inspector would have to make well over 600 visits a year to cope. It follows:

1 That inspectors inevitably go to those work places which are known or expected to be hazardous;
and
2 That other visits depend upon accident or tip-off.

Therefore, the effectiveness of the Act depends to a great extent upon co-ordination from management and employees. In the main, trade unions accept that their vigilance may bring safety for their members. The key to this approach is held by the shop steward.

What is wrong with this example?

A machine operative refuses to wear his safety spectacles. The foreman and the safety officer speak to him but he does not mend his ways. The personnel manager (or other employers' representative) calls the offender into his office and brings the shop steward to represent the man's interests.

'There is nothing wrong' you say? Then you are echoing the views of the majority of British managers. But in fact you (and they) are starting on the old, wretched trail of ill-will and misunderstanding. Above all in health and safety matters, the steward should be representing his men not by taking their side when they refuse to take reasonable precautions for their safety. He should be leaning on them to comply with your requirements – for their sake.

To achieve this result, employers must stop introducing the disciplinary procedures at the start of their health and safety routines. If the foreman's efforts fail, then the shop steward should be approached and asked to speak to his member. Most will do so. If that fails and you have to give disciplinary warning the trade union representative should be on your side.

Naturally, if the steward himself is refusing to wear the protective spectacles (or ear muffs or boots – or to keep the guard on his machine), you are in trouble. But then far too many foremen and other managers walk around the plant unprotected. Leadership means example.

Equally, if you have the misfortune to deal with a steward who refuses to help, you (and his members) are equally unlucky. The chances are, though, that you have approached him in the wrong way.

Any factory inspector will confirm that one of the main reasons for the unexpected proliferation of prohibition and improvement notices has been the acceptance of the usefulness of those notices – and of the inspectorate – by both trade unions and managers.

'Please don't say it came from me or I'll lose my job', says the voice on the phone. 'But there's a dangerous practice going on in our works. . . .'

The inspector arrives; and usually, he finds that the report is justified. Either the management puts matters right or a notice is served.

Sometimes it is the union that complains – unable to convince the employers to take action. Sometimes, though, it is a manager who is anxious for the welfare of his men and who cannot convince his superiors to spend money on change.

Even before the Health and Safety Regulations, Code and Guidance on safety representatives come into force, the 'watchdog' system is starting to work.

Chapter 16

Enquiries and Accidents

No Parliament can ban accidents. So Section 14 of the new Act looks to the miseries of life. It decides what may now happen if a serious accident afflicts your business.

Where there is any 'accident, occurrence, situation or other matter whatsoever' which the Health and Safety Commission 'thinks it necessary or expedient to investigate', then it is given two options. First, it may direct the Health and Safety Executive or authorise any other person to investigate and to make a special report on any such matter. Second, with the consent of the Secretary of State, the Commission may 'direct an enquiry to be held into any such matter'.

Unfortunately, it is often an 'accident' which throws into relief the need for a change in the rules. So the same powers apply where the Commission considers that new regulations may have to be made.

Either the Commission itself, then, or some other body may march into your premises, in an attempt to prevent any recurrence of the circumstances leading to the accident concerned. And you will have to co-operate.

Once again, regulations control the way in which the enquiry is held. You may be fortunate and find that it is conducted in private. But, in general, the enquiry will be public – 'except where or to the extent that the regulations provide otherwise'.

The regulations confer on the person holding the enquiry any necessary rights to summon witnesses, require them to give evidence or produce documents or to make declarations or statements under oath.

As with the enquiry, so with the report which emerges from it. The Commission may cause the report 'or so much of it as it thinks fit' to be made public 'in such time and in such manner' as it wishes. What, then, if you or your company get slammed in the report? What steps can you take to protect your own good name?

Here we run into the law of defamation. Anyone who speaks ill of anyone else 'defames' him. If the statement is made orally or in some other ephemeral form, then it is a slander. If it is in writing or some other permanent form (such as on television) then it is a libel. Either way, the person who has been brought into 'hatred, ridicule and contempt' has a good 'cause of action'.

There are, though, some very excellent defences which, in practice, make defamation actions rare and risky. First, the maker of the statement may maintain that it is justified – no one is entitled to a good name which he has not earned. Second – and much more important – are the rules on 'privilege'.

Suppose that you are sued for damages for negligence. A witness (or for that matter, the defendant or the Judge), makes unworthy statements about your competence. These are reported in the Press. Unfortunately for you, you have no claim against either the maker or the reporter. As in Parliament, so in all Courts – the occasions are absolutely privileged. No matter how evil the tongue nor how malicious the mind of the maker, he cannot be successfully sued in defamation.

As for the reporter, he is fully entitled to give a fair and accurate account of what happened in Court. So you have no rights against him either.

Now suppose that you are asked for a reference for an employee whom you have dismissed because he is accident prone. Are you entitled to speak your mind, without fear of a libel action?

The law recognises that while you are under no legal obligation to provide a reference, you have a moral duty to do so. Therefore any reference you give is privileged – with one qualification. If your object is to harm the person named rather than to help the person to whom the reference is supplied, then you are said to have acted out of 'malice'. And the privilege disappears.

What, then, of the public enquiry? The occasion is certainly privileged. Depending on the circumstances, the privilege will be either absolute or qualified. Either way, your chances of making a successful attack on the defamer are remote. Even if the company is private, the report published afterwards will be privileged too. And those whose job it is to inform the public will be entitled to report the proceedings with due accuracy.

That, after all, is one of the objects of holding the enquiry in public. Others must learn from your accidents or mistakes. There will be no privacy for those whose activities have led to disaster.

Chapter 17

Defending Yourself and Your Company from Prosecution and Punishment

There are four available defences under the Act:

1 *Not Guilty*. That is: We deny having committed any offence . . . we did take all proper steps to avoid causing risk to the health or safety of our employees (or visitors, or customers, or as the case may be). Or: we did not impede the inspector we did carry out all necessary research and testing – or as the case may be. Remember that *you* do not have to prove your innocence – it is for the prosecution to prove what you deny having done.

2 *Not Guilty: Further steps 'not reasonably practicable'.* That is: We admit that we did not take enough care – but further steps would not have been 'reasonably practicable' in the circumstances. The burden of proving 'lack of reasonable practicability' rests upon the accused.

3 *Not Guilty: It was not our fault.* We set up a proper system . . . the company made all the appropriate arrangements . . . the failure properly to carry out that system or to implement those arrangements was due to the act or default of someone else (which, as we shall see, could include another executive or employee – including the injured party, if any)

4 *Not Guilty: technicalities*, e.g. a defect in prohibition notice or improvement notice.

Note: The absence of any actual accident or (still less) of

injury, no more provides a defence to a charge under the Act than 'provocation' allows an assault. Absence of disaster will provide a powerful argument in mitigation of sentence, but will not prevent a conviction.

Anyway, if you do receive a summons under the Act, panic not. Take stock of the available defences; and discuss them with your lawyers.

Question 1: Are you in breach of the Act?

The prosecution must first prove its case beyond reasonable doubt, Initially, it is not for you to prove your innocence but for those who seek to establish your guilt to do so with certainty.

So you must assess the facts and consider whether you have any (and if so what) prospect of an acquittal. Only an experienced lawyer with all the facts at his fingertips; equipped with any expert evidence that may be necessary; and with all the documents before him, can hope to assess the odds – unless, of course, guilt is obvious. Too many cases are not only hopeless but obviously so.

If the prosecution cannot get to first base by proving such facts as may be necessary to establish guilt, then you should plead not guilty.

Question 2: Do you hope to fight the case in the Magistrates' Court or before a jury?

Trial in a Magistrates' Court is meant to be quick – and hence 'summary'. Trial at the Crown Court is said to be 'on indictment' – you are indicted to stand trial before a jury.

In proceedings under the 1974 Act, you are unlikely to be given the choice. In practice, the prosecution decides where the case will be taken. And the vast majority have come before Magistrates' Courts.

Still, you may be given the choice – and if so, you must balance the joys of a jury trial against the miseries thereof.

There is one, massive advantage of trial by jury (in legal terms 'on indictment'). The chances of acquittal are greater. Whatever the charge, the acquittal rate is likely to be far higher when the case is heard by twelve fellow citizens; honest and true – and not nearly as cynical as many magistrates are (stipendary or lay) who have 'heard it all' many times before.

Disadvantages of trial by jury:

1 The cost is always much greater. You will need Counsel – a 'junior' certainly and possibly, in important cases, a

Queen's Counsel (or 'silk'). Solicitors' fees are higher. The trial will be longer.

2 Also, the case will take longer to reach trial. 'Summary proceedings' (as they are called) are not only swifter when they arrive but the queue outside the Magistrates' Court is far shorter. With the magistrates, you may get your case on and over in days or weeks – you may wait months before your turn arrives before the jury. This may make not one iota of difference for the company but may be extremely worrying for any individual concerned, with the legal sword of Damocles (including the peril of prison hanging hideously over his head). But in some parts of the country – especially if your case is long and you are pleading not guilty – the magistrates may take just as long as the Crown Court.

3 Above all: the possible penalties, if convicted, are far higher when the trial is on indictment than in the case of summary proceedings. A £400 fine is the maximum for the magistrates. Unlimited fines and potential prison looms ahead for those convicted by juries.

There are, of course, other factors, impossible to assess in advance. For instance, there is the Bench which sentences.

Experienced lawyers know their judges. Some are fierce, others kindly; some tend to sentence heavily on a particular class of offence and to be gentle with other classes – which, in their turn, are treated harshly by colleagues who may be especially understanding in other matters. The accused cannot pick his court and will not even know its identity until (at the earliest) the night before the hearing.

Question 3: If the prosecution can prove its case, can you show that it was not 'reasonably practicable' for you to have taken other steps than you did, in order to avoid the dangerous situation?

Remember always that once a dangerous practice has been proved (and the prosecution rarely has any problems about this), the burden of proving that you could not reasonably have done anything else shifts firmly onto you. How do you discharge it?

'Reasonableness' (as always, in law) depends upon all the circumstances of the case. Here you will undoubtedly need the best technical evidence available. You must find yourself a top consultant, able to advise you on the prospects; to prepare a report; and to give firm and powerful evidence if need be on your behalf.

A plea that further steps were not 'reasonably practicable' may be worth making, even if it is likely to fail. At best, it could secure an acquittal; at worst, it should go in mitigation of sentence.

Still: if you plead guilty and the matter is dealt with swiftly and before magistrates, there may be less adverse publicity for you or for your business than if the case is fought out. Once you do battle, the sound of the crashing weapons tends to reverberate through the media.

On the other hand, even if you plead guilty, there can be no guarantee of silence. And then you can never protest: 'The court was wrong . . . we should not have been convicted. . .'.

Your lawyers will advise – on expert evidence, on your prospects of success, and on the best plea. They will also look into the technicalities. The chances of (for example) a prohibition or improvement notice being incorrect on its face are not great – but mistakes are made. Your lawyers will watch out for them.

That leaves the question of reliance on someone else's mistake – which we shall consider in the next chapter.

Note: For the Scots, although the names of the Courts, and the formalities, are different, the arguments about whether or not you should ask for trial by jury are the same.

Chapter 18

The Art of Passing the Buck

The Act places a new and shining premium on passing the legal buck.

An able seaman sat an examination for promotion. One of the questions read: 'Correct the following: It were me that done it.' The lad wrote: 'It were *NOT* me what done it.' If you can show that it were not you what committed the offence, you will be entitled to be acquitted. So: 'It were my superior what did not follow my recommendation that the system be altered . . . the machine replaced . . . the instructions to line management altered . . .' Alternatively: 'I laid down clear, precise and reasonable arrangements to avoid dangers and accidents. It was not my fault that the rules were not followed.'

The famous case of *Tesco Supermarkets Limited* v. *Nattrass* points the way to the successful blaming of managers for the sins of the company. Potential defences open to those charged with 'applying false trade descriptions' to goods or services are much the same as those steps to protect the health, safety or welfare of employees at work or of others affected by that work.

Washing powder was displayed at a Tesco Supermarket at a reduced price. A pensioner tried to find a packet at the special offer rate but was told that there was none in stock. She bought one at the higher price and reported the company to the Weights and Measures Authorities, who prosecuted under Section 11 of the Trade Descriptions Act, which makes it an offence to offer to supply goods after giving 'by whatever means, any indication likely to be taken as an indication that goods are being offered at a price less than that at which they are in fact being offered'.

There was no dispute on the facts, but Tesco's relied on a special defence. They claimed 'that the commission of the offence was due to a mistake or to reliance on information supplied to them or to the act or default of another person, an accident or some other cause beyond their control' – and maintained that they 'took all reasonable precautions and exercised all due diligence to avoid the commission of such an offence by themselves or any person under their control'.

They proved that they had set up an excellent system and that the offence resulted from the failure of their manager properly to operate the system. He (they said) was 'another person'.

The magistrates held that the manager was not 'another person' but was acting as servant or agent of the company and that therefore the company could not rely on his failure to do his job. The company appealed and the Divisional Court held that the manager *was* 'another person' but that as a person 'acting in a managerial or supervisory capacity' had failed to exercise due diligence, the company must take the legal responsibility. Tesco's appealed to the House of Lords.

'I find it almost impossible to suppose', said Lord Reid, 'that Parliament or any reasonable body of men would as a matter of policy think it right to make employers criminally liable for the acts of some of their servants but not for those of others. I find it incredible that a draftsman, aware of that intention, would fail to insert any words to express it . . . I think that it was plainly intended to make a just and reasonable distinction between the employer who is wholly blameless and ought to be acquitted and the employer who is in some way at fault, leaving it to the employer to prove that he was in no way to blame.

'What good purpose would be served by making an employer criminally responsible for the misdeeds of some of his servants but not for those of others? A board of directors can delegate part of their functions of management so as to make their delegate an embodiment of the company. . . .

'But here the board never delegated any part of their functions. They set up a chain of command through . . . supervisors, but they remained in control. The shop managers had to obey their general directions and also to take orders from their supervisors. The acts or omissions of shop managers were not acts of the company itself.'

This remarkable view – that the acts of managers, supervisors or other executives are not in the circumstances 'acts of the company itself' – was supported by all the other law lords. Lord Dilhorne, for instance, said that managers in a large business 'cannot properly be regarded as part of the company's directing mind and will and so can come within the reference to "another person".'

'To treat the duty of an employer to exercise due diligence as unperformed unless due diligence is also exercised by all his servants to whom he has reasonably given proper instructions and on whom he could reasonably rely to carry them out', said Lord Diplock, 'would destroy the power of the defence provided and 'thwart the clear intention of parliament'.'

There are those who maintain that it could *not* have been 'the clear intention of parliament' that managers should be prosecuted in place of companies. But while there is considerable variation of approach and system as between enforcement authorities in various parts of the country, managers – sometimes together with their companies, sometimes on their own – are feeling the full force of the old law. They must now beware of further miseries.

Section 36 of the Act provides that where 'the commission by any person of an offence under any of the relevant statutory provisions is due to the act or default of some other person, that other person shall be guilty of the offence, and a person may be charged with and convicted of the offence by virtue of this sub-section whether or not proceedings are taken against the first mentioned person.'

Whether or not the company is prosecuted, the executive is at risk. The company which wishes either to preserve its high reputation for looking after the health, safety and welfare of its employees – or which is merely mean and nasty and ready and willing to cast off the blame on individuals, when it can – may certainly rely upon this section which, in combination with the decision in Tesco's case, will provide it with a let-out – provided, of course, that the company – like Tesco – had set up a first-class system and that it was the manager who was himself at fault.

So while the company may elbow its way out of trouble by legal buck-passing, the executive may himself be in the front rank of the accused, thanks to another section of the Act, aimed directly at him – as the next chapter will show.

Chapter 19

An Executive's Personal Liability

The object of the Act? To save lives and limbs . . . to cut down the rate of industrial injuries, physical and mental – caused by over a quarter of a million accidents at work, each year.

No one enjoys imposing fines on business enterprises or on their executives nor, still less, sending company directors or secretaries, managers or executives, shop stewards or workers to prison. Punishment is the last resort – but if making an example of a few will save the lives of many, then watch out. The Act puts everyone in peril, from the bottom of the industrial or commercial heap to the peak of achievement.

The company itself may be fined but it can scarcely languish behind the wrong sort of bars. That privilege is reserved for those by whom it acts.

Section 37: 'Where an offence committed . . . by a body corporate' – that is, a company, a statutory or local authority or anyone other than an individual or a firm – 'is proved to have been committed with the *consent* or *connivance* of, or to have been attributable to any *neglect* on the part of' the individuals named, they will be guilty of the offence. 'Consent' . . . 'connivance' . . . 'neglect' – those are the key words. The individuals? 'Any *director*, *manager*, *secretary* or other similar officer of the body corporate or a person who was purporting to act in any such capacity'. Any executive, then, or anyone who is acting in an executive role.

The company may still be convicted, but the individual himself will be guilty and 'liable to be proceeded against and punished accordingly'.

'Where the affairs of the body corporate are managed by its members, the preceding . . . shall apply in relation to the act and defaults of a member in connection with his functions of management as if he were a director of the body corporate'. Members of boards, or corporations and of other 'bodies' must watch out.

Naturally, the mere fact that you are a servant or agent, an executive or officer of a company will not itself make you criminally liable – under this Act or any other – for its wrongdoings. You must have played some personal part in the affair.

A woman was chairman of a company that operated gaming establishments. The company failed to obtain appropriate licences and she was prosecuted and convicted.

The conviction was set aside on appeal. The chairman was non-executive; she had no knowledge of the offence; she had played no part in it – and on the wording of the statute concerned, she was not to be held personally liable merely because she held office.

In the 1974 Act, the prosecution must prove 'consent', 'connivance' or 'neglect'.

To 'consent' means to agree to the commission of the offence. To 'connive' at its commission imports not merely a positive approval but some sort of active role – perhaps a deliberate closing of both eyes.

It is the word 'neglect' though which provides wider scope. You 'neglect' your duties if you are guilty of some act or omission which has led directly or indirectly, to the commission of the offence. If you are a mere non-executive director, then 'neglect' may not bother you. But if the Act is flouted and you should have done something to ensure that it was complied with – perhaps through better training or supervision . . . personally or by delegation . . . then you are one of those at whom the Act points an accusing finger. You may find yourself (literally as well as metaphorically) in the dock.

Now, Section 7 of the Act places a direct responsibility on the individual employee. 'While at work' he must 'take reasonable care for the health and safety of himself and of other persons who may be affected by his acts or omissions at work'.

In addition, 'as regards any duty or requirement imposed on his employer or any other person by or under any of the relevant statutory provisions', he must 'co-operate with him so far as is necessary to enable that duty or requirement to be performed or complied with'.

The employee, then, must take reasonable care for the safety of others and must 'co-operate' with his employers to that end. No law has or will require the employee to co-operate for the improvement of productivity or to do a better job. That is a matter for negotiation and personnel management. Safety, though, requires all hands safely on deck and every employee to exercise a duty of care towards his 'neighbour'.

In practice, though, the inspectorate generally leans on manager rather than on man. This is for two reasons – and you may or may not disagree with either or with both of them, but they still represent reality:

1 If an employee does not follow the safety rules, then clearly he has not been submitted to sufficient 'persuasion and propaganda' to induce him to take care. Your efforts were insufficient to do the trick.

'They always blame the manager, don't they?' Which is reasonably fair, but the fact remains that if someone under your management disobeys the rules and therefore creates danger for himself or for others, you have failed. Maybe it was not your fault. Maybe you could prove that you took all such steps as were reasonably practicable. Still, you will have to do the proving.

2 More important, if the Act is to produce the desired results, the support of the workers is vital.

From the positive side, employees must be convinced and satisfied that the Act is designed to help them to avoid death and injury at work. If this approach is accepted, then employees in general and their trade unions in particular will co-operate both with management and with the inspectorate in seeing that the Act works.

Conversely and from the negative angle, if and in so far as the Act is regarded as a flail, designed or used to harass or to harm employees or their organisations, then – as a latter-day Industrial Relations Act – it will wither and die.

After all, even with a few hundred extra inspectors, enforcement must be from shop floor upwards. The Act must be self-policing and that can only happen if employees regard the provisions as their own.

Suppose, then, that an obdurate employee – perhaps one who refuses to wear his safety spectacles – is prosecuted. If the trade union or the workforce generally regard the prosecution as reasonable and fair, the industrial relations spin-off will do no harm.

Suppose, though, that the employee considers that he has been victimised. 'I'm not the only one, am I? Others have done the same and nothing has happened to them, has it? Why pick on me?'

If that man is then convicted and fined, will he pay? Or will he prefer to be martyred in an unworthy cause? If so, will his mates wish to show solidarity?

We have learned that direct confrontation does not present the best way to industrial harmony generally. In the health and safety field, co-operation from the workforce is vital.

In the days of the Industrial Relations Act, a handful of dockers nearly managed to bring the entire country to a halt. One of them stood outside the walls of the prison declaring: 'It's a bloody liberty'. He did so not when he was put inside but when he was let out. The day had come when a politically acute British workman wanted to be jailed. It was indeed a day of industrial disaster. At least we have learned from it.

So prosecutions of individual workmen are few. There have been some; more will follow; but management will simply have to understand and accept that part of the red cross that they bear is the personal responsibility in keeping blood off the factory floor.

* * *

Section 8: 'No person shall intentionally or recklessly interfere with or misuse anything provided in the interests of health, safety or welfare in pursuance of any relevant statutory provisions'.

It is a criminal offence to interfere with safety equipment. Latter-day Luddites – beware.

Chapter 20

Civil Liability

If you are in breach of the Act you commit a criminal offence and may be prosecuted. If as a result of your breach an accident occurs, you may also be sued for damages for negligence in a civil court. One act or omission may lead to two separate sets of proceedings.

The object of the criminal law is to set up standards and to ensure that these are complied with. In addition or alternatively, the individual, firm or company harmed as a result of your wrongful (and possibly but not necessarily criminal) act may claim his civil remedy. The civil law is designed to provide rights as between citizens and/or their businesses.

Now suppose that you are driving your car on a business journey. Your concentration waivers and you cause an accident. You may be prosecuted for road traffic offences and if convicted, you may suffer criminal penalties – ranging from an absolute or conditional discharge, through disqualification from driving and a fine to (at worst) imprisonment.

Your punishment may put the sweet scent of revenge into the nostrils of the other driver who has suffered injury, loss or damage through your carelessness, but he will want money. He cannot get it from the criminal court. But he may sue you for damages – and if you have been convicted of a criminal offence, he is almost certain to be successful in his civil suit.

The converse does not apply. Even if the prosecution fail to prove beyond reasonable doubt that you were guilty of a crime, the other driver (or, for that matter, his passenger or yours) may still show that – on the balance of probabilities (which is the burden of proof in a civil case) – you did not come up to the standard of care which would be expected of a reasonably prudent driver. Once again, then, one wrongful act could lead to both civil and criminal consequences.

Now suppose that your company applies a false trade description to goods or services. Someone is deceived. You may be prosecuted and, if convicted, fined. But this time the criminal courts have special power – they may award up to £400 compensation to the innocent victim of your misleading statement. A criminal court may apply a civil remedy in certain cases, and frequently does so.

The Magistrates' Court or the Crown Court (at the higher level – and incidentally, the Old Bailey is the Crown Court for the City of London) has similar powers in other cases, including the power to require payment of compensation by those who cause malicious damage to your property. But in general, the wrongs to society are dealt with by the Magistrates' Court or the Crown Court; the wrongs to the individual by the County Court (which normally takes claims up to £1000, soon to be increased to £2000) or (in more costly cases) by the High Court.

Suppose that one of your employees assaults another. From the criminal viewpoint, he has been guilty of the crime of assault. If injury was caused, then it may be an assault causing actual bodily harm; if the injury is serious, then it will be an assault causing grievous bodily harm; and if the person assaulted dies, it may be manslaughter or murder.

Even the criminal law provides defences – self-defence is the only one likely to succeed in an assault case. Provocation may help in mitigation of sentence, but it will not prevent a conviction.

An assault is also a 'trespass to the person'. The sufferer may sue for damages to compensate him for his injuries.

The Criminal Injuries Compensation Board may provide the victim with what amounts to damages, if he suffered his injury through another person's criminal act. All too often, the assailant has either disappeared or is not worth suing. The Criminal Injuries Compensation Board has paid out millions of pounds to unfortunate victims of crimes. So criminal and civil law often interlock. The Act creates a huge new realm of liability imposed on employers and industrialists – and on those who insure them.

Section 47: 'Nothing in this part shall be construed as conferring a right of action in any civil proceedings in respect of any failure to comply with any duty imposed by Sections 2 to 7 or any contravention of Section 8'.

The intention is that there should be no civil liability in respec of any contravention of these Sections, which create new duties and obligations. But the Act also is not meant to 'affect the extent (if any) to which breach of a duty imposed by any of the existing statutory provisions is actionable'. So breach of statutor duty under (for example) the Factories Act or the Offices, Shops and Railway Premises Act or the Employers' Laibility (Defective Equipment) Act, remains unaffected. And the operation of the Nuclear Installations Act – which provides a right to compensation in certain cases – remains the same.

So there is no new civil liability, the Act says. Except: 'Breach of a duty imposed by health and safety *regulations* . . . shall, so far as it causes damages, be actionable except in so far as the regulations provide otherwise'. The italics are mine. The regulations are the Government's.

Suppose, then, that an accident occurs as a result of an act or omission which is itself a breach of some duty imposed by Sections 2 to 7. The above rules [says Section 47(4)] 'are withou prejudice to any right of action which exists apart from the provisions of this Act. . .'. So the injured person may sue.

Take an ordinary case. As a result of an employer's failure to take adequate safety precautions, an employee is injured. If he can prove breach of a statutory duty on the part of the employer – perhaps a failure properly to guard machinery, in breach of Section 14 of the Factories Act – then he can claim damages for breach of that duty.

Equally if there is a breach of (say) the Abrasive Wheels Regulations which resulted in injury to his eyes, the employee may claim damages arising out of that breach. But he cannot simply claim on the basis that the employer failed to comply with his duty under Section 2 of the Act – that the company (for example) failed to take reasonably practicable steps to provide him with a safe place of work or a safe system of working.

What will the employee do? As before the Act, he will claim

damages for common law negligence. He will maintain that he was submitted to unnecessary risk. And in his Statement of Claim (in the High Court) or in his Particulars of Claim (in the County Court) he will specifically plead and rely upon any conviction of the employers arising out of the breach relied upon.

The criminal offence created by the employer's breach of his statutory duty will not create a new civil 'cause of action'. But in practice, the employee who sues for damages in common law will be able to call in aid the employer's criminal failure to comply with his obligations.

It follows that where an employer (whether company, firm or individual) or an executive is convicted of an offence under Sections 2 to 8 of the Act, and where that incident caused injury, loss or damage, the victim is almost certain to succeed in a civil action arising out of that incident. There may be no new civil liability, but none is needed. The employer who is found 'beyond all reasonable doubt' to have failed to take proper steps for the health, safety or welfare of his employees in circumstances which gave rise to injury, loss or damage has about as much hope of avoiding liability in civil law as the fabled snowball in hell. Insurers, please note.

Chapter 21

Building Regulations

Part 3 of the Act is devoted to alterations to and amendments in various building regulations. Far more important than any changes made by the Act itself are those which may be made in the future, thanks to Governmental powers to make regulations.

Under the amended *Public Health Act, 1936* – reproduced as Part 2 of Schedule 6 of the Act – is the right to make regulations to 'secure the health, safety, welfare and convenience of persons in or about buildings and of others who may be affected by buildings or matters connected with buildings'. Just as the word 'welfare' is not defined for the general purposes of Section 2 of the Act, so the term 'convenience' will take its normal meaning – which is a very broad one indeed.

Still, it is Section 64 which is likely to have the most bite. Parliament did not forget the disastrous fire in the Isle of Man, with lives lost by the tragic dozen because material was used for the roof which melted away in the heat of the flames, pouring death on the crowds below. Now building regulations may be made to bar the use of 'a type of material or component' for inclusion as part of a building, if such material or components 'is likely to be unsuitable for use in the construction of a particular part of a permanent building in the absence of conditions with respect to the use of the building or with respect to any material or component of that type used in the construction of a part of that description'.

In addition, regulations may 'prescribe a type of service, fitting or equipment. . .' if that type is likely to be 'unsuitable for provision in or in connection with a permanent building in the absence of conditions with respect to the use of the building or with respect to any service, fitting or equipment of that type so provided'. Once prescribed, special restrictions apply to the use of equipment, etc.

Apart from a fine of up to £400, an offender under this Section may be fined a further £50 for each day on which the offence continues or on which the work or building is allowed to remain after conviction. And that is without prejudice to the right of the local authority to remove the work or building where prescribed, and to charge the offender with the cost of that removal.

On the other hand, if the Minister considers 'that the operation of any requirement of building regulations would be unreasonable in relation to any particular type of building matter', he may give a direction which dispenses with or relaxes the requirement. He may do so of his own volition or as a result of an application made to him and the relaxation may be conditional or unconditional. Section 66 provides a useful discretion. Apply for it, as required.

In addition, Section 69 provides that where an appeal is made to the Secretary of State, he may in many cases afford to the appellant and to the local authority concerned the opportunity of putting the case before an inspector and of being heard. The Section provides detailed procedures for such appeals.

Architects, surveyors, builders and others whose life's work involves the use and understanding of building regulations should check carefully through Part 3 of the Act in so far as it applies to them. Part 3 is included in full, for their benefit. The Part 3 rules apply only to them – but the general rules explained in this book apply to them, together with all other employers, occupiers, managers and men.

Chapter 22

Finding Your Way Round the Act

Until a law receives the Royal Assent, it is merely a 'bill', divided into 'clauses'. Once it gets on the statute book, it becomes an 'Act', split into 'sections'. Either way, if you get faced with a statute – like the 1974 Act, or the Factories Act, or the Fair Trading Act or any other – it is vital to know your way around it. Follow a few basic rules and all those statutes sitting in your drawer suddenly become intelligible.

No Act has an alphabetical index. But there are two inevitable pointers:–

1 At the very beginning come the contents, called the 'Arrangement of Sections'. Here are your chapter headings and sub-headings. Invariably, there are parts. (Part I of the 1974 Act contains nearly everything you will want – including 'general duties' and the powers of the Health and Safety Commission and Executive – plus enforcement and penalties.)

2 The definition section (or 'Interpretations'). Towards the end of the statute concerned, or in some cases (as in the case of the 1974 Act – Section 53) towards the end of the Part concerned, the interpretations not only provide the meanings of words but also lead the reader to the section sought.

So when you want to know what a word means under the Act (or any other), look at the definition Section. If you find no definition at all, then give the word its ordinary meaning in the English language. As a late Lord Chief Justice once remarked: 'A sausage is a sausage'. So 'welfare' is 'welfare' – at least until a superior court sees fit to limit the application of the word.

Or take 'article for use at work'. Section 53 of the Act defines this as meaning 'any plant designed for use or operation . . . by persons at work' and 'any article designed for use as a component in any plant'. The fact that an article is in fact used at work is not the criterion. If it was 'designed' for use at work, then it must comply with the rules – even if it is used elsewhere; and if it was not 'designed' for use at work, then the rules will not apply to it – even if a particular item happens to be used by those who labour.

Or consider 'premises'. This is defined as including (amongst other 'places'), any 'vehicle, vessel, aircraft or hovercraft'. Your lorries are 'places', your 'premises' are subject to the Act; the 'working environment' and 'welfare facilities' in your transport may well be called into legal question. But then so may they in any 'tent or moveable structure' – on land or the foreshore or resting on the sea bed.

Suppose that you want to find out who is going to enforce a particular provision of the Act. You will look for 'enforcement' and instead find 'enforcing authority'. This term 'has the meaning assigned by Section 18(7)'. You go to Section 18 (7) and find that it means the Executive. Back you turn to the interpretation section which refers you to Section 10 (5) – which provides for the general constitution of the Executive. From thereon, the path forward is an easy one.

At the back of the Act comes the answers to two other vital questions; *When* and *where*?

When? Some statutes come into force all at the same time. Others (such as the 1974 Act) are brought in piecemeal, as ordered by the Secretary of State; 1 April 1975 was the ultimate date for the Act. Meanwhile, the Commission and the Executive had to be set up and the organisation prepared. . . .

Where? In the main, in the whole of Great Britain. Certain exceptions for Northern Ireland. Details in the penultimate section: 'Extent and application. . .'.

It is vital to know the bare bones of what is in the Act – like all other crucial statutes. But to know the lot is impossible. To find the route to knowledge, use the 'Arrangement of Sections'; the interpretations clause; and know what is at the end.

"THAT COMPLETES THE MINUTES — NOW FOR 'ANY OTHER BUSINESS'!"

Part Three

Safety Committees and Representatives

Chapter 23

Safety Committees: Are You Ready for Them?

The 1st October 1978 is the date now fixed for the implementation of the new regulations and Code, requiring the setting up of safety committees and consultation with both committees and with union-appointed safety representatives. What is their essence and how can you prepare for their implementation?

* * *

A Parliamentary Committee recently described a committee as a 'cul de sac into which ideas are lured, there to be quietly strangled to death'. A camel (goes the well known saying) is a horse, invented by a committee. If Moses had been a committee (said a sage), the Israelites would still be in Egypt. Why, then, this new emphasis on committees for health and safety?

The appointment of a few hundred more inspectors cannot conceivably achieve the enforcement of the Health and Safety at Work Act nor the removal of the dreadful toll of human death and destruction in our industry. That can only be the result of efforts by management and the workforce – together. Bill Simpson (Chairman of the Health and Safety Commission since its inception) insists that the Act must be 'self-policing'. Individual policemen have little effect. They must be combined into a force. And as a force requires organisation from all sides, it can only be achieved by unions on the one hand meeting together with management on the other. That means – committees.

Safety committees should be constituted so as to achieve the maximum effect. Traditionally, they are manned by a majority from management. As Bill Simpson (again) pointed out: 'Safety committees do not run companies and there can be no philosophical or practical reason why the workforce should not consider these committees as their own'.

The management may decide on the size of the committee. This will depend, of course, on the nature of the site or establishment or operation.

Take a typical, large union with (say) 12 safety representatives. Maybe you decide on four or five managers with intimate concern for safety – plus a number of safety representatives, spread across the operations so as really to represent the workforces. You must try to set up a system which really works. Perhaps you will have departmental committees with an overall steering committee at the centre. Maybe you can manage better with one committee for the entire operation. As the Guidance Notes say: 'Detailed arrangements . . . should evolve from discussion and negotiation between employers and the appointed safety representatives who are best able to interpret the needs of the particular workplace or places with which the committee is to concern itself. . .'.

The relationship of the safety committee to other works committees 'is a matter for local organisation'. But the work of the safety committee 'has a separate identity' and safety matters must not become 'interposed in the agenda for other meetings'.

The Commission recommends that safety committees 'be related to a single establishment rather than to a collection of geographically distinct places' but where the workplace is large, a single committee may become unwieldy – but if kept small, it may become too remote. So several committees 'with adequate arrangements for co-ordination' may have to be set up.

The object of a safety committee is to 'keep under review the measures taken to ensure the health and safety at work of the employees'. Once you have established your committee, you should immediately consider the drawing up of agreed objectives or terms of reference. The object: 'The promotion of co-operation between employers and employees in instigating, developing and carrying out measures to ensure the health and safety at work of the employees'.

So you decide on the size and number of your safety committees; you agree with the unions on the set up and the objectives; you shepherd management resources and harness the enthusiasm of your workforce by encouraging maximum union participation; and you avoid what Bill Simpson described as 'the start of a conflict situation'. Instead of seating 'them' on one side of the table and 'us' on the other, you regard the operation as a joint, life-saving exercise. Experience shows that where numbers are equal or the committee is regarded as a mere arm of management, the trade union representatives tend to gather before the meeting and to prepare 'their' approaches – in the same way as some directors of some companies organise Board meetings long before they are held.

Works engineers, personnel managers, supervisors – all should be included. But 'the number of management representatives should not exceed the number of employees' representatives'.

Membership of the safety committee should be 'regarded as part of an individual's normal work'. Naturally, his pay must not be docked because he sits on the committee, which should meet 'as often as necessary . . .' having in mind 'local conditions, the size of the workplace, numbers employed, the kind of work carried on and the degree of risk inherent. . . . And 'sufficient time should be allowed during each meeting to ensure full discussion of all business'.

Unfortunately, meetings of safety committees are frequently cancelled or postponed because of 'business exigencies', 'emergencies', 'pressing problems afflicting the manager who is taking the chair' – or any other excuse (usually, but not always, genuine). Only in 'very exceptional circumstances', says the Commission, should meetings be put off.

As in the case of all other committees, minutes should be kept, displayed or circulated; agendas should be prepared and provided; rules for the conduct of the meeting should be drawn up, 'including procedures by which committees might reach decisions' – and, in fact, all sensible arrangements should be made for the conduct of these committees – like all others.

The decisions of safety committees are not binding on anyone. They make recommendations. But as an employer must take all such steps as are 'reasonably practicable' to ensure the health and safety of employees at work, they must think many times before turning down a suggestion.

Suppose that an employee is killed on a site for which you are responsible. The inspector considers that he would have lived had the management only carried out a recommendation of the site safety committee. How can the manager prove (as he must, if he wishes to be acquitted of a criminal offence) that he did all that was 'reasonably practicable' to save that man's life?

The Health and Safety at Work Act is only now beginning to bite. Safety committees will give it teeth. The time to set them up is now. Details follow . . .

Chapter 24

Committees and Representatives: Checklist

The Act lays down the rules; the Code helps explain how to carry them into force; the Guidance Notes add further suggestions. This chapter summarises all three.

* * *

1 Have you sought and reached agreement with all recognised trade unions concerned?

Safety representatives must be appointed by trade unions; trade unions must be consulted about the new set up; 'full and proper use of the existing agreed industrial relations machinery' must be made, so as 'to reach the degree of agreement necessary to achieve the purpose of the Regulations and in order to resolve any differences'; and if agreement is reached and implemented, the new rules should cause you no trouble.

The purpose of the Regulations and of the Code 'is to provide a framework within which each undertaking can develop effective working arrangements'. Is your framework established on an agreed basis?

2 Have your recognised trade unions appointed their safety representatives?

A trade union recognised for bargaining purposes 'may' appoint safety representatives, who must be employees concerned (and not outsiders). If a trade union has notified you of the identity of its representative, then you must recognise him and permit him to carry out his functions. Normally, he must either have been with you for at least two years or have had at least two years' experience in similar employment elsewhere.

3 *Have you agreed on areas for representation?*

Normally, unions will appoint representatives to represent a group or groups of workers of a class for which the union has negotiating rights. However, exceptions may be made. For instance, within the organisation of a small employer when the number of recognised trade unions is high, relative to the numbers employed – or where it is more convenient to make some other division for some other reason – exceptions may certainly be made. As usual, everything depends upon mutual agreement. You should consider these problems in advance. Have you done so?

4 *How many representatives do you need?*

The number of safety representatives will depend upon: the total number of employees; the variety and different occupations; the size of the work place and the variety of work place locations; the operation of shift systems; the type of work activity and the degree and character of the inherent dangers. In other words – all the circumstances of the case must be taken into account. Have you done so?

5 *How flexible must you be?*

Flexibility is essential – especially in (among others) the following cases:

(a) If the majority of employees in your work place are engaged in low risk activities, but if there are special risks attached to particular places or processes. (Where do you keep your explosive or inflammable substances?)

(b) If your employees (or some of them) move around in the course of their duties. (Do you send out sales or maintenance engineers?).

(c) If a wide variety of different work activities are going on in the same place.

(d) If your work place has a specially high process risk (do you carry out research? Are there any construction or demolition processes going on in your premises?).

6 *Have you agreed on and established the functions of your safety representatives?*

The safety reps' functions should include the following:

(a) Representation of employees in consultation with employer on health and safety matters. You must consult with them 'with a view to the making and maintenance of arrangements which will enable effective co-operation in promoting and developing measures to ensure the health and safety at work of employees and checking the effectiveness of those measures'.

(b) The investigation of potential hazards and dangerous occurrences at the work place and examination of causes of accidents.

(c) The investigation of complaints by any employee represented by the representative concerning that employee's health, safety or welfare at work.

(d) The making of representations to the employer of matters arising out of the above.

(e) The making of representations to the employer on general matters affecting the health, safety and welfare at work of employees.

(f) The carrying out of inspections in accordance with the Regulations.

(g) The representation of the employees in consultations with inspectors.

(h) The receiving of information from inspectors.

(i) The attending of meetings of safety committees in the capacity of safety representative.

7 Will a safety representative be liable at law if he carries out his duties negligently?

No. The regulations specifically provide that no function given to a safety representative shall be construed as imposing any duty on him – other, of course, than the ordinary duties which he undertakes as an employee, to take such steps as are reasonably practicable to protect his own safety and that of his colleagues at work.

In addition, the Health and Safety Commission has directed the Executive not to institute criminal proceedings against any safety representative for any act or omission by him in respect of the performance and functions assigned to him by the Regulations or indicated by the Code of Practice. Every effort must be made to avoid frightening people out of doing this extra, voluntary service.

8 What time off work should we allow safety representatives in order to do their jobs?

The Regulations say that a representative shall be allowed to take such time off with pay as is necessary for him to perform his above functions and to undergo necessary training for that purpose. Details are set out in a Schedule as to how that payment is to be calculated. Briefly, he should not lose money as a result of performing his function. And that includes paid time off for courses of training in safety problems – provided by you or by his union.

9 Are there any special steps we should take to help safety representatives to perform their functions?

Yes. The Code of Practice says that the representatives themselves should take all reasonably practicable steps to keep themselves fully informed about legal requirements concerning health and safety, particular hazards of the work place concerned and the health and safety policy of their employers. They should encourage co-operation in promoting safety measures and should bring to their employer's notice, 'normally in writing', any unsafe or unhealthy conditions or working practices or unsatisfactory arrangements for welfare at work which comes to their attention.

You should do everything you can to assist the representative to perform his functions. You should give him 'ready access' to you or to your representatives and enable more complaints to be taken up without delay.

10 If safety representatives wish to consult with management, what channel should they use?

(a) Normal trade union methods of communication.
(b) Special relationships with other safety representatives, whom they should know directly.
(c) Ready access to the employer or his representatives.

11 What records should be kept by safety representatives when they make inspections?

A safety representative should fill in a form and give a copy to the employer. There are two samples which are included in the Guidance Notes.

A

Date of inspection	*Area or Workplace inspected*	*Name(s) of safety representative(s) taking part in inspection*

(This record does not imply that the conditions are safe and healthy or that the arrangements for welfare at work are satisfactory.)
Signature(s) of safety representative(s) . . . .
Date . . . .

B Sample of suggested form to be used for notifying to the employer, or his representative, unsafe and unhealthy conditions and working practices and unsatisfactory arrangements for welfare at work.

Date of inspection or matter observed	*Particulars of matter(s) notified to employer or his representative (include location where appropriate).*	*Name(s) of safety representative notifying matter(s) to employer (or his representative).*	*Remedial action taken (with date) or explanation if not taken*

(This report does not imply that the conditions are safe and healthy or that the arrangements for welfare at work are satisfactory in all other respects.)

Signature(s) of safety representative(s) . . . .
Date . . . .
Signature of employer
(or his representative) . . . .
Date . . . .

12 What inspections should be made by the safety representatives – and how?

The Regulations provide that a representative is entitled to inspect the workplace or any part of it, provided that he gives the employer reasonable notice in writing of his intention to do so and provided that he has not inspected the same area during the previous three months. By agreement, inspections may be more frequent.

The Guidance Notes suggest that where there is 'high risk activity or rapidly changing circumstances . . . confined to a particular area of the workplace or sector of an employee's activities', more frequent inspections may be advisable.

Where there has been 'a substantial change in the conditions of work' since the previous inspection, then a representative may inspect however recently his previous inspection took place. But the Commission considers that 'a programme of formal inspections' should be planned in advance – subject to agreed variations.

The employer must then provide 'such facilities and assistance as the safety representative may reasonably require' – but the employer or his representative may remain present during the inspection.

The Commission 'sees advantages' in these formal inspections being carried out jointly by employer and employee together, but independent investigations are proper and often advisable.

Safety representatives should co-ordinate their work so as to avoid unnecessary duplication and, where appropriate, a safety officer or specialist advisers should be available to give technical advice on the problems that arise during the course of the inspection.

13 What sort of inspection should be carried out?

The Commission suggests three types:-

(a) Safety tours – that is, general inspections of the workplace.

(b) Safety sampling – that is, systematic sampling of particular dangerous activities, processes or areas.

(c) Safety surveys – that is, general inspections of a particular dangerous activity, process or area.

The representatives and the employers should agree on the numbers of representatives to take part in the particular inspection.

If there has been a notifiable accident, i.e. one causing three or more days off work, or a dangerous occurrence or notifiable disease, then the safety representatives may carry out such inspection as is necessary in order to 'determine the cause' – and to prevent repetition. Once again, employers should provide new assistance.

In all these cases, there should be maximum flexibility. For instance, at a large workplace, different groups of safety representatives may carry out different inspections.

If remedial action is taken, then representatives should re-inspect in order to satisfy themselves that the trouble has been overcome.

As in all other cases, employers and employees should seek agreement at every stage.

14 How much information must be given to a safety representative and what documents must you disclose?

The representative is entitled to inspect and take copies of 'any document relevant to the workplace or to the employees . . . which the employer is required to keep' by virtue of any industrial safety statute. These include, of course, any accident books or records. The representative must give to the employer 'reasonable notice' of his wish to inspect or to have copies.

As to information, it is laid down by the Code of Practice under five heads. Here they are:

- *(a)* information about the plans and performance of the undertaking and any changes proposed in so far as they affect the health and safety at work of their employees;
- *(b)* information of a technical nature about hazards to health and safety and precautions deemed necessary to eliminate or minimise them – in respect of machinery, equipment, plant and processes, systems of work and substances in use at work (including any relevant information provided by consultants or designers or by the manufacturer, importer or supplier of any article or substance used, or proposed to be used, at work by their employees);
- *(c)* information which the employer keeps, relating to the occurrence of any accident, dangerous occurrence or notifiable industrial disease and any statistical records relating to such accidents, dangerous occurrences or cases of notifiable industrial disease;
- *(d)* any other information specifically related to matters affecting the health and safety at work of his employees, including the results of any measurements taken by the employer or persons acting on his behalf in the course of checking the effectiveness of his health and safety arrangements;
- *(e)* information on articles or substances which an employer issues to home workers.

The exceptions to the rule are almost the same as those (in the Employment Act) which free an employer from his normal duty to disclose information to recognised, independent trade unions during the course of collective bargaining. He will not have to harm national secutiry or give information related to an individual without his consent, nor information obtained in connection with legal proceedings. Above all, he may keep to himself any information 'the disclosure of which would, for reasons other than its effect on health, safety or welfare at work, cause substantial injury to the employer's undertaking or, where the information was supplied to him by some other person, the undertaking of that other person'.

Still, you should not be looking for the exceptions but doing your best to comply with the rule.

As the Guidance Notes say: 'Appointed safety representatives will need to be given information and knowledge over and above that necessary for employees generally – so as to enable them to play an informed part in promoting health and safety at work'.

15 When must we establish a safety committee?

Whenever at least two safety representatives request you to do so in writing. You must then consult with safety representatives who made the request and with the representatives of recognised trade unions whose members work in any workplace in respect of which you propose that the committee should function. You must post a notice stating the composition of the committee and the workplace or workplaces to be covered by it, somewhere where it may be easily read by the employees. Your committee must be established not later than three months after the representatives have asked for it.

Detailed arrangements (say the Guidance Notes) should 'evolve from discussion and negotiation between employers and the appointed safety representatives'. Circumstances and workplaces vary – but certain rules are vital. These include the following:

(a) The safety committee must have a separate identity so that safety matters do not 'become interposed in the agenda for other meetings'.

(b) Safety committees should generally be related to a single establishment rather than to a collection of 'geographically distinct places' – although you may have a group or company safety committee, co-ordinating the work of the smaller ones.

(c) The safety committee should draw up agreed objec-

tives and terms of reference, defining its function.

(d) The membership and structure of the committee should be agreed between the parties but the size should be 'as reasonably compact as possible'. The number of management representatives should certainly not exceed the number of employees' representatives. From the management side, works engineers and personnel managers should be included. So should any company doctor or safety officer directly concerned with this work.

(e) Safety representatives should suffer no loss of pay through attendance at meetings.

(f) Meetings should be given priority; they should be prepared well ahead and only cancelled or postponed in case of true emergency.

(g) The meetings should be run in a businesslike way with an agenda and minutes – the latter made available to employees.

16 What can happen if we do not follow the rules?

If you do not comply with the regulations you are in breach of the law. The Factory Inspector may prosecute in the same way as for any other breach – and in addition, a safety representative who has not been given paid time off for his safety functions may himself complain to an Industrial Tribunal. If breach of the rules results in an unsafe practice, you also risk prosecution under Section 2 or 3.

* * *

So the Regulations have the force of law; the Code may be quoted in evidence against you if you do not comply with it; Guidance Notes should be followed, so as to avoid clashing with the Regulations or with the Code. Disagreements should be settled through normal machinery for the resolution of industrial relations practice. But the entire operation should be regarded as a means of involving the workforce in the avoidance of unnecessary accident, injury and death – from which they will suffer and for which you may be held criminally responsible.

Chapter 25

Chairing a Safety Committee

A safety committee (like any other) needs a chairman. He may be a manager – the managing director, perhaps, or the personnel chief or the company doctor. Or one of the safety representatives may himself be an experienced chairman – perhaps a local councillor? The law does not prescribe the identity of the chairman of a safety committee nor prescribe how he should do his job. But success of the committee's work will depend on how he carries out this important function. So here are some hints to help him (or you) to do this vital job.

* * *

(a) Do your homework. This means:

1 Read and understand the new Regulations, Code and Guidance Notes. You will find the full text set out in Appendix 2 to this book. You can get further copies in a neat pamphlet from the Health and Safety Commission (Baynards House, 1 Chepstow Place, London W2 4DF. Telephone: 01-220 3456).

2 Read the Minutes of previous meetings, so that you know what has been discussed and decided in the past – otherwise you are bound to forget to check on implementation of decisions and/or to waste time going over old territory again.

3 Study the safety set-up, organisation and problems within the unit concerned – if necessary, taking guidance from representatives or other committee members – so that you can guide the discussion in an informed and helpful way.

(b) Prepare your agenda in advance. As in the case of all other meetings, you must know what is to be discussed. Typical agenda would read:

1 Apologies for non-attendance.
2 Minutes of last meeting.
3 Matters arising from Minutes, not included under later items.
4 Correspondence.
5 Reports of safety representatives on incidents – including accidents or hazards occurring since last meeting.
6 Report of safety officer.
7 Report of medical officer/nurse.
8 Recommendations for action.
9 Any other business.

(c) Ensure that someone on the committee is capable of taking careful Minutes; that he in fact does so; and that the Minutes are circularised to all members before the meeting – so that at the start you can say: 'Minutes have been circularised. May I sign these as a correct record of what occurred at the last meeting?' If there are any alleged inaccuracies, these should be sorted out. Remember: the Minutes are neither more nor less than a record. They set out what happened – not what you or anyone else would have preferred to have happened.

(d) Prepare the rest of the meeting in advance, in so far as can. Help the safety representatives to have their reports ready and encourage them to discuss with you beforehand any queries on presentation. You may also find items which it would be better for the safety representative (at least initially) to deal with behind the scenes rather than in public. The job of the chairman is to get results – and not to encourage disputes. Conversely: the more harmony he can achieve, the better.

(e) Encourage full discussion and take special care to bring

into it those whose views may be valuable but who may be reticent or inarticulate. Particularly when dealing with people who have practical safety experience or interest but who are not used to committee work, it is the chairman who can make them feel valuable – and so encourage in their efforts.

(f) Guide the discussion so that it stays within the intended limits – of health, safety and welfare. Do not allow the meeting to turn into a battleground, with discussion or argument ranging over other areas. If a safety committee trespasses into the arena of (for instance) collective bargaining, union and management are likely to move back to their own sides of the table – whereas in a safety committee they should be brought and kept together.

(g) Unlike chairing committees with two sides, the safety committee chairman's job is to focus attention all the time on the united purpose of management and unions – to preserve life and limb. There should not be two sides. If you are successful in bringing and keeping people happily together for this purpose, then you may indeed change the atmosphere for all other purposes. But if management and unions cannot combine successfully for safety purposes, what hope can there be for industrial peace?

(h) If disputes arise over the composition of the committee, check back to the Commission's Guidance Notes. Yours is a practical committee with one, sole, crucial job – to reduce the risks of accidents. Keep your mind concentrated on that task – and ensure that the discussion does not drift away from that specific task.

(i) As in the case of all chairmen, keep cool; retain your good humour; and use tact, courtesy – and flattery – rather than sarcasm or the stick. A firm approach (especially when dealing with deviations from the health and safety area) should be fully acceptable.

(j) Always try to achieve a consensus of opinion. But do not be afraid to call for a vote. Votes are rare on boards of directors but frequent at trade union meetings. Directors who chair safety

committees are often too chary of calling for a vote where clarification of views becomes necessary. You will sometimes find that the vote brings results which are quite different from those that you would have expected from the discussion.

(k) Always fix the date of the next meeting – and make sure it is one that is suitable for yourself. The Commission stresses that meetings should only be cancelled or postponed in the most rare emergencies. If you expect others to give priority to your committee and to its decisions and deliberations, you must do so yourself. A chairman's job is to lead. Chairmen of safety committees are leading the way into a safer industrial world.

Chapter 26

Why Always the Unions?

From 1 October 1978 employers will be *required* to appoint safety committees and to consult with appointed representatives of independent, recognised trade unions. There will be no legal requirement that they consult with non-union representatives.

If you employ non-union labour, you would most certainly be wise to do so. But the 'safety watchdogs' will be appointed by the organised workforce and it will be a criminal offence not to consult with them and with union safety committees.

Why this insistence on the independent trade union? The answer lies partly in the law and partly in the realm of practical politics and philosophy.

Ever since *The Trade Union and Labour Relations Act, 1974*, a whole series of measures have been introduced designed to strengthen independent trade unions. A union is 'independent' (in broad terms) if it is not under the direct or indirect control of employers. The certificate of independence granted by the Certification Officer is absolute proof of independence.

Most independent trade unions are affiliated to the TUC. Many are not.

Advantages enjoyed by trade unions include the following:

> The law now requires consultation with independent trade unions concerning intended redundancies of any of their

members. Failure to consult entitles the union (and not the member) to apply to an Industrial Tribunal for a 'protective award'. If successful, the union will win money (approximately equivalent to the sum which the employee would have received during the period during which consultation should have taken place), which the employer must pay to the employees threatened with redundancy. Still, it is the union that applies and only union members in practice can obtain such an award. The rest have to rely on the employer's duty to inform the Department of Employment in the case of any intended redundancy exceeding 10 in number at any one establishment during a period of 30 days.

There is, of course, nothing to prevent your giving information of intended redundancies to non-union employees – and good management requires you to do so. Not, though, the law.

Soon, employers will be required (thanks, again, to the Employment Protection Act) to disclose information for the purposes of collective bargaining to those independent trade unions who require it. You may (and indeed should) give information to everyone. The legal requirement will be confined to trade unions.

When worker participation legislation appears (and that day cannot be far away), it will be the trade union representatives who will sit on Boards and not elected representatives of the entire shop floor.

Why this constant preferment of trade unions? Whether or not you agree with the reasons, they are as follows:

1 The Government and the unions have come to an agreement. In return for the unions supporting the Government's efforts to balance the economy (and to stay in power), the Government has undertaken to attempt to strengthen the organised trade union movement.

This, incidentally, is not a particularly revolutionary idea – during the Industrial Relations Act debates, the previous Government frequently emphasised its wish to strengthen trade unions and to weaken 'wild cats'.

2 The Trade Union and Labour Relations Act (repealing the Industrial Relations Act but re-enacting the unfair dismissal rules – strengthened) was the first stage in implementing the above agreement; the Employment Protection Act followed; worker participation will be the third stage. The Health and Safety at Work Act, though, was in the main a non-party/all-party effort. Even here, though, the Government has implemented the decision to insist upon trade union involvement – and (via the Employment Protection Act) abolished the power of the Employment Secretary to require consultation with elected shop floor representatives (see above).

3 Politics apart (and you cannot remove their effect from the law-making process), the philosophy behind the giving of these powers to trade unions is a simple one: It is the trade unions that have:

(a) The organised strength to build health and safety awareness and understanding among the workforce; to influence colleagues to comply with the rules; and (if necessary) to face up to management, if the need arises.

(b) The back-up organisation to make the appropriate arrangements and (hopefully) to provide training additional to that laid on by the management (in the health and safety field, so as to comply with Section 2 obligations).

(c) The power to make and to enforce collective bargains – with you and with the government of the day.

"AREN'T YOU TAKING THIS 'PROTECTIVE CLOTHING' IDEA TOO FAR, HARGREAVES?"

Part Four

Your Questions Answered

Introduction

This Part is devoted to answering those questions about the Act which are most frequently asked in industrial and commercial practice. Some cover new ground; some have been touched upon or hinted at in Parts 1-3 of this book; others apply tests or information already supplied, so as to solve new problems. Section A deals with general questions and Section B with those that stem directly from the impending arrival of safety committees and representatives.

When lecturing to embattled executives, questions can be asked and answered in the course of the day. Interplay between lecturer and businessman brings the subject to life – but this cannot be transferred to a book. This Part provides the next best arrangement and has the advantage of being a permanent record. To all those keen-witted executives who originally asked me the questions, my thanks. They bear no responsibility for the answers which follow; neither questions nor answers are in any particular order; but the pot-pourri of legal and industrial expertise which now follows may be used by readers to test their own recollection or knowledge, or that of their colleagues or employees to whom they must explain the intricacies of the Act in full operation.

Your Questions Answered

Section A: General

1 What goes into our written safety statement?

We are preparing a written statement of our general policy with respect to the Health and Safety at Work of our employees and of the organisation and arrangements for the time being in force for carrying out that policy, as required by Section 2(3) of the Health and Safety at Work Act. Can you advise us, in general terms, as to what ought to be included?

* * *

You should set out your general policy in broad terms but your precise procedures in detail, in connection with each hazardous operation. Detailed, specific rules are vital. But you could refer to specific job instructions, and these should themselves incorporate the safety element.

Some employers argue that a document will be useless if it is too full, because employees will not trouble to read it, whereas a shorter document would be more effective. But while it is certainly sensible to cut out any unnecessary padding, the intention of the Act is that the safety rules should be set out as fully as is necessary so as to enable the inspector and the employee alike to see that the arrangements are totally adequate.

2 Whom must you protect – and how?

The Act requires employers and others to take care for the safety of all those affected by their work or by premises under their control. How far does this responsibility stretch; and what steps should we take in practice, to avoid being successfully prosecuted for failing to comply with that duty?

* * *

Everyone is covered – visitors, neighbours, sub-contractors and their employers and employees alike.

Any visitor who is likely to be submitted to risk should certainly be warned in advance. And that warning should where possible be given in writing, not merely so as to drive it home to the visitor but also so that you can prove if necessary that you have provided it.

Where contractors come onto your premises, you should always make them aware of their own duties and responsibilities. Take special care with the contractual documentation, to ensure that these matters are fully covered – even though nothing in the documents can free you from liability under the new Act. By all means refer to any required standards or Codes of Practice. And if you have any works' rules or other guidance, then these should be provided.

As to the wider public – neighbours, visitors and the like – you must take great care not to expose them to unnecessary risk. Your premises; your goods in transit; your operations – all are included.

If you engage in any sort of construction work, take special care. A very high proportion of industrial accidents involve construction, which causes risk not only to employees but to the public at large.

3 How does the Act affect agriculture?

To what extent does the Act apply to agriculture?

* * *

All employees, including those in agriculture, are covered by the safety measures and if engaged in agriculture you must comply with the new rules. These apply not only to shops (including garden centres), to offices, to launderettes and to factories and works, but also to farms and agricultural holdings. It is a common and dangerous misunderstanding to believe that agricultural employees are excluded.

Schools, hospitals, research establishments, hotels, entertainment centres – all are brought under the one unified umbrella. Agricultural operations came into the Act for the purposes of the new duties and requirements but at first they stood apart for the purposes of enforcement. Since 1976 that too has been changed by the Employment Protection Act.

4 How does the Act modify other legislation?

How does the Act affect our position under the Offices, Shops and Railway Premises Act?

* * *

The former legislation remains in full force. The Offices, Shops and Railway Premises Act; the Factories Act; all regulations made under them – indeed, almost all existing law – remains as binding as previously.

The new enforcement rules (including 'improvement notices' and 'prohibition notices'), requiring you – either immediately or within a stated time – to mend your ways apply to all existing legislation and to the new Act and regulations made under it as time goes on. The new penalties, in the main, apply to the old law as well as to the new. But that law remains unchanged and you must continue to comply with it, now and in the future as in the past.

5 What is 'reasonable'?

In the Act, employers are required in many cases to do what is 'reasonably practicable' for the safety, health and welfare of employees. The question of what is 'reasonably practicable' is very difficult to answer. Does the Act provide any guidance?

The words 'reasonably practicable' are not defined. What is 'reasonable' depends on all the circumstances of the case. It may be that there is a stricter obligation than in ordinary, common law cases involving 'reasonableness' – but in practice, I doubt it. If you have taken those steps which a reasonable, intelligent, average, prudent employer would take, then the average, reasonable, sensible court should consider that you have done enough. In other words, both you and the court will apply the rules of common sense. But as views as to 'reasonableness' differ, you should certainly lean in favour of extra caution.

Note, though, that if you admit that certain steps were not taken but your defence is that it was not 'reasonably practicable' for you to take them, then the burden of proving lack of practicability will rest on your bowed shoulders. The burden of proof, that is, shifts from the prosecution onto you.

6 Can we afford the changes?

Can we afford the cost of the changes required by the Health and Safety at Work Act?

* * *

You cannot afford the cost of having a prohibition notice slapped on your company and a machine or system or even the entire works.

So you must balance the cost of the safety measures and your ability to bear it against the risk to human life or limb if you do not add it to the possibility of being forced to make the changes in the inspector's time rather than your own.

And apart from the suffering and misery it causes, have you ever sat down and worked out how much it costs, in terms of managers' time, lost production, sick pay, preparing reports and documents, discussing the responsibility . . . just for a relatively minor accident?

7 What is my liability to cleaners' children?

Many of the ladies who clean our premises bring their children to work with them. What are our responsibilities towards those children, both at common law and under the Act?

* * *

You owe a 'common duty of care' to cleaners' children under *The Occupiers' Liability Act, 1957.* If you fail to take such care for their safety as is reasonable in all the circumstances, then you will be liable to pay damages if as a result of that breach of your duty the child suffers injury. You must also (says the Act) bear in mind that a child will take less care of itself than would an adult in similar circumstances. The problems are examined more closely in the chapter on 'Looking after children' in Book 2.

Under the 1974 Act, a similar duty is imposed – and if you are in breach of that duty, you will be liable to prosecution. Thanks to Section 3 of the Act, you must 'conduct your undertaking in such a way as to ensure, in so far as is reasonably practicable, that persons not in your employment who may be affected thereby are not thereby exposed to risks to their health or safety'. So you must take 'reasonably practicable' steps, to protect your cleaners' children against risks to their 'health or safety'.

You may insure against risks imposed by the Act but you cannot insure against your criminal liabilities. So you should certainly consider with care – and with your cleaners – whether their children are safe while on your premises. It is no longer good enough simply to leave it to the common sense of the mother. You must take your own, objective judgement – as a court would do if you were prosecuted. Remember, too, that if it is shown that you did not take sufficient steps to protect the child, but you argue that it was not 'reasonably practicable' for you to do more, then the burden of proving lack of reasonable practicality will rest upon you.

The same rules apply to children brought onto your premises by your drivers – or other peoples'.

8 Can you charge for lost protective clothing?

Like many other employers, we provide protective clothing free of charge – but we have always made employees pay for replacement when employees lose that clothing. Is it true that we are no longer able to charge even when clothing is lost?

* * *

Some protective clothing or equipment is provided as a result of specific statutory requirements – such as safety spectacles, required by the Protection of Eyes Regulations. In cases where the provision is 'in pursuance of any specific requirement' or a 'relevant statutory provision', then you will not be entitled to make any charge, either in respect of the initial provision or, almost certainly, in respect of any provision as a replacement.

However, Section 9 of the new Act has no reference to those cases – and they are the majority – in which the protective clothing or equipment is provided out of caution and common sense, rather than as a result of 'any specific statutory requirement'. In those cases, you may still charge for replacements – in the same way as many employers require employees to contribute towards even the initial cost of protective shoes.

9 How does this Act affect interference with machinery?

To what extent does the Act change the duty which the Factories Act places on employees not to interfere with machinery?

* * *

Section 143 of the Factories Act makes it an offence to interfere with or to misuse equipment 'wilfully'. Section 8 of the new Act rules that 'no person' (whether employed or not) shall 'intentionally' or 'recklessly' interfere with or misuse anything provided 'in the interests of health, safety or welfare' in pursuance of any relevant statutory provision.

It is easier to prove an 'intention' or 'recklessness' than to show what a court has described as 'an element of peversity'. To convict under the Factories Act, the prosecution must show both intention and 'wilfulness' – intention to interfere with or misuse will suffice under the new legislation.

In addition, an employee may be charged with the further

count of failing to take reasonable care for the health and safety of himself or of some other person affected by his work; or with failing to co-operate with his employers so far as is necessary to enable his employer to carry out his (that is, the employer's) obligations under the Act – contrary to Section 7.

An employer's duties under the new Act are more extensive and difficult to comply with than under the old legislation, and so are those now imposed on employees.

10 How do we deal with unco-operative employees?

We have a long-term employee who simply refuses to wear his safety spectacles. He says: 'I have been doing it this way all my life and I'm not changing now. . .'. We do not want to dismiss him. But we are afraid of a prosecution. He says: 'It's my eyes, not yours . . . I'm not affecting anyone else. . .'. We say: 'You are putting us in jeopardy. As your employers, we are liable to be taken to court.' What do you advise?

* * *

First, you must use all reasonable persuasion and propaganda to induce him to change his mind and to follow the rules. Apart from talking to him yourself, have you got his union or his mates onto the trail?

Second, can you prove your efforts to convince him? Have you written to him . . . warned him . . . and either obtained a signature from him or else recorded on your file that he refused to sign?

If you are prosecuted because there has been a breach of the Protection of Eyes Regulations or under Section 2 of the 1974 Act, you must be in a position to show that you have taken 'all steps that are reasonably practicable'. You are not under an absolute liability to ensure that your employees stay safe. A court would ask: 'Have you done all that a reasonable, prudent kindly, decent, sensible employer would have done in the circumstances?'

Dismissal is the last resort and if you were to dismiss the man having gone through all these stages, the dismissal would probably be 'fair'.

Equally, if you have really done everything in your power to get the man to comply and he still refuses, it is extremely unlikely that a court would convict you of a criminal offence merely because you kept him on. The situation would be different, of course, if the man were hazarding other people's safety.

Still, you have to ask yourself: What is the extent of the risk? Which is the less unpleasant of the two alternatives – to allow the man to stay on when he may lose his eyesight or dismiss him so that he loses his livelihood?

11 What are my new duties to visitors?

We are insured in case anyone is injured when visiting our premises. Can we insure against our responsibilities under the Act? How do our duties and liabilities differ under the new rules?

* * *

The old laws are mainly laid down by *The Occupiers' Liability Act, 1957,* which remains in force. The main effect of the new Act is to introduce new criminal liabilities which can be imposed on those who do not take proper care for the safety of their visitors.

Under the Occupiers' Liability Act, you owe a 'common duty of care' to all your visitors. The extent of that duty depends upon the visitor – for instance, you must be far more careful for the safety of children than you would be for that of those who visit you 'in the exercise of their calling' (sub-contractors, window cleaners and the like).

Still, if someone is injured, you will be covered by insurance. And the Employers' Liability (Compulsory Insurance) Act ensures that you insure at least for the safety of your employees. But prudent occupiers also carry full insurance against public liability.

No insurer, though, can or will cover you against potential fines. Still less will the insurers take your place in the dock or cell. So remember Sections 4 and 5 of the Act, which cover people 'in control of premises'. You must see that your premises (shop, works or anywhere else) are safe for visitors (or 'third parties'). You must take care that, if in due course your premises are 'prescribed' by regulations, you take all reasonably practicable steps to see that any 'noxious or offensive emissions' from your premises are rendered harmless and inoffensive.

12 How are the self-employed and partners affected?

We know that companies are covered by the Act. But we operate our business in partnership. Are self-employed people or partners covered by the new rules?

* * *

Yes. The self-employed person comes under the Act in three main ways. First, in so far as he is covered by existing legislation (such as the Offices, Shops and Railway Premises Act or the Factories Act or regulations made under them), he is subject to the new enforcement procedures and penalties, in the same way as anyone else.

If, for instance, you fail properly to heat your premises for the benefit of your employees or if you use machinery which is not properly guarded, then you may have an improvement notice or a prohibition notice served on you; your right of appeal lies to the Industrial Tribunal; and if convicted of an offence, then the maximum penalties will be a fine of unlimited amount and/or two years imprisonment.

It is, of course, highly unlikely that any such penalty will be imposed – but self-employed people and partners are at risk under the new Act in the same way as company executives.

Second, self-employed people come under Section 2 as employers of others. They are under the new duty to take all reasonably practicable steps for the safety, health and welfare of their employees.

Third; under Section 3 of the Act, self-employed people and partners must ensure in so far as is reasonably practicable that they do not endanger themselves or others through their work. If you are an individual who works for gain or reward otherwise than under a contract of employment, then (whether or not you employ other people) you are included within the definition of 'self-employed' and will have to comply with the rules.

13 What is the extent of an inspector's powers?

Under the new Act, inspectors are given considerably increased powers – including the right to seize and destroy an article or substance which is considered likely to cause 'imminent danger of serious personal injury'. How can an inspector be prevented from abusing that power? And what of his right to demand information which is highly confidential?

* * *

An inspector is only entitled to seize and destroy in highly dangerous emergencies. Even then, there must be prior consultation about the danger; and if it is practicable for the inspector to take a sample of the substance or article and to provide a marked proportion of that sample to 'a responsible person' on the premises concerned, then he must do so – before he acts. Subsequently, he must prepare a detailed report and give a copy to the owner of the premises and to the 'responsible person'.

An inspector who takes unjustifiable action to seize or destroy any article or substance may be sued in a civil court. And if he discloses information which he obtained in the course of his duties with respect to 'any trade secret', then if that disclosure was unnecessary for the purpose of carrying out his duties or for legal proceedings or unless he has the consent of the owner, then he commits an offence.

In practice, these powers are exercised rarely and with discretion. But there are provisions designed to prevent abuse.

14 What are your duties to employees travelling abroad?

Like many manufacturers, we organise our own transport and our lorries deliver our products overseas. What are our liabilities under the Act, once our vehicles cross the Channel?

* * *

Section 2 imposes a duty on 'all employers' to take all such steps as are 'reasonably practicable' to ensure the 'health, safety and welfare at work of all employees.' There is no restriction on where the employees are working.

An employer must, in particular, take proper steps to ensure that an employee's 'place of work' is safe and healthy. And 'place' is defined as including transport.

So you must provide mobile places of work, both within the United Kingdom and outside it – under UK legislation, you must comply with the new Act or you may be liable to be prosecuted. Equally, your insurance will no doubt cover you against risks, wherever your transport may be. In civil and in criminal law, you do not get rid of your responsibilities when your vehicle leaves the jurisdiction of the English court.

On the other hand, once your vehicles and their occupants are overseas, they come under the jurisdiction of other courts – and must comply with the laws of the countries in which they are operating. If, for instance, they fail to comply with local transport regulations or road traffic laws, then the drivers and your company may both be prosecuted.

Still, it is not clear to what extent the Act applies to installations on the Continental shelf, or to installations or transport overseas, but Section 84 gives power to the Government to make Orders in Council, extending the rules outside Great Britain. Extensive regulations as to safety on oil installations were made in any case, under a different Act.

15 How absolute is my duty?

We are proud of our safety record and do our best to look after our employees. But with the best will in the world, accidents do happen. If we have taken all reasonable steps to comply with our duties, both under the previous legislation and under the Act, could we successfully be prosecuted?

* * *

You must insure against liability to your employees because the Employers' Liability (Compulsory Insurance) Act and commonsense both so require. But, in general, you are only liable under the old law or the new if you fail to take such steps as are reasonably necessary to protect your employees against unnecessary risk. What is 'reasonable' always depends upon the circumstances of the case.

Who decides what is 'reasonable'? It may be the factory inspector; the lawyers who are negotiating a settlement; or, at worst, a court. And the same applies to the general duty imposed under the new Act to do what is 'reasonably practicable' for the safety of employees.

If you follow the rules laid down by regulations and codes of practice; adopt the best methods known to avoid injury or accidents; follow the advice and guidance given by your factories inspector – then all should be well.

Remember, though, that under the Act if it is proved that you did not take adequate steps to protect employees (or, for that matter, other people affected by operations under your control) and you say that the reason is that it would not have been 'reasonably practicable' for you to do more, then the burden of proving lack of 'reasonable practicability' will rest on you.

Normally, you are only bound, then, to take reasonable steps to guard against those accidents which a reasonably farsighted person would have expected to occur. You must protect employees against 'reasonably foreseeable' injuries. But there are exceptions where absolute liability is imposed and where liability in no way depends upon knowledge of the peril.

You are absolutely liable if you knock down a pedestrian on a zebra crossing, provided that his foot was on the stripes before your wheels crossed the studs – even if you had no chance in fact to avoid the disaster. In the same way, the requirements of the Asbestos Regulations concerning notification of intention to work with certain dangerous materials are absolute and even if you could not really have had knowledge of the risk, you will still be responsible.

In general, though, foreseeability is as good a rule of legal thumb as any, when considering liability in civil or criminal law, new or old.

16 How does a court fix penalties?

Under the Act, enormous potential penalties are now in force even for existing legislation such as the Offices, Shops and Railway Premises Act. How will a court in fact decide on the extent of the fine to be imposed – or whether or not to send a director or manager to prison?

* * *

In deciding on the penalty, any court will consider both the offence and the offender. So where health and safety are concerned, the court would certainly look at the extent of the hazard; the efforts made to put matters right; and all the circumstances of the case.

Then the court would consider whether the accused had previous convictions for the same or similar offences; the extent of his resources; and what was said by his solicitor or counsel in 'mitigation'.

The Act frequently says that 'a person' is under a duty. The word 'person' means both an individual and a company or authority or other 'corporate body'. Corporations, of course, cannot be sent to prison; their directors, managers, secretaries and 'other similar officers' may be; but you may expect the ultimate sanction to be used only in those rare and extremely serious cases in which there is vast peril to life or limb and persistent failure to comply with the rules.

17 What are the duties of a manufacturer, designer or supplier?

If a product is defective and causes harm to 'the ultimate consumer', he may sue the manufacturer in a civil court, claiming damages for negligence. If the product is not in accordance with contract, then other parties to that contract may claim damages – again in a civil court – for breach of contract. The new Act imposes a new criminal liability on manufacturers. What is its extent and how can we guard against the danger of prosecution under the new rules?

* * *

The civil rules quoted apply to anything manufactured. The Act refers specifically and only to articles *designed* for use at work – which means, in effect, plant or components; plus 'substances' (liquid or solid) intended for use at work. So the scope of the Act is far more limited than that of the civil law.

If you *manufacture, import, design* or *supply* articles or substances for use at work, though, you must take special care to provide full information about any known dangers; to carry out all necessary testing and research, except in so far as you can prove that someone else has already carried out the particular procedures (which you are not then bound to repeat) and except in so far as you can obtain a written undertaking from your customer that he has taken specified precautions; and unless the article or substance is absolutely innocuous, then you should certainly give the purchaser or customer specific warnings and accurate information – in letters, documents and/or on labels. And you should check your own sampling systems.

You may also have to change your marketing methods. In one recent case, a coroner criticised a supplier of a particular alloy which contained cadmium. The bulk package was suitably labelled with adequate warnings. But the contents of the package could be and were sold off separately. The individual items were not marked; the alloy was used by a plumber; and he died.

So in the case of any product which may be dangerous, you should consider your entire procedures, from beginning to end, with new vigilance and, if necessary, with the help and kindness of your factory inspector.

18 How are directors' reports affected?

Is it true that directors' reports will soon have to contain details of health and safety matters?

* * *

Probably. Section 79 provides that the Secretary of State may make regulations requiring directors' reports to contain prescribed information 'about the arrangements in force in that year for securing the health, safety and welfare at work of employees of the company and its subsidiaries' and also 'for protecting other persons against risks to health or safety arising out of or in connection with the activities at work of those employees'. The regulations have yet to be made.

19 Who starts proceedings?

There are heavy penalties for offenders under the new Act. Could anyone who wishes to get us into trouble start a prosecution? Suppose, for instance, that we want to prosecute one of our workmen, who refuses to give up unsafe practices – or, more likely, what if a trade union decides to have a go at us?

* * *

Only an inspector may institute proceedings, except in the rare cases where the Director of Public Prosecutions gives his consent to someone else doing so. In Scotland, it is the job of the Crown Office to decide on prosecution, no doubt on the advice of the inspector. Enforcement comes under the aegis of the executive; local authorities will take such responsibilities as required by law; but it will be the inspectors who start the prosecutions – not you, not your company, not your employees and not the trade unions. The Act will be activated by or on behalf of the public. It sets up standards of conduct required by society as a whole and is not to be used (directly at least) as a private flail.

20 What are the new duties of the Crown?

Are public servants protected by the new Act in the same way as private employees?

* * *

In general, yes. With rare exceptions, 'persons in the public service of the Crown' are protected in the same way as all other persons. But the Crown cannot be prosecuted in its own courts, although it may be sued for damages (in a civil action).

21 What happens in canteens and catering?

Most large concerns operate canteens – either directly or by bringing in outside caterers. Canteen staff tend to suffer from a high accident rate, however much care is taken to keep the floors clean and dry. So we encourage our girls to wear non-slip shoes. But some say that they simply cannot afford to buy the kind of specialised footwear which they would like. Is there any requirement – now or in the future – that we must supply special footwear to our cooks, waitresses and cleaners?

* * *

In civil law, you are bound to take reasonable care for the safety of your employees. From your question, you seem to recognise that non-slip shoes are necessary for your canteen staff and if you fail to provide them – or to ensure that the employees supply their own – you may be liable, if an accident occurs.

The new Act has no direct reference to such shoes, nor are there any regulations in force at present requiring them to be worn or provided. But regulations may be made – and there is no reason why you should wait until you are forced to take action before you do.

If in due course there is a specific requirement that these shoes be provided, you will not be able to make any charge for them. Meanwhile, there is nothing in law to prevent you from paying, say, half the cost – so as to encourage and enable those ladies who wish to wear safety shoes to do so. You should also consider very carefully whether you should not both pay for shoes, in whole or in part, and require them to be worn.

22 To what extent can I insure?

We can insure against having to pay damages to injured employees or visitors. Can we insure against fines which may be imposed on us under the new Act?

* * *

No. It would be 'contrary to public policy' for any insurer to cover his client against that sort of liability.

23 Can we insure against legal costs?

We appreciate that if we are convicted of an offence under any of the Industrial Safety Statutes, we will have to pay the fines ourselves and no insurer can cover us.

We have read, though, that we are able to insure against the costs involved in any such proceedings. Is this correct and if so is it lawful?

* * *

Suppose that you have an accident in your car or van or lorry. If you were at fault, your insurers will have to foot the bill.

If you are prosecuted under the Road Traffic Act and are convicted, the chances of your insurers avoiding liability are almost nil. Conversely, if you are acquitted, they stand at least a fighting chance of avoiding paying at least part of the damages which they would otherwise have to produce. So they clearly have a considerable interest in the outcome of the criminal proceedings. And they frequently pay the costs of the defence of their assured, so as to protect that interest.

These principles apply equally to industrial safety cases. It is possible to insure against the legal costs of the defence, including the fees of solicitor, counsel and expert witnesses and even any prosecution costs if awarded against you.

It is in your interests and in those of your insurers that you obtain the best possible advice and help in connection with your defence. Therefore they may ensure that you do so if you are insured against that risk.

To find out whether you are already covered against this risk, look at your insurance policy. The contracts made between insurers and their assured are variable and varied. To discover what you have bought for your premium, look at the policy document which contains the terms of your contract. If you wish to extend those terms – either with the same insurers or with others – you will have to be prepared to pay more out in premiums so as to achieve greater cover than you have at present

24 What is an insurer's liability?

We pay an annual premium to insurers but have no policy to show what it covers.

A short time ago, a 23 year old lad who worked for us was killed in a tragic accident, entirely caused through his own negligence. Our insurers have refused to pay out anything to his widow or three children. Are they within their rights?

* * *

Under the Employers Liability (Compulsory Insurance) Act, every employer is bound to carry insurance against liability to employees injured or killed at work due to any fault on the part of the employers, their servants or agents. You carry this insurance – but its precise extent will depend totally upon the nature and details of the policy concerned. An insurance contract is like any other – its terms depend upon agreement between the parties. Nobody can advise you on the terms of your policy without seeing it. You say that you 'have no policy' – what you really mean is that you have no copy of the policy. You could certainly ask your insurers to provide a copy, so that you could know how far you are covered.

Unfortunately, it is likely that your policy will only cover you in so far as you were liable to your employee. In other words, your insurers would step into your shoes and acquire your liability. It follows that if you have no liability – because you were not at fault – your insurers would not have to cover you.

In your case, you say that the accident was the lad's fault. If that is correct and there was no element of fault on your part, then it is extraordinarily unlikely that your insurers would have to pay out anything to your employee's unfortunate widow or children.

25 What is the Act's effect on equipment replacement?

We know that there is certain machinery which is a good deal safer than that which we are now using. But the cost of buying and installing it would be prohibitive. If we cannot afford safety measures which we would like to take, could we fairly say that it is not 'reasonably practicable' for us to re-equip?

* * *

Everything would depend on all the circumstances of the case and the burden of proving lack of reasonable practicability would rest on you. There are bound to be court decisions on this important point, before long. But the chances are that if re-equipment would mean going out of business then – unless there is substantial risk of serious injury – it would probably be 'reasonable' for you to carry on as you are.

26 What is our liability for sub-contractors?

Sub-contractors are at the moment finishing the electrical work on half of one floor of our factory. There is a strict time limit to the work and they are pretty efficient. But they are leaving wires, tools, and equipment all over the passageway – and people are liable to trip and fall. What should I do about it?

* * *

You would be responsible under the new Act because your place of work is not safe. Equally, the contractors would bear responsibility because they are causing danger as a result of procedures under their control. Why not have a word with the top man in the contracting outfit and ask him to lean on his own employees? If you try to influence them directly, then they may down tools – or alternatively (courteously or otherwise) tell you to mind your own business – even if (as is the case) their carelessness on your business premises is now your concern as well as theirs.

27 Are the rules on women at work to be changed?

There are still some special rules regarding the employment of women. These seem ridiculous in the light of the new legislation. Why, for instance, should an employer have to get the permis-

sion of the Factory Inspector if he wants to employ a woman at night?

* * *

In a recent Parliamentary answer, the responsible Minister said this: 'Section 55 of *The Sex Discrimination Act, 1975,* places a duty on the Equal Opportunities Commission to keep under review, in consultation with the Health and Safety Commission, the relevant statutory provisions (as defined in Section 53 of *The Health and Safety at Work etc. Act, 1974*) in so far as they require men and women to be treated differently. The majority of the provisions to be reviewed are to be found in *The Factories Act, 1961*, the Regulations made under that Act and in associated legislation such as *The Hours of Employment (Conventions) Act, 1936.*

'I have asked the Chairman of the Equal Opportunities Commission to give priority to the review and I have required the Commission to complete a report on all the provisions concerned and to let me have it, with recommendations, by the end of 1978.'

Change will probably come – later rather than sooner.

28 How is the employment of the disabled affected?

We have always employed more than our share of disabled people. But surely the new Act – placing such heavy duties on us for the health and safety of our employees – must discourage our taking on any responsibilities over and above those which we cannot avoid?

* * *

You will still be required to employ your quota of disabled people and it is earnestly hoped that you will continue to go beyond the legal minimum. True, the degree of care you must take will depend upon the employee concerned and obviously you must pay special attention to the needs of the disabled – as well as those of (for instance) young people.

29 What is our liability to those who work at home?

We employ outworkers to work for the company in their own homes. Are those premises then regarded as workplaces, covered by the new Act? And if one of them is injured at home while working for us, are we responsible in law?

* * *

No. These are domestic premises. Except in those rare cases where premises are actually provided for carrying out the company's work, it is not a criminal offence to fail to keep those premises safe. Representatives and others must take proper care of and in their own homes, for their own safety and that of their visitors. And it is up to them to carry any necessary insurance.

If an employee is injured and wishes to obtain damages against her employers, she would have to show that she was hurt through some fault on their part. If, for example, you provided defective equipment which caused harm, you will be responsible. If, however, there was no negligence on your part, the fact that your employee was injured while doing your work will no more make you (or your insurers) liable than if she was injured on your premises without your being at fault.

If you fail to take reasonable care for the safety of your employees while they are 'at work' for you, you may be held criminally liable under the Health and Safety at Work Act. The fact that they were working in their own homes would not remove your responsibility. Employers owe a duty to outworkers as well as to those who labour under their observant eyes. Indeed, in some ways, there is a greater duty towards outside than there is towards inside workers – you need to train people better if you can supervise them less.

Still, if your outworkers work in their own homes, their prospects of obtaining any compensation from you in the event of them suffering injury are not great.

30 How liable are we for O and M systems?

We employ O and M specialists. If one of them sets up a system for us which he regards as safe, how far is the company protected against a prosecution if someone is injured through a defect in that system?

* * *

If it was reasonable for the company to follow the specialist's advice; if the company had taken all 'reasonably practicable' steps, to make the system safe; if a reasonably prudent employer would not have done more; if there were no indications in practice that the system was likely to create danger to health or safety – then the company should be in the clear. But the expert may himself be at risk if he did not carry out any necessary research or testing, to ensure the safety of the system which he had created.

31 What is my responsibility for a supervisor's negligence?

We bought some new forklift trucks. A supervisor tried out one of them and tipped it over the edge of a dock. He was lucky to escape death. Could we be convicted of an offence under the new Act?

* * *

You are bound to provide adequate training and instruction for your supervisors, as well as for those whom they control. If, then, you submitted your supervisor to unnecessary risk by not giving him sufficient information or training in the use of the new machine, then you could well be liable – in both civil and criminal law. He is a supervisor, but he is nevertheless an employee – and you are bound to take care for his safety.

32 How will the Act affect medical examinations?

At present, only youngsters and the drivers of heavy goods vehicles must be medically examined. Do you expect this rule to be extended to other employees?

Yes. The Act contains powers for the making of regulations for medical examinations and tests and I do not believe that an employer can adequately care for the 'health' of employees, unless that health is examined – both when the employee is taken on and periodically or as necessary thereafter. Even without regulations, you should certainly consider instituting full and proper health testing and examination, if you do not already carry it out.

33 What are the 'welfare' hazards?

In civil law, you must not unnecessarily risk the health or the safety of employees. But there is no mention of 'welfare'. Does the new Act not extend far beyond the realm of the civil law? And will it not reverberate back by making employers who do not provide adequate welfare arrangements – and who are convicted of a criminal offence – liable also in civil law?

* * *

Yes, the criminal law does in this respect extend beyond the boundaries of existing civil liability. No, the employee will not have any new civil rights, unless there are special regulations regarding welfare which are flouted – and then only if the employee can prove that he has suffered injury, loss or damage as a result. And this is highly unlikely.

34 How far must we go in catering for the welfare of immigrants?

We have to provide adequate welfare arrangements for our employees. We employ large numbers of Indians. Could we get prosecuted for not giving them chapatis?

* * *

No. But if a large proportion of your workforce does come from overseas and you make no allowances for their tastes, can you really say that you are taking reasonable steps for their welfare? Or suppose that your employees do not eat pork (Muslims) or beef (Hindus) or any meat at all (because they are vegetarians) – or unkosher meat, because they are orthodox Jews. If you provide no alternatives to the forbidden foods, do you really feel that you are taking their sensibilities into account in a way that a reasonable, kindly, sensible employer would do?

The word 'welfare' is not defined by the Act; and the question of the adequacy of welfare facilities is one of fact. Ask yourselves the appropriate questions and you should come up with the answers which a court is likely to give in your case.

35 Does an improvement or prohibition notice mean prosecution?

If we are served with an improvement or prohibition notice, is this always a forerunner of court proceedings?

* * *

No. In most cases, the recipients of the notice will probably comply and either 'improve' the situation as required or stop the practice which is 'prohibited'.

Court proceedings may usually come about in two ways. The recipient may appeal to the Industrial Tribunal against the notice; and from the Tribunal, he has a right to make a further appeal to the Court of Appeal on a point of law.

Alternatively, if he flouts the notice, he may confidently expect to be prosecuted in a Magistrates' Court or in a Crown Court.

36 Who is a 'manager'?

The Act refers to the duties of a 'manager', but the word is not defined. Is every sort of 'manager' included, whatever his title?

* * *

Yes, top, middle and line management . . . personnel managers, safety managers, foremen – all are included. Those who 'manage' others must take care for their health and safety at work. Anyway, the same section which places responsibilities on 'managers' refers also to 'other officers of the company' and to those who 'purport to act' in a managerial capacity. There is no escape from duties under this statute.

37 Who decides to prosecute whom?

It is a defence under the Act to prove that the offence was caused through the act or default of some other person. And we understand that the 'other person' may be the person to whom you delegated the responsibility – or, for that matter, your own superior who failed to give you enough authority or support or staff or cash to do the job properly.

Who decides whom to prosecute? Surely if each person is afraid of a heavy fine or even a prison sentence and starts trying to pass the buck, this is going to lead to great ill will?

* * *

The inspector will initially decide whether or not to prosecute and if so then who is to bear the blame. The buck-passing process is indeed extremely unpleasant; but it is inevitable. The Act seeks to place criminal responsibility where the blame lies for a default. And that is fair.

38 How are specialist designers affected by the Act?

We often employ technical advisers who prepare and design processes. Are they covered by the Act?

* * *

As employers, they must take care for the safety of their own employees; as controllers of work or premises, they must take care for others affected by their work or workplace; but while the designers of articles or substances for use at work are criminally responsible if they fail to take proper care to ensure that those articles and substances are safe, there appears to be no equivalent rule which covers technical advisers, in that respect.

39 Who decides what is 'reasonable'?

The Act frequently says that we must take 'reasonably practicable' measures. Who decides as to what is or is not 'reasonable' and what standards do they apply?

* * *

Initially, you must make the decision. If the inspector disagrees with you, then he will have to decide whether or not to prosecute. And ultimately, if you are prosecuted and plead not guilty, the question of reasonableness will be decided by the court. But if you agree that a certain practice was unsafe but say that it was not reasonably practicable for you to do otherwise, then the burden of proving reasonableness rests upon you.

What is or is not 'reasonable' always depends in law upon all the circumstances of the particular case. You – together with your colleagues; the Safety Committee or others concerned; the inspector; the court – each must apply the standard as best he can.

40 What happens if the inspectors disagree?

We have three factories in different parts of the country. We find that the inspectors are still setting different standards in different places. We are rather apprehensive about pointing out to the inspector who is being tough that his colleague elsewhere is more reasonable because this might have the effect of toughening up the reasonable one rather than inducing the tough one to see sense. What do you think?

* * *

This sort of tactical matter can only be decided on the

ground and not in theory. You know the people and must judge the tactics. But if you do want to know where you stand and to obtain a reasonable overall standard, you should contact either the area chiefs of the Health and Safety Executive or get in direct touch with HQ in London – Health and Safety Executive, Baynards House, 1 Chepstow Place, London W2 4TF. Telephone: 01-229 3456.

41 What are a woman's duties?

The Act always refers to 'his' duty. How about the girls?

* * *

As Churchill once remarked, 'man embraces woman'. In law, the masculine includes the feminine.

42 What is my liability for a customer's injuries?

If a customer is injured through a defect in goods which we manufacture, are we criminally liable under the new Act?

* * *

No. The Act only applies criminal penalties in this respect to the manufacture of plant or components *designed* – or substances *intended* – for use at work.

Naturally, the customer has his rights in civil law. He may sue his supplier in contract or, if he suffers injury, loss or damage through negligence in manufacture, he may sue the manufacturer, in 'tort' – that is, in the civil wrong of negligence.

43 Who is liable at point of sale?

A salesman is erecting point of sale material. He climbs a ladder and falls. Who is liable?

* * *

In civil law, his employer was bound to take reasonable care for his safety – and that included providing a safe ladder and proper instruction in the carrying out of his job. The same duty, in effect, rests on the employer under the 1974 Act. So if the employer is in breach of his duty, he will be liable – both civilly and criminally.

The occupier of the premises owes similar duties. Under *The Occupiers' Liability Act, 1957,* he is bound to take reasonable care for the safety of his visitor – but as the representative is visiting the premises 'in the exercise of his calling', the occupier is entitled to expect that the representative will take all such steps as are reasonably necessary to protect himself against risks ordinarily incidental to that calling – such as checking that the ladder is firmly footed.

Finally, the representative must take proper care for his own safety. In civil law, his damages will be reduced in direct proportion to his own responsibility for the mishap. Section 7 of the 1974 Act requires him to co-operate in the taking of all necessary steps to preserve his own safety.

So ask yourself the question: Whose fault was it that the accident occurred? Almost certainly, it will be the culprit who will have to bear the blame – civilly and criminally alike.

44 How far must we protect a caretaker?

Our caretaker lives in a flat which we provide. Could we be prosecuted if we fail to take sufficient steps for his health in his home?

* * *

Probably not. Domestic premises are excluded – and 'domestic' includes not only your home but that of your employee, even if you have provided it for him – unless it is so provided as a place of work. If your home or that of your employee is used partly for business purposes – perhaps for bringing and storing of materials, interviewing customers or representatives or keeping books – it will still be extremely unlikely that a court would apply new legislation to that home.

45 What do you need to do to protect employees from criminal attacks?

We run a betting shop and have been advised that we ought to put in protective glass screening because of the danger of hold-ups. We are not convinced that this is worthwhile. What do you think?

* * *

You must take such steps as are reasonably practicable to protect your staff against predictable dangers.

All businesses which handle cash run into these dangers to some degree. Rent collectors and retailers . . . firms that bring in cash from the bank to pay wages or take cash to the bank on deposit . . . theatres, cinemas and garages with box offices or tills . . . and betting shops like yours. In every case, the employer must balance the risk against the cost of carrying out the work – and include any added loss of productivity or difficulty in doing the job. But if he turns down a request such as you have had, he bears a heavy potential liability.

46 What is an individual's civil liability?

An individual employee may be liable in criminal law if he is negligent and causes danger to himself or to others while at work. Does he bear the same liability in civil law? Could he be forced to pay damages to someone who was injured by his carelessness in the course of his duty?

* * *

An *employee* is bound to take reasonable care for the safety of others. Recent decisions suggest that his company would be bound to indemnify him against any such liability, but the legal position still needs to be settled finally, one way or the other. The *employer* is (or certainly should be) fully insured against such risks, while the employee is not. And (as one judge suggested, not long ago) if employees have to meet this sort of liability they will have to insure and will therefore expect increases in their pay to cover any premiums.

47 Can we be prosecuted if no improvement or prohibition notice has been served?

If no prohibition notice or improvement notice is served on us, can we be prosecuted under the new Act?

* * *

Yes. Most prosecutions will probably be brought against people who fail to comply with notices. But an inspector is not bound to serve a notice before he prosecutes.

Suppose, for instance, that you have carried on a dangerous process which causes an accident. You stop the process – too late. You may still be prosecuted for your past misdeed.

48 Must an inspector give warning of prosecution?

If an inspector intends to prosecute, must he warn the proposed accused?

* * *

No. Unlike a serious motoring offence, where the delinquent driver must be warned at the time that a prosecution may be contemplated or given written notice of intention to prosecute within 14 days of the incident, the employer or other person who is to be prosecuted under the Act is entitled to no warning.

In practice, though, a prosecution is likely to be used only as a last resort and when persuasion and warnings have failed to bring the action desired by the inspector.

49 How are men on the move affected?

We employ people who move about in the course of their work. How can we be expected to supervise them in the same way as those whose jobs are static?

* * *

You may not be able to supervise them as carefully, so you should train them better. Neither the civil nor the criminal law expects you to stand over your employees, but both the old law and the new require you to take reasonably practicable steps to ensure their safety.

50 How far can you rely on an inspector's approval?

A machine is passed by the Factory Inspector. An accident occurs to the operative who is using it. Can we be made liable, either to pay damages or in criminal law?

* * *

The machine may have been passed as safe but was it used in a safe and proper manner? Was it properly maintained? Was the operative properly supervised? Did you take all reasonably practicable steps to protect him while using the machine? The fact that the machine itself may be adequately designed or guarded is a good start – but by no means the finish of the problem. Moreover, the inspector's opinion is not *necessarily* conclusive, e.g. if the machine does not comply with the regulations and an accident occurs which leads to a civil action by the injured party.

51 How liable are we during prototype development?

We are developing prototype machines. During the development the guarding is insufficient. If there is an accident during the course of design, can we be held responsible?

* * *

The design is itself an industrial process and must be carried on in a careful manner. You must recognise the risks involved and guard against them as best you can – or risk having to pay damages to the injured party and/or being prosecuted under the new Act. The fact that a machine is a prototype in no way gives you carte blanche to be careless.

52 Should we rely on suppliers' promises to test?

Suppliers promise that they will test a new machine. In use, though, it turns out to be defective and an accident is caused. Who is responsible?

* * *

If it was the defect in the machine which caused the trouble – rather than your failure to recognise the possibilitiy of teething trouble or otherwise to guard against that risk – then both civil and criminal liability would probably be laid at the supplier's door and not at yours. But to give a definite answer, you or the inspector or the court would have to know all the facts.

53 What does 'health' mean?

The Act requires employers to take care for the 'health' of employees. Does this word refer to physical or mental health or both?

* * *

Both. If you employ disabled people, you must take special care to protect them against extra risks which may be caused as a result of that disablement – whether the employee's defect is one of mind or body. Indeed, it is likely that you will eventually be bound by law as well as by common sense to provide sufficient medical examinations for both new and existing employees so that, where possible, illness or disability can be spotted and dealt with. Problems of mental health in industry and commerce – particularly those caused by excess strain – are likely to become increasingly prominent.

54 How far does liability extend in the home?

Could we now be prosecuted if our gardener or au pair girl is injured?

No. The Act, only applies to business premises. All employees are covered, wherever they work, with the exception of people in private homes, doing domestic work. In my view, that would include work in the garden.

55 What happens if a notice is unjustified?

If we are served with a prohibition notice which turns out to be unjustified and is set aside by the Industrial Tribunal, will we be entitled to compensation from the erring inspector or out of public funds? Our loss may be immense.

* * *

Nobody yet knows whether the inspector can be made liable to pay compensation if he exceeds his powers. As for the Crown meeting the bill out of public funds; the Act says that if damages are awarded against an inspector they may be reimbursed to him out of public money. More simply, if (but only if) the inspector himself is liable, the Crown (as his employer) is likely to be liable as well.

56 Is it enough to obey the inspector?

If we do all that the inspector requires but there is still an accident, who is responsible? Would we avoid liability under the Act – and could the inspector be made personally responsible?

* * *

You are expected to do everything that is 'reasonably practicable' to keep your employees and others affected by your work in safety and good health. If the inspector has made his enquiries and given you a clean bill, then you should have an excellent defence in connection with the risks about which the inspector's advice has been given.

However, it may be that you did not reveal the full truth or all the facts to the inspector, or steered him round the risk, in which case his advice may not provide you with a particularly stout shield. And in any event, the Act is not designed as a flail to be used against him.

57 What must we do in the case of bomb warnings?

We have received a number of hoax bomb warnings and the police refuse to take the responsibility of telling us whether or not we must evacuate the premises each time a warning is received. What do we do?

* * *

You take the best advice available, bearing in mind that if you decide not to evacuate and there is in fact an explosion which causes death or dire injury, you will have not only a potential legal responsibility but a heavy moral one as well. If in doubt, evacuate if you can; if you decide not to do so, at least try to get some expert to accept the responsibility for advising you that it would not be 'reasonably practicable' or necessary for you to do so in your particular circumstances.

58 When can you get compensation for criminal injuries?

If we evacuate premises as a result of a bomb warning and a bomb does actually explode and in spite of our efforts people are injured and property is damaged, who pays?

* * *

If personal injury is suffered as a result of a crime of violence, then the sufferer should be able to obtain compensation from the Criminal Injuries Compensation Board. But property is not covered, though there is a separate scheme covering property in Northern Ireland. That is a matter for your insurers; and you should certainly check your insurance policies to ensure that there is no exclusion which applies to risks of this sort.

Anyway, as you have taken all reasonable precautions and have been in no way negligent, neither you nor your company should be liable either in civil or in criminal law as a result of the disaster.

59 How are accident-prone employees affected?

Some employees are accident prone. How are they affected by the 1974 Act?

* * *

They are required by Section 7 to take reasonable care for their own safety and well-being. If *you* know that a person is particularly liable to suffer from accidents, then the degree of care which you should exercise for his safety must necessarily be greater than that which you would need for the average employee.

60 When do fines for continuing offences run from?

Section 33(5) of the Act provides for fines of £50 a day where there is a continuing offence. From what date does this liability to a fine begin – does it start with the date when the offence is spotted by the inspector; the date of the improvement or prohibition notice; or date of the conviction?

* * *

The daily fine only arises after conviction.

61 Who is a child?

We know that we must take special care for the safety of children, both under the Occupiers' Liability Act and thanks to the 1974 Act. When does a person cease to be a child?

* * *

The word is not defined by either Act. Under the Factories

Act, of course, special rules apply to the young persons under the age of 18. But childhood and maturity are questions of physical and mental fact, rather than of legislation, when it comes to civil or criminal liability in connection with health and safety rules not specifically covered by statute.

62 Have Building Regulations been made under the Act?

What regulations have been made under Section 64 of the Health and Safety at Work Act? What major changes have occurred in building control as a result of the Act?

* * *

As we go to press – none. As long ago as the 24 June 1976, the Minister concerned stated in the Commons that 'consultation exercises' were taking place with the industries concerned about the future of building control in the light of the new powers available and in particular the extent to which quality of construction could be assured.

63 Does the Act affect our car parks?

We provide a car park for the use of both employees and visitors. If there is an accident on that car park, are we liable – in civil or in criminal law?

* * *

As occupiers of the car park, you must take such steps as are reasonable to ensure that those who use it are reasonably safe, but you are not the insurer of the users. So you will only be liable in damages if it can be shown that the accident resulted from your breach of your duty. Even then, unless and until the law is changed (as it may be), you are free to exclude your liability by agreement with the user. This may be express or implied – and is often imposed by the provision of the appropriate tickets or the exhibition of a sign, saying that the facilities are provided at the user's own risk.

Under the 1974 Act, Section 2 required you to take all such steps as are reasonably practicable for the safety and health of your employees while they are at work. It would be a question of fact as to whether they were at work when using the car park on any particular occasion.

Section 3 – which requires you to take all reasonably practicable steps to ensure that danger to health and safety is not caused through operations under your control – does not cover danger to property. Still, when there is liable to be an accident with a vehicle, there will probably be danger to both. So you must certainly take care to ensure that your car park is in proper condition.

64 Does the Act affect liability for accidents at the sports ground?

We provide recreational facilities for our employees. These include a sports centre and some football pitches.

What are the rights of our employees against us and generally if they are injured while at play, rather than while at work?

* * *

In the case of *Regina* v. *National Insurance Commission, ex parte Michael*, the Court of Appeal held that even a policeman who is 'expected' to play in a football team (even though he is not 'required' to do so) is not 'at work' when he is 'at play'. If he is injured during a game, he is not entitled to industrial injury benefit under *The National Insurance (Industrial Injuries) Act, 1965.* He is doing something incidental to his employment and not part of it. It also means that the full rigour of the 1974 Act will not apply to you.

Equally, an employee who injures someone else while at play will not make his employer liable to compensate the injured person, even if the injury was caused by negligence.

As an employer, you are only 'vicariously liable' for injuries caused by one employee to another in the course of his employment. You are not responsible if he was merely doing some activity incidental to the employment and not part of it.

It would be different, of course, if you yourself were guilty of negligence which caused the accident.

If you provide facilities, for instance, then you must exercise reasonable care to ensure that those facilities are in proper and safe condition. If – but only if – the cause of the accident is your negligence will the employee at play have enforceable rights against you.

Under the Act, you may also be criminally liable if you fail to take such steps as are reasonably practicable to protect people who are not your employees but who make use of facilities which you provide. So watch out for the other team – or, for that matter, for your employees' guests.

Finally, an employee who plays football usually does so at his own risk because of the old doctrine – *volenti non fit injuria* – a person has no right to claim damages for injuries which he suffered through undertaking voluntarily a risk the extent of which he knew and should have understood. Footballers – and to a large extent those who watch them at play – take their recreation at their own risk.

65 What are the dangers of importing?

We import machinery for use in our works. We also buy plant from local suppliers. Are we at risk under the Health and Safety at Work Act if the machinery proves dangerous in operation?

* * *

If you buy locally, then your problems are minimal. Your supplier will be liable if he has failed to take such steps as are reasonably practicable to ensure that the plant is safe.

If, on the other hand, you import, you will find yourself covered by Section 6 of the Act: 'It shall be the duty of any person who designs, manufactures, *imports* or supplies any article for use at work . . . to ensure, so far as is reasonably practicable, that the article is so designed to construct and is to be safe and without risk to health when properly used'.

Let someone else import for you as principal in the operation and the responsibility rests on him. Do the importing yourself and you must 'carry out or arrange for the carrying out of such testing and examination as may be necessary . . .' and provide 'adequate information' about how to use the plant safely. You do not have to repeat any testing done by your supplier – but you should make certain that you are in a position to prove that you have taken all reasonable steps to ensure that adequate testing and research has been done by your overseas suppliers.

The logic of all this, of course, is that our courts have jurisdiction over those who supply within the UK but none whatever over those who export from other countries. If you bring dangerous goods onto your factory floor, then you (as well as any employee put at risk) must expect consequences.

66 What is our liability for dismissing sick employees?

We have an assistant who has suffered a great deal from ill health and we are soon going to have to dismiss her. If it turns out that the dismissal is regarded as 'unfair', will the tribunal take into account the ill health when assessing compensation for loss of future earnings?

* * *

Yes. The Employment Appeal Tribunal pointed out in a recent case that compensation awarded to an employee must cover 'loss sustained by him in consequence of his dismissal' and would include 'a reasonable estimate of his financial loss while he remains unemployed'. Where the loss due to any additional period of unemployment results from the employee's 'personal characteristics . . .' then the tribunal must take the ill health into account when assessing compensation.

Of course, you should try to avoid this situation arising by treating the employee with the utmost fairness. For instance, you should give your assistant at least one written warning that if her health does not improve, and if she is unable to cope with her job within a specified (and reasonable) period, you will most regretfully have to dismiss her. And you might add a sentence to say that if and when (as you hope) her health recovers, you will of course do your best to find a place for her in your business.

67 How do we cope with promotions?

We recently promoted a first-class operative to foreman. Unfortunately, he is not coping with his new responsibilities. He does not seem to have the ability, in particular, to get his men to follow the safety rules – about which we are extremely particular. Are we entitled to demote him – or, if he refuses to go back (and this is likely) to dismiss him? He has been with us for about five years, but he has only been employed as a foreman for a couple of months.

* * *

The law provides what amounts to a statutory trial period during which you can and should check on the performance of new employees. Normally, an employee only has protection against unfair dismissal after he has been continuously employed for 26 weeks. Until then, he is, of course, entitled to his proper notice or pay in lieu (unless he has 'repudiated' his contract – that is, done something so desperately serious as to strike at the root of it and to give you the right to dismiss him summarily). But he is not entitled to an unfair dismissal remedy.

The exceptions: where the employee is dismissed for discrimination of one of three kinds:

1 *Trade union rights*, i.e. for wanting to join or to take part in the activities of an independent trade union or for refusing to join or take part in the activities of a non-independent (or 'tame') union (or staff association); or
2 *Sex discrimination* – which protects men and women, and married people – but not the single; or
3 *Race discrimination* (on the grounds of race, colour, ethnic or national origin or – thanks to the new Race Relations Act – nationality).

It follows that you may dismiss an employee for any reason (other than discrimination) or none, provided that he has not been with you for the statutory 26 weeks. Beware, though: For the purposes of the rules, a week is one during any part of which the employee has worked. If, for example, the employee starts work on a Friday and ends on a Monday, both the first and the last week will count in full. So 26 statutory weeks could be 24 weeks and 2 days of actual work.

This period during which you may normally dismiss without fear of unfair dismissal or reprisals is a period of 'continuous employment' by the same employer (or, usually, by his predecessor). It counts from the first day that the employee starts work for the particular employer – and not from the date when he changes his position within the company or firm.

In your case, the employee has been on the company's books for far more than the statutory 26 weeks. The fact that he was promoted only a short time ago is irrelevant. For the purposes of his protection under the Trade Union and Labour Relations Act and now the Employment Protection Act, he is far outside the trial period.

This does not mean, though, that you are debarred from dismissing him. If he is incompetent at his new job, then you must consider his case like that of any other. Maybe you are mistaken and you could induce him to move back down the ladder. If you can achieve a demotion by agreement, the contract will have been varied by consent and all will be (legally) well.

Alternatively, are you sure that you cannot train the man to cope with his new responsibilities or provide him with some additional backing, even if only on a temporary basis?

If you must consider dismissal, then you would certainly have a reason which came within the statute. He does not have, you would say, the 'capabilities' to do the job properly. He lacks the skill which you were entitled to expect of him.

The man would prove that he was dismissed; you would show the reason; and then you would have to prove positively that you acted 'reasonably' in treating that reason as sufficient to warrant depriving the employee of his daily bread. Could you do so? If you are in doubt, then you should consult the Advisory, Conciliation and Arbitration Service (ACAS) or your solicitors. Yours would be the sort of borderline case which you should prepare with care.

The longer that an employee works for you, the more difficult it becomes to show that he is not capable of doing the job properly. And promotions are at your legal risk as well as that of the employee promoted. Once he has been with you for the statutory period starting with the day that he entered your employment, he is well protected by the new rules.

68 Are offshore oil installations affected?

Does the Health and Safety at Work Act apply offshore?

* * *

As we go to press – no. But an Order in Council will be made under Section 84(3) of the Act so as to cover oil rigs; consultation with industry on the draft of the Order has taken place; and it is expected that the Order will come into effect in late summer 1977. At that time, all installations 'beyond territorial waters' are likely to be covered by the same safety rules on land or within territorial waters. Meanwhile, everyone concerned with work on oil rigs and the like will need to be familiar with the extensive and detailed safety regulations – laid down in the rather cumbersomely named *Offshore Installations (Operational Safety, Health and Welfare) Regulations, 1976* – which came into force in November 1976.

Section B: Committees and Representatives

69 Do we still need safety officers?

Does the safety representative legislation remove the need for safety officers?

* * *

No. The more emphasis that is laid on safety, the greater the need will be for experienced, trained safety officers. Safety representatives will be appointed by trade unions; safety officers by the company – and among the duty of the officers will be the provision to the reps of the information without which the reps will not be able adequately to do their jobs.

70 What are the rules on sites with many unions?

If we only had to deal with one union, life would be easy. But we have a number which we recognise in our works. How do we deal with this situation, from the safety angle? Who will do the inspection and appoint the representatives?

* * *

You need the agreement of the unions on this. It may be that you should encourage them to set up an overall steering committee. Perhaps you will have separate committees for each union or department and share the information and the responsibility. Anyway, the unions will decide on their representatives and (as in all other well conducted industrial relations procedures), you should do whatever you can to help the unions to achieve agreement among themselves.

71 What are the rights of minority unions?

The numbers of safety representatives have been agreed by management and unions. What if a minority union then wants representation disproportionate to its numbers?

* * *

Every effort should be made to achieve agreement. If there is none, then the same procedures should be followed as are operative in respect of representation for bargaining purposes.

72 Can safety representatives stop the machines?

How do management deal with the over-zealous representatives who could stop a large number of machines for minor safety complaints?

* * *

No safety representative acting in that capacity has the power to stop any machine. He may, of course, spark off industrial action – but there is nothing new about this. Or he could tip off the factory inspector who might bang on an improvement or a prohibition notice. More likely, though, he would refer a complaint to the safety committee. Management ignores the recommendations of a safety committee at its own risk as well as at that of the operative concerned.

73 How should we train our representatives?

We recognise both supervisory and manual unions in our factory. How do we train safety representatives from the various levels?

* * *

You should try to get them to work together. Where there are differences in status involved, this may create problems. But if you can establish the right relationship with the leaders of the various unions concerned in your business, you should succeed in convincing them that co-operation is essential for the common good. Some unions are working on joint problem-solving exercises in the safety field, to good effect. These efforts should, of course, be encouraged.

74 How will the new rules affect relationships with inspectors?

How will the safety representative and committee regulations affect our relationship with our inspectors?

* * *

Your inspector would normally be pleased to discuss your representative and committee problems with you, at your work place – although there is some apprehension in the ranks that the inspectors may be deluged with demands for assistance. They will not denigrate from your responsibility to inform, train and supervise your work force in connection with safety. But they will do what they can to help you to cope with practical problems.

When the inspector visits your site, he will want to see and to talk to the safety representative – on behalf of those whom he represents. So if you know that the inspector is coming, you should make sure that the representative is available.

Your personal relationship with your inspector should not be affected. It will simply be given a new dimension.

Remember, though, that inspectors will not *decide* how many representatives are necessary; how many meetings your committee should have; or any other practical matters which come within your area. These decisions must be made by you in consultation with the trade unions. And the inspectors are there to help, to guide and, in case of non-compliance with the law, to ensure enforcement.

75 How do the regulations deal with contractors?

We sometimes have contractors or sub-contractors, erectors or installers working on our site for considerable periods. Are we required to have representatives from their trade unions on our safety committees?

* * *

There is no requirement of law. But safety committees may (and often should) include people who work on the site, even if they are not employed by you.

76 Information – who gives it?

We know that we will have to make more safety information available. Who will be entitled to require it and who should be available to give it?

* * *

Machinery is needed for the exchange of information. This should be an item on the agenda at an early meeting of your safety committee.

77 What are the key problems?

What specific difficulties do you foresee in implementing the rules on safety committees and representatives?

* * *

Problems are as varied as workplaces and people. The larger the business, though, the more varied the anxieties. Among common questions which need to be answered are: Which unions appoint representatives and which representatives sit on committees? How do you divide the work place up for this purpose? Do you have a committee for example, specifically for one area of work or one type of employee or for the whole plant? Do you include contractors or sub-contractors? If you employ a sales force or others who work outside your supervision or control, how do you deal with what are sometimes called 'wandering work places'?

At the first (or next) meeting of your safety committee, you should list the problems that you see from the viewpoint of your business. Then discuss them with your managers concerned and with the trade union representatives. The more the problems are identified and kicked around in the open, the more obvious their solutions usually become.

78 What are the best areas for co-operation?

Can you suggest some specific areas in which co-operation between safety committees and management would be likely to bring particularly good results?

* * *

You should study all accidents and discuss their origins; recommend corrective action; consider reports from representatives and from inspectors; keep an eye on the effectiveness of safety training and publicity within your unit; and involve your committee in discussions on how to promote better co-operation.

79 What formalities should we have for safety meetings?

Can you advise us on the procedures which should be followed so as to get the best results from our safety committees?

* * *

You should follow the same formula as that at any other sort of successful committee. You need a firm, fair chairman who gives a hearing to all and especially to people who are shy to intervene but who have helpful suggestions to make. All members should receive an agenda for the meeting in advance, setting out the subjects to be discussed – especially where any prior thought or preparation is necessary. Proper minutes should be kept and made available either to members or on the notice board or (preferably) both.

Sub-committees should only be appointed if they are really necessary such as where there is a special subject to consider.

Dates for committee meetings should be fixed well in advance and adhered to except in dire emergency. Management members of committees should regard attendance as a top priority and should lead through example.

The objectives of the committee should be formulated at the first meeting and followed thereafter.

80 Two sides of the table?

Should safety committees be organised so as to provide a balance between employers and employees?

* * *

No. The Commission insists that there should never be more than 50 per cent management representation and its officials recommended less. Every effort should be made to bring the part to one side of the table – through recognition that there are two sides in heaven or in hell and that it is in the interests of all that each should keep both feet firmly planted on the soil of this world – and firmly attached to his body.

81 When must a committee be set up?

When must a committee be set up and how will failure to comply with the committee rules be enforced?

* * *

A committee must be set up if the management is required to do so by at least two representatives. No special form of committee is required. But as soon as you receive a request for a committee, you should immediately start consultations with a view to setting it up.

The Commission consider it very unlikely that there will in practice be much difficulty in enforcing the setting up of committee. But steps may be taken if a time limit is exceeded; if there is no consultation; or in the (hopefully, remote) eventuality of a refusal.

The far greater practical risk is that a committee will be set up and simply allowed to go to sleep. Inspectors are likely to ask for minutes of the latest committee meeting and to crack down if they find that the rules are being flouted. They may use the same enforcement procedures (including prohibition and improvement notices) in respect of these Regulations as they may to achieve enforcement of any other industrial safety rules.

82 Is a safety representative part of the management team?

Does a safety representative become a member of management?

* * *

A safety representative has no managerial functions and there is no loss of managerial prerogative – nor of managerial responsibility to avoid consenting to, conniving at or permitting through neglect any breach of the safety regulations.

Naturally, a trade union representative who considers that the interests of those whom he represents are being ignored may back up his wishes through industrial relations sanctions. But that represents no change from the previous situation.

Whether or not the regulations prove onerous or irksome to the management will depend upon the safety measures in current operation. They cannot push off their duties or responsibilities onto the safety representatives. The representatives, though, may spur them into action.

Remember, too, that although the representatives have no power to prosecute under the Act (there are no private prosecutions other than with the consent of the Director of Public Prosecutions – which means that there are none whatever), many trade union representatives have reported their companies to the Factory Inspectorate for failure to comply with safety rules.

If the safety representatives are given and accept duties in respect of safety, they would then acquire legal liabilities. They are not acting merely as 'safety watchdogs' but have acquired managerial functions. This may lead to problems – especially as the law and industrial relations questions are inextricably mixed.

83 How can departmental managers help?

We have been asked by our departmental managers how they can help get our safety committees and representatives into action. What should they be asked to do?

* * *

Get them to start mapping out a sensible programme – a timetable for progress. If they have a positive approach to the rules, that will be a great help. They should meet the representatives in and from their departments and draw up an agenda for meetings. The greater the personal involvement, the less the likelihood of conflict.

You are lucky that your managers want to get cracking. Bill Simpson said that managers who regard the new regulations and Code as a misery are engaged in self-fulfilling prophecy.

84 Are piggy-back meetings recommended?

Do you recommend the attaching of a safety committee meeting to the end of another meeting at which many or most of the same people are present?

* * *

No. Meetings should neither be tagged on to the end of other meetings nor to the end of a day, otherwise you devalue them. They should be treated as important by you if you wish their outcome to be regarded as important by those who they are designed to protect.

85 Must the inspector give information to the safety representative?

Is there any legal requirement on an inspector to give information to a safety representative?

* * *

Yes – under Section 28(8) of the Act.

You may expect safety representatives to engage in a new dialogue, backed up by far more information than was available to the unions in the past.

86 Do tradesmen inspect?

In a large factory with many unions involved, would the area committees inspect the entire factory? Which area should be inspected by a tradesman whose area of work stretches all over the site?

* * *

Safety committees should not do general inspections. Inspection procedures should be related to a particular problem or area and should be undertaken by the representatives of those most concerned in it.

87 How will the regulations affect shopkeepers?

To what extent will the safety committee representative requirements apply to the ordinary retailer? Surely we won't need a committee to organise safety in our shop?

* * *

That all depends on the size of your shop or of your total business and whether or not you 'recognise' an independent trade union for bargaining purposes.

If you have employees who are members of a union (probably the Union of Shop, Distributive and Allied Workers or the Transport and General Workers' Union, or one of the supervisory unions) – then the union will be entitled to appoint safety representatives. If you recognise the union, you will have to consult with them. If two or more representatives ask you to set up a safety committee, then you will have to do so.

It follows that many of the larger retail concerns will be covered by the new Regulations, Code and Guidance. They should already be using the lead-in period in order to set up arrangements.

Still, if you are a small trader, you will not be forced to appoint or to recognise a safety representative or to have a safety committee. You must, of course comply with the safety rules contained in the Health and Safety at Work Act and in the Offices, Shops and Railway Premises Act and in any Regulations made under them. So you should consider how best to consult your staff, so as to ensure that everything you do is as safe as is reasonably practicable.

88 Must we make special arrangements for research workers?

We know that our research and development department is not a 'factory' and therefore is only covered by the 1974 Act. How far are we entitled to expect that research workers – who are, after all, experts in their own field – will themselves guard against dangers inherent in their work in that field? Should they have their own safety committees?

An employer must take all reasonably practicable steps to set up and maintain in operation a safe system of working. He must ensure in so far as is within his power that hazards are identified, controlled or guarded against. And if he does not employ people with sufficient qualifications to do so from within his own staff, he should call in independent experts and obtain and follow their advice.

The Flixborough disaster occurred because the employers concerned had no one available who could identify the risk. The dogleg pipe which split and caused the tragedy was (said the enquiry) the result of the management's failure to take proper precautions.

It follows that the more qualified the people you employ, the less likely it is that you will have to rely upon outside guidance and wisdom. But the mere fact that you have qualified people on your staff will not free you from liability. You must also train them to take care – and provide them with all necessary means for doing so.

You are certainly right that research establishments have come under the wing of the criminal law for the first time. So special care is essential. Whether or not it will be wise to have a safety committee for your research and development department will depend on its size and nature.

89 What are the rules about the smallest companies?

We are only a minnow in our industry. Will we have to operate safety committees and if so should we include safety reps? What do we do about people who are not members of our various unions?

* * *

There is no provision excluding even small companies from the rules regarding safety committees and safety representatives. You do not have to put out a statement setting out your safety policy, organisation and arrangements unless you employ five or more people. But if a 'recognised trade union' wishes to appoint safety representatives, then it may do so and you will have to consult with them.

If you receive a written request from at least two safety representatives to establish a safety committee, then you will be bound to do so. You must consult with the representatives who made the request and with the representatives of recognised trade unions whose members work in your workplace. Together with them, you should work out the composition of the committee. If they agree to the inclusion of non-union representatives, then by all means include them. Then post a notice at the workplace, stating the composition of the committee; the places or areas to be covered by it; and then you must establish your committee not more than three months after the request for it.

90 Who should be a safety representative?

We appreciate that safety representatives will be selected by our unions – but we have a very good relationship with them and would be interested to know whether you consider that it is or is not better for safety representatives to be selected from among our shop stewards.

* * *

There are two schools of thought on this one. On the one hand, it is argued that a shop steward has influence and power and can achieve results better than anyone else. On the other hand, has he time, energy and willingness to spare for the extra job? And has he the expertise?

So others believe that you are better to take a safety enthusiast – with experience and time – who is not a shop steward. Unions will probably appoint him as an 'official', so giving him status and credentials.

Then there are some unions who are afraid that there will be a conflict between financial interests of their members – represented by the shop stewards and safety – represented by the safety representatives. (They may be wrong, but it is a commonly held view.)

Of course, if you can find a shop steward with time, energy, enthusiasm and safety knowledge, who wants to serve as a safety rep. . . .

91 Conflicts of interest

I don't understand why there could or should be any conflict between the financial interests of union members, represented by their shop stewards, and safety, represented by the safety representatives. Please explain.

* * *

There may only be a certain amount of money in the kitty. The unions will be bargaining for that money to be used in the best interests of their members and may prefer to have any cash available used to improve pay (or, perhaps, pensions).

The safety representatives, though, may feel that the union has its priorities wrong and that available money should be spent on safety. So they will be fighting the management from their side for more expenditure on safety while their unions want the available money for other purposes.

If the safety representatives are correct in their view, they should impress this on their union colleagues who should give priority to safety. This conflict therefore should not arise. But it sometimes does.

92 Who should prepare our safety policy?

To what extent can responsibility for formulating policy statements be passed on to safety committees?

* * *

Not at all. Under Section 2(3) of the Health and Safety at Work Act, it is made 'the duty of every employer' to prepare and (where necessary) to revise these statements.

Guidance Notes from the Health and Safety Commission suggest, though, that: 'It would be sensible for an employer to consult his employees, through their safety representatives and to heed to the advice of the safety committees (where these exist), so as to ensure that the best arrangements and organisations for safety and health are evolved and maintained.' However: 'Such consultation does not diminish the employer's responsibility; it is clearly part of his greater responsibility' under the Act.

So by all means discuss the statements with your employees' representatives, but the responsibility for drafting and promulgating the statements is yours.

93 Who wins when the Safety Committee votes?

Are decisions taken at a safety committee by a simply majority, a two-thirds majority or by consensus?

* * *

That is entirely a matter for your own arrangements, in agreement with your unions.

Glacier Metals, who are the pioneers in worker participation in Britain, operate their committees on the basis that a decision is only binding on the company's board of directors if there is total unanimity on the works' committee. Most boards never have a vote at all but operate by consensus – which is sometimes more apparent than real. Trade unions, on the other hand, are used to resolving an apparent dispute by vote – which may be by secret ballot but which is normally by show of hands. The vote sometimes produces surprising results. It sharpens feelings and attitudes and encourages people who may be apprehensive about speaking their minds to show their views.

Safety committee procedures may be decided in advance or may evolve through time and experience. The key to their successful operation, though, lies with the chairman.

94 Mr Chairman – who is he?

Who should take the chair at a safety committee and what are his powers?

* * *

The chairman should be elected. Glacier Metals choose some independent person who at present happens to be the company accountant but who has been the medical officer or a union official. The members of the committee should come to an agreement as to the person who is best suited to conduct their meetings in a firm, fair, effective and brisk manner. This is not necessarily a negotiating committee, so the quality of the chairman is more important than striking a balance between 'sides'.

Once in the chair, the chairman's decisions on procedure are normally final. But there is no law which lays down the procedure for such meetings any more than there is for most meetings. Different committees operate in different ways and you and your trade unions are free to organise your ways so as to achieve the best effect.

95 What must we tell the committee?

How much information is a safety committee entitled to obtain and where will they get it?

* * *

The committee should have the maximum information and should ask the appropriate manager to get that information for it. Curiously, while all the emphasis has been on the additional information which will be made available to trade unions through these committees and other worker participation efforts, management itself will become much better informed. Not only will safety officers have more information and hence more power, but so will management negotiators in every field.

96 Why have a law?

We have operated a safety committee for some time. We are wondering why there has to be a law about it? Surely evolution is a better arrangement than legislation?

* * *

Unfortunately, far too many managers have not followed your good example. Laws are necessary in order to bring people up to minimum standards.

There are various reasons why management has shied away from participatory practices. Most of them are based on fear:

1 Fear of the individual manager that he will be more open to criticism when he is liable to be questioned.
2 Fear of most managers that if they lose their right to keep secrets, they forfeit part of their authority.
3 Corporate fear – bred by generations of secretive behaviour – that leakages of information will become likely and will damage the business.

This defensive armour against active co-partnership is slowly being split open not only by safety committees but through required consultation over intended redundancies and through required disclosures of information during the course of (and for the purposes of) collective bargaining.

97 No union – no committee?

We have no recognised trade unions in our works. What are our rights and duties in connection with safety committees?

* * *

The Commission's Guidance Notes cover situations such as yours. They point, first, to your statutory duty under Section 2 of the Health and Safety at Work Act 'to ensure, in so far as is reasonably practicable, the health, safety and welfare at work of all employees'. To do that, you need to inform your employees of your safety policy and of the arrangements for carrying out that policy – and to instruct employees of their own duties under the Act to take care.

It follows that you will find it necessary 'to involve your employees in the development of health and safety procedures and to obtain their co-operation in the improvement of safety performance'.

Therefore: 'The Commission consider that except in the smaller establishments a suitable approach in many cases might be for an employer to set up a safety committee consisting of members drawn from both management and employees.

'Where no such formal machinery exists, these employees

will need to consider carefully what kind of safety committee would be appropriate in their undertakings and in particular how to achieve an adequate representation on the committee of appropriate management skills and of employees chosen freely by their fellow workers.

'The committee should then consider its objectives and in so doing ought to ensure that they are in line with the objectives of the Act.

'Some employers and employees already operate safety committees, and others have worker councils or similar machinery. In these cases it should not prove difficult to develop joint consultation on health and safety matters'.

So even though the law will not force you to set up a committee in your case, you would certainly be well advised to do so. And if you want further guidance about this, you can consult your Inspector or the Health and Safety Executive itself.

98 Safety committees – and collective bargaining

To what extent should our safety committees be slotted into our general collective bargaining procedures?

* * *

Not at all. It should be entirely separate. Indeed, the people on it are likely to be different.

Naturally, though, if you operate a successful safety committee and are on good terms with its members, the goodwill should spill over into other aspects of your relationships with trade unions – including, of course, collective bargaining.

99 Convincing the stewards

How do we convince our shop stewards that they should be on our side in safety matters? This becomes particularly important if the difficult steward is on our safety committee.

* * *

Communication is vital to success here, as in all other industrial relations respects. So you should try to convince your steward through your efforts and those of your colleagues and if that fails you should call in an outsider who may be more effective if only because he is less familiar.

If the steward maintains that the law has no place on the shop floor, ask him whether he believes that a colleague who drives when drunk and knocks down a woman outside the works should be prosecuted. When he accepts that he should, put the case of the man who comes to work drunk; drives a forklift truck; then due to his carelessness driving or stacking kills the same woman inside the factory. Should he not be prosecuted? If the steward says 'No', then he will almost certainly be out on a limb, with none of his mates agreeing.

The more the steward disagrees, the less suited he is for your committee and the more it should be left to his mates to isolate him. Provided that you make it plain that your safety committe is for the benefit of your employees, you should not leave them for long on the opposite side of the table.

100 Who can help us?

We are doing our best to comply with the new rules on safety representatives and committees but we are running into a series of snags. We need help. Where do we get it?

* * *

Try your factory inspector or the Health and Safety Commission. If they cannot advise you, they can probably put you onto someone who can.

101 Codes of Waffle

Why are Codes of Practice put out by the Health and Safety Commission – including the approved Code concerning safety committees and representatives – so vague? We have also found the same with most of the Codes produced by the Advisory, Conciliation and Arbitration Service (ACAS).

The Commission drafts its documents on the basis 'that it would be undesirable to restrict unnecessarily the freedom of employers and trade unions to make arrangements suitable to the circumstances of each undertaking'. Nothing 'would prevent employers and employees continuing existing agreed arrangements which are satisfactory to both sides, or drawing up alternative arrangements for joint consultation over health and safety at work which do not follow the provisions of the proposed Regulations . . . Code . . . or Advice (Guidance)'. But the existing or alternative arrangements must at least come up to the minimum standards created by the Regulations – and the Code is designed to guide employers as to the best way of doing so.

Statutes and Regulations are (where possible) precise. Codes are almost always more vague because they are intended as generalised guidance (quotable in court against you, if you do not comply with them – but without the force of law). 'Guidance' or advice is even more vague.

102 Can we bring private prosecutions for safety infractions?

What are the prospects in practice of private prosecutions being brought for failure to comply with the safety representatives' rules – by trade unions against employers, or employers against trade unions or by members of the public?

* * *

On 9 March 1977 – when the Act had been in force for some two years – the Attorney General informed Parliament that there had been no private prosecutions and only two requests to the Director of Public Prosecutions for his leave to bring such a prosecution under the Act. So the Act is being operated as intended – by and on behalf of the public and not by private citizens. It is unlikely that this will change – because of the safety representative rule rules or for any other reason.

BOOK 2

STATUTE AND COMMON LAW LIABILITY – BEFORE AND AFTER THE ACT

An employee who wishes to obtain damages as a result of an injury suffered at work must prove three elements. First, he must show a duty of care, owed to him. This is seldom a problem. Every employer owes a duty to his employee to avoid negligence and to comply with his statutory duties towards those on his payroll.

Second, the employee must prove a breach of duty – that his employer was negligent or that he had failed to exercise reasonable care to protect him from unnecessary risk or that he was in breach of a duty imposed by a statute or by a regulation made under a statute.

Third, to obtain damages, the plaintiff must prove loss or damage arising out of the breach.

Book Two explains an employer's duties and an employee's rights. It cannot provide more than a survey of relevant statutes; an understanding of the most important rules on negligence and nuisance; a look at the laws on damages and on the assessment of damage in financial terms; and some hints on courts and their procedures.

This law existed before the new Act and will now flourish at its side.

"HE SAYS HE'S FROM THE NEW INTEGRATED INSPECTORATE . . ."

Part Five

Statutory Duties

Introduction

On 31 December 1973, there were 202,588 registered factories; 1202 docks, wharves and quays; 2612 warehouses; and 273 premises registered under Section 179 of the Factories Act – a grand total of nearly 206,000 units.

Factory inspectors made 160,841 visits to factories – less than one per factory per year. The average workplace has been visited only about once in four years. The number of prosecutions (informations laid) in 1973 was 3,983, but the number of notifiable accidents reported was 272,518 – of which 549 were fatal. Reported dangerous occurrences were 1881.

Of prosecutions in 1973, the vast majority were successful – 3725 out of 3983. Inspectors are normally very sure of their ground before they prosecute. Soon, there will be more inspectors; more prosecutions – and, it is hoped, far fewer deaths and injuries.

Of the 549 fatal accidents in the year, 31 resulted from reported electrical accidents – and 230 from individual construction processes including building and engineering construction operations. Building and engineering industries must be under special scrutiny.

These details come from the annual report of HM Chief Inspector of Factories for 1973.

The Inspectorate was greatly changed – in its size, its organisation and its powers – as a result of the 1974 Act. Manpower is still scarce, but the inspectors have more power. The existing legislation – especially *The Factories Act, 1961* – remains in force, until it is gradually replaced with newer, more up-to-date rules. Against this background we will now consider the main outline of the existing statutory duties, mainly imposed by the Factories Act and by the Offices, Shops and Railway Premises Act, and by regulations made under them.

Chapter 27

What is a Factory?

Section 175 of *The Factories Act, 1961,* says that in general: 'the expression "factory" means any premises in which, or within the close or curtilage or precincts of which, persons are employed in manual labour in any process for or incidental to any of the following purposes, namely:

(a) the making of any article or part of any article; or
(b) the altering, repairing, ornamenting, finishing, cleaning, or washing or the breaking-up or demolition of any article; or
(c) the adapting for sale of any article; or
(d) the slaughtering of cattle, sheep, swine, goats, horses, mules or asses; or (in general)
(e) the confinement of such animals as aforesaid while awaiting slaughter at other premises. . . .

being premises in which, or within the close or curtilage or precincts of which, the work is carried on by way of trade or for purposes of gain and to or over which the employer of the persons employed therein has the right of access or control.'

As if this is not enough, the Section goes on specifically to include various places which might otherwise not be factories.

Note also that if two or more people carry on any work in any particular place and the nature of the work is such that the work-place would be a factory if the people concerned were employed by the owners or occupiers of the premises, it will still in almost every case be a factory for the purposes of the Act. But where somewhere within the 'close, curtilage or precincts forming a factory' there is some place 'solely used for some purpose other than the processes carried on in the factory, that place shall not be deemed to form part of the factory for the purposes of this Act'. If otherwise it would be a factory, then it will be a separate factory and not part of the factory within whose grounds it stands. But if the separate building is not itself a 'factory', the distinction is important, and the boundary must be drawn, even if (in the words of one Judge) the result is 'absurd'. The test is whether the function of the separate building is 'incidental to' the main function of the factory – an administration block, for instance. Premises owned or occupied by the Crown or any municipal or other public authority may be just as much a factory as one in private occupation.

In throwing its net so widely over factories and works (in the widest possible sense of both words), the Act does its best to protect those who work in them – sometimes even those who are not employed by the owners or occupiers themselves. If the object of the business is 'trade or gain', the chances are that the premises are covered. But a prison workshop is not a factory, nor is a technical institute conducted by a municipal or public authority to instruct or train pupils in work involving the use of dangerous machinery. Equally, where a man was employed as a porter in a chemist's shop, the fact that he did manual labour did not make the shop a factory – but if others had been employed on manual labour, so that the premises were generally used for the purpose of employments involving such labour, then a factory it would have been. Indeed, where girls made wreaths and floral decorations out of natural flowers, the fact that they also served customers did not prevent their work-place from being covered by the Act, nor did the light nature of the work itself.

As for the 'premises', these are usually marked off by walls or fences. The hangar of an airfield was a factory – and so was its apron. 'Premises' need not be a building – a scrapyard in the open has been held to be included. But an unfenced site where a new factory was being built, and crushing machinery was used, was held to be outside the Act.

If you are ever in doubt as to whether your works or any part of them have to be treated as a factory, you should ask your lawyer for his advice. And to show just how difficult it is for that advice to be accurate, contrast some examples of premises where manual work done on premises was held to be 'adapting an article for sale', so that the premises were factories, with some other instances where the processes were held to be outside the scope of the legislation.

Bottling beer by hand is within the Act, but washing bottles and filling them with beer by machine is outside it; testing propellers and modifying and adjusting them where necessary is in, but testing anchors, cables and prototype vehicles and their parts is out; sorting rags in a warehouse is in, but sorting them by passing them through a machine to remove dust and dirt, ready for sale to manufacturers of paper and shoddy, is out; separating refuse into saleable and unsaleable parts is in, and so is compressing waste paper, but while in one case repairing motors, making none of the parts used for the repair, was held to be out, most repair shops or service departments of electrical appliance shops and the like have been held to be 'factories'.

In another case, the workroom at the back of a radio and TV shop, in which a skilled engineer diagnosed faults in equipment and then repaired them, was held to be a 'factory'. The question here, the court decided, was whether any person was engaged in 'manual labour'. The test to be applied is whether (as in the case of a shop assistant, who may have to move stock or carry out minor repairs or alterations) the manual work is incidental to the main purpose of the employment – in which case, the place of work is not a 'factory' – or whether (as in the case of the radio and TV repair man who used his non-manual skills to diagnose faults), the non-manual worker is incidental to the main purpose of the employment – itself manual – in which case the place of work is a factory.

The question, 'When is a factory not a factory?' is not nearly as silly as it sounds – nor nearly as easy to answer as to ask. But upon the answer depends the issue of civil or criminal liability (or both), in hundreds of cases, every month of the year. So, if in doubt about any premises you occupy, either comply with the Act or confirm with your solicitor that you are not running unnecessary risks by failing to do so.

Chapter 28

The Fencing of Machinery – and the Safety of Your Operatives

'Every dangerous part of any machinery, other than prime movers and transmission machinery, shall be securely fenced unless it is in such a position or of such construction as to be as safe to every person employed or working on the premises as it would be if securely fenced.'

This part of Section 14 of *The Factories Act, 1961* (repeating provisions formerly in Section 14 of the 1937 Act) is the most fertile breeding ground for court decisions provided by any factory legislation. To understand the Section is a considerable task. Over the course of time, certain basic principles have evolved. Here are some of them – and the cases from which they arose.

A Mr Kinder was an operator of a machine for compressing waste paper into bales. The paper was put into a box with a moveable top, described as a plunger. As the box was filled, the plunger was pressed down by hand, the additional power required to compress it being applied by means of a lever upon which the operator pressed. As the paper was compressed, the plunger went still farther down and was kept in position by cogs or studs, with the result that the lever was fixed until it was released. In order to fill up the box from time to time, there was (by means of a second handle) a method of releasing the gear which held the plunger in position. While Mr Kinder was attempting to release the gears so as to put some paper into the box, the release took place, not under his control, but quite suddenly, with the result that the handle flew up and struck Mr Kinder, knocking out several teeth.

Mr Kinder sued. He claimed that he had suffered his injuries as a result of the negligence of his employers. He also claimed that there was a breach of Section 14 of the Factories Act.

The then Lord Chief Justice had to consider whether or not the machine was dangerous, and he found this very difficult. 'Anything in a manner of speaking', he said, 'is dangerous if it may cause danger either owing to negligence or owing to the fact that it is impossible for everybody on every occasion, however carefully they may conduct themselves, to avoid some mischance whereby hand or eye injury might be caused; and this particular piece of apparatus does not come within the class of cases where the moment a button is pressed or a handle is turned, the machine begins to operate without the man-handling of the operator . . . it is not inherently more dangerous than the starting handle of a motor-car which may become dangerous the moment it is operated by hand.'

'That states a principle,' said the Lord Chief Justice, 'upon which a decision may be given, but it is not very easy to apply. If a machine has been used for a number of years and no fence has been required or used, and accidents have been very scarce, I suppose it might be said that in the ordinary course of human affairs it might be reasonably anticipated that the use of it without protection did not result in accidents.

'On the whole, I find this machine was dangerous, since in the ordinary course of business, danger may reasonably be expected from the use of it without protection . . . I think danger may be reasonably anticipated, and it is only the very great care of the operators which has prevented accidents happening of the sort which happened in this present case.'

There, then, is the general rule. If in the ordinary course of human affairs, danger may be reasonably anticipated from the use of the machinery or part without protection, then it must be protected. And to decide whether a particular part needs protection, all the facts in the particular case must be taken into account. 'The question whether part of a machine is a dangerous part, is one of fact in each case', as another authority put it.

But the facts must be considered in accordance with the law. In a case brought by a Mr Smith against the Chesterfield and District Co-operative Society, Mr Smith worked a machine which rolled out puff pastry at a bakery. A guard was provided to protect the operator from coming into contact with the rollers. But disregarding instructions, the plaintiff, while operating the machine, put his hand under the guard to press against the rollers pieces of dough which had escaped them. His hand came into contact with the rollers and he was injured. The judge who originally heard the case upheld the view that as the plaintiff had deliberately put his hand underneath the guard, that was equivalent to breaking or taking away the guard. The defendants were not liable. Mr Smith appealed.

The Court of Appeal decided that there had been a breach of statutory duty. While the facts have to be considered by the trial judge in each case, nevertheless his findings can be interfered with if he has drawn the wrong inferences in accordance with the law. Here the trial judge held, as Lord Goddard put it, 'that because the plaintiff put a hand underneath the guard, i.e. through the space which was left between the guard and the bed of the machine, that was equivalent to breaking or taking away the guard, and that, therefore, the employers were not liable'.

'With all respect to the learned judge, I do not agree with that view. It was possible for an operator, without breaking the guard, to get a hand in contact with the rollers. Therefore, it seems to me that it is impossible to say that the dangerous part of the machine, the moving rollers, was "securely fenced". For this reason, I think that there was a breach of statutory duty on the part of the defendants.'

'The plaintiff, however, was guilty of contributory negligence, because he did a deliberate act against which he had been warned and which he ought to have known was highly dangerous. That the danger was foreseeable by the employers is clear, both because the guard was provided to prevent it and because the employees were instructed about it. The guard was not adequate, but the plaintiff was guilty of doing what he did, in direct disobedience of orders. Therefore, he cannot recover the whole of the damages . . . he should be given 40 per cent of whatever sum may be awarded.' The other judges agreed.

You will note at once that even where there has been a breach of statutory duty which could lead to the employers being prosecuted, this will not of itself give an injured employee a right to damages. If the cause of the accident was the employee's negligence, he will get nothing. If his negligence contributed towards the accident, then his damages will be reduced proportionately to his share in the responsibility for the mishap.

In law, then, a part of a machine is dangerous if it is a reasonable foreseeable cause of injury to anybody acting in a way a human being might reasonably be expected to act in circumstances which may reasonably be expected to occur. The possibility of 'inadvertent or indolent conduct' by the employee must be taken into account.

Take, for instance, the recent case of *Rushton* v. *Turner Brothers Asbestos Company Limited.* Mr Rushton was a fibre packer. He suffered a crushing of the tips of the forefingers of his left hand; amputation took place at the first joint of three of the fingers; and there was also a sliced amputation of the index finger. He had been with the defendants quite a considerable time before the accident, and had been employed as a packer, but at his own request he was transferred to operating a crushing machine. One part of the machine was a floor or pan, within which there were two stones connected by a central pin. They rotated round the edge of the pan, which also rotated as it moved round the circumference. In the pan, from time to time, a bag of asbestos fibres was placed, and the purpose of the stones was to crush the fibres as they rotated. The transition took about eight minutes and it was Mr Rushton's task to fetch a bag or sack, empty it into a chute into the machine, and then, after eight minutes, to collect the crushed fibre from the outlet chute and take it away. In order to permit the crushed fibre to leave the pan, there was what the judge described as a 'trap-door or slide'. This was operated by handles screwed into the trap-door, much like the starting handle on a car, the handle being turned until the trap-door slid open. The trap-door moved in grooves along its right-hand and left-hand sides.

As the fibre was discharged out of the trap-door into the chute, from time to time parts of it tended to collect in these two grooves on either side of the trap-door. As the process went on, it appears that the material which collected in the grooves tended to harden (or to become impacted) on the sides of the grooves. If sufficient material had collected, it was clearly difficult to close the trap-door effectively and, therefore, it was necessary from time to time during a day's shift to clean the grooves. It was the operator's task, and, bearing in mind that the stones were rotating round the pan and that in between the stones there were scrapers, cleaning the surface of the pan, the judge took the view that for a man to place his hand in the trap-door while the machine was in motion was 'about as foolish a piece of negligence as anyone could conceive'.

'I am quite satisfied,' said the judge, 'on all the evidence that the idea of cleaning the grooves when the machine was in motion was something which the defendants, from the common-sense angle, had barely any reason to contemplate as being likely to occur; but one must remember that it is not only the sensible workman who is within the scope of the protection given by the Factories Act. . . . They should have contemplated as a matter of law that one day a man would be foolish enough to do it without stopping the machine, and it is against that sort of risk, as I find, that the Factories Act . . . was passed. . . . Fencing clearly could have been applied to the opening because, since the accident, a form of wire guard or barrier has been installed. . . . I find that this particular part was dangerous and it was not fenced at all'.

But none the less, 'the plaintiff was the sole author of his own misfortune. For this reason there must be judgement for the defendants'.

So even where there was a liability to fence, and even where that liability was completely ignored, the employers may still win their case.

'*What sort of parts have been held to be dangerous?*'

There have been any number of decisions on this point. For instance, the gears of a mixer and of a reeling machine have been held to be dangerous. So have calender rollers, a guillotine machine, worm gears of ovens and the gear wheel of a mechanical excavator, parts with a propensity to fly off, a grinding wheel, and a power press for cutting off ends of springs. Conversely, the worm of an extruder, a screwing-machine and a horizontal milling machine have been held not to be dangerous parts.

Incidentally, whereas the Act requires that the machinery that is dangerous when in motion should be fenced, it does not require that material which is dangerous when in motion *in a machine* should be fenced.

One recent case on the point was brought by a Mr Eaves against Morris Motors. Mr Eaves was engaged in the task of putting bolts, two at a time, through a milling machine driven by hydraulic power. He usually hoped to deal with 3000 during the night shift. He stood at a metal table on which was a vice or block into which he inserted two bolts standing upright. He secured them by tightening a nut. He then pulled the starting handle, whereupon the metal table together with the block traversed a few inches towards the cutting knives of the machine, moving fairly fast. The knives had a guard of vertical bars, which allowed the block to pass underneath them and the projecting bolts to pass between them. Thus there was no danger of his hand coming into contact with the knives. While the bolts were being milled by the knives, the block momentarily halted. The block (and table) then reversed, the block still holding the bolts emerged once more from within the guard, and returned to the position whence it started. The metal table and block would then halt. The plaintiff would then loosen the nut and remove the bolts. He would insert two fresh bolts, pull the starting handle again, and the whole operation would be repeated.

On the occasion of the accident, the machine 'repeated' or 'performed an uncovenanted stroke'. Instead of remaining stationary on the completion of its task, it suddenly for no apparent reason started off on its journey again without the plaintiff pulling the starting handle. He was just in the act of removing the finished bolts when this happened. He hastily withdrew his hand to avoid its being drawn towards and against the guard and in doing so cut his hand on a tiny burr or irregularity on the bolt head. This trivial cut became septic and he lost his finger.

The first question the Court of Appeal eventually had to consider was, 'Was the failure to fence within Section 14 of the Factories Act?'

'Dangerous machinery is only required by Section 14 to be fenced against danger of a particular and limited kind', said Lord Justice Holroyd Pearce, 'namely, danger from workmen coming into contact with the machine. There is no protection under Section 14 against a class of obvious perils caused by dangerous machinery, namely, perils which arise from a dangerous machine ejecting at the worker pieces of the material or even pieces of the machinery itself. Thus, there is now left a gap in the law which neither logic nor common sense appears to justify.'

Because judges do not like this artificial distinction, however, they try to make sure that the line is not drawn too technically. Consider the recent case of *Wearing* v. *Pirelli Limited*. Mr Wearing worked at Pirelli's tyre factory, operating a revolving drum. The judge at the trial decided that the drum was dangerous; it went round at 20 miles an hour; and it was not fenced. Mr Wearing fractured his wrist, by touching not the drum itself but a sheet of rubber, one sixteenth of an inch thick, that was wrapped round the drum as part of the tyre-making process.

The defendants argued that they were not liable because the injury to Mr Wearing had not been caused by contact with the dangerous machine at all, but only with the sheet of rubber which encased it.

The House of Lords held that the cause of the accident had to be looked at in a practical way. To all intents and purposes the presence of the rubber sheeting made no difference. To decide any other way, said Lord Edmund-Davies, would be a 'denial of justice'. So the claim succeeded.

'But to what machinery does the Section refer? How far are you responsible if you manufacture unfenced machinery for others to use?'

You are not responsible at all under the Factories Act. The word refers to machinery used in the factory for production and not to machinery which is a product of the factory. And anyway, the word has its ordinary, sensible meaning. For instance, in one case a cable-way was unfenced. It was used for transporting materials. It was held not to be 'machinery' within the meaning of the Section. And nor was a truck used for conveying materials produced. But a mobile crane was held to be 'machinery – with startling consequences, as explained in Chapter 30.

In certain cases, the obligation to fence dangerous parts has been modified by special Regulations coming within Section 76 of the 1961 Act. This Section gives power for the making of special Regulations for safety and health, and in fact dozens of these Regulations have been made. To find out whether any apply to your own particular industry, inquire of your factory inspector and he will certainly tell you. And the Section gives power to 'modify or extend . . . requirements as to health or safety', so many factory occupiers are relieved from the duty to fence where Regulations give this relief.

'In so far as the safety of a dangerous part of any machinery cannot by reason of the nature of the operations be secured by means of a fixed guard', Section 14 itself goes on, 'the requirements of subsection 1 of this section (as to fencing) shall be deemed to have been complied with if a device is provided which automatically prevents the operator from coming into contact with that part'. So you can fence out the operator instead of fencing in the machine.

'Where the Minister is satisfied that there is available and suitable for use in connection with machinery of any class any type or description of safety device which:

(a) prevents the exposure of a dangerous part of machinery whilst in motion; or
(b) stops a machine forthwith in case of danger;

he may make regulations directing that the type or description of device shall be provided for use in connection with such class of machinery as may be specified in the regulations.' Once again, to see whether there are Regulations which you ought to know about, inquire.

'Any part of a stock bar which projects beyond the headstock of a lathe shall be securely fenced, unless it is in such a position as to be as safe to every person employed or working on the premises as it would be if securely fenced.' That part of the Section speaks for itself.

And finally, an exception to the rule about the fencing of materials. 'The Minister may, as respects any machine or any process in which a machine is used, make regulations requiring the fencing of materials or articles which are dangerous while in motion in the machine.' It is a power which as yet does not seem to have been used.

The next problem comes in deciding whether any part of machinery 'is in such a position or of such construction as to be as safe to every person employed or working on the premises as it would be if securely fenced'. Here the rules are laid down by Section 15.

'(a) No account shall be taken of any person carrying out,

while the part of the machinery is in motion, an examination thereof or any lubrication or adjustment shown by the examination to be immediately necessary, if the examination, lubrication or adjustment can only be carried out while the part of the machinery is in motion; and

(b) in the case of any part of transmission machinery used in any such process as may be specified in regulations made by the Minister, being a process where owing to the continuous nature thereof the stopping of that part would seriously interfere with the carrying on of the process, no account shall be taken of any person carrying out, by such methods and in such circumstances as may be specified in the regulations, any lubrication or any mounting or shipping of belts.'

Provided that 'the examination, lubrication or other operation' is carried out by men who are at least 18 years old, running examinations, lubrications or adjustments will not be taken into account.

As for the fencing itself, Section 16 says that this 'shall be of substantial construction and constantly maintained and kept in position while the parts required to be fenced or safeguarded are in motion or use, except when any such parts are necessarily exposed for examination and for any lubrication or adjustment shown by the examination to be immediately necessary'. And that, at least, is common sense. But of course, where there has been a complete failure to fence, this exception will not help the employer. If the employee is examining, lubricating or adjusting a machine which has a fence which is not in use, that is one thing. It is quite another if he is doing the same to a machine which should be fenced but has not been.

By contrast to the strict attitude of courts in deciding whether maintenance is 'necessary', there is the difficulty of deciding when machinery is actually 'in motion or in use'.

In the case of *Kelly* v. *John Dale Limited,* Dale's employed Miss Kelly in their factory, cleaning the rollers of a printing machine. The rollers had to be exposed by means of a so-called 'inching button'. The button inched and the employee's hand was trapped by one of the rollers. She claimed damages. The Judge held that the machinery was not 'in motion or in use' at the time, so that it did not matter that the guard was not in place.

In *Stanbrook* v. *Waterlow & Sons*, decided by the Court of Appeal a month after Kelly's case, the judges held that 'a printing machine which is being moved in short jerks by way of preparatory work is 'in motion' within Section 16 of the Act'. The law, too, 'moves' in a mysterious way.

Never forget, though, that even the employer who escapes liability under the Regulations may still be liable irrespective of any statute (that is, by 'common law') for operating a negligent system of work – a point easily forgotten in the tussle over interpreting the Regulations, (as Lord Edmund-Davies remarked in Wearing's case).

Finally, consider some other cases on Section 14. First, *Woodley* v. *Meason Freers & Company Limited.*

Meason Freers occupied a factory in which there was a plastic-grinding machine into which plastic scrap was fed. The topmost part of the machine, which was some 4¾ ft from the floor, consisted of a hopper with a square top feed and a side feed to a trap inlet. Larger forms of plastic scrap were fed into the top feed, came down the inside of the hopper, passed a constricted space known as the throat, and were then cut by a revolving cylindrical cutter, the top of the blades of which were 20 inches below the top of the hopper. Occasionally, the plastic scrap would stick within the hopper, and it was then necessary to push it down.

Unknown to Meason Freers, the operatives used to stand on boxes to reach inside the hopper in order to push down the material which had stuck. If the machine was stopped, there was no risk of injury. Meason Freers told their operatives to be careful and to mind their hands and had, at one time, fitted two or three metal bars across the top of the hopper to emphasise warnings against the insertion of hands into the hopper. The machine had been in use for three years without mishap and without complaint by the factory inspector.

One day, an operative inserted his left hand inside the top feed of the hopper to press down material that had stuck. His fingers were injured by the blades of the cutter. The inspector instituted proceedings against the company under Section 14. He maintained that the cutters of the machine were not securely fenced. The magistrates decided that the cutters were not a 'reasonably foreseeable cause of injury' to anyone acting in a way in which a person employed might reasonably be expected to act. The information was dismissed and the inspector appealed.

The appeal was heard by a Divisional Court presided over by the Lord Chief Justice. He pointed out that if the machine is turned off, there is no risk of injury. But 'any employer must contemplate that an employee may forget to turn off the machine, and, once one has got that far, it is quite clear that the respondents quite properly realised that a hand would go into the machine, and that there was a danger. . . . It seems to me that, once the danger is recognised of not turning off the machine and of getting a hand into the hopper, then it is very little more to contemplate that the hand will go down a little farther than it should. . . . There was really only one inference which could be drawn, namely, that these cutters, contrary to the findings of the justices, were a reasonably foreseeable cause of injury to anyone acting in the way which a person employed might be reasonably expected to act.' And his brother judges agreed with him.

Finally, *Cross* v. *Midland & Low Moor Iron and Steel Company.* Mr Cross is an inspector of factories. He brought proceedings before the Rotherham Justices against the respondents, who were occupiers of a factory. An employee who was feeding bent metal bars into the leading-in rollers of a power-driven machine for the purpose of straightening them, was distracted by a noise. He turned and his hand was drawn along and nipped between the metal bar and a leading-in roller. The leading-in rollers were not fenced. But the magistrates dismissed the case on the grounds that the Section 'did not impose a duty to fence against danger created by juxtaposition of a moving piece of material and a part of a machine not in itself dangerous'.

The Divisional Court held that where a machine is being worked as it was designed to work and a part of the machine (and not merely the material being worked) becomes dangerous for the operation of the machine, that part is a dangerous part of machinery, for the purposes of Section 14 of the Act. It must therefore be securely fenced. Thus, the danger being foreseeable, the company had contravened Section 14. The case would be remitted to the justices with a direction to convict.

Ancient rabbis recommended that a fence be put about the Law, to preserve it from being whittled away by non-observance. But in Britain, the law requires that a fence be put about machinery which is in itself dangerous or which has dangerous parts, in order that employees who operate it may be saved from harm. But it is one thing to make a law and quite another to interpret it. Even those who wish to comply with the Factories Act do not always find it easy to do so. And that is hardly surprising when one knows how often lawyers (and even Judges) disagree on the subject.

Chapter 29

Floors and Passages

The Factories Act requires that 'all floors, steps, stairs, passages and gangways shall be of sound construction and properly maintained, so far as is reasonably practicable, be kept free from any obstruction and from any substance likely to cause persons to slip.'

Exactly the same rules also apply to offices, shops and railway premises, and the new Act also covers 'access and egress' to work-places. But what does all this mean?

Consider the case of *Dorman Long (Steel) Limited* v. *Bell,* which reached the highest court in the land.

Thomas Henry Bell was employed by Dorman Long as a burner at one of their factories. One night, he was required to help in maintenance work. Having turned on some gas cylinders, he made his way back to the place where he was working. He had to go round a large plinth and he stepped on to two large, heavy plates lying on the floor, one on top of the other. He slipped or tripped and fell. He was injured. He sued for damages.

First, he claimed that his employers had been in breach of their statutory duty to him, to keep the floor clear of obstruction and from a substance likely to cause people to slip. The plates were an obstruction and they were slippery. Alternatively, he argued that every employer is bound to take reasonable care for his employees' safety. This includes a duty to see that the place of work is reasonably safe. It was not. As a result he was injured. He was entitled to damages.

The employers retorted that there had been no breach of the Factories Act. They said, in effect, that if Mr Bell slipped, that was caused by a 'slippery film on the plates, and not by anything on the floor'. The statutory obligation, they said, 'is only to keep the floor free from slippery substances and it does not apply to anything which is not actually on the floor'. As for common law negligences, this, too, they denied. They said that there was plenty of room for the man to walk round the plates. He had no need to trip over them. His downfall was entirely due to his own negligence, this, too, they denied; in not looking where he was going contributed to the accident.

The judge who heard the case decided that the employers were in breach of the statute but that the employee's own carelessness was a 50 per cent cause of the trouble. So his damages were reduced by 50 per cent. And the House of Lords (via the Court of Appeal) upheld the judge.

Lord Reid in the House of Lords said that he was quite unable to accept the employer's arguments about the Act only requiring slippery things to be kept off the floor – and not off objects on the floor. 'It would mean that if there is something slippery on a tarpaulin or even a sheet of paper lying on the floor', he said, 'then the statutory protection does not apply. I think that keeping the floor free means preventing the presence of or removing slippery substances on which anyone is likely to step, and it is quite immaterial whether or not the slippery substance is actually in contact with the floor. In this case, the danger was caused by a combination of the slope of the plates and the slippery film on the surface and I would prefer to regard this as a case of an obstruction which had become slippery. It does not matter whether the man tripped or slipped. It was the presence of the obstruction in the state in which it was that caused the accident.'

But what of the employer's argument that it was not 'reasonably practicable' to keep the floor clear? No attempt having been made to clear the covers off the floor, 'it cannot be said that it was not reasonably practicable' to remove them. Dorman Long's appeal was dismissed.

It follows from this that employers and others with factory premises (together with their brethren who occupy offices or shops) must see that floors are clear of obstruction. Slippery substances must be swept or kept away or mopped or cleaned up. If they are allowed to remain and as a result an employee is injured, damages will be payable. And even if insurers actually do the paying, the occupier cannot shrug his shoulders. Premiums have a nasty way of going up, along with the claims made under the policy.

But that is not the end of it. Even if there is no actual accident, the employer may be taken to court and prosecuted. The maximum fine used to be a relatively modest £60, plus £15 for each day for which the offence continues after conviction. Under the new Act, the penalties have been increased to the full extent of those for breaches of the Act itself: up to two years' imprisonment or an unlimited fine on indictment or a £400 fine in the Magistrates' Court (which may soon be increased to £1000). If the court makes an order requiring the convicted party to remedy the unsafe practice, he may also be fined £50 a day thereafter, until things *are* put right.

Nor is it simply the company which can be fined. If the offence is found to have been committed 'with the consent or connivance of, or to have been facilitated by any neglect on the part of, any director, manager, secretary, or other officer of the company, he, as well as the company, shall be deemed to be guilty of the offence and shall be liable to be proceeded against and punished accordingly'.

These rules (laid down by Section 155 of the Act) are common not only to this particular offence, but to all others for which the Factories Act lays down no special penalty. What matters is that the safety of the employee is the concern of Parliament and not merely of his employer. It is your duty to protect your staff, not only so that you do not have to compensate them if they are injured – but also to keep yourself out of the criminal courts, even if they are not injured. A breach of the Factories Act can bring you before a Criminal Court, even if good fortune prevents anyone from being hurt as a result. Conversely, even if you are not prosecuted, an injured person may rely upon your breach of statutory rules, if he is injured as a result. Civil and criminal law go hand in hand to protect the employee. And as the House of Lords showed in *Dorman Long* v. *Bell*, this being a benevolent statute, designed to protect employees, the courts are unlikely to stretch themselves to interpret it to the employer's benefit.

Chapter 30

Factory Safety

Mr Eddie Donaghey was a construction worker, who found himself on the roof of a hanger being built by main contractors, who had sub-contracted the roof work to Boulton & Paul. They had in turn sub-contracted the laying of asbestos sheeting on the roof to a firm called O'Briens – which employed Mr Donaghey. One day, Mr Donaghey was removing damaged asbestos sheets and relaying the lowest tier next to the gutter. The foreman noticed that one of the relaid sheets was out of place. He told Mr Donaghwy and his mate to put it right. Boultons had provided crawling boards. But these were on ground level, and the plaintiff, Mr Donaghey, did not use them. His foreman did not insist. He stood on the outside of the roof, tugged at the sheet and it came loose. He lost his balance and fell through an open space created by the removal of the asbestos sheet. He was severely injured – and sued his employers, O'Briens, and Boulton & Paul. He alleged breaches of Building Regulations. O'Briens filed a defence but did not appear at the trial. It was said that they were without funds and not insured against claims such as that brought by Mr Donaghey.

Now the Regulations say: 'Where work is being done on or near roofs or ceilings covered with fragile materials through which a person is liable to fall a distance of more than 10 ft and where workmen have to pass over or work above such fragile materials, suitable and sufficient ladders, duck-boards, or crawling-boards (which shall be securely supported) shall be provided and used. . . .' Mr Donaghey, through his lawyers, alleged that it was the duty both of his employers and of their head contractors (the defendants) to provide and secure the use of crawling-boards.

'Work was being done on a roof covered with fragile materials through which a person was liable to fall more than ten feet', said Viscount Dilhorne. 'The plaintiff and his mate were working above such fragile materials . . . so suitable and sufficient ladders, duck-boards or crawling boards should have been provided and used. They were not. Crawling-boards were available on the ground, but they were not on the roof and they were not used. . . .' The trial judge had found negligence against O'Briens and had said that Boulton & Paul had failed to take sufficient precautions by the use of crawling-boards to prevent the plaintiff from falling. So 'it was not possible to say that the breach of Regulation . . . was not the cause of the accident. . . . As a result of that breach, the plaintiff suffered injury by falling from the roof. It was the kind of accident at which that Regulation was directed. And it mattered not that when he fell he did not happen to fall on and through the fragile material'.

But why should Boultons be liable? They had sub-contracted the work to others. 'The duty to comply . . . fell on every contractor and employer who undertook any of the operations to which the Regulation applies in relation to any work, act or operation performed or about to be performed by such contractor or employer'.

So was the work 'performed' by Boultons? That in its turn depended upon the contract between Boultons and O'Briens. And as on the evidence it did not appear that Boultons had 'divested themselves of control over the roofing of the hangar', they were liable. They provided all the materials for the roofing, and 'though the actual labour might have been provided by a number of gangs, of which O'Briens' was one, the work was being performed by Boultons . . . the appeal must be allowed'.

So while you do not have to 'nursemaid your staff', where a Regulation says that you must secure the use of the safety equipment which you must provide, it means what it says. Provision alone is not enough. And if by chance you subcontract any of your work, remember that it is only if you 'divest yourself of your control over that work' so that you are not 'performing' it that you are likely to avoid liability if failure to comply with statutory obligations leads to disaster.

On the other hand, if the required safety equipment would not have been used even if it had been provided, the liability may be different. If, for instance, the employer can show that the injured employee would have refused to wear a safety harness whatever attempts were made to persuade him, the employer may prove that the accident was not caused by his failure to ensure that the regulations were obeyed. For an example of this rule, see Chapter 45.

A mobile crane was mounted by vertical shaft on a chassis with four rubber-tyred wheels. It could move about under its own power. It consisted of a jib, which could be operated from a cab by means of machinery enclosed in a large casing. And it was mounted in such a way that it could be rotated as a whole on the chassis.

The plaintiff, Mr Thomas Liptrot, suffered injuries when he was employed as a slinger in a scrap metal yard which was a 'factory' within the meaning of the Factories Act. His body was caught between the upper swivelling part of the crane and one of its wheels. He alleged that there was a breach of Section 14 (1) of the Factories Act. This says that 'Every dangerous part of any machinery . . . shall be securely fenced. . . .'

'Not at all,' answered the defendants. 'It was long ago decided that a mobile truck is not within the section'.

'Wrong', said the House of Lords. 'The decision in which the rule was decided was incorrect.'

'The object of the Act,' said Viscount Dilhorne, 'is to make safety provisions for those employed in or working in factories. To that end, every dangerous part of any machinery in a factory requires to be securely fenced. That is an absolute obligation which does not depend on whether the machinery is a fixed part of the equipment of the factory or is on wheels and capable of moving under its own power from one part of the factory to another or outside it'.

But is a 'vehicle' the same as 'machinery'? No, but 'it might contain machinery . . . and if the vehicle forms part of the equipment of the factory Section 14 imposes an absolute obligation . . . to fence securely every dangerous part of the machinery it contains' (subject to the limited proviso in the section).

So if a car or a lorry visits a factory, it would 'not be part of its equipment' and the Act would not apply to it. But the judges could 'see no reason for excluding any part of the equipment of a factory which contains machinery from the operation of the Act on the ground that it is mobile or could be described as a vehicle'.

The French have a famous saying: 'If my aunt had wheels she would be a bicycle'. The reverse no longer applies in English factories. The fact that equipment has wheels does not prevent it from being machinery, and if that machinery is 'dangerous' it must be fenced, as firmly and securely as if it were utterly immobile. The duty to see that the fencing is done rests on those who supervise the safety and operations of the factory itself.

Chapter 31

The Offices, Shops and Railway Premises Act, 1963

The Offices, Shops and Railway Premises Act, 1963, applies to the three types of premises named – which are individually divided.

'Office premises, means a building or part of a building . . . the sole principal use of which is as an office or for office purposes'. 'Office purposes' include 'the purposes of administration, clerical work, handling money and telephone and telegraph operating'; and 'clerical work' includes 'writing, bookkeeping, sorting papers, filing, typing, duplicating, machine calculating, drawing and the editorial preparation of matter for publication.'

'For the purposes of this Act, premises occupied together with office premises for the purposes of the activities there carried on shall be treated as forming part of the office premises'. So where you have office premises attached to a workshop and the two work in conjunction, both are covered by the Act.

As for 'shop premises', this means not only a shop, in the ordinary sense of the word, but also 'a building . . . of which the sole or principal use is the carrying on there of retail trade or business', 'a building occupied by wholesale dealers or merchants where goods are kept for sale wholesale' to persons resorting to the premises, and 'a building to which members of the public are invited to resort for the purpose of delivering there goods for repair or other treatment'.

Finally, 'railway premises' are defined as meaning 'a building occupied by railway undertakers for the purposes of the railway undertaking carried on by them and situate in the immediate vicinity of the permanent way or a part (so occupied) of a building so situate. . . .'

If your premises are covered by the Act, then it is up to you to ensure that they have been registered, and that you have complied with the Act and the Regulations made under it. The most important of which concern the 'health, safety and welfare of employees'. 'All premises to which this Act applies,' says Section 14, 'and all furniture, furnishings and fittings in such premises shall be kept in a clean state'. No room in such premises shall be overcrowded, and 'effective provision shall be made for securing and maintaining a reasonable temperature in every room comprised in, or constituting premises . . . in which persons are employed to work otherwise than for short periods.'

How cold is 'reasonable'? Where the work going on 'does not involve severe physical effort', the temperature must not be less than 60.8°F (16°C) 'after the first hour'. How hot? Surprisingly, the Act fixes no limit, but common sense and the need for efficient employees usually fill the gap.

Exceptions? Rooms where members of the public are 'invited to resort' and in which 'the maintenance of a reasonable temperature is not reasonably practicable' and rooms where the maintenance of a reasonable temperature 'would cause deterioration of goods'. But people who are employed to work in a room that comes under one of these exceptions must have 'conveniently accessible and effective means of enabling them to warm themselves'.

And just to make sure that employees know that they are getting proper treatment, 'a thermometer of a kind suitable for enabling the temperature in any room . . . to be readily determined' must be kept on every floor.

'Effective and suitable provision shall be made for securing and maintaining, by the circulation of adequate supplies of fresh or artificially purified air, the ventilation of every room . . . in which persons are employed to work' and 'for securing and maintaining . . . sufficient and suitable lighting, whether natural or artificial' and 'suitable and sufficient sanitary conveniences'.

Regulations have already been made as to these items – and

in particular, these provide that where people of both sexes are employed on the premises, there must usually be separate lavatories.

'There shall . . . be provided, at places conveniently accessible to the persons employed to work in the premises, suitable and sufficient washing facilities, including a supply of clean, running hot and cold or warm water and, in addition, soap and clean towels or other suitable means of cleaning or drying.'

This section alone caused a minor office revolution. No more may employees come to work clutching their soap and towel. Now, both have to be provided – and the manufacturers of hot-air machines, rotary towels, disposable towels and the like are enjoying a boom.

'There shall . . . be provided and maintained . . . an adequate supply of wholesome drinking water.' If it 'is not piped, it must be contained in suitable vessels and . . . renewed at least daily', and if 'delivered otherwise than in a jet from which persons can conveniently drink, there shall either be provided, and renewed as often as occasion requires, a supply of drinking vessels of a kind designed to be discarded after use, or . . . a sufficient number of drinking vessels of a kind other than as aforesaid, together with facilities for rinsing them in clean water'.

In American offices, the water fountain is commonplace. In British offices and shops, it soon will be.

Accommodation must be made available for 'such of the clothing of the persons employed to work . . . as is not worn by them during working hours', and for any special clothing so worn by them. No more hanging of clothes over the back of chairs or on hangers suspended from door-knobs. But so long as the lockers or coat hooks are there, there is no special obligation to keep away the light-fingered. An employer has no special duty to look after the safety of his employee's belongings.

Sitting facilities must be provided for the use of employees, together with foot-rests, and 'it shall be the duty of the employer of persons for whose use facilities are provided in pursuance of . . . this section to permit them to use them whenever the use thereof does not interfere with their work, and if he fails to do so he shall be guilty of an offence'. There must be a foot-rest for the short-legged typist.

'All floors, stairs, steps, passages and gangways . . . shall be of sound construction and properly maintained and shall, so far as is reasonably practicable, be kept free from obstruction and from any substance likely to cause persons to slip.' Which is common sense.

'For every staircase . . . a substantial handrail shall be provided and maintained and . . . in the case of a staircase having two open sides or of a staircase, which, owing to the nature of its construction or the condition of the surface of the steps . . . is specially liable to cause accidents, such a hand rail . . . shall be provided and maintained on both sides.'

Again, 'any open side of a staircase . . . shall also be guarded by the provision and maintenance' of a lower rail or other effective means, and 'all openings in floors . . . shall be securely fenced, except in so far as the nature of the work renders such fencing impracticable'.

Employees must mind their step – but employers must see that if their step goes astray, they will have something to hold on to.

Section 17: The fencing of exposed parts of dangerous machinery in offices, shops and railway premises is required, in much the same way as in factories (*see* Chapter 28). Special provisions are made for the training and supervision of people under eighteen, working such 'dangerous machines'. And the Secretary for Employment is empowered to make 'special regulations' for protecting the people employed in premises to which the Act applies 'against risks of bodily injury to health arising out of the use of any machinery, plant, equipment, appliance or substance, the carrying on of any operation or the use of any process'.

The Secretary of State 'may impose obligations, restrictions and prohibitions on those who employ persons to work as aforesaid, on persons employed so to work and on others'. So whichever side of the unfenced machine you may be on – watch out.

If your work brings you into contact with dangerous machines in these premises, you will have to study Sections 17 to 20 with special care. But even if you operate some of the more modern office equipment, you will find that fences and guards may be needed to satisfy the provisions of the Act.

'In the case of all premises to which this Act applies, there shall be provided so as to be readily accessible a first-aid box

. . . or a first-aid cupboard . . . and, where the number of persons employed to work in the premises exceeds 150 at any one time', an additional such box or cupboard must contain such 'first-aid requisites and appliances' as the Minister may order, and contain 'no articles other than first-aid requisites or appliances'.

Special regulations deal with fire precautions. 'Fire certificates' have to be obtained in the case of larger premises and the appropriate authority has to make sure that there are appropriate 'means of escape in case of fire' and proper 'safety provisions'. All premises concerned have to be 'provided with effective means, capable of being operated without exposing any person to undue risk, of giving warning in case of fire' – so automatic fire alarms have become obligatory. The Regulations require that there must be 'provided and maintained appropriate means for fighting fire, which shall be so placed as to be readily available for use'. So fire extinguishers must be bought, if they are not already available. Even more important, in the light of some past tragedies, outward-opening or sliding exit doors must be provided, and 'conspicuously marked' as such. Nor must they be barred so that those in the building cannot escape.

'Where an accident . . . causes loss of life to a person employed to work in the premises or disables any such person for more than three days from doing his usual work', notice has to be given in the proper form – as has long been the case where there is a factory accident.

Nor can any part of the Act be lightly ignored. Apart from the employer's new liability to his servants, he becomes liable to a criminal prosecution, and the by now familiar penalties of up to two years' jail and an unlimited fine.

Chapter 32

Good Workmen and Bad Tools

An employer must provide and maintain in good working order all necessary plant, materials and appliances. Irrespective of the Factories Act or any other statute, he is under a legal duty to provide a safe system of working, and this includes not only the supply of safety equipment as such, but also of safe equipment.

Some time ago, a highly reputable employer supplied a workman with a new drift, bought from equally renowned suppliers. Unfortunately, when the man struck the drift with a hammer, a splinter flew into his eye and blinded him. The cause? A defect in the manufacture of the drift.

The injured workman sued his employers who replied (with total truth): 'The fault was not our's. We were not negligent. We took all reasonable steps to protect you by purchasing what should have been a totally adequate tool from honourable and normally reliable manufacturers.'

Because an employer is not under any absolute liability to his employers the mere fact that an employee is injured at work will not give him any rights against his boss; if he wants damages he must normally prove that his injuries were due to some negligence or breach of statutory duty on his employer's part. On that basis, the unfortunate, one-eyed man lost his case. His employers, after all, had in no way acted carelessly, nor had they contravened any statutory rule or regulation, designed for their employees' safety.

'So why did the workman not sue the manufacturers of the defective drift, so as to make liable those whose manufacturing methods were not reliable?' you ask.

Maybe they were in liquidation; perhaps they were abroad or otherwise difficult to sue. There were and are many reasons why it is infinitely more convenient and satisfactory for a workman to be able to sue his own employers and not to have to look to some potentially distant or insolvent third party, however negligent he may have been.

Accepting this view, Parliament passed *The Employer's Liability (Defective Equipment) Act, 1969,* closely followed by *The Employer's Liability (Compulsory Insurance) Act, 1969.* These two statutes between them overruled the decision in the case of *Davie* v. *New Merton Mills* (for such was the name of the drift case), and while imposing an absolute liability onto employers to provide tools which are not defective in manufacture, it also ensures that they insure against potential liability to their employees.

The effect of the Employer's Liability (Defective Equipment) Act is simply this. Where an employee is injured at work due to a defect in equipment supplied by the employer, the employer is 'deemed' to have been negligent. And however ridiculous it may be, Parliament can arrange for anything to be 'deemed' to be anything else and – lo and behold – it is! By a rub of its magic lamp, Parliament has produced employers' negligence (and hence new employees' rights) out of the air of Westminster.

Naturally, if you get impaled on this thorn, you are still entitled to seek your legal remedy against the real culprit – the supplier of the defective tool or equipment. You are (or at least should be) in a far better position if necessary to chase the culprit across the seven legal seas. And anyway, if there is no money in the manufacturer's kitty, you will be insured.

The second Act – the Employer's Liability (Compulsory Insurances) Act – is of far less practical importance to the prudent employer than the first, because he would in any event have carried insurance. But that which was previously merely an intelligent precaution is now a requirement of law – at least as far as claims from employees are concerned. And to make sure that you comply with it, you must duly frame and exhibit the certificate with which your insurers will have supplied you. Insurance cover must not only be obtained but manifestly seen to be obtained. The ghost of *Davie* v. *New Merton Mills* has been laid low and publicly embalmed.

Chapter 33

Children, Minors and Young Persons

The days when child labour could be lawfully exploited are long since past. Today, children (people not over compulsory school age), young persons (aged between 16 and 17 inclusive) and 'minors' (people under 18) are specially protected by the law.

First, take children. No child may be employed in any factory in any capacity whatsoever. Nor may he be employed in any 'industrial undertaking' unless only members of the same family are employed there. The only exception is for schemes of 'work experience' during the last year of compulsory schooling.

Once school days are over, the newly fledged 'young person' is put by the Factories Act into much the same protected category as a woman worker. Weekdays, they may work from 7 a.m. until 6 p.m., but not in general for more than 44 hours, exclusive of intervals for rest and meals. Once they are 16 they may work overtime, but whereas women may be employed until 9 p.m., young persons may not. And whilst hours of work for women may be increased by the Minister in factories subject to special or seasonal pressure, the same does not apply to young persons. But Regulations may allow overtime employment for young persons in such factories provided that the people concerned are not employed during more than 100 of the hours of overtime employment allowed for the factory in any one year.

Sections 86, 89, 91, 92, 93, 96, 100, 101, 102, 104, 107 and 109 to 114 inclusive of the Act lay down rules for young persons, of which I have only provided a few samples. If you wish to employ youngsters, it is up to you to know those rules in detail. And what with Sections 86, 87, 88, 116 . . . Parliament made sure that there should be no exploitation of the young.

These laws are there to be read. In a way more intriguing are the rules which have evolved through the decisions of judges, providing extra protection for the under 18s.

A minor is only bound by a contract if it is, when looked at as a whole, for his benefit. Business contracts never come into that category. You do business with an under-18 at your peril. If he borrows money from you and does not repay it, waste no time in suing him. You will lose. If he orders goods and does not accept delivery, you had better sell them elsewhere. If he engages you to perform services for him and then cancels the contract before it has begun, you had better hunt for work elsewhere.

Quite apart from business purchases, a minor is only bound to accept and pay for goods if they are 'necessaries' – reasonably necessary for him at the time when he buys them, having regard to his actual needs at that time and to his 'station in life'. Giving credit to minors is asking for trouble.

But happily for those who employ apprentices, education is regarded as thoroughly 'necessary'. Apprentices are bound by their indentures. Even if they are paid a pittance, they cannot avoid their responsibilities because they could earn a good deal more elsewhere. Provided that the contract as a whole is beneficial to the apprentice, the law will hold him to it.

Every factory, then, must have a register in a prescribed form and entered in it or attached to it must be prescribed particulars about the young persons employed in the factory and showing every special exception of which the employer makes use. Every works, engineering site, repair shop or other place which comes within the definition of a 'factory' must have available details of the young persons employed. Up to the age of 18, the eyes of the authorities must be directed at the youngsters employed.

"DEAR SIR, WITH REGARD TO YOUR NEGLIGENCE CLAIM AGAINST YOUR EMPLOYERS . . . "

Part Six

Negligence, Nuisance and an Employer's Liability

Chapter 34

Acts, Omissions – and the Law of Negligence

A person is guilty of negligence when he causes injury, loss or danage through a breach of a duty of care. Where he is under an obligation to take care and he fails to comply with that obligation, then the sufferer is entitled to damages, to compensate him for any loss that he suffers as a result of that failure.

In its turn, the failure may be either an act or an omission – that is, a wrongful failure to act. And courts have often had to decide on whether a particular omission was or was not negligent.

First, the law makes a distinction between two sorts of situation. There may be a failure in the course of doing something which is itself a bad way of doing that thing. Maybe you are driving home one night, dead tired, and you fail to notice a 'Halt' sign. You crash into another vehicle. You *omit* to stop at the 'Halt' sign – but you *positively* smash into the other vehicle.

Second (and much more complicated) is the category of total failure to do an act.

In one case, a judge said that a man may watch a child drown in two feet of water without making any effort to help and he will incur no liability: 'There is no obligation on anyone to play the Good Samaritan'. You may see an accident and drive straight on, even if you know that someone has been injured. Morally, you may regard yourself as a worm. Legally, you incur no obligation.

'An omission on the part of one or other of the defendants would not furnish the plaintiff with any cause of action in the absence of some duty to act owed by the defendants to the plaintiff', said one judge. However, the converse applies: Where there is 'some duty to act', inaction is itself legally actionable.

"If a father were to watch his child drown in two feet of water', says one authority, 'without attempting to rescue, he will be liable since the circumstances of the parent/child relationship impose a positive duty'.

Doctor/patient; teacher/pupil; parent/child; club leader/club member; employer/employee . . . the categories of duty are wide.

Similar rules apply to the failure to provide advice or information. An omission may even amount to a false trade description.

Suppose that you are asked to provide a reference. You are not bound to do so. But once you have agreed to oblige, you have undertaken a duty of care. If you then provide a negligent reference, you could be in trouble.

Are you bound to speak evil of your fellow man? Certainly not. On occasion, silence may be golden; but sometimes it can be damning. 'Yes, she did work for me during the period specified.' FULL STOP.

To avoid liability, then, the first step is to keep away from what lawyers call a 'duty situation'. Unless you owe an obligation to take care, carelessness is not actionable.

Chapter 35

Negligence – Gratuitous and Otherwise

The milk of human kindness can be a very expensive commodity. The law has no sympathy for those who do harm in the course of doing good. We all owe a 'duty of care' to our neighbours – whether or not we are paid a bob or more for the jobs done.

Let us start with the snail that created legal history way back in 1932. It was quietly decomposing in the opaque depths of a ginger-bottle when it was rudely disturbed by a Miss Donoghue, who had been given the drink by a friend. She consumed the alleged beverage and as a result became seriously ill. She sued the manufacturers. 'Ridiculous', they retorted. "We don't know you. We owed no duty to you. Even if we were negligent in our preparation of the ginger beer, you should have sued the person who gave you the drink'. 'Wrong', pronounced the House of Lords. Lord Atkin said this:

'You must take reasonable care to avoid acts or omissions which you can reasonably foresee would be likely to injure your neighbour. Who, then, in law is my neighbour? The answer seems to be – persons who are so closely and directly affected by my act that I ought reasonably to have them in contemplation as being so affected when I am directing my mind to the acts or omissions which are called in question.'

The most hard-hearted soft-drink maker must realise that the person likely to drink his poison is not the person who buys it from him, but 'the ultimate consumer'. Miss Donoghue was the 'neighbour' of the manufacturers. And she won a triumphant victory.

The next great leap forward came in 1963, in another House of Lords case:

'If a reasonable man knows that he is being trusted or that his skill and judgement are being relied on', said the learned Law Lords, in effect, 'and he gives the information or advice sought without that reflection or enquiry which a careful answer would require, and as a result of his negligent behaviour the enquirer suffers loss or damage, he will be liable in damages.'

The defendants in question wriggled off the hook thanks to their disclaimer. But we know that anyone who gives advice, provides information or does any sort of service for anyone else is under a legal duty to take proper care– especially if he has some financial interest in the matter, as in one case where the representatives of a petrol company negligently overstated the throughput of a garage to a potential tenant. If the defendant is negligent and his negligence causes damage, it will be no excuse to say: 'You didn't pay me . . . I only acted out of pure goodness of nature. . . .' Even a completely gratuitous kindness must be carefully performed.

So be sparing with your free advice. If you do not wish to deprive others of the benefit of your counsel, cover yourself by saying that the recipient of your wisdom follows it at his own risk . . . that you give your reference 'without responsibility' . . . that you can accept no liability if your recipe produces poisonous results, your old-fashioned remedy paralyses the patient or your recommended short cuts run the car over a cliff. The odds are that you will be legally in the clear.

Chapter 36

Res ipsa loquitur

Each year, several dozen people are killed by 'bombing' from scaffolds. Rocks, bricks, chunks of metal – even small ones can kill if they land with sufficient velocity on the head beneath. Damages prove a poor solace to the widow or other dependants. But even the mourners must live.

Where an object falls off a building or scaffold, those in occupation have problems if they wish to avoid legal responsibility. The general rule in law? He who seeks damages must prove negligence. But some negligence is so apparent that 'the thing speaks for itself'. In legal Latin: *Res ipsa loquitur*.

The first case on record concerned a barrel of flour which toppled off a building. The owner of the building maintained that he should not be liable. The court held that – in those rare circumstances – the accident spoke for itself. The person in charge of the building (or the barrel) must positively disprove negligence, if he wishes to avoid liability.

Then came the car (or was it a cart, coach or carriage?) which rode up on the pavement, knocking down a pedestrian. The roads are for 'passing or repassing'. When a vehicle goes on a pavement (said the court) negligence will be presumed.

The drive may be able to show that he was in full control of his vehicle until some totally unexpected and unforeseeable accident occurred. Maybe his steering packed up or a new tyre burst. He may be able to shift the presumption of negligence. He can try – good luck to him.

The classic example? The surgeon who sews up a swab inside his patient. Something has gone amiss with the procedures. Had the nurse or the surgeon or both done their arithmetic with elementary precision, all would have been well.

And just to show how wide the principle can be, consider this case: Mrs Ward slipped on a pool of spilt yoghurt on the floor of Tesco's supermarket in Liverpool. She couldn't prove who spilt it – it might have been a customer for whom Tesco's would not be responsible. But *res ipsa loquitur* saved her. It shouldn't have been there. And Tesco's couldn't prove that they took enough precautions to mop up spills. Moral? It may be no use crying over spilt milk, but sometimes it *is* worth suing!

Those who have to draft statements of claim in actions involving personal injury during the course of construction work often plead *res ipsa loquitur*. A bridge collapses: a 'bomb' falls off a scaffold; a structure disintegrates. It is not for the plaintiff to prove his case but for the defendant to establish his innocence – if he can.

This is a 'common law' rule, embellished by decades of legal decisions. And negligence (as opposed to statutory liability) is a common law offence.

If your employee is injured – whether through a falling object or due to any other cause – a lawyer would ask two questions: Was there negligence at common law? And was there a breach of statutory duty? If there was either or both, the man has a case. And if that case speaks for itself, then it should be won. But while an employer is bound to insure for the safety of his employees, he is not the insurer of those employees. The mere fact that they are injured at work will not of itself give them any rights to damages.

One day, the law may change. Fault will cease to be the touchstone for damages. Meanwhile, it is the sole initial criterion.

Chapter 37

Nuisance – in Law

Engineering and most others works are inevitably noisy. Neighbours are disturbed. Unfortunately for them, the law says that even though noise, dust, vibration or smoke may create a nuisance in fact, it only becomes one in law if it goes beyond that which the ordinary, sensible person would expect to put up with. As Mr Justice Plowman put it in the important recent case of *Emms* v. *Polya*, the question is whether the disturbance is 'such as materially to interfere with the ordinary comfort, physically, of human existence in the plaintiff's premises according to plain, simple and sober notions among English people, or whether it affects the plaintiff only because he is hyper-sensitive to noise'.

In assessing the degree of nuisance, the judge will look at the area. If your company, firm or client carries out work in an industrial neighbourhood, then he can reasonably create far more disturbance than would be reasonable in a quiet, residential neighbourhood. That which is a nuisance in Mayfair may not be alongside the Manchester Ship Canal.

Equally, it is the standard of the ordinary, healthy, average man that the court applies. A nightshift worker has no greater right to daytime quiet than his day-shift colleague. Even a man at death's door can demand no greater silence than his robust neighbour.

Mr Emms was a playwright. Mr Polya, who carried out works of conversion in parts of the house occupied by Mr Emms, maintained that the man was hyper-sensitive to noise. Mr Justice Plowman held that Mr Emms 'expected and felt entitled to a higher degree of quiet than an ordinary man who had a flat in a residential part of Hampstead would expect'. But making every allowance for that, the judge still decided that 'the degree of noise occasioned by the defendant's operations was such as to constitute a nuisance. . . .'

You may need quiet for at least part of your work, so that you can concentrate and produce the best results. But you are not entitled to any special legal freedom from disturbance. Still (as Mr Justice Plowman held) provided that your complaints are not caused by hyper-sensitivity, you have no less right than the next man.

So Mr Polya's activities had overstepped the bounds of reasonableness. Next question: Could he bring himself into the exception created by the famous case of *Andreae* v. *Selfridge & Company* by proving 'that he carried out the works with all proper care and skills so as to prevent a nuisance as far as possible?'

There is no law which required Mr Polya to employ a consultant or an expert – Mr Polya took over plans for the conversion of the house which had been prepared on behalf of the previous owner 'by a consultant'. Apparently, said the judge, 'he consulted the person in question from time to time when the construction work was being carried out, but otherwise the man took no part in the work'. He acted as his own supervisor, even though he lived some distance away and was not on site all the time the men were working, especially early and late in the day. He got his labour mainly by advertising for it, and he admitted 'that he was not always satisfied that the men he employed were competent'. He agreed 'that they were unreliable in respect of time-keeping and were not always temperate' – but then who is? He claimed that he was 'on the whole satisfied with the way they did their work'.

Had he, then, taken all proper care and skill so as to prevent a nuisance as far as possible?

'Having no architect and no surveyor', said the judge, 'he had no advice on how to keep the noise level down so as not to cause a nuisance. The truth of the matter was that he took no precautions whatever to mitigate the effect of his operations' – other than once asking one of the workman not to use a transistor radio.

So Mr Emms won his case. Originally, he had asked for an injunction – the ordinary remedy in nuisance actions. He had claimed an Order, restraining the defendant from continuing to behave in the unlawful and unneighbourly way complained of. But by the time the case reached trial, he was on the point of quitting the premises for good. So he claimed damages.

It is always very difficult to assess the amount of damages in nuisance actions. It is hard enough for courts to follow precedents when deciding the value of an amputated or broken leg or of a lost eye. When it comes to assessing human misery caused by an excess of noise or other disturbance, a judge must make a stab in the legal dark; as when the Court of Appeal recently had to fix the damages for twelve years' worth of the smell from a badly run pig farm (£1000).

Mr Justice Plowman came up with the sum of £350. More important to the plaintiff, though – the defendant was required to pay his costs.

The costs of even a modest High Court action – especially paying the bill for both sides – are likely to run well into four figures. The chances are that had Mr Polya paid a consultant of his own, he would have saved a good deal of money in the long run. No doubt the old maxims about pennywise pound foolish and spoiling a ship for a ha'porth of tar are by now well known to him. Maybe if the work of conversion had only gone on for a few weeks, he might have made a profit by his do-it-yourself consultancy, supplemented by a word with the man who drew up the plans. As it was, although the Law Report does not tell us how long the job continued, it was obviously a major work of reconstruction, occupying probably many months.

Chapter 38

Coming to a Nuisance

Dr Sturges built a consulting room next door to a factory. 'What better place for business?' he asked himself, rhetorically. The answer came in the form of bangs and hisses, squeals, rattles and clattering – all the row of particularly noisy modern machinery. The result? The doctor could not hear himself diagnose or prescribe, nor listen to the complaints of his patients. The time had come, he decided, to make his own complaints.

'Sorry', said the factory people. 'We've been carrying on business in this industrial area for a long time. You decided to set up shop next door to us. That was your decision and not ours. We have to make a living. You will just have to put up with the noise and vibration as best you can – or move out to the foreign parts whence you came.'

But Dr Sturges was not a man to be easily moved (literally, if not metaphorically). Instead, he sued the proprietors of the factory.

Now, no one is allowed to use his land in such a way as unreasonably to disturb his neighbour's enjoyment of his property. But what is or is not 'reasonable' in any particular case is (as we have seen) a question of fact and often has to be hammered out with a great deal of (very dignified, of course) sound and fury in a court of law. And that is where the case of Dr Sturges ended up.

The doctor won his day. Lord Justice Thesiger held that the degree of disturbance caused to the good physician was more than that which an ordinary, reasonable individual would expect to have to endure as 'part of the give and take of neighbourly life'. Having regard to all the circumstances of the case, including the nature of the neighbourhood, the factory created a 'nuisance'. The doctor was entitled to an injunction, restraining the factory owners from continuing this unlawful behaviour.

Many morals may be drawn. First, the fact that you 'come to a nuisance' does not mean that you cannot complain of it. You are entitled to reasonable quiet for your work, no matter how new you are to a particular district. But the district you are in does matter.

As Lord Justice Thesiger said, 'Whether anything is a nuisance or not is a question to be determined, nor merely by an abstract consideration of the thing itself, but in reference to its circumstances; what would be a nuisance in Belgrave Square would not necessarily be so in Bermondsey; and where a locality is devoted to a particular trade or manufacture carried on by the traders or manufacturers in a particular and established manner not constituting a public nuisance, judges and juries would be justified in finding, and may be trusted to find, that the trade or manufacture so carried on in that locality is not a private or actionable wrong'.

So you cannot expect the same quiet in your industrial premises as you would in your hallowed precincts of Harrow or Harley Street. The neighbours *can* expect, though, that wherever they live their property will not suffer physical damage by your industrial activities next door. Residents of a street in Fulham, who found when they parked their cars outside that acid smuts from a nearby oil refinery ate holes in the paintwork, won their case for an injunction although they lived in an industrial district.

Chapter 39

The Occupier's Liability Act, 1957 – Duties to Your Visitors

Until 1957, visitors were divided into all sorts of complicated categories, and an occupiers' responsibility varied according to the category of the visitor. But no more. *The Occupiers' Liability Act, 1957,* lays down a 'common duty of care', owed by the occupier of premises to all his visitors. He must 'take such care as in all the circumstances of the case is reasonable to see that the visitor will be reasonably safe in using the premises for the purposes for which he is invited or permitted by the occupier to be there'.

So whether it is mother-in-law on a rampage, the postman with the mail, someone else's employee making deliveries, sub-contractors . . . provided that the visitor has your consent, express or implied, to be there, you must take reasonable care to see that they are safe. Which is pretty reasonable law – but, in practice, exceedingly difficult to apply because every case has to be decided upon its own individual facts.

The Act helps a little. It starts by saying that among the circumstances that have to be considered are: 'the degree of care, and want of care, which would ordinarily be looked for in such a visitor, so that (for example) in proper cases – (*a*) an occupier must be prepared for children to be less careful than adults; and (*b*) an occupier may expect that a person, in the exercise of his calling, will appreciate and guard against any special risks ordinarily incident to it, so far as the occupier leaves him free to do so'.

So the ordinary rule that each of us must look after himself applies here, too. But if you let children in, then watch out. You must take more care of them than of adults. But if it is a window-cleaner, a repairer, a builder or some other independent contractor, who regulates his own way of working, then your responsibility is less. Certainly he must be expected to look out for the ordinary risks of his calling. A window-cleaner who does not test the window frames to see whether they are safe is a foolish man. But if one of your own employees (or some-one else's), working under your charge, were to clean a window and fall because of a defective frame, you might be in trouble.

'In determining whether the occupier of premises has discharged the common duty of care to a visitor', the Act continues, 'regard is to be had to all the circumstances, so that (for example) –

(a) where damage is caused to a visitor by a danger due to the faulty execution of any work of construction, maintenance or repair by an independent contractor employed by the occupier, the occupier is not to be treated by reason of this alone as answerable for the danger if in all the circumstances he had acted reasonably in entrusting the work to an independent contractor and had taken such steps (if any) as he reasonably should in order to satisfy himself that the contractor was competent and that the work had been properly done'.

So if you put up signs warning people to watch their step, this may or may not be enough to protect you. Certainly the fact that people have been warned would not of itself free you from liability.

On the other hand, if you call in an independent contractor, and he negligently causes broken bones for your unwary and unsuspecting visitors, you should be in the clear. Assuming that you had picked a reasonably suitable contractor and had taken ordinary precautions to see that he was doing his work properly, you have nothing to worry about.

Note: There is a distinction drawn by the law between a warning (such as *Beware of the missing steps*) and a notice disclaiming liability. You may want to let certain people in – perhaps visitors to an open day – only on condition that you are not liable if they are mauled by your machinery. You can opt out of liability with a sufficiently clearly worded notice. Still, judges look very carefully at the wording, so it must be checked first with an expert, and the law may soon be amended so as to reduce the practice of disclaiming liability.

'And what of the chap who insists upon inspecting your place, even though he knows that dangerous processes are being carried on?'

The Act says that 'the common duty of care does not impose on an occupier any obligation to a visitor in respect of risks willingly accepted as his by the visitor (the question whether a risk was so accepted to be decided on the same principles as in other cases in which one person owes a duty of care to another).

So if you really had warned him of the risks, and, with his eyes open, he insisted upon charging around the place, the injury would be his own liability.

In a word, the law requires you to be 'reasonable' in the care you take for the safety of your visitors. And, as usual, 'reasonableness' is an objective matter, regarded with common sense and decided by the courts in the light of what the 'ordinary, reasonable man' would have done in the circumstances of the case. Take reasonable care then, and all should be well. And even if it is not, the responsibility is unlikely to be thrust upon you.

Breach of your duties under *The Occupiers' Liability Act, 1957*, could result in an accident which, in its turn, could force you to compensate the sufferer. But you could not be prosecuted for the breach. That misery now awaits those who are in breach of similar duties created by the new Act.

A final warning about guard dogs. A new Act of Parliament, *The Guard Dogs Act, 1975*, makes it a criminal offence to keep guard dogs on your premises – apart from farms and private houses – unless there is a handler to look after them and a clear warning notice. Maximum penalty: a £400 fine. In addition, you may be liable if your fierce dog bites a visitor (even a trespasser) if the court decides that keeping a fierce dog on the premises was unreasonable.

Chapter 40

Looking after Children

Thanks to a series of important recent cases, employers must now take special care for children, even those who are technically 'trespassers', arriving uninvited and unwanted.

* * *

Each of us owes a so-called 'duty of care' to his 'neighbour'. We must take reasonable care to avoid acts or omissions which are likely to cause danger to our 'neighbours'. A judge once said: 'Who is my neighbour?' In this sense, he replied, it is any person who we ought reasonably to contemplate would be likely to suffer, as a result of our carelessness.

Clearly, anyone lawfully on your premises is your 'neighbour' – and you must exercise proper care for his safety, as required by *The Occupiers' Liability Act, 1957*, (Chapter 39). That Act specifically reminds us that we must expect children to be less careful than adults. So a standard of care which may be quite reasonable for an adult may be utterly inadequate for youngsters.

Again, the Act says that it may or may not be enough simply to give or to exhibit a warning. You may have a 'DANGER' sign on the door of the room which houses your high-voltage machinery. In glorious scarlet, complete with 'high voltage' signals, it may be quite enough for the protection of a literate, English-speaking adult. But if you are dealing with youngsters who have not learned to read – or, for that matter, with immigrants who cannot cope with the English language – it may be totally inadequate. A court would have to look at all the facts.

These rules are designed to protect those who lawfully enter your premises. But what of the trespasser?

In general, the unlawful guest must take care of himself. The occupier must not set a trap for him, but he is not liable in law to the person who comes without any invitation, express or implied. If an adult climbs over your wall, then he normally does so at his own risk and not at yours. All this was clear until the important Court of Appeal decision in the case of *Pannett* v. *P. McGuinness & Company Limited.*

Manchester Corporation employed Messrs McGuinness to demolish a warehouse alongside a public park in a thickly populated area. Many children played in the park, especially after school hours.

When the contractors had almost finished work, they took down the hoardings and started burning the rubbish inside, preparatory to knocking down the warehouse walls.

One afternoon, five-year-old James Pannett came from the park, wrongfully and unlawfully entered the demolition site; and a short time later the park gardener saw him running down the road with his clothes and hair burning and 'screaming his head off'. He was severely burned, and his parents sued McGuinness on his behalf.

The contractors argued that the boy was a trespasser. Children were persistently chased away – but still came back. Indeed, young Jimmy had been specifically warned to keep away and his mother had told him not to go there. How, then, could the contractors be liable?

Lord Denning answered that nowadays there is 'no general rule to be applied to all trespassers. Each case depends on whether, in the circumstances, a duty was owed to the trespasser.

'Even if children are trespassers', said the judge, 'precautions must be taken if the activity is going on in a place where it could be anticipated that the children might come'.

In one case a child was hurt while playing alongside an

electric railway line. The railway authority was held not to have taken sufficient steps to protect him, even though he should not have been there.

Children have been held not to be 'trespassers' when they were playing with trucks alongside a mine. Although they were unwanted guests, the occupiers had not done enough (said the court) either to keep the children away or to protect them when they came. Those who have machinery, equipment or facilities on their premises which amount to an 'allurement' must protect the young.

James Pannett won his case because lighting a fire 'heightened the danger, alluring the child, and the heightened danger called for extra steps. . . . The previous warnings were not enough to meet the situation. The contractors, by their men, should have kept a proper lookout to warn off children. . . .'

A four-year-old who fell from an upstairs window of a derelict house won damages from the local council (who owned it) because they had not bricked it up to keep out trespassers.

The court must look at 'the prevailing circumstances' to see whether the occupiers have done enough to save 'even a trespassing child from harm'.

So if you operate premises with walls that can be scaled or broken down by the young – watch out. Even if they trespass, you will be held liable if you knew or ought to have known that children would come in, unwanted. And even if children find their way through some part of an indoor establishment where they are not meant to go, the fact that they are 'trespassers' will not necessarily free you from liability. Even the trespasser is entitled now to some protection – particularly if he happens to be a child.

Chapter 41

The Industrial Training Act, 1964 – and the Training of Your Employees

In 1964, Parliament passed an Act 'to make further provision for industrial and commercial training; to raise the limit on contributions out of the National Insurance Fund towards the expenses of . . . providing training courses; and for purposes connected with those matters'. Here is a breakdown of its main features.

First, the Secretary of State is empowered to make an order setting up an industrial training board, for the purpose of making better provision 'for the training of persons over compulsory school age (in Scotland, school age) for employment in any activities of industry or commerce'. Before making an industrial training order, the Minister must consult any organisation or association of organisations appearing to him to be representative of substantial numbers of employers engaged in, or of employees employed in, those activities. And if the industry concerned is nationalised, then the body in charge must be consulted.

An industrial training board is ordinarily given seven main functions. It must provide or secure the provision of 'such courses and other facilities (which may include residential accommodation) for the training of persons employed or intending to be employed in the industry as may be required, having regard to any course or facilities otherwise available to such persons'. If there are any other courses or facilities so available, then it 'may approve such courses and facilities'; from time to time, it will consider 'such employment in the industry as appears to require consideration' and will make recommendations 'about the nature and legnth of the training for such employment and the further education to be associated with the training, the persons by and to whom the training ought to be given, the standards to be attained as a result of the training and the methods of ascertaining whether those standards have been attained'.

Then the board may apply or make arrangements for the application of 'selection tests and of tests or other methods of ascertaining the attainment of any standards recommended by the board and may award certificates of the attainment of those standards'. It may assist people to find facilities for training for employment in the industry; it may take part in any arrangements made by the Minister for training and, finally, it may carry on or assist other people in carrying on research into any matter 'relating to training for employment in the industry'.

In other words, a board is clothed with immense responsibility for ensuring that there are proper facilities for training in a particular industry, setting up proper standards, and seeing that those standards are adhered to. What is more, it is entitled to enter into contracts of service or apprenticeship with people who intend to be employed in the industry and to attend courses or avail themselves of other facilities provided or approved by the board. It may itself, then, take on the role of employer or apprentice-master. And one board may help another by providing courses or other facilities. Finally, it is empowered to pay maintenance and travelling allowances to people attending courses it provides or approves, to make grants or loans to such people and to pay fees to those providing further education in association with training courses provided or approved by the board.

The board is empowered to appoint committees, either on its own or in conjunction with other industrial training boards, and the committees (whose members may receive expenses and whose chairman may be paid) will act as the executive arm.

The Minister may make a 'levy order' and in accordance with it the board will impose a levy on employers in the industry (other than any employers who are specially exempted).

The manner of assessment is laid down in the particular levy order. If you do not think a particular order is fair, then you have a right to appeal to a special tribunal set up under the Act.

But happily, the industry does not necessarily bear the whole burden. The Minister, with Treasury approval, may 'make grants and loans' to a board, out of public funds. These funds are voted by Parliament. What's more, a board may, with the Minister's consent or on his authority, 'borrow temporarily from any other person by way of overdraft or otherwise such sums as it may require'. A maximum is laid down as the aggregate of the grants and loans to be made, but the Minister may from time to time allocate a larger sum. But any increase has to be approved by Parliament.

Once a board has been established, the Minister may require employers in the industry to furnish returns of information and to keep records and to produce them for examination. A board which is assessing and collecting a levy may then inspect the returns and information and require a production of the records. But these details may not, without the employer's consent, be disclosed to anyone other than to the Minister or one of his officers or to a board or its committee or officer. This is not intended as a statutory outlet for confidential information which your competitors would dearly love to possess. But if legal proceedings have to be taken as a result of the Act, or indeed 'any criminal proceedings' at all, disclosure may be made. And the appropriate summaries may also be published, provided they do not reveal information about any particular business.

If you refuse to reveal the information, you may be fined up to £100 by a Magistrates' Court – or £200, on a second conviction. And for any person who may 'knowingly or recklessly' make false returns or false records or discloses information which is provided confidentially to the board or the Minister or his officers, the maximum penalty which a Magistrates' Court can impose is three months imprisonment or a £100 fine or both. But if a jury convicts, then the maximum is two years imprisonment or a fine of an unlimited amount, or both. The law is given a very strong arm. And if one of these offences is committed by a company 'with the consent or connivance of, or attributable to any neglect on the part of, any director, manager, secretary or other similar officer' or anyone purporting to act in that capacity, then he may be punished, as well as his company.

Industrial training boards, of course, are responsible to the Minister and must report to him. They must keep proper accounts and, if things go wrong, the Minister is entitled to amend an industrial training order or to revoke it altogether.

After giving power to the Minister to set up industrial training boards with respect to training for overseas employment, the Act then sets out the constitution of a board. Its members are appointed by the Minister. It must have a chairman with industrial or commercial experience, an equal number of representatives of employers and employees within the industry, plus people appointed by the Minister (presumably, educationalists). A deputy chairman may be appointed, and various departments are empowered to send one person to meetings of the board, with the right to take part in its proceedings.

These, then, are the bare bones of the Act. Apart from some of the more detailed provisions, the flesh is being added as the Act continues in operation. Employers must continue to watch with interest and concern to ensure that interference in their affairs – and especially, with their pocket books – is kept within reasonable bounds.

Part Seven

An Employer's Duties

Chapter 42

Contributory Negligence

How far can an employee be held responsible for his own accident? If you are injured at work how will the rules on 'contributory negligence' apply to you?

* * *

To recover damages for negligence, you must prove that your mishap was caused through the failure of someone else to take due care for your safety. Before 1945, even if you could prove that the defendant had been negligent, he could avoid having to pay you any damages whatsoever by showing that your own lack of due care contributed to some extent at least to the accident. But since *The Law Reform (Contributory Negligence) Act, 1945,* this rule has been returned to the limbo where it belongs. The full extent of that return was shown by the House of Lords, in the very important case of *Smith* v. *National Coal Board.*

Section 1 says: 'where any person suffers damage as a result partly of his own fault and partly of the fault of any other person or persons, a claim in respect of that damage shall not be defeated by reason of the fault of the person suffering the damage, but the damages recoverable in respect thereof shall be reduced to such extent as the court thinks just and equitable having regard to the claimant's share in the responsibility for the damage'. In general, you can reckon that the damages recovered by the plaintiff will be reduced proportionately to his own share in the blame.

Suppose, for instance, that you are involved in a crossroads collision. Neither of you was taking proper care and you are each 50 per cent responsible. Before 1945, neither could obtain any damages from the other. But today the damage of each would be totted up and divided by two. Suppose, for instance, that the proper recompense for your pain and suffering, loss of salary whilst off work and repair costs for your vehicle amount to £1000. Those of the other driver come to £500. You are entitled to 50 per cent of your £1000 against him and he to half of his £500 against you. Since you will both be insured, in practice you can do quite well out of this arrangement – it would even work out to the advantage of both sides if the figures were the same.

Usually, where only damage is involved, the insurers on each side may settle on a knock-for-knock basis, leaving you without your no-claims bonus (if you had one). If the case comes to court and the liability is divided that way, that is how the figures would work out.

Suppose, now, that you are injured at work. If the entire fault was that of your employer, you recover damages in full. If you were wholly to blame and your employers in no way negligent, then the fact that you suffered your injuries during the course of your employment would not make them liable in damages. And if they were partly at fault, then they (or their insurers) would doubtless do their best to attribute as much contributory negligence to you as reasonably possible.

The case of *Smith* v. *National Coal Board* arose from the tragic death of a shunter, run over by a train of three wagons being moved from one siding to another. The employers maintained that if the deceased had paid proper attention to his own safety, he would not have been killed. His widow contended that if the NCB had conducted their business with proper care, the accident would never have occurred and that they were entirely to blame. By a majority of three to two, the House of Lords found the deceased one quarter to blame and reduced his widow's damages by 25 per cent.

'An employer', we are told, 'or those for whom he is responsible, must always have in mind not only the careful man but also the man who is inattentive to such a degree as can normally be expected'. You cannot expect your employees to be on the alert all the time. You are entitled to expect them to take proper care of themselves, but you must make allowances for normal, human failings. You are not responsible for the safety of others only in their brighter moments. Allowances must be made for their times of inattention. Once again, the law accepts that it is made for the protection of the fallible. And while a failing on the part of the sufferer may reduce the amount of damages awarded, it in no way absolves the other party from his duty of care.

So even if the injured party was asleep on the job, the law was not. In spite of the finding by a majority of their Lordships that the deceased was guilty of contributory negligence, the shunter's widow got £3792. It would only have taken one more of their Lordships to have absolved him altogether of liability and the majority would have gone the other way. Do you wonder that lawyers are cagey when asked to assess the odds in litigation?

In practice, whenever there is an industrial accident, the employer's insurers ask themselves the question: 'Who caused the mishap?' If the answer is clear, then the only question that remains is: 'How much?' If the answer is in doubt, then the haggling begins – and the injured man is certainly wise to put his own solicitors on the trail. If there is any sort of settlement, the chances are that his legal costs will be paid by the employer's insurers.

If no agreement can be reached, then legal proceedings are likely to be issued. Happily, most cases are settled long before they reach trial. But if there is no settlement, then a judge will eventually have to answer precisely the same question: who was negligent?

To the extent that the employee was careless and his carelessness contributed towards his accident, his damages will be reduced. Employers must not expose their staff to unnecessary risk. They must provide and maintain proper equipment. The workplace and the system of work must be reasonably safe.

On the other hand, the employee must take care what he does. The employee who causes his own injuries entirely through his own stupidity will get no compensation from the company.

Chapter 43

An Employee's Responsibilities – for Life or for Death

The employer who makes his own mistakes which cause injury, loss or damage must bear both legal and moral responsibility. But how far is he responsible for wrongs committed by his 'servants or agents'? If, for instance, your assistant makes an error that proves fatal, can you be held legally liable?

Your assistant is your 'servant or agent'. He is probably employed by you under a contract of service. Alternatively, he may act for you as your agent for the purpose of dealing with your work or your clients.

As principle, you are responsible for the acts of your employee or agent. Your responsibility rests both in contract and in 'tort' (generally, civil wrong of negligence).

Suppose, for instance, that your agent (who may be your assistant or secretary, your manager or clerk – or, for that matter, your wife) orders equipment for your office or supplies for your home. If the agent had your actual authority to place the order, then obviously you are bound by it. You cannot creep out of your responsibilities by saying: 'I don't want the stuff'. You have, by your agent, entered into just as binding a contract as if you had placed the order personally, by your own unsteady hand or erring mouth.

Equally, you are bound by your agent's contracts if they are made with your 'apparent' or 'ostensible' authority. If you have placed your agent in such a position that the other contracting party reasonably believes that he had your authority to place the order or to purchase the goods (as the case may be), then you are bound by the contract made on your behalf. This is sometimes called 'the doctrine of holding out' (which, you will note, has nothing to do with the crime of indecent exposure).

The law says: 'You must not put others into such a position that they reasonably believe that you have given your authority to someone, whereas in fact you have not'. 'Ostensible' authority is just as effective, from the point of view of the innocent stranger, as actual authority. Either way, the principal will have acquired obligations – whether he likes them or not.

Naturally, you can avoid these difficulties if the other party knows (expressly or by implication) of the limitation on the agent's authority. You may say to a supplier: 'My assistant (or secretary or as the case may be) has my authority to place orders of up to £X per week/month'. If orders are placed and accepted in excess of that sum, then the supplier has been 'put on notice' of the limit placed on the agent's powers and he accepts the excess orders at his own risk.

In criminal law, the situation is rather different. You are only liable for the crimes of those whom you employ if you are party to them. If, for instance, you employ your assistant to erect a structure in breach of regulations, you are liable because he is doing it for you and on your behalf and is acting as your agent. It is not only the man who holds the murder weapon who may commit the unlawful killing.

On the other hand, if the agent is off on a 'frolic of his own' (in the charming legal phrase), then you cannot be held responsible – particularly for committing a crime in which you took no part. The mere fact that your servant turns out to be a criminal will not put you behind bars.

In 'tort', the law asks only one question: 'Was the employee acting within the scope of his employment?' If he was doing his job – albeit in a thoroughly wrongful, improper and forbidden manner – then the principal is liable for the results of the negligence, nuisance, defamation or other wrong committed. If, on the other hand, the agent was independently frolicing, the principal is not liable.

Suppose, for instance, that your assistant is driving his car (or your's, for that matter) during his own free time. He is not about your business. Through his carelessness, he smashes into another vehicle and causes injury to passengers. You are not responsible.

But when your assistant is sitting behind his desk (or your's), and making your appointments on your behalf, you are most definitely responsible for the errors of his ways. You obtain the benefits of his good deeds? Then the law will lumber you with liability for the unhappy results of his misdeeds.

Naturally, you must instruct your assistant. Fail properly to teach him how to behave in a way that is safe and you yourself will have been negligent. An employer is under a duty to provide reasonably competent fellow employees, properly trained and supervised.

However: Do not think that merely because you give proper instructions and take all due care, your responsibilities are at an end? The law imposes the sins of the agent upon the purse of the principal. And that is one reason why the wise principal is fully insured.

Chapter 44

An Employer's 'Vicarious' Liability

The crane driver had not grown up. He still thought that his equipment was a toy. And as a result of his 'skylarking' with the machine, the plaintiff was injured. He sued his employers for damages.

'We are not responsible for our employee's injuries,' retorted counsel for the company, 'because although he was engaged in his employment when he was injured, the accident was caused by behaviour on the part of a fellow employee which came right outside the scope of the man's employment. He was not doing anything which he was employed to do. He was on an independent frolic of his own. His job was to drive the crane, not to fool around.'

But the judge held otherwise. He decided that although the injury was caused by an employee who was skylarking, that skylarking was itself 'within the course of the crane driver's employment'. If the employer saw fit to have as their crane driver someone so inexperienced or stupid as to 'fool around' with a crane, they must bear the responsibility and pay the damages if that fooling around resulted in injury to another employee.

This decision throws into relief the whole question of an employer's responsibilities for damage caused through the unauthorised or forbidden fun and games of his employees, while at work. When is an employer 'vicariously liable' for the results of his employees' negligence? And when can he avoid responsibility by saying that the fault was that of his servant and not of himself?

The general rule is that an employer is just as responsible for the havoc inflicted through the negligence of his servants as he would be if he had done the damage with his own hand. In a world where companies rule, this must obviously be right. A company has no human existence apart from those who hold its shares, run its affairs and work for it. The company itself can do no wrong – its troubles all arise through the misdemeanours of those who work for it.

The exception to this rule applies where the wrongful act complained of occurred outside the scope of the person's employment. The company will be responsible if an employee breaks the arm of another through tripping him in the workshop, but if the same employee were to commit the same wrong against the same unhappy injured party, at a dance held in the local hall in the evening, the master would not be responsible. The wrong was caused far from the place and time and circumstances of the employment. Just as an employee's spare time is, generally speaking, his own, so the employer is not usually responsible, vicariously or otherwise, for damage caused during that spare time.

The real difficulty in all these cases comes in deciding whether or not a wrongful act was committed 'within the scope of the servant's employment'. Consider the questions as they arise.

'We do not allow smoking in our plant. We deal with inflammable materials and no one is allowed even a puff anywhere inside the building, except in the canteen. In breach of our orders an operative smoked, caused a fire and an explosion in which another employee was injured. Is the company responsible?'

Almost certainly, yes. The test is not whether the employee who caused the damage was doing something unauthorised or forbidden, but whether or not he was 'engaged in his employment'. Ask yourself the question, 'Was he doing something which he was employed to do – albeit in a thoroughly wrongful way – or was he doing something which came right outside the course of his employment?' If he was performing an act which came within his employment, then the fact that he did so wrongfully, contrary to instructions, stupidly or negligently, is irrelevant for this purpose. He was acting in the course of his employment and his employer is responsible for his misdeeds.

The leading case involved an attendant at a petrol pump. He knew perfectly well that he must not throw matches around. But he did. He lit up, flicked away his match and the inevitable explosion occurred. His employers met the plaintiff's claim with the defence that the man was acting right outside the scope of his employment, doing an improper and forbidden act. He was on an 'independent frolic'. The employers claimed that they should not be held liable for its results. But they lost their case. The man was employed to fill customers' tanks. That was what he was doing. And the fact that he did so in an improper way would not free the employer from responsibility for the damage he caused while doing it.

So if the person who was smoking on the job was on the job while smoking, his master is responsible for the results.

Then came the case of the milk roundsman. A Mr Plenty was expressly forbidden by his employees to let children on to his milk float, still less to employ them as assistants. But that was exactly what he did to 13-year-old Leslie Rose. He paid the boy to collect and to bring back the empties, as he went down the street, and the boy rode on the milk float between stops. Mr Plenty cut a corner, and young Leslie's foot was caught in the wheel.

Although the employers had expressly forbidden Mr Rose to carry a child with him, the Court of Appeal, by a majority, said that they were liable for the boy's injuries. Why? Because it was a way (albeit a *forbidden* one) of doing the very thing for which Mr Plenty was employed.

'One of our vans was involved in a crash. It was off its route. Will we be held liable?

That all depends on how far the driver was off his route, and why. If he was delivering your goods in an improper way and by an unorthorised route, you will still be responsible. If, on the other hand, he was not doing your work at all, you will not. If, to take the extreme example, he was engaged in stealing your property – or even if he had 'taken and driven away' your vehicle without your consent, to take his family to the seaside or his girl friend to a dance – then his behaviour would have taken the act outside the scope of his employment.

'Does it make any difference if the injured party is another employee, rather than a stranger?'

None at all. There used to be a rule known as the 'doctrine of common employment' under which a master was not liable for damage resulting from the misdeeds of someone in 'common employment' with the injured person. But happily, this doctrine is no longer any part of our law. No matter whether the injured person is another servant of the company, at whatever level, or whether he is a complete stranger, the company will still be vicariously liable for the trouble, if it was caused within the scope of the employment.

So the plaintiff succeeded in the skylarking case because the skylarking was committed within the course of the employment. The inefficient, stupid, inexperienced and negligent crane driver was playing about with his crane. He was employed to work a crane, he was working it in an improper, unauthorised and forbidden way. But the employer was still liable.

Chapter 45

Statute and Common Law – and a Causal Connection

An employer must take proper care for the safety of his servants. The common law, as prescribed in the decisions of judges (quite apart from any statutory rules), requires that you shall take proper steps to see that your employees' system of work is reasonably safe, that they are properly supervised in or about their work and that reasonable precautions are taken to see that they are not submitted to unreasonable risk.

So there are two duties laid upon an employer, then. One is to take reasonable care. This is a common law duty. And the second is to comply with any statutory regulations affecting the particular work.

In the case of *McWilliams* v. *Sir William Arrol & Company Limited,* The House of Lords had to consider an important aspect of both these duties. In essence, the question was simply this – if an employer has been guilty of breach of statutory duty and/or of his common law duties, and if as a result a servant is injured, how far must the injured person (or his heirs, if the injuries prove fatal) prove a causal connection between the accident and the breach of duty? In other words, if there was a breach of duty, but it does not appear that this actually caused the accident, can a claim against the employers succeed?

The Lord Chancellor said that 'Mr McWilliams, an experienced steel erector, was employed by Sir William Arrol & Company Limited, in connection with a steel lattice-work tower of a tower crane which they were constructing. . . . Prior to the accident, the deceased man had been working in connection with the erection of the staging at a point about seventy feet above the ground. While it was not established exactly what he had been doing at the time of the accident, it was not disputed that he fell from about the point where the staging was being erected to the ground, sustaining fatal injuries. Safety belts, the wearing of which would have prevented the death, had been available until two or three days before the accident, but had then been removed to another site. The widow's case against the employers was that for work of this nature, it was their duty under Section 26 of the Factories Act to have provided her husband with a safety belt and to have instructed him to wear it. . . .'

The Lord Chancellor agreed with the judge in the court below that there had been a breach of the Factories Act and also of the employers' common law duty. But then he went on like this: 'The evidence demonstrated to a high degree of probability that if safety belts had been available, the deceased would in any event not have worn one. . . . No witness deposed to having even seen a safety belt worn in the course of such work . . . there had been overwhelming evidence that the deceased did not normally wear a safety belt and in particular it was proved that he had been engaged in erecting riveters' scaffolds on the crane from which he fell, at heights greater than that from which he fell, and at times when safety belts were available, and that he had not on such occasions worn or asked for a safety belt. In my opinion, it was clearly open to a court to infer that the deceased would not have worn a safety belt even if it had been available'.

And the Lord Chancellor decided that, in the circumstances, it was not the breach of duty, statutory or common law, which caused the accident. The widow therefore could recover nothing.

Viscount Simonds put it like this: 'It is a part of the law of Scotland', he said, 'as it is part of the law of England, that a causal connection must be established between a breach by an employer of his duty at common law or under a statute and the damage suffered by his employee. . . .' There was no such causal connection in the present case.

Lord Reid added that 'It was quite unnecessary to give the deceased information. The device was not new. He was no novice. The work he was doing was his ordinary work. He was well aware of the advantages and disadvantages of wearing a safety belt. It was not maintained that he should have been ordered to wear it. . . . I can therefore find nothing to justify holding either that there ought to have been a general practice to exhort skilled and experienced steel erectors to use these belts or that this man ought to have been specially urged to use a belt when doing work on this tower.

The effect of this decision can be stated quite simply. If you are in breach of your duties under the Factories Act, you may be prosecuted. It is a criminal offence. Equally, if you are guilty of a breach of a common law duty of care, you are asking for trouble. You may be sued in a civil court, for damages. But in either case, any damages which would be recoverable against you must arise out of the breach of duty. It is not enough that there was a breach – that breach must have caused the injury. If, then, you can prove that even if you had taken reasonable care for your employee's safety and put into effect such precautions as the law would require, these would not have prevented the accident, you will win your case. And if *you* are unfortunate enough to suffer any injury and you wish to recover damages against your employers because they have failed in one of their duties to you, you must prove that this failure caused or contributed to the accident. There must be a 'causal connection' between the two. If there is not, your action will fail.

"I SOON GOT OVER MY INDUSTRIAL ACCIDENT —
I HAD THE BEST VETERINARY SURGEON IN LONDON!"

Part Eight

Courts and Cases

Chapter 46

Legal Aid

One of the greatest joys of winning your case is collecting the costs from the loser. 'Costs go with the event', says the law. He who emerges triumphant from court is entitled to have at least the bulk of his costs paid by the other side. But what happens if the loser has Legal Aid.

Conversely, what are your chances (as a business concern or as a private individual) of having your litigation financed as part of the wonders of the Welfare State? If you need solicitor and counsel, it is best to be rich or poor. But the middle-grade executive or professional man is out of luck.

So let us look at legal aid from every industrial and commercial angle.

* * *

If one of your operatives is injured and wishes to sue you, the chances are that he will get legal aid. This will not necessarily be free. His income will be assessed; various items of expenditure will be deducted; and if the balance is sufficiently high, he will have to make a contribution towards his costs. Still, the chances are that his legal battle will cost him far less than it would if he had to finance it on his own.

Perhaps the greatest advantage of legal aid comes to the

loser. The chances are that he will have to contribute exactly the same towards the costs of the winner as he does to the Legal Aid Fund for his certificate. If his contribution was nil, then the winner will probably have to bear all his own costs, even if he emerged from court, unruffled and triumphant in every respect.

No winner can be sure of getting all his costs. Generally, these will be 'taxed' (or assessed, by an official of the court) and the loser will have to pay those which are regarded as essential for the doing of justice ('party and party' costs, so called). There is usually a balance ('solicitor and client' costs) which the winner will have to pay in any event. Litigation is always a luxury, to be avoided where possible.

Still, it is possible in most cases to rescue a great deal from the wreckage if you can only convince the court of the justice of your cause. But when you fight a legally assisted person, whatever happens you are almost always bound to lose. If you cave in at the start and pay up, the chances are that you will not only save time, worry and aggravation but that you will have to pay out less than if you had taken the case to court and fought it to a conclusion. In other words, if you are advised by your solicitors that if you win against a legally assisted person your own costs will exceed the amount of his claim, the sooner you come to a sensible compromise, the better. This is a form of blackmail, if you like. But it is legitimate and it works.

'What about my litigation, then?' you say. 'If I want my doctor on the National Health, I can have him. Can I force the State to pay for my lawyer as well?'

The chances are that – as a reader of this book – your income will exceed the prescribed limit for Legal Aid. If you operate through a company, then even if it is on the rocks . . . about to go up the spout . . . operating at a loss . . . legal aid certainly will not be available to that company. If you are an individual and your income exceeds the limit, the fact that you cannot afford to litigate without legal aid does not mean that the State will help you by paying one single farthing towards your costs – or by saving you from the grim necessity of finding the costs of the other party, if you lose.

The departmental manager of a substantial factory recently settled a High Court case. He dropped his claim and even agreed to pay his own costs. His counsel pointed out to the judge that if the hearing were to last, as expected, for the best part of a week, to lose would have meant complete financial ruin. The stakes were too high. He had to throw in his hand and lose every penny that he had spent on the litigation.

'I sometimes feel,' said the judge, 'that our courts are like the restaurant in the Ritz. In theory, they are open to all. . . .'

American lawyers avoid this problem by agreeing to work on a contingency basis. If the client loses, he may pay nothing. If he wins, as much as 50 per cent of the proceeds may go to the lawyers. This system is forbidden to counsel and solicitors in Britain. There are many who feel that while both the rich and the poor are better off without it, at least it would enable the industrial and commercial executive, professional man, and even the better paid modern operative or engineer to fight cases which he ought to win but which today he does not even dare to fight. It is a brave man who risks ruin, even when his cause is just.

There is still, of course, insurance. If you are insured for liability in respect of personal injuries suffered by employees at work, then the insurance almost always covers the lawyer's bills for contesting the case, win or lose.

Chapter 47

Your Employee in Court

'Compensation neurosis' is no crime. The law recognises that many honest, decent litigants recover their health with miraculous swiftness the moment their legal action ceases to hang over their heads. Without any conscious exaggeration, the symptoms prevail, persist and even deepen – until the battle is over. Then the strain lifts.

Even if the doctors were agreed that the prognosis is excellent and that (as so many practitioners put it in their reports – in a way that sends a shudder through the spine of the plaintiff's counsel), 'I am confident that when the legal issues are resolved, the patient will have a full and swift recovery'; meanwhile the suffering is genuine and the victim is entitled to his money.

Still, the amount of the money will be far less if the prognosis is good.

On the other hand, there are too many sufferers from 'plumbi-pendulosis' – the ancient, self-induced illness of swinging the lead. Compensation neurosis is still a genuine neurosis for which compensation is payable. Dishonest exaggeration is at best worth nothing and at worst deserves a generous sentence for perjury.

Good judges recognise that they are bad doctors and they therefore rely on medical reports for guidance as to the seriousness and as to the genuineness of a patient's complaint. And that means not merely the final report but the doctor's notes and comments as from the time when he is first brought onto the scene.

Now suppose that the doctor falls ill, dies, emigrates or is not available at the trial for some other reason. His partner or successor will have inherited the cards, along with the case. That unfortunate man will then have to attempt to explain the meaning of the records – and will often fail to do so either to his own satisfaction or to that of the court.

When a policeman goes into the witness box, he is entitled to refer to his notebook. He may refresh his memory from contemporaneous documents.

In the same way, the doctor in the witness box may look at his records – and indeed, any reasonable judge or magistrate would expect him to do so. How else can he remember the details?

On one hand, the doctor may resent the prying eyes of the law, peering into his patient's records. On the other hand, he may be grateful that he is not forced to rely upon his memory.

Laboratory reports, hospital reports, X-rays – these speak for themselves.

Even though the law, in general, bans 'hearsay' – that is, the witness may say what he saw or heard, but not what someone else told him that he (the other person) had seen or heard – doctors are entitled to put into their reports what patients have said to them. After all, unless they can describe their patient's synptoms out of their own mouths they may be unable to describe them at all. The court may rule out the evidence as inadmissible – but that is a matter for the court.

If your doctor has obtained reports from other doctors, then those reports may only be put in evidence in one of two ways. Maybe the other party will agree to their production; alternatively, the other doctors may themselves be called.

Suppose, now, that the doctor has prepared his reports. Who is entitled to see them?

Technically, ownership of the patient's hospital records is vested in the local hospital authority. In practice, where a patient wants copies of his reports for the purpose of litigation, then they should where possible be provided – either to the patient or (more likely) to his solicitor or to his medical adviser.

Naturally, if the doctor is in doubt as to diagnosis, treatment or prognosis and the case is likely to result in litigation, he will obtain a further opinion. When a solicitor needs further help, he goes to junior counsel. If the barrister feels that the case is too big or too complicated for him that he requires a second opinion, he asks for a Queen's Counsel (or 'leader') to be instructed. If the client is legally aided, then normally the certificate has to be extended to allow for the extra expense.

As with lawyers, so with doctors. The more serious or worrying the case, the more essential it becomes to get a second opinion from a specialist in the field.

One advantage of the solicitor/counsel relationship is that the barrister is further removed from the client's personality. He can apply a concerned and uncommitted mind to the problem – and one which is not emotionally involved.

Chapter 48

Witness in Court

Whether you like it or not (and you will probably dislike it very much), you must be prepared to have to go to court one day. If you are fortunate, you will succeed in being neither litigant nor (still less) accused, but a mere witness as to fact or opinion.

Every lawyer knows that litigation is for others. One way to preserve your confidence if you get to court is to know how to handle yourself in the witness box – and how to deal with the questions you are likely to be asked.

One of the most misleading phrases in the English language? 'That's a leading question'. The fact that a question may be unpleasant does not make it 'leading'.

For instance, your own counsel or solicitor (or the advocate appearing on behalf of your company) may not ask you leading questions. He may not by his question suggest the answer. He may say: 'What did you find?' 'What did you observe?' 'What happened next?' Or 'What were the injuries?' He may not ask: 'Did you notice such and such?' Or 'He showed you the bruising, didn't he?' – that is, not unless there is no dispute on the matter. Your own counsel may not lead you to the answer to his own questions.

Cross-examining counsel, on the other hand, may lead to his heart's content. Take an ordinary assault case as an example. The accused is alleged to have caused an injury to your employee. You testify as to the bruises or wounds that you observed.

'I suggest to you,' says counsel, 'that the same symptoms could have been caused by a fall?'

Your employee's advocate could not make any suggestion to him. The other side may suggest, as he wishes.

So what is your answer? Could the bruises have been caused through some cause other than that which your employee contends?

Do not be tempted to gild the lily. In one famous case, a patient complained of injury to his shoulder. *Cross-examining counsel:* 'Mr Jones, I understand that you are having pain from your shoulder and restriction of movement?'

Plaintiff: 'That is right, Sir.'

Counsel: 'Then show my lord the height to which you are able to raise your arm.'

With much moaning and hesitation, the patient manages to raise his arm a few inches.

Counsel: 'Now show my lord how high you were able to raise your arm before the accident.'

The plaintiff, with neither thought nor hesitation, raises his arm up high. He has lost his case.

So you are in the witness box. You are being examined 'in chief', or cross-examined. How can you make the most of your case or that of your company? Follow some simple rules.

First: when heading for court, remember to take with you all the records and documents that you will require – documentation is often vital.

Second: Treat the judge with respect.

Third: You must be heard. The more complicated and detailed your evidence, the more vital it becomes to speak your piece with clarity – and sufficiently loudly to get through to the judge, who may be a little deaf.

The judge must also take full notes. Some do so swiftly: others are painfully slow. Watch the judge's pen and try not to race ahead of it. Counsel who is questioning you should be doing the same – but when you have a long answer to give, do not aggravate the judge by giving your evidence too fast. If there are technical terms which the judge may or may not know how to spell, do not be afraid to repeat the term – and to give the spelling, if necessary. The witness who gives extra help to the judge will be greeted with gratitude.

Fourth: Answer the questions that you are asked. It is a basic rule for all witnesses, expert or otherwise. It is also the one most frequently ignored. If you can give a brief and precise answer, then do so. Add afterwards: 'May I please add to that answer, my lord?' Permission will almost invariably be granted. But the witness who either fences with counsel or is always trying to be one-up will soon find himself trodden under.

Finally: Remember that however important your demeanour may be in the witness box (and it is very important indeed), many judges take even more note of a witness's behaviour when he (the witness) does not know that he is being observed. Preserve your dignity and your cool when you are sitting in court, waiting to be called – or after your evidence is complete. The judge will be watching you.

Perhaps the most important rule of all? Do not take personal offence or affront at your treatment in court. The lawyers and the judge alike are doing their job as best they can. Like witnesses, they vary in their quality but they do their best. The witness's job is said to be 'to assist the court'. The greater the assistance you can give – and the more apparent the effort to provide it – the more effective the evidence is bound to be.

Chapter 49

Suing the Doctor

The law of England is contained in some four dozen volumes of Statutes; an equivalent number of tomes of text; libraries full of case law; and enough text books (going speedily out of date, of course) to bring delight to the heart of numerous publishers and their shareholders. It is a wonder that anyone manages to keep within the law for any reasonable period of time. A sad and human fact; it is the few (mighty businessmen or minor criminals) who tend to fill up a remarkable proportion of all available pages.

As with lawyers and MPs, so with doctors. If even a substantial fraction of their patients fell ill at the same time, they would collapse under the strain as, of course, would BUPA if too many of its members succumbed to the same plague. From the point of view of doctor and insurer, death is generally preferable to disease and comes as a merciful release.

As with ordinary medical practice, so with the doctor's unhappy errors. Most of them lead nowhere. The patient does not even know that the doctor has made a mistake but merely believes that his illness has taken an unusual course. Alternatively, nature cures. It is the exceptions that delight the journalists.

Headline in recent edition of the *Daily Telegraph:* 'Wrong Hospital Danger in Rare Cancer Cases'. Innuendo: If doctors only spotted the disease early enough and referred the patient to the correct hospital for adequate treatment, a lot more patients would live a great deal longer. Problem: These diseases are mercifully rare; only an occasional patient contracts one; and few can survive more than one in a lifetime; so how can even the most alert general practitioner be blamed for mistaking the symptoms or consigning his patient to the wrong hospital?

Ask a wise lawyer whether he is going to win his case and the usual reply will be: 'You have a reasonable prospect of success; I believe that you should win; given the right judge – and if such-and-such a witness says in the witness box the same as he has put into his statement . . . everything should be all right.' 'Should be' are the key words.

Happily, most doctors are able most of the time to set the minds of most patients at rest. 'Whatever it is, it's nothing to worry about. . . .' To the anxious relative or friend, these words are balm indeed. But what if they are spoken in error?

Your chances of obtaining damages against your lawyer if he is unduly hopeful about the results of a legal case are slight – for two reasons. First, no barrister – and probably no solicitor either – can be successfully sued for negligence in connection with his advocacy.

This curious rule is designed largely to cope with two problems. First, the law does not like the reopening of trials and the rehearing of a concluded case, under the guise of an attack upon the lawyer's conduct of one side of that case. Second: Lawyers owe a duty to the court. There are many occasions when solicitor or counsel must refuse to follow instructions – or must give information to the court – or must draw the judge's attention to case law which is against him – even though he is doing a disservice to his own client in the process.

Second, the fact that a lawyer thought that a case would be won when in fact it was lost is not itself a sign of negligence. Litigation is a very chancy business. Just as the surgeon's knife should be regarded as a last resort for the patient, so the businessman should keep away from litigation in connection with his own affairs in so far as and whenever he can.

The problem facing the potential plaintiff (or his executor) who wishes to sue his doctor rather than his lawyer comes in two unhappy parts. First: Can they prove that the defendant doctor was negligent and not just mistaken? No negligence means no damages. Second: Even if there was a failure to take sufficient care, how can they possibly prove that – on the balance of probabilities – the patient would have lived (and if so, then for how long)?

Problems of proof are so great and the prospects of success so small that litigation of this sort is almost as rare as some of the varieties of disease which the careful physician fails to recognise. The doctor may be glad of this. His patient must simply accept it as one of the facts of death.

Chapter 50

Accidents and Injuries

Just as more than one person may be injured in an accident, so more than one may be liable for it. If, for example, you are a consultant engineer, both you and your client may be liable for its results. Consider *Driver* v. *William Willett (Contractors) Limited and R.G. Richardson-Hill & Partners.*

Rodney Driver sued his employers (Willett) and Richardson-Hill (consultant safety and inspecting engineers). He had been employed as a general labourer on a building site. A scaffold board fell from a hoist and he was seriously injured.

The court held that the employers were negligent and in breach of their statutory duty because they permitted the hoist to be used in an unsafe manner. 'Not our fault', they retorted. 'We contracted with the engineers, who had agreed to advise us on safety requirements and compliance with the relevant regulations. They undertook the duties of a safety officer under the Building Regulations then in force. They had not advised us to discontinue the unsafe use of the hoist.'

'It is plain from the evidence', said Mr Justice Rees, 'that the consultants knew and could reasonably foresee that the employers' employees would be working on the site and that their safety would be endangered if the safety regulations were not observed or the work not safely conducted. In my judgment, the consultants also knew that the employers relied on them for advice as to the steps to be taken in relation to the safety precautions on the site generally and, in particular, as to the safety of the hoistway. . . .'

'The Plaintiff fell clearly within the class of persons whom the consultants must have reasonably foreseen would be injured if they failed to give advice to the employers as to the safety precautions to be taken, and they therefore owed a duty to the Plaintiff. . . .'

'We were not in breach of that duty', argued the consultants. The Judge disagreed. They had 'clearly failed in their duty to advise the employers to have the hoistway enclosed by wire mesh as soon as their site inspectors observed that the hoist was adapted for carrying scaffold boards and long timbers. They must have observed the state of affairs several months at least before the accident.'

'But even if we had complied with our duty and given the proper advice, that advice would not have been accepted and the precautions advised taken and the accident prevented', said the engineers.

'I am satisfied on the balance of probabilities', said the Judge, 'that the employers would have implemented that advice'. The result? Responsibility was apportioned in the ratio of 40 per cent to the employers and 60 per cent to the consultants. But the employers were entitled to recover from the consultants as damages for breach of contract such sum as the Plaintiff was awarded against the employers. Although the injured man could have recovered from either defendants, for the 'tort' of negligence, the engineers were in breach of their contract and were liable to indemnify the employers in full. This was no joke. The trial Judge assessed the damages at £21,646.

Moral: Damages and responsibilities may be divisible – but are not necessarily payable in the same proportions. Watch out for the wording of contracts. Make sure that you are insured.

Chapter 51

Compensation for Criminal Injuries

If you are looking for danger, you do not have to volunteer to work in Belfast. You may, of course, be somewhat safer in a factory or office – but by no means always. Bombs go off in the most unexpected places.

Then there is the police. They will not make up their minds, will they? One moment they tell you to 'have a go', and complain bitterly at 'public apathy' when ordinary mortals leave the men in blue to fight out their own business battles with the criminals. Then when some courageous member of the public – armed only with umbrella – succeeds in getting clobbered while interfering in some moment of criminal violence, like as not the 'police spokesman' (whomever he may be) will say: 'The public are advised not to attempt to restrain criminals. They may be armed.' So what are you to do?

Suppose, then, that you – whether out of courage or instinct, it matters not – seek to protect your wife, your child or your employee, your home or your office from the depredations of a burglar . . . a drug addict on the loose . . . a psychopath out of control. . . .

Or suppose that one of your staff does the same. Who will pay if bravery is rewarded with injury? Or what if someone is injured in a bomb outrage?

The inhumanity of the general law on personal injury and liability has been tempered by the efforts of the Criminal

Injuries Compensation Board. Every employer should know of these, for his own potential sake, as well as that of his employees'.

The normal rule is clear: No liability without negligence. No compensation without liability. And those who volunteer for risk cannot normally recover damages if that risk breeds trouble.

Happily, though, Parliament established not long ago the so-called 'Criminal Injuries Compensation Board'. This benevolent tribunal has handed out (literally) millions of pounds to those who have been injured through the commission of crimes of violence.

If your employee is hurt while defending your property, he will only have a right to damages against you if he can show that you exposed him to unnecessary risk. If, for instance, you knew that an ex-employee was on the warpath and you failed to warn your staff – or, perhaps, to inform the police and to follow their advice as to the precautions which you ought to take – then you might bear personal responsibility for the injuries of your employee. But otherwise, the fact that the man was injured on the job will not of itself give him any rights against you.

Today, though, he can apply to the Criminal Injuries Compensation Board for damages. And, in theory at least, these are assessed on the same basis as damages for personal injuries in negligence cases.

In the same way, if you are battered over the head by a visiting villain, you may properly claim compensation out of public funds. If your unwanted guest is caught, then he could be made personally liable for his villainy. That's the theory. Assault is not only a criminal offence, giving rise to potential fines or imprisonment, but also a civil offence, giving the person assaulted a right to damages.

Still, villains are seldom worth suing. With luck, they are in gaol. If they are on the loose, then they are unlikely to have money – or anyway, you would probably be better off not to mix with them any further.

So get your doctor to provide you with a report on your cracked skull, bruised flesh or tormented nerves. Let a solicitor prepare your case, if necessary, for submission to the Board. And then hope that when the Board comes to consider your case, its members will be in a benevolent and generous mood. One of the problems with this particular Tribunal is the lack of any general right of appeal against its decisions. Still, with good fortune on your side, you may not want to appeal.

INSURANCE AND HEALTH & SAFETY AT WORK

Part Nine

Damages, Insurances and Wills

Chapter 52

Damages for Negligence

It is not enough for an employee to prove that you have been negligent. He must also show that as a result of that negligence, he suffered personal injury, loss or damage. And if he wishes to recover damages, then he must prove the amount of that loss.

In the case of personal injuries, 'special damage' is normally easy to calculate. It includes all those items – loss of remuneration, cost of repair to motor vehicle, cost of hire of replacement – which can be totted up in terms of pounds and pence.

'General damage' is another proposition. The value of a lost limb or of a tortured mind is assessed on the basis of precedent. Judges do their (often pathetic) best, on the basis of medical or psychiatric reports.

'Special damage' can usually be calculated, without too much difficulty. 'General damage' should be left to solicitors, skilled in the arts of calculation.

Another, curious and important problem on damages was discussed by the Court of Appeal in the recent case of *Simple Simon Catering Limited* v. *Binstock Miller & Company*. Solicitors had been negligent. But on what basis could their client claim compensation?

The catering company took on the lease of new premises. Their solicitors made a mistake and instead of a rent of £30 a week, they put in £50. Instead of giving their clients (the tenants) the exclusive use of the kitchen, they let the landlords put in a term that they and those with their authority would be entitled to use the kitchen when they wished. The solicitors failed to draw their clients' attention to these facts or, still less, to explain them.

The trial judge held that the solicitors had been negligent. The extra rent could be compensated for by payment to the clients of £1750; but only nominal damages were awarded in respect of the term regarding shared premises. The landlords were very unlikely to make use of their theoretical right and anyway there would appear to be no access to the kitchen without the consent of the tenants. The tenants appealed.

The Court of Appeal first commented that the clause concerned was 'so unusual that it had hardly ever been heard of .... No restaurant keeper would ever agree to it . . . the defendants were liable in damages in consequence of it. . . .' But how much?

Normally, damages are designed to compensate the injured party for loss suffered. But how do you assess loss in cases of this sort?

Lord Denning referred to the famous case of *Philips* v. *Ward*. As a result of the negligent advice of a surveyor, who said that the property was in good condition, Mr Philips paid £25,000 for it. In fact it was in poor condition and was worth only £21,000. The loss occasioned to the buyer by the bad advice was £4000. 'In those cases', said Lord Denning, 'it is the difference between the price actually paid for the property on the basis that the advice was good and the price at which it would be bought as it was in fact.'

Next came *Ford* v. *White*, in which the judge considered the problem of a man who saw a picture on sale for £100. He consulted an art expert who negligently told him that the picture was an old master worth £50,000. The man bought the picture but could not find a purchaser willing to pay more than £5 for it. Was his 'measure of damages' £95 or £49,996?

Unanimously, all courts have held that it is the £95 figure that represents the true damage. That is the real loss suffered by the innocent party.

The catering company maintained that the same principle should apply in their case. Overhanging their lease was 'a right, of which they were not told, of the landlords coming in and having a possible right to use the kitchen. . . .' This is a loss (said Lord Denning) 'not to be measured necessarily by the difference in value of the reversion and so forth, but as a matter of general expectation of loss.' This would be 'such as should be compensated for in damages, having regard to the possibility that the landlords might come down and demand their right under the lease. Alternatively, if there were a question of the place being sold, there would be the difficulty of selling it with such a clause.'

Nominal damages would not be enough. But it was not for the Court of Appeal to assess the correct sum. The case was remitted – that is, sent back to the trial judge, so that correct (and not merely nominal) damages could be assessed.

These principles, of course, apply not merely to solicitors but to all professional men – including doctors – who cause loss to their patients. The court will look to see not only the actual, provable loss, but also the 'general expectation of loss' likely to follow as a result of the negligence proved. The patient is entitled to expect careful consideration. If this fails, then loss will result – and have to be paid for by the guilty party.

So 'special damage' remains easy to assess. But in yet another sphere, the courts have emphasised that – in the law of 'tort' (or civil wrong) as opposed to that of contract – failure to prove loss with sufficient particularity will not prevent the plaintiff from getting his money. Patients have a 'general expectation of life' and anyone who cuts down that expectation is liable in damages. Equally, if he acquires an expectation of loss as a result of the employer's failure to take care for his safety, then the law will – stabbing away in the dark with its blunt scalpel – attempt to assess that loss in monetary terms.

Chapter 53

Cancer – and a Forty-year Incubation

We live and we learn – alternatively, we learn too late and we die. From both the legal and the medical viewpoint, the sad case of Mr Albert Tams, the rubber worker who died of cancer of the bladder, has many morals.

Recording a verdict of death from industrial disease on 69-year-old Mr Tams, the City Coroner of Stoke-on-Trent said that the deceased had been employed curing rubber at the local Michelin Tyre Factory. The Coroner stated that people like Mr Tams could develop bladder cancer caused by a chemical used in the factory only until 1949.

Mr Tams had worked in the curing department for nine years until 1949, and had inhaled fumes from the chemical, beta naphthylamine. The head of Michelin's medical department said that his company had stopped using the chemical when the danger was first noticed, some 22 years earlier. But it was not until much later that tests were perfected.

All former employees who had been exposed had been informed – but while some 2000 to 3000 people may have been involved, only about 10 per cent were contacted. 'Some have moved and some have died. . . .' Checks showed that those in contact with the chemical had 'a higher incidence of bladder cancer' – which can take up to 40 years to incubate.

The Coroner urged all former employees of the factory to get in touch with Michelin 'in the interests of their health'.

One day, it may be too late to say: 'If only we had known. . . .'

There are, of course, two aspects to this unhappy tale. One is purely medical. Knowledge and prevention may produce avoidance of danger, or, if necessary, a cure. Knowledge of legal rights and their exercise in due time may (if the worst comes to the unhappy worst) at least provide financial solace.

The law says that if you do not exercise your rights within the appropriate time, you will lose them. It lays down a specified 'period of limitation', within which legal proceedings must be started, if they are to be sustained.

Where a claim is to be brought against the estate of a deceased person, the period is one year from the date of the grant of probate (where the deceased died having made a will) or the taking out of 'letters of administration' (where the deceased was intestate).

In personal injury cases, the period of limitation is three years – and these normally run from the date of the accident. Suppose, for instance, that the haggling goes beyond the three-year period and no writ has been issued. Any claim is then 'statute barred'. If the defendants rely upon their rights under the statute of limitations, the claimant will have lost his chance unless, under a dispensation created by recent legislation, the judge is persuaded that it is 'equitable' to allow the case to be heard.

What, then, of the claimant who suffers from a disease contracted years ago, but which did not become apparent until lately? Under recent legislation, the period of limitation starts to run from the date when he knew of his illness, and knew also that it was the defendant's fault that he was ill. Ignorance of the law is rarely an excuse. In this case at least, it will not help if the reason for the delay is that he did not know that he had a right in law to make a claim.

In all other negligence actions – arising, perhaps, out of damage to a vehicle in a road accident – the limitation period is six years. And that is the same period as in ordinary cases of contract or of 'tort'.

In general, if you wish to claim damages for breach of contract – or arising out of some other civil wrong (such as defamation or nuisance, for instance) you must bring your claim within six years from the date when the wrongful act was committed.

The same six-year period applies to debts. But here the period runs either from the date when the debt was incurred or from the date when it was last acknowledged in writing. Suppose that you write to a creditor. 'I admit that I owe you this money – and I will pay it to you when circumstances permit. . . .' The period of limitation may have almost expired, but it will start running all over again, as from the date of your letter.

To obtain a right over land, the limitation period is twelve years. Suppose, for example, that you fence off property at the end of your works or garden, and you 'exercise exclusive possession' over it. If the owner does not take some step to establish his right within twelve years, he will lose those rights forever.

In every case in which valuable rights are at stake and a time limit is beginning to run, my advice is: Go to your solicitor. If he forgets to take the appropriate action within the prescribed period, then the fault will be his – and you will have a potential negligence action against him. This action, in its turn, may be brought at any time within six years from the date when the solicitor ought to have issued the writ on your behalf.

Once the writ is issued, it need not be served for 12 months. Even then, the time for service may be extended. But in due course, the law says that if you wish to make use of its facilities, you must get cracking. Delay in pursuing your legal rights (or 'laches', to use the legal term) may spell the death of those rights.

Anyway, we live in a dangerous and polluted world. If negligence can be proved against those who cause the danger, then they may be called financially to account. And as lawyers and doctors alike appreciate the time it takes for danger today to produce death tomorrow, so 'the periods of limitation' have been extended. This will bring little joy to the deceased – but may be of assistance to their heirs.

Chapter 54

The Value of Life and Limb

The most likely place for anyone to suffer injury is on the road. But there are accidents in every place of work and even the most sedate and middle-aged executive may (literally) fall down on the job.

So assume the worst. You are injured. You are entitled to damages against the other driver – or against your employers – because you can prove that your injuries were (wholly or in part) the result of their negligence or breach of statutory duty. How much will you get?

First, there are those items which can be assessed in terms of hard cash. These include loss of wages or salary (minus the tax which would have been paid on it and also less one-half any National Insurance Benefits received – but not minus any benefits you may get from personal insurance cover). There are convalescent and medical expenses, the cost of repairing or replacing a damaged vehicle – in fact, all those items which can be totted up in precise figures.

But what of your physical injuries? Who can put a price on human life or limb? You would not exchange your right arm for all the gold in Threadneedle Street? But if it has to be amputated because of someone else's negligence, you will require compensation – in pounds, shillings and pence. And if the case gets to court, a judge will have to decide how much you receive. Your life and those of your family and friends could not be bought at any price. But where there is a fatal accident, caused by negligence, a judge may have to assess the damages payable to dependants of the deceased. How? If you are involved in this sort of trouble, how much 'damages' will you get?

The answer depends on the sums awarded by courts in respect of similar injuries suffered by others as unfortunate as yourself. This is how insurers decide how much to offer to settle a case – and happily, the majority of claims are haggled to a satisfactory compromise, long before they get to court. This is how lawyers base their advice on the proper amount to accept – and the nearer the case gets to court, the more likely it is that lawyers have become involved.

The experts delve into the Law Reports and their own memories for awards in similar cases. Like as not, they discuss the problems with their colleagues – the more experience you can concentrate on the problem, the more likely you are to reach a sensible result.

But no two injuries are ever identical. And even if they were, people's reactions to pain differ enormously. If two people are knocked down the same way by a car, one may walk away with a shrug whilst the other dies. Everything depends upon the person's constitution. One man has a thick skull (literally). Another's is thin and brittle. One man can shrug off a severe shock with minimal after-effects. Another will suffer months of depression from a minor blow. In law, 'you take your victim as you find him'. Every case, like every victim, is different. And lawyers and insurers can never work out prospective damages for personal injuries with any absolute certainty.

Suppose, for instance, that a singer or a lawyer suffers damage to his vocal cords. He may lose his livelihood. But if the same man loses a leg, however mighty his misery, his loss of earnings may (if he is lucky) turn out to be minimal.

But suppose that the victim of the same accident was a labourer. His leg and his earning power go together. Even though his earnings may be a fraction of those of the limbless lawyer or artiste, his damages might be fifty times as great. But if the labourer lost his power of speech, his financial loss might be minimal. Lawyer, labourer, performer – and man of commerce – alike may obtain the same sort of award in respect of their pain and suffering. But there may be spectacular differences in their loss of actual and prospective earnings.

So reported awards cannot do much to help the layman to estimate what he would get for his injuries. There are too many variables. Newspaper summaries are too brief – or too full of the human-interest angle which interests the reader but which may obscure the legal issue.

So if you get involved in a claim for damages for personal injuries, do not try to deal with it on your own. If you are at the receiving end of the trouble, then the odds are that your insurers will be behind you and you will have to do as they say. But if you are the claimant, it is most unwise to attempt to assess your own damages.

If your claim is to succeed, then you have nothing to fear from getting the help of a solicitor. The odds are that your case will settle and as part of the bargain your costs will be paid. If you are merely claiming lost cash (such as the cost of repairing your van, lorry or car), then you can probably assess the amount of that claim, without too much difficulty. But when it comes to personal injuries, the chances of your being able to assess the right answer are remote. The more serious the injury, the greater the claim, the more vital it is that you should consult an experienced solicitor at the first possible moment.

Solicitors' services are often dispensable – but never for the potential litigant with a serious, personal injuries claim. The lawyer will not only push for a quick settlement, where this is advisable, but (often equally important) not allow you to settle too early, when the course of the illness or injury and hence its after-effects are unclear. He will make certain that if you require Legal Aid, you will get it – and that if medical reports are necessary, they are obtained. If counsel's opinion is required, either as to your prospects of success or as to the damages you are likely to recover, he will obtain it. He will see that you do not lose your rights through suing too late, nor your money through settling too soon.

Chapter 55

The Value of a Broken Bone

'Will I get any compensation, doctor?' asked your employee patient, nursing his injured foot.

'If you can show that the accident was caused through someone else's negligence – or through your employer's failure to comply with his duties under *The Factories Act, 1961*, or *The Offices, Shops and Railway Premises Act, 1963*,' the knowledgeable doctor replied. 'The mere fact that you are injured – or even injured at work – will give you no legal claim to damages. But if and in so far as you can show that someone else's fault caused the accident, you will be entitled to damages.'

Then comes the crunch. 'What will I get for my broken foot, then?' One answer appeared from the Court of Appeal decision in the case of *Parry* v. *English Electric Company Limited*, in 1971.

Jane Parry worked in a factory. A stacker truck ran over her foot. According to the agreed medical reports, she had suffered fracture of the neck of the fifth metatarsal of her left foot. The foot was put in a walking plaster which she used for three weeks. When it was removed, the fracture had united satisfactorily. She attended hospital from time to time and was off work for a total of about ten weeks. She had endured a certain amount of pain and suffering and in addition to the fracture, there was 'some bruising and grazing on both feet'.

The lady's employers denied liability. But the County Court judge held that they were 60 per cent responsible for the mishap. 'Special damages' were agreed – and the amount of wages that the plaintiff had lost during her period off work. But what of 'general damages?' How much should the plaintiff get for her pain and suffering? '£75', replied the County Court judge. '£75, minus 40 per cent, of course, that representing the plaintiff's contributory negligence.' The plaintiff appealed.

Now, the Court of Appeal will seldom interfere in an award of damages. Only where that award is 'wholly inappropriate' will the judges interfere with the discretion of their colleague who first heard the case. 'The award is far too low', argued the plaintiff's counsel. 'Where there is a broken bone and a claim worth pursuing in court, the award should never be less than £100.'

Lord Justice Widgery said this: 'I have come to the conclusion that the figure of £75 was one at which the judge was perfectly entitled to arrive. No one wishes to try to minimise the sufferings of others, but this was in any view a very slight injury, and I for my part would be disinclined to say that the award was in any way out of scale or too low. Certainly . . . it is not so low as to justify interference by us. . . .'

'Out of scale'? Some professionals have scales for some of their charges, but there is no 'scale', as such, for assessing the value of personal injuries.

On the other hand, the assessment of 'general damages' is invariably done by direct reference to previous decisions, involving similar injuries. Judges will look at decisions of other courts, in cases along similar lines.

That said, the award of damages depends very much upon the impression made by the particular plaintiff and her medical witnesses – or, as in the case of Parry – by the agreed medical reports.

Still, some judges are notoriously mean, others well known for their generosity. Some (for instance) pay high regard to depressive or nervous illness, while others think that neuroses and nervous ailments should be largely disregarded.

If you are the defendant in a personal injuries case, you 'take your victim as you find him'. Knock down a man with a thin skull and it will provide you with no answer to say: 'If his skull had been of normal strength, I would not have killed him'. Similarly, you take your judge as you find him – and often you do not know until the night before the case is heard which judge you are likely to get. You will find, though, that plaintiffs are generally amenable to reason, when offered a settlement outside the door of the court of a judge renowned for his parsimony.

Anyway, Lord Justice Cross delivered the final word in Parry's case. Counsel for the plaintiff had argued, in effect, that 'having regard to the fall in the value of money and the cost of proceedings in the County Court, an award of less than £100 is only appropriate where the injury can properly be described as trifling – an injury scarcely justifying a claim being brought at all. Once one can say, the argument runs, that the injury was not trifling there ought to be an award of more than £100, even though the injury was as slight as that sustained in this case. 'For my part', said the judge, 'I cannot accept that argument and I agree this appeal should be dismissed'.

Judges, like everyone else, are aware of the ravages of inflation. An accident that happened in 1969 and which resulted in an award of £75 might be worth the same as an award of £200 today. Still, if your employee's injuries are minor, his damages will be small. If he suffers a broken bone in the foot, £75 – plus an element for inflation – may still be all he gets.

Chapter 56

Noise – and Damages for Deafness

There are some who have eyes and see not and others who lose their hearing but do not realise that they are deaf. In the past, anyone who did not bring a claim for damages for personal injuries within three years of the cause of the trouble lost his rights forever. Today, the sufferer has three years from the date when he became aware of his injury, within which to issue his writ. But there is a limit even to that doctrine – as appeared from the judgment of Mr Justice Ashworth, in the fascinating, recent case of *Berry* v. *Stone Manganese Marine Limited.*

Mr Berry was employed in a workshop in which the noise 'frightened him out of his life'. One witness described it as 'bordering on the threshold of pain'. Tolerable noise is about 90 decibels. Technically, the noise in the shop amounted to 115 to 120 decibels.

Now, employers must take reasonable steps to protect their employees against unnecessary risk. This duty includes an obligation to provide necessary protective clothing and other devices. All the experts agreed that Mr Berry should have been provided with earmuffs – the earplugs which he was offered were inadequate.

'Even if muffs had been supplied in 1957, when the trouble began', argued the defendants, 'Mr Berry would not have worn them.' He had suffered partial loss of hearing due to his own negligence, and not that of his employers.

The Judge was 'not satisfied that, given adequate propaganda, Mr Berry would have been so foolish in 1957 as to refuse to wear muffs'.

Anyway, Mr Berry became aware of his loss of hearing by the end of 1960. He did nothing about it until 1964, when he consulted his doctor. 'From 1960 onwards', said the Judge, 'he knew perfectly well that the noise at work was the cause of his deafness. He decided to, and did, consult his trade union in 1968'.

I wonder whether the doctor whom he saw in 1964 advised him to consult his trade union or his solicitor right away? Probably not. It is no part of a doctor's duty in law to ship off his patient to a lawyer. The doctor, you say, has quite enough trouble looking after physical and mental ailments, without getting involved in legal complications. Perhaps so – but it would have been a kindness.

By the time that the case came to court in December 1971, 'the crucial issue was whether, in the circumstances, the material facts relating to Mr Berry's cause of action were, or included, facts of a decisive nature which were before 2 April 1967 (three years before the writ was issued) outside Mr Berry's knowledge actual or constructive'.

In so far as Mr Berry was claiming damages for injuries about which he knew or ought to have known three years before the writ was issued, his claim had become 'statute barred'. And the Judge decided that he could only award compensation for deterioration in the man's hearing, occurring since 2 April 1967.

Had the claim been brought in good time, it would have been worth about £2500. Weight had to be given to the fact that 'to make a man already deaf still deafer was to increase his handicap very considerably – he had fewer decibels to spare'. He was awarded £1250.

Deprive a man of the sight in one eye and he may get £5000. Deprive him of his sight altogether and his claim will not be confined to £10,000 or thereabouts. It may well be nearer £30,000. The loss of two eyes is far more serious than double the loss of one eye. The law does not operate on an eye for an eye and two eyes for two eyes – nor does it necessarily assess the value of damage to a man's jaw by the number of teeth that he loses. Each case is considered on its own facts.

Still, Mr Berry had delayed too long. Had he – or, perhaps his doctor – realised the cost of delay, no doubt proceedings would have been started within three years of 1957.

Suppose that Mr Berry had gone to a solicitor within the three-year period and he had failed to issue a writ – what then? The chances are that the solicitor would have been negligent and the client could have claimed from him the same amount of money as he would have got from the employers, had the claim been brought in time. It is worth knowing when not to go to a lawyer – but worth a good deal more to understand when a solicitor's services are indispensable. In my opinion, serious personal injury cases warrant the attentions not just of a doctor of medicine but also those of a man of law.

In the old days, lawyers are reputed to have chased ambulances, in the hope of getting custom. It would be both pleasant and helpful if those who look after people delivered to hospital or surgery, whether by ambulance or otherwise, would refer their patients to the law. The trouble with legal rights is that they get lost by those who do not know of them – and exercise them – with sufficient speed.

Three years for personal injury claims; six years for other 'torts' – negligence, nuisance, defamation and the like; six years for claims for damages for breach of contract; six years for debt – with the time running either from the date when the debt accrued, or from the last date when the debtor admitted in writing that he owed the money; and twelve years for a claim to property – in general, for 'squatter's rights'. These are the statutory 'periods of limitation'. So do yourself a legal favour remembering that just as disease must be tackled at an early date, if it is to be destroyed, so legal rights must be exercised in due time if they are not to be 'statute barred'.

Finally, if your employee must endure noise at work, check the Code of Practice on noise. Failure to comply with it will be used in evidence against you in any proceedings brought against you by a sufferer – or, of course, in any prosecution under the new Act, based on the noise in your premises.

Chapter 57

Foreseeing the Consequences

Never resign – unless you have a better job to go to. If you leave voluntarily, then (by definition) you are not 'dismissed'. You have therefore no prospect of getting compensation for unfair dismissal; damages for wrongful dismissal (because you did not get proper notice or pay in lieu); or redundancy pay.

Conversely: If you wish to be rid of an employee, then if you can induce him to resign (as opposed to 'constructively dismissing him' – by forcing him out the door), you will be lucky. The law only helps those who hold tight.

The law has also become involved in a whole string of so-called 'escape' cases. These mainly come from two directions.

Consider: If a dog rushes under your wheels or a cow strays into your path, will its owner be liable to compensate you for your injuries, loss or damage – and will you be liable to the animal's owner?

Suppose that you are driving at your usual moderate speed, along a narrow lane. Suddenly and without warning, a cow ambles in front of you and you slam into its unwary side. The animal has to be destroyed; your car is damaged; and you are injured.

Clearly, as you were driving carefully, no damages for negligence could be awarded against you, if the owner of the cow were to sue. But what of your rights against him?

Until the recent Animals Act, you would have been out of luck. While it is a farmer's duty to fence in his own cattle, he was never liable if animals strayed onto the highway.

Today, that ancient rule has gone. Your prospects of recovering damages against the farmer will be excellent – and if he knows his business, he will have insured against this (unhappily common) risk.

A Mr Horwood left his horse unattended in the street. There were children nearby, one of whom threw a stone at the horse which promptly took fright and bolted.

Mr Haynes was a brave policeman. He leapt at the runaway horse and was seriously injured.

Mr Haynes sued for damages.

The Court of Appeal held that Mr Harwood ought to have realised that if he left the horse as he did in an area where children were wandering around, he should have foreseen the possibility of the horse being frightened and of an intelligent bystander taking action as Mr Haynes had done.

Mr Haynes was entitled to his damages.

On the other hand, a Mr Cutler lost his case against United Dairies. The driver of a horse-drawn milk float lost control and the horse ended up in a field. He called out for help and Mr Cutler went to his assistance, held the horse and was injured.

Mr Cutler's claim failed because the court held that at the time when he had intervened, the danger was over; his action was unnecessary, in spite of the appeal for help; and he had therefore 'eclipsed the defendant's wrong in creating the danger' by his own 'conscious act of volition'.

The decisions are the law student's nightmare – and, in my view, are totally inconsistent. But the idea of a 'chain of causation' is not.

Suppose you are an engineer and you or your assistant produce inadequate or defective plans or drawings. You have been negligent. You will be liable to compensate your client (or possibly third parties) for loss which you ought reasonably to have foreseen might arise from your carelessness. But you will only be liable for 'foreseeable loss'.

Equally, if you have been negligent and the damage was caused to your client or to the third party through some new, intervening act – which may even be his own failure to take reasonable, sensible care – then you will escape from your liability. The law tries to be sensible, even if it does not always succeed.

Or take the road builders who carelessly cut through a cable. They cut off electricity – not merely from adjoining properties but (almost inevitably) from premises some distance away. Is the damage too remote from the carelessness? Does the fact that the electricity supply is interrupted at some distance from the damage caused free the contractors from legal liability?

Not long ago, a court considered just this case. These were the rules applied:

First: Each of us owes a duty to take care for the safety of his 'neighbour' – and your 'neighbour' includes anyone whom you ought reasonably to have foreseen would be likely to be caused damage if you applied your mind to the particular act or omission complained of.

Secondly: Construction people ought to realise that if they cut cables, damage would not merely be caused to adjoining frontages, but to people with premises some distance away.

Thirdly: At some stage, the distance away would make the damage unforeseeable – but three miles should have been within the reasonable contemplation of all concerned – so the contractors were held liable.

Finally, suppose that you accumulate water or some other substance, in the course of your operations. You are under an absolute liability, if it escapes and causes damage. Whether the water (for instance) is in a tank or an artificial pond or reservoir, if you have seen fit to bring it on to property which you control then you owe a 'stricter liability' to others, to ensure that it is kept under control. Even without negligence, you will be responsible if the substance escapes.

Chapter 58

Getting the Needle

The unfortunate Reginald William Brazier nursed a broken needle in his buttock. To make things worse, it shifted to the area of the groin. Luckily for him, it was eventually extracted after a successful operation. Mr Brazier, who was at the time employed as a deep-sea diver by the Admiralty, clearing up the aftermath of the Suez campaign, had been treated for his infected hand by the sick bay on HMS Forth. He claimed that the needle had broken off because the sick berth attendant 'held the syringe in his closed fist like a dagger and plunged the needle into the right buttock from a distance of about 12 inches'. . . .

In due course, he sued the Admiralty and the case came before Mr Justice McNair in the High Court.

Not surprisingly, the Admiralty denied negligence, claiming that their employee had done the needle plunging in a perfectly proper manner. And the Judge? He decided that the Admiralty was right. But how then 'did the needle, which was properly inserted in a recognised manner, come adrift from its seating in the stub of the syringe as it did? The breaking of a needle in this kind of operation occurred very rarely indeed. The defendants had given an explanation that the injection had been given without negligence and that the needle had broken because of a latent defect. On the balance of probabilities, having regard to the fact that the operation was properly conducted, it was more probable than not that the needle broke in the way it did by reason of a latent defect in the shaft of the needle. In the circumstances, the Plaintiff's claim failed.'

Now comes the interesting point. What of the manufacturers of the defective needle? If it can be shown that a medical appliance is defective and as a result of the defect a patient suffers injury, then there is an excellent chance that the manufacturers can be held responsible. Not only will the doctor obtain an indemnity from them, if he is sued, but the patient may sue the manufacturer direct.

In one famous case, the decomposing remains of a small, black snail was found in the bottom of a ginger beer bottle – but not until the drink had been consumed and not by the person who bought it, but by a friend. The friend sued the manufacturers. The manufacturers retorted that they had no contractual relationship with the friend and were therefore not responsible.

But the court decided, once and for all, that we each owe a 'duty of care' to our neighbour – and 'neighbour' includes anyone whom we must reasonably expect to be affected by our careless act, if we apply our mind to the matter. Any manufacturer must, then, realise the probability that his goods will not be used or consumed by the person who buys them but by someone else. And as a result of the case of the snail in the bottle, the manufacturer is now held liable to the 'ultimate consumer', if some defect in manufactured goods, caused by negligence in the manufacture, results in injury, loss or damage to that 'ultimate consumer'.

The same rule that applies to ginger ale, then, applies also to those who 'consume' needles. So were it not for the unhappy fact that Mr Brazier had allowed so many years to pass that he could no longer succeed in an action against the manufacturer, he might have been all right after all. But, alas, he now has no remedy against anyone. Not only was it vital that his injection be quickly given but that his legal action be quickly taken when the needle broke. Three years is the limit for most actions for damages for personal injuries. And the Suez campaign was long, long ago. The law, like medicine, requires alacrity.

Chapter 59

Remoteness of Damage

Just as you are not liable to pay damages merely because there is an accident in your office, shop, factory, works or other premises, so damages are not payable in respect of every injury for which you are responsible. Anyone who wants damages from you must prove that you were negligent or in breach of statutory duty and that the damages claimed are not 'too remote'.

Suppose that you yourself are injured. Perhaps you tripped over an obstruction which someone had carelessly left in a passageway or into a pool of oil, negligently allowed to accumulate alongside a machine. You break your leg; you are carted off to hospital; you are off work for a month, and return grinning bravely, supported by crutches.

Your company is insured against employer's liability and you claim. What would you get?

First, there is your actual provable, financial loss. If you were paid while off work, your 'special damage' would probably be quite small. Maybe there were medical or convalescent expenses. Next, there are damages for pain and suffering. Their amount would depend upon the nature and seriousness of the injury and whether or not you will suffer after-effects (quite minor injuries, for instance, may trigger off painful osteo-arthritic conditions).

Now suppose that the day following the accident you were due to attend an interview for another post. Had you been successful in your application, you would have improved your salary and working conditions. Instead of sitting in the interview room, you are lying on your hospital bed. You lose the job.

Immediately you can get to a telephone, you speak to your proposed interviewer. 'I am terribly sorry,' he says, 'but the matter was urgent. We have appointed another man. I'm sure that you would have had an excellent chance of obtaining the position . . . but. . . .'

'The company was negligent', you tell your lawyer.

'I am therefore entitled to damages to compensate me in so far as possible for my financial loss'. Correct?

'Agreed.'

'I did not lose a mere few weeks' pay, but an immensely important opportunity to improve my financial position on a permanent basis.'

The lawyer shakes his head. 'The damage is too remote', he says.

Unfortunately, unless you can show that the loss actually flowed from the accident as a reasonably foreseeable result, you get no damages.

In the Court of Appeal decision in the case of *Hinz* v. *Berry*, the judges unanimously decided that, in certain circumstances, damages for 'nervous shock' arising out of an accident which occurred to someone are not 'too remote' to be recoverable.

The unfortunate Mrs Hinz had been married for ten years. She had four children and the lady was again two months pregnant. In addition, she was looking after four foster children. She and her husband drove in their Dormobile van down to Canvey Island. On their way back, they pulled into a lay-by and Mr Hinz was making the tea. His wife and one child walked across the road to pick bluebells.

At this moment, a Jaguar car went out of control – a tyre had burst. The car crashed into the Dormobile. Mr Hinz was injured and a few hours later he died. The other children who had been in the Dormobile were injured.

Mrs Hinz heard the crash. She turned around and saw the disaster. She ran across the road and did her best to comfort her husband and care for her children.

In due course, Mrs Hinz claimed damages. She was awarded £15,000 in respect of the pecuniary loss which she suffered as a result of her husband's death. But what of the damages for the shock she suffered 'by turning round and seeing her husband injured and the children strewn about'?

Damages, said the court, could be given for 'nervous shock caused by the sight of the accident'. This is not too remote.

On the other hand, 'by English law no damages are awarded for grief or sorrow caused by another's death, or for worry about children, or for the difficulty of adjusting to a new life'. There are many wrongs for which the law provides no remedy. (In similar circumstances in Scotland a widow would be entitled to claim damages in respect of the grief and suffering caused to her by her husband's death.)

'Damages', said the Master of the Rolls, 'are recoverable for medical effects, the nervous shock, and any recognised psychiatric injury. In some way the line has to be drawn so as not to give damages for grief and sorrow but for the medical consequences of the injury to health.'

There was 'telling evidence' that poor Mrs Hinz suffered 'far more than a widow would have done had her husband been killed in an accident 50 miles away'. A 'sound, level-headed, robust, hardworking capable woman', she might in the course of time have got over it. But in fact she was suffering from 'a morbid depression', two years later. She was 'physically ill'. And she was 'entitled to be compensated effectively for the extreme mental anguish that she had suffered during the past five years as a result of being present at the scene of the disaster'.

The trial judge had awarded the lady £4000 damages. Although this may have been a high figure, it was upheld by the Court of Appeal.

Chapter 60

Traps in Contracts of Insurance

Every employer insures. Far too many lose the cover they have paid for. To avoid trouble, it is essential to know the law.

If you want to know whether or not you are covered against a particular disaster, then you must look at your contract. In return for your agreeing to pay a specified premium, the insurers undertake to provide you with certain cover. But unlike almost every other contract you make, the one with your insurers is 'based on the utmost good faith'. If you do not comply with this very high obligation, the contract may be avoided by the insurers.

If you are selling your services or those of your company or firm, then you must tell no untruths. You must make no misrepresentation. Apply a 'false trade description' to goods or services and you may be prosecuted for an offence under the Trade Descriptions Act.

On the other hand, you are not bound to tell the whole truth any more than your doctor is forced to reveal all to his suffering patient.

Equally, the Sale of Goods Act may imply a term into a contract that the goods will be 'of merchantable quality' and 'reasonably suitable for the purpose supplied'. But if the buyer misleads himself and buys goods which he does not want but which are otherwise satisfactory, he has only himself to blame.

A buyer is normally under no obligation whatsoever to give any information to a seller. If you buy equipment for your work, the seller is not normally bound to tell you anything about it. Equally, you are not bound to give any information to the seller – if you pay your money, you will be entitled to your goods.

When you buy insurance, though, you are under 'a duty to disclose material facts'. The insurer is entitled to know 'every circumstance which in the ordinary course of business ought to be known to him'. You must disclose 'every material fact . . . every circumstance which would influence the judgement of a prudent insurer in fixing the premium or determining whether or not he will take the risk'.

After all, if your insurer knew all the facts he might charge you a higher premium or decline to cover you at all. And as you are the only person who knows 'every circumstance', you are bound to make full disclosure.

Normally, the relevant questions are contained in a proposal form. This provides the basis of the whole deal. You may be asked to answer specific questions and your answers are vital. Give false, inadequate or insufficient information and the contract may be avoided.

Still, even if your insurers do not ask questions, you are bound to disclose material facts.

What facts are 'material'? One expert puts it like this: 'Generally speaking, facts may be material because their existence renders the subject matter of the insurance peculiarly susceptible to a peril to be insured against, or because they indicate that the assured is a person whose proposal needs special consideration'.

In one recent, startling case, a woman was taking the Pill. She applied and obtained a life insurance policy. She died and her husband claimed the £1500 benefit. The insurers refused to pay on the ground that the woman was on the Pill and should have told them. Mr Justice Kerr decided in favour of the insurers. He held that this was a material fact which should have been brought to the attention of the company.

The Life Offices Association stated that women must tell insurers if they are taking the Pill when they apply for a life policy and if they do not, companies may refuse to pay out in cases of death. If they go on the Pill afterwards, there is no need to inform insurers – the contract is made.

The situation is similar with a man who smokes. Obviously the non-smoker is likely to live longer. He must reveal his smoking habits when he fills in his proposal form for life insurance. If, thereafter, he becomes addicted to the weed he is (it seems) not bound to tell the insurers. The vital time is when the contract is made.

An even more worrying case concerned a jeweller who was robbed of some £30,000. He claimed on his insurance policy. His insurers discovered that – some fifteen years previously – the man had been convicted of an offence involving fraud.

In fact the insurance had been arranged through a broker who did know of the previous conviction and the policy was actually issued to the man's company, rather than to himself.

The Court of Appeal decided that this conviction – so many years ago – was undoubtedly a 'material fact' which might have affected the mind of the insurers. Maybe they would have preferred not to have covered the man at all. Maybe the premium would have been higher. Or perhaps it would have made no difference at all – but it would certainly have been taken into account. The unfortunate jeweller lost his case.

A man suffered from a detached retina. He alleged that this resulted from an accident at work. He claimed under his insurance policy but it turned out that when he had filled in his proposal form, he had said nothing about any defect in his eyesight. An operation years before remained undisclosed. The insurers avoided paying out under the policy.

Suppose that you honestly believe a statement to be true – or that it is unnecessary to make a particular disclosure. No matter. Innocence is irrelevant. In general, even an innocent misrepresentation or material non-disclosure may make void an insurance contract.

Suppose, now, that you have filled in your proposal form, fully and adequately. You have paid your premium. Then your premises are flooded, your employees injured or some other circumstance insured against occurs. You must still take care if you do not want to lose your cover.

The policy usually stipulates the time and way in which – and the people to whom – you must notify the event or loss giving rise to the claim. If you do not comply with the rules then, even if you were in no way at fault, you may lose your cover. But where you are required to give notice 'immediately' this will be interpreted as meaning within a reasonable time and without unjustifiable delay.

Minor inaccuracies will not destroy the effectiveness of the agreement. But any fraudulent claim entitles the insurer to avoid the contract.

'Mere exaggeration', we are told, is not 'conclusive evidence' of fraud – but if the claim is out of all proportion to the true loss, then even if the cause was gross negligence, the assured will have trouble in collecting his money.

Anyway, the burden of proving both the loss and the fact that it was caused by perils insured against rests on the assured. He must prove, if necessary, that he did not under-insure – so as to pay less than the premium that he would have had to produce, had he declared the full value of the goods. Equally, if he over-insures he may be in trouble. So it is vital to assess the correct value of (for instance) goods or equipment insured, in so far as you can. So if you have not revalued your buildings or equipment (or, for that matter, your home and its contents) for some time, now is an excellent time to do so.

Finally, what of the biggest insurance bugbear of all, in everyday practice – the knock-for-knock agreement? If you are involved in a collision due to the fault of another driver, do you risk losing your no claims bonus if you fill in a form and the insurers settle on a knock-for-knock basis?

If you are not to blame for the accident, there is no reason why you should lose your no-claims bonus – even if your insurers do settle on a knock-for-knock basis. But it is essential that you should make it plain to your insurers that you are not making a claim.

The knock-for-knock system has been set up by the insurers, as between themselves, so that they give up arguing about apportionment of blame; they keep down their legal costs; and in the long run, they satisfy their customers. But whether in any particular case the no-claims bonus is affected will depend upon all the circumstances.

Under a knock-for-knock arrangement, each insurer pays his own client. Suppose, then, that you were to blame for the accident – wholly or in part. In that case, your no claims bonus would either disappear or go down (depending on the terms of your policy). Conversely, if you were in no way to blame, there is no reason why you should suffer any financial loss because your insurers decide to deal with the matter on the basis of knock-for-knock – so as to please themselves.

Of course, the fact that you consider that you were free from blame does not necessarily mean that everyone else will agree with you. If you were in a stationary vehicle and a car ran into your rear then – assuming that you could prove your case – you should win it. But otherwise, if there is room for argument, you would certainly be wise to inform your insurers of the accident, so as to make certain that if there is any trouble, you will be able to rely upon your policy.

In one case, a driver thought that the people in the other vehicle were totally unhurt, and so did they. But one of them suffered from delayed shock which kept him away from work for several weeks. The driver had not informed his insurers in accordance with the terms of his policy and had to pay the damages out of his own pocket.

So write to your insurers. Fill in the form, giving the details of the accident. But say: 'At this stage, I am not making a claim on my policy. I am informing you of the details of the accident.' No claim equals no problem with the no-claims bonus.

Suppose that you do make a claim. How much will this cost you?

Some insurers operate a 'step or step back no-claims bonus system'. Maybe your no-claims bonus is a certain percentage after one year with no claim; a higher percentage after two years, three years, four years and five years. Maybe one claim means one step back. In some cases, you may find yourself knocked three stages down the ladder – and if you are not on maximum bonus, you may be forced back to scratch.

How, then, do insurers consider this sort of case?

Many ask themselves the question: Without a knock-for-knock arrangement, could we get full recompense from the insurers of the other driver? If the answer is yes, the no-claims bonus should not be affected; if it is no, then the person insured was at least partly at fault and he cannot pretend that there has been no claim.

Put it differently: If insurers believe that they could recover their full outlay for the accident or damage to the car they insure from the other insurers, then the policy holder's no-claim bonus should not be affected. Conversely, if they would have had to pay part or all of the cost of putting their own insured vehicle into proper order, then they can batten on to the no-claims bonus so as to recover at least part of their loss that way.

'It's all unfair', you may say. 'Why should my insurers pay for damage to my car, which was caused by the other man's negligent driving?'

Your insurers would answer: 'You are not losing out. On the swings and roundabouts we break even – in fact, we are saving money because we are avoiding making unnecessary payments to the lawyers. We are settling damage claims more speedily and keeping administration costs down. And in that way, we are preventing premiums from going up still further.'

You may not agree with this reasoning. But what matters is not to worry about losing your no-claims bonus, if you are really blameless.

One warning: If the other man refuses to fill in a claim form, then he will be liable; he cannot make his insurers liable, because he has not filled in his forms; and the knock-for-knock agreement cannot be confirmed between the insurers. You will then have to rely on getting your money from the other man or let your insurers step into your shoes, sue the other driver in your name and, if they win, then you will not need to rely upon the money which you would otherwise have got from them.

Chapter 61

Where There's a Will

Accidents cause deaths. . . . The shoemaker's children go barefoot – and the doctor takes insufficient care of his own health. The wise lawyer will avoid personal litigation, if he can – but you will find few solicitors too busy to make their own wills. The businessman knows the uncertainty of human life, and should know better than to leave it, intestate.

If you die 'intestate' – that is, without making a will – the law lays down some fairly complicated rules on the succession to your property. As these rules are an effort to provide a common denominator for all, it would be surprising if they provided precisely what you would wish, had you set out your intentions on paper.

Anyway, it takes longer and costs more to 'take out letters of administration', where the deceased died intestate, than it does to 'obtain a grant of probate', where he leaves a will. If you wish to be kind to those who come after you, then take the trouble to make a will.

There is no law that says that a will must be made on paper or parchment. A will written on an eggshell was once upheld as valid. So was another. inscribed on a brown paper bag. But informal documents have grave perils.

First, a will must be properly executed and witnessed. Second, if money is left to a witness, the bequest almost always dies with the testator – if anyone asks you to witness his will, make sure that he is not planning on leaving you anything.

Then there are technical rules which you could never know, without professional advice. Some years ago, an ex-neighbour of mine died, his wife having pre-deceased him. Without mentioning anything to me, he made me executor under his will. I therefore automatically became guardian of his fifteen-year-old daughter. I am certain that he had no idea that he was blessing me with an extra member of my household.

So get a solicitor to draw up your will for you. Assuming that you are not asking him to prepare an elaborate trust, but you are merely giving your money, property, goods and chattels to your wife or children or other relatives or friends, it can all be done simply and at little expense. Ask your lawyer what he would charge you – and you will probably be pleasantly surprised.

Once made, a will may always be revoked. You could tear it up, with the intention of destroying it. Or you might remarry – in which case the law presumes that you would not wish your original intentions to remain valid. But if you have children, you should make sure that they are provided for, one by one.

You need not make a new will, if you wish to add to or vary the original. You may make a codicil – but this requires the same formalities as the will itself.

As before, you can buy a printed form at your local stationers, if you wish. It will explain the formalities – but cannot set out all the law that the testator needs to know. This is one time when a solicitor's help is needed.

Even when the will is properly made, there are occasions when the law will upset it. For instance, someone who is left out of the financial reckoning may allege that the testator was under the 'undue influence' of some major beneficiary. 'The old man was senile . . . He was out of his mind. . . . He did not know what he was doing. . . . He was fraudulently induced to sign. . . . He was incapable of understanding the nature or effect of the document. . . .'

If a wife or a young child is left penniless, the court may intervene, and provide a required inheritance. But it often happens that a father leaves his money to one child – and his other children are left to whistle for their share. Assuming that they are capable of earning their own livings, the law cannot help them.

If you die intestate in some foreign land, very complicated questions of 'domicile' may arise. Were you merely working abroad or had you sunk your roots into the foreign soil? Where was your permanent home? Had you lost your 'domicile of origin' and taken up a 'domicile of choice'? Which law would apply in your case – that of your country of origin or that of your place of death?

Estate duty, too (now called Capital Transfer Tax), is not peculiar to our law. Who will levy tax on your estate – and how much?

The more you travel – and the further afield you go – the more important it becomes for you to prepare the future of your assets in this world, before you step into the next. But even if you never move beyond the jurisdiction of our courts, the better you plan, the more you are likely to leave for your heirs and the less for the Revenue.

You may, of course, give away everything you own and leave nothing in your will. Until recently, this would have enabled you to keep your assets from the clutches of the Revenue, provided you acted sufficiently far in advance of your death. Capital Transfer Tax now ensures that even gifts may be liable to be taxed. Moreover, you are then in the hands of the recipients of your bounty. And however much you trust your son or daughter, you may have to contend with your in-laws. Far too many folk die in penury because they have placed too much trust in their young.

Anyway, where there's a will, there's generally a way to achieve a satisfactory conclusion for your worldly affairs. I wish you a well-drawn up will – and many years of good health in which to vary it.

"WELL, GENTLEMEN – THAT'S ENOUGH WORRIES ABOUT A SAFE SYSTEM OF WORK – YOU'RE ALL FIRED."

Endpiece

The law on safety is on the move – thrust forward by both Parliament and the courts. This book has summarised the rules as they are at present. Readers must now prepare for rapid change. Courts will interpret Parliament's meaning; codes of practice will be made and interpreted; above all, the Secretary of State will make regulations – by the dozen.

With the background provided by this book, new law will be intelligible. But whether in connection with safety committees or safety arrangements in directors' reports; whether in connection with procedures to be followed by inspectors or to regulate specific activities as recommended by the Commission – regulations are inevitable. Watch out for them – and good luck to you.

The tightening up of the law on health, safety and welfare at work should continue to cut accidents and improve health – but it certainly imposes a new and heavy burden on all executives and managers – personally. Those who fail in their duties are liable not only to pay heavy damages but, more important, to be fined or even imprisoned. The old law was reasonably gentle in its approach and application; the new law is potentially fiercesome indeed.

"WHICH IS THE SECTION ON NEUTRALIZING BURGLAR ALARMS?"

Appendices

Appendix 1

The Health and Safety at Work etc. Act, 1974 (as amended)

The Act as printed here includes the amendments made by *The Employment Protection Act, 1975*. Parts repealed by the 1975 Act are indicated by dots and parts added or amended are enclosed in square brackets.

ARRANGEMENT OF SECTIONS

PART I

HEALTH, SAFETY AND WELFARE IN CONNECTION WITH WORK, AND CONTROL OF DANGEROUS SUBSTANCES AND CERTAIN EMISSIONS INTO THE ATMOSPHERE

Preliminary

Section
1. Preliminary.

General duties

2. General duties of employers to their employees.
3. General duties of employers and self-employed to persons other than their employees.
4. General duties of persons concerned with premises to persons other than their employees.
5. General duty of persons in control of certain premises in relation to harmful emissions into atmosphere.
6. General duties of manufacturers etc. as regards articles and substances for use at work.
7. General duties of employees at work.
8. Duty not to interfere with or misuse things provided pursuant to certain provisions.
9. Duty not to charge employees for things done or provided pursuant to certain specific requirements.

The Health and Safety Commission and the Health and Safety Executive

10. Establishment of the Commission and the Executive.
11. General functions of the Commission and the Executive.
12. Control of the Commission by the Secretary of State.
13. Other powers of the Commission.
14. Power of the Commission to direct investigations and inquiries.

Enforcement

Obtaining and disclosure of information

Provisions as to offences

Financial provisions

Miscellaneous and supplementary

48. Application to Crown.
49. Adaptation of enactments to metric units or appropriate metric units.
50. Regulations under relevant statutory provisions.
51. Exclusion of application to domestic employment.
52. Meaning of work and at work.
53. General interpretation of Part I.
54. Application of Part I to Isles of Scilly.

PART II

THE EMPLOYMENT MEDICAL ADVISORY SERVICE

55. Functions of, and responsibility for maintaining, employment medical advisory service.
56. Functions of authority responsible for maintaining the service.
57. Fees.
58. Other financial provisions.
59. Duty of responsible authority to keep accounts and to report.
60. Supplementary.

PART III

BUILDING REGULATIONS AND AMENDMENT OF BUILDING (SCOTLAND) ACT 1959

61. Amendments of enactments relating to building regulations.
62. Further matters for which building regulations may provide.
63. Miscellaneous provisions as to the approval of plans.
64. Special provisions as to materials etc. unsuitable for permanent buildings.
65. Continuing requirements.
66. Type relaxation of building regulations.
67. Power of Secretary of State to approve types of building etc.
68. Power to require or carry out tests for conformity with building regulations.
69. Provisions relating to appeals etc. to the Secretary of State under certain provisions.
70. Power to make building regulations for Inner London.
71. Civil liability.
72. Application to Crown.
73. Application to United Kingdom Atomic Energy Authority.

PART IV

MISCELLANEOUS AND GENERAL

SCHEDULES:

Health and Safety at Work etc. Act 1974

1974 CHAPTER 37

An Act to make further provision for securing the health, safety and welfare of persons at work, for protecting others against risks to health or safety in connection with the activities of persons at work, for controlling the keeping and use and preventing the unlawful acquisition, possession and use of dangerous substances, and for controlling certain emissions into the atmosphere; to make further provision with respect to the employment medical advisory service; to amend the law relating to building regulations, and the Building (Scotland) Act 1959; and for connected purposes. [31st July 1974]

BE IT ENACTED by the Queen's most Excellent Majesty, by and with the advice and consent of the Lords Spiritual and Temporal, and Commons, in this present Parliament assembled, and by the authority of the same, as follows:—

PART I

HEALTH, SAFETY AND WELFARE IN CONNECTION WITH WORK, AND CONTROL OF DANGEROUS SUBSTANCES AND CERTAIN EMISSIONS INTO THE ATMOSPHERE

Preliminary

1.—(1) The provisions of this Part shall have effect with a view to— Preliminary.

(*a*) securing the health, safety and welfare of persons at work;

(*b*) protecting persons other than persons at work against risks to health or safety arising out of or in connection with the activities of persons at work;

PART I

(*c*) controlling the keeping and use of explosive or highly flammable or otherwise dangerous substances, and generally preventing the unlawful acquisition, possession and use of such substances; and

(*d*) controlling the emission into the atmosphere of noxious or offensive substances from premises of any class prescribed for the purposes of this paragraph.

(2) The provisions of this Part relating to the making of health and safety regulations . . .

. . . and the preparation and approval of codes of practice shall in particular have effect with a view to enabling the enactments specified in the third column of Schedule 1 and the regulations, orders and other instruments in force under those enactments to be progressively replaced by a system of regulations and approved codes of practice operating in combination with the other provisions of this Part and designed to maintain or improve the standards of health, safety and welfare established by or under those enactments.

(3) For the purposes of this Part risks arising out of or in connection with the activities of persons at work shall be treated as including risks attributable to the manner of conducting an undertaking, the plant or substances used for the purposes of an undertaking and the condition of premises so used or any part of them.

(4) References in this Part to the general purposes of this Part are references to the purposes mentioned in subsection (1) above.

General duties

General duties of employers to their employees.

2.—(1) It shall be the duty of every employer to ensure, so far as is reasonably practicable, the health, safety and welfare at work of all his employees.

(2) Without prejudice to the generality of an employer's duty under the preceding subsection, the matters to which that duty extends include in particular—

(*a*) the provision and maintenance of plant and systems of work that are, so far as is reasonably practicable, safe and without risks to health;

(*b*) arrangements for ensuring, so far as is reasonably practicable, safety and absence of risks to health in connection with the use, handling, storage and transport of articles and substances;

(*c*) the provision of such information, instruction, training and supervision as is necessary to ensure, so far as is reasonably practicable, the health and safety at work of his employees;

(*d*) so far as is reasonably practicable as regards any place of work under the employer's control, the maintenance of it in a condition that is safe and without risks to health and the provision and maintenance of means of access to and egress from it that are safe and without such risks ; PART I

(*e*) the provision and maintenance of a working environment for his employees that is, so far as is reasonably practicable, safe, without risks to health, and adequate as regards facilities and arrangements for their welfare at work.

(3) Except in such cases as may be prescribed, it shall be the duty of every employer to prepare and as often as may be appropriate revise a written statement of his general policy with respect to the health and safety at work of his employees and the organisation and arrangements for the time being in force for carrying out that policy, and to bring the statement and any revision of it to the notice of all of his employees.

(4) Regulations made by the Secretary of State may provide for the appointment in prescribed cases by recognised trade unions (within the meaning of the regulations) of safety representatives from amongst the employees, and those representatives shall represent the employees in consultations with the employers under subsection (6) below and shall have such other functions as may be prescribed.

• • •

(6) It shall be the duty of every employer to consult any such representatives with a view to the making and maintenance of arrangements which will enable him and his employees to co-operate effectively in promoting and developing measures to ensure the health and safety at work of the employees, and in checking the effectiveness of such measures.

(7) In such cases as may be prescribed it shall be the duty of every employer, if requested to do so by the safety representatives mentioned in subsection (4) • • • above, to establish, in accordance with regulations made by the Secretary of State, a safety committee having the function of keeping under review the measures taken to ensure the health and safety at work of his employees and such other functions as may be prescribed.

PART I

General duties of employers and self-employed to persons other than their employees.

3.—(1) It shall be the duty of every employer to conduct his undertaking in such a way as to ensure, so far as is reasonably practicable, that persons not in his employment who may be affected thereby are not thereby exposed to risks to their health or safety.

(2) It shall be the duty of every self-employed person to conduct his undertaking in such a way as to ensure, so far as is reasonably practicable, that he and other persons (not being his employees) who may be affected thereby are not thereby exposed to risks to their health or safety.

(3) In such cases as may be prescribed, it shall be the duty of every employer and every self-employed person, in the prescribed circumstances and in the prescribed manner, to give to persons (not being his employees) who may be affected by the way in which he conducts his undertaking the prescribed information about such aspects of the way in which he conducts his undertaking as might affect their health or safety.

General duties of persons concerned with premises to persons other than their employees.

4.—(1) This section has effect for imposing on persons duties in relation to those who—

(*a*) are not their employees; but

(*b*) use non-domestic premises made available to them as a place of work or as a place where they may use plant or substances provided for their use there,

and applies to premises so made available and other non-domestic premises used in connection with them.

(2) It shall be the duty of each person who has, to any extent, control of premises to which this section applies or of the means of access thereto or egress therefrom or of any plant or substance in such premises to take such measures as it is reasonable for a person in his position to take to ensure, so far as is reasonably practicable, that the premises, all means of access thereto or egress therefrom available for use by persons using the premises, and any plant or substance in the premises or, as the case may be, provided for use there, is or are safe and without risks to health.

(3) Where a person has, by virtue of any contract or tenancy, an obligation of any extent in relation to—

(*a*) the maintenance or repair of any premises to which this section applies or any means of access thereto or egress therefrom; or

(*b*) the safety of or the absence of risks to health arising from plant or substances in any such premises;

that person shall be treated, for the purposes of subsection (2) above, as being a person who has control of the matters to which his obligation extends.

(4) Any reference in this section to a person having control of any premises or matter is a reference to a person having control of the premises or matter in connection with the carrying on by him of a trade, business or other undertaking (whether for profit or not). **PART I**

General duty of persons in control of certain premises in relation to harmful emissions into atmosphere.

5.—(1) It shall be the duty of the person having control of any premises of a class prescribed for the purposes of section 1(1)(*d*) to use the best practicable means for preventing the emission into the atmosphere from the premises of noxious or offensive substances and for rendering harmless and inoffensive such substances as may be so emitted.

(2) The reference in subsection (1) above to the means to be used for the purposes there mentioned includes a reference to the manner in which the plant provided for those purposes is used and to the supervision of any operation involving the emission of the substances to which that subsection applies.

(3) Any substance or a substance of any description prescribed for the purposes of subsection (1) above as noxious or offensive shall be a noxious or, as the case may be, an offensive substance for those purposes whether or not it would be so apart from this subsection.

(4) Any reference in this section to a person having control of any premises is a reference to a person having control of the premises in connection with the carrying on by him of a trade, business or other undertaking (whether for profit or not) and any duty imposed on any such person by this section shall extend only to matters within his control.

General duties of manufacturers etc. as regards articles and substances for use at work.

6.—(1) It shall be the duty of any person who designs, manufactures, imports or supplies any article for use at work—

(*a*) to ensure, so far as is reasonably practicable, that the article is so designed and constructed as to be safe and without risks to health when properly used ;

(*b*) to carry out or arrange for the carrying out of such testing and examination as may be necessary for the performance of the duty imposed on him by the preceding paragraph ;

(*c*) to take such steps as are necessary to secure that there will be available in connection with the use of the article at work adequate information about the use for which it is designed and has been tested, and about any conditions necessary to ensure that, when put to that use, it will be safe and without risks to health.

(2) It shall be the duty of any person who undertakes the design or manufacture of any article for use at work to carry out

PART I or arrange for the carrying out of any necessary research with a view to the discovery and, so far as is reasonably practicable, the elimination or minimisation of any risks to health or safety to which the design or article may give rise.

(3) It shall be the duty of any person who erects or installs any article for use at work in any premises where that article is to be used by persons at work to ensure, so far as is reasonably practicable, that nothing about the way in which it is erected or installed makes it unsafe or a risk to health when properly used.

(4) It shall be the duty of any person who manufactures, imports or supplies any substance for use at work—

(*a*) to ensure, so far as is reasonably practicable, that the substance is safe and without risks to health when properly used ;

(*b*) to carry out or arrange for the carrying out of such testing and examination as may be necessary for the performance of the duty imposed on him by the preceding paragraph ;

(*c*) to take such steps as are necessary to secure that there will be available in connection with the use of the substance at work adequate information about the results of any relevant tests which have been carried out on or in connection with the substance and about any conditions necessary to ensure that it will be safe and without risks to health when properly used.

(5) It shall be the duty of any person who undertakes the manufacture of any substance for use at work to carry out or arrange for the carrying out of any necessary research with a view to the discovery and, so far as is reasonably practicable, the elimination or minimisation of any risks to health or safety to which the substance may give rise.

(6) Nothing in the preceding provisions of this section shall be taken to require a person to repeat any testing, examination or research which has been carried out otherwise than by him or at his instance, in so far as it is reasonable for him to rely on the results thereof for the purposes of those provisions.

(7) Any duty imposed on any person by any of the preceding provisions of this section shall extend only to things done in the course of a trade, business or other undertaking carried on by him (whether for profit or not) and to matters within his control.

(8) Where a person designs, manufactures, imports or supplies an article for or to another on the basis of a written undertaking by that other to take specified steps sufficient to ensure, so far as is reasonably practicable, that the article will be safe and

without risks to health when properly used, the undertaking shall have the effect of relieving the first-mentioned person from the duty imposed by subsection (1)(*a*) above to such extent as is reasonable having regard to the terms of the undertaking.

(9) Where a person ("the ostensible supplier") supplies any article for use at work or substance for use at work to another ("the customer") under a hire-purchase agreement, conditional sale agreement or credit-sale agreement, and the ostensible supplier—

(*a*) carries on the business of financing the acquisition of goods by others by means of such agreements; and

(*b*) in the course of that business acquired his interest in the article or substance supplied to the customer as a means of financing its acquisition by the customer from a third person ("the effective supplier"),

the effective supplier and not the ostensible supplier shall be treated for the purposes of this section as supplying the article or substance to the customer, and any duty imposed by the preceding provisions of this section on suppliers shall accordingly fall on the effective supplier and not on the ostensible supplier.

(10) For the purposes of this section an article or substance is not to be regarded as properly used where it is used without regard to any relevant information or advice relating to its use which has been made available by a person by whom it was designed, manufactured, imported or supplied.

General duties of employees at work.

7. It shall be the duty of every employee while at work—

(*a*) to take reasonable care for the health and safety of himself and of other persons who may be affected by his acts or omissions at work; and

(*b*) as regards any duty or requirement imposed on his employer or any other person by or under any of the relevant statutory provisions, to co-operate with him so far as is necessary to enable that duty or requirement to be performed or complied with.

Duty not to interfere with or misuse things provided pursuant to certain provisions.

8. No person shall intentionally or recklessly interfere with or misuse anything provided in the interests of health, safety or welfare in pursuance of any of the relevant statutory provisions.

Duty not to charge employees for things done or provided pursuant to certain specific requirements.

9. No employer shall levy or permit to be levied on any employee of his any charge in respect of anything done or provided in pursuance of any specific requirement of the relevant statutory provisions.

PART I

The Health and Safety Commission and the Health and Safety Executive

Establishment of the Commission and the Executive.

10.—(1) There shall be two bodies corporate to be called the Health and Safety Commission and the Health and Safety Executive which shall be constituted in accordance with the following provisions of this section.

(2) The Health and Safety Commission (hereafter in this Act referred to as " the Commission ") shall consist of a chairman appointed by the Secretary of State and not less than six nor more than nine other members appointed by the Secretary of State in accordance with subsection (3) below.

(3) Before appointing the members of the Commission (other than the chairman) the Secretary of State shall—

(*a*) as to three of them, consult such organisations representing employers as he considers appropriate ;

(*b*) as to three others, consult such organisations representing employees as he considers appropriate ; and

(*c*) as to any other members he may appoint, consult such organisations representing local authorities and such other organisations, including professional bodies, the activities of whose members are concerned with matters relating to any of the general purposes of this Part, as he considers appropriate.

(4) The Secretary of State may appoint one of the members to be deputy chairman of the Commission.

(5) The Health and Safety Executive (hereafter in this Act referred to as " the Executive ") shall consist of three persons of whom one shall be appointed by the Commission with the approval of the Secretary of State to be the director of the Executive and the others shall be appointed by the Commission with the like approval after consultation with the said director.

(6) The provisions of Schedule 2 shall have effect with respect to the Commission and the Executive.

(7) The functions of the Commission and of the Executive, and of their officers and servants, shall be performed on behalf of the Crown.

" (8) For the purposes of any civil proceedings arising out of those functions, the Crown Proceedings Act 1947 and the Crown Suits (Scotland) Act 1857 shall apply to the Commission and the Executive as if they were government departments within the meaning of the said Act of 1947 or, as the case may be, public departments within the meaning of the said Act of 1857.".

General functions of the Commission and the Executive.

11.—(1) In addition to the other functions conferred on the Commission by virtue of this Act, but subject to subsection (3) below, it shall be the general duty of the Commission to do such things and make such arrangements as it considers appropriate for the general purposes of this Part • • •

(2) It shall be the duty of the Commission • • • **PART I**

(*a*) to assist and encourage persons concerned with matters relevant to any of the general purposes of this Part to further those purposes;

(*b*) to make such arrangements as it considers appropriate for the carrying out of research, the publication of the results of research and the provision of training and information in connection with those purposes, and to encourage research and the provision of training and information in that connection by others;

(*c*) to make such arrangements as it considers appropriate for securing that government departments, employers, employees, organisations representing employers and employees respectively, and other persons concerned with matters relevant to any of those purposes are provided with an information and advisory service and are kept informed of, and adequately advised on, such matters;

(*d*) to submit from time to time to the authority having power to make regulations under any of the relevant statutory provisions such proposals as the Commission considers appropriate for the making of regulations under that power.

(3) It shall be the duty of the Commission—

(*a*) to submit to the Secretary of State from time to time particulars of what it proposes to do for the purpose of performing its functions; and

(*b*) subject to the following paragraph, to ensure that its activities are in accordance with proposals approved by the Secretary of State; and

(*c*) to give effect to any directions given to it by the Secretary of State.

(4) In addition to any other functions conferred on the Executive by virtue of this Part, it shall be the duty of the Executive—

(*a*) to exercise on behalf of the Commission such of the Commission's functions as the Commission directs it to exercise; and

(*b*) to give effect to any directions given to it by the Commission otherwise than in pursuance of paragraph (*a*) above;

but, except for the purpose of giving effect to directions given to the Commission by the Secretary of State, the Commission shall not give to the Executive any directions as to the enforcement of any of the relevant statutory provisions in a particular case.

PART I

(5) Without prejudice to subsection (2) above, it shall be the duty of the Executive, if so requested by a Minister of the Crown—

(*a*) to provide him with information about the activities of the Executive in connection with any matter with which he is concerned ; and

(*b*) to provide him with advice on any matter with which he is concerned on which relevant expert advice is obtainable from any of the officers or servants of the Executive but which is not relevant to any of the general purposes of this Part.

(6) The Commission and the Executive shall, subject to any directions given to it in pursuance of this Part, have power to do anything (except borrow money) which is calculated to facilitate, or is conducive or incidental to, the performance of any function of the Commission or, as the case may be, the Executive (including a function conferred on it by virtue of this subsection).

Control of the Commission by the Secretary of State.

12. The Secretary of State may—

(*a*) approve, with or without modifications, any proposals submitted to him in pursuance of section 11(3)(*a*) ;

(*b*) give to the Commission at any time such directions as he thinks fit with respect to its functions (including directions modifying its functions, but not directions conferring on it functions other than any of which it was deprived by previous directions given by virtue of this paragraph), and any directions which it appears to him requisite or expedient to give in the interests of the safety of the State.

Other powers of the Commission.

13.—(1) The Commission shall have power—

(*a*) to make agreements with any government department or other person for that department or person to perform on behalf of the Commission or the Executive (with or without payment) any of the functions of the Commission or, as the case may be, of the Executive ;

(*b*) subject to subsection (2) below, to make agreements with any Minister of the Crown, government department or other public authority for the Commission to perform on behalf of that Minister, department or authority (with or without payment) functions exercisable by the Minister, department or authority (including, in the case of a Minister, functions not conferred by an enactment), being functions which in the opinion of the Secretary of State can appropriately be performed by the Commission in connection with any of the Commission's functions ;

(*c*) to provide (with or without payment) services or facilities required otherwise than for the general purposes of this Part in so far as they are required by any government department or other public authority in connection with the exercise by that department or authority of any of its functions;

(*d*) to appoint persons or committees of persons to provide the Commission with advice in connection with any of its functions and (without prejudice to the generality of the following paragraph) to pay to persons so appointed such remuneration as the Secretary of State may with the approval of the Minister for the Civil Service determine;

(*e*) in connection with any of the functions of the Commission, to pay to any person such travelling and subsistence allowances and such compensation for loss of remunerative time as the Secretary of State may with the approval of the Minister for the Civil Service determine;

(*f*) to carry out or arrange for or make payments in respect of research into any matter connected with any of the Commission's functions, and to disseminate or arrange for or make payments in respect of the dissemination of information derived from such research;

(*g*) to include, in any arrangements made by the Commission for the provision of facilities or services by it or on its behalf, provision for the making of payments to the Commission or any person acting on its behalf by other parties to the arrangements and by persons who use those facilities or services.

(2) Nothing in subsection (1)(*b*) shall authorise the Commission to perform any function of a Minister, department or authority which consists of a power to make regulations or other instruments of a legislative character.

Power of the Commission to direct investigations and inquiries.

14.—(1) This section applies to the following matters, that is to say any accident, occurrence, situation or other matter whatsoever which the Commission thinks it necessary or expedient to investigate for any of the general purposes of this Part or with a view to the making of regulations for those purposes; and for the purposes of this subsection it is immaterial whether the Executive is or is not responsible for securing the enforcement of such (if any) of the relevant statutory provisions as relate to the matter in question.

(2) The Commission may at any time—

(*a*) direct the Executive or authorise any other person to investigate and make a special report on any matter to which this section applies; or

PART I

(*b*) with the consent of the Secretary of State direct an inquiry to be held into any such matter ; . . .

(3) Any inquiry held by virtue of subsection (2)(*b*) above shall be held in accordance with regulations made for the purposes of this subsection by the Secretary of State, and shall be held in public except where or to the extent that the regulations provide otherwise.

(4) Regulations made for the purposes of subsection (3) above may in particular include provision—

(*a*) conferring on the person holding any such inquiry, and any person assisting him in the inquiry, powers of entry and inspection ;

(*b*) conferring on any such person powers of summoning witnesses to give evidence or produce documents and power to take evidence on oath and administer oaths or require the making of declarations ;

(*c*) requiring any such inquiry to be held otherwise than in public where or to the extent that a Minister of the Crown so directs.

(5) In the case of a special report made by virtue of subsection (2)(*a*) above or a report made by the person holding an inquiry held by virtue of subsection (2)(*b*) above, the Commission may cause the report, or so much of it as the Commission thinks fit, to be made public at such time and in such manner as the Commission thinks fit.

(6) The Commission—

(*a*) in the case of an investigation and special report made by virtue of subsection (2)(*a*) above (otherwise than by an officer or servant of the Executive), may pay to the person making it such remuneration and expenses as the Secretary of State may, with the approval of the Minister for the Civil Service, determine ;

(*b*) in the case of an inquiry held by virtue of subsection (2)(*b*) above, may pay to the person holding it and to any assessor appointed to assist him such remuneration and expenses, and to persons attending the inquiry as witnesses such expenses, as the Secretary of State may, with the like approval, determine ; and

(*c*) may, to such extent as the Secretary of State may determine, defray the other costs, if any, of any such investigation and special report or inquiry.

(7) Where an inquiry is directed to be held by virtue of subsection (2)(*b*) above into any matter to which this section applies arising in Scotland, being a matter which causes the death of any person, no inquiry with regard to that death shall, unless the Lord Advocate otherwise directs, be held in pursuance of the Fatal Accidents Inquiry (Scotland) Act 1895. **PART I** **1895 c.** 36.

Health and safety regulations and approved codes of practice

Health **and** safety regulations**.**

" (1) Subject to the provisions of section 50, the Secretary of State, the Minister of Agriculture, Fisheries and Food or the Secretary of State and that Minister acting jointly shall have power to make regulations under this section for any of the general purposes of this Part (and regulations so made are in this Part referred to as " health and safety regulations ").".

(2) Without prejudice to the generality of the preceding subsection, health and safety regulations may for any of the general purposes of this Part make provision for any of the purposes mentioned in Schedule 3.

(3) Health and safety regulations—

(*a*) may repeal or modify any of the existing statutory provisions;

(*b*) may exclude or modify in relation to any specified class of case any of the provisions of sections 2 to 9 or any of the existing statutory provisions;

(*c*) may make a specified authority or class of authorities responsible, to such extent as may be specified, for the enforcement of any of the relevant statutory provisions.

(4) Health and safety regulations—

(*a*) may impose requirements by reference to the approval of the Commission or any other specified body or person;

(*b*) may provide for references in the regulations to any specified document to operate as references to that document as revised or re-issued from time to time.

(5) Health and safety regulations—

(*a*) may provide (either unconditionally or subject to conditions, and with or without limit of time) for exemptions from any requirement or prohibition imposed by or under any of the relevant statutory provisions;

(*b*) may enable exemptions from any requirement or prohibition imposed by or under any of the relevant

PART I

statutory provisions to be granted (either unconditionally or subject to conditions, and with or without limit of time) by any specified person or by any person authorised in that behalf by a specified authority.

(6) Health and safety regulations—

(*a*) may specify the persons or classes of persons who, in the event of a contravention of a requirement or prohibition imposed by or under the regulations, are to be guilty of an offence, whether in addition to or to the exclusion of other persons or classes of persons;

(*b*) may provide for any specified defence to be available in proceedings for any offence under the relevant statutory provisions either generally or in specified circumstances;

(*c*) may exclude proceedings on indictment in relation to offences consisting of a contravention of a requirement or prohibition imposed by or under any of the existing statutory provisions, sections 2 to 9 or health and safety regulations;

(*d*) may restrict the punishments which can be imposed in respect of any such offence as is mentioned in paragraph (*c*) above.

(7) Without prejudice to section 35, health and safety regulations may make provision for enabling offences under any of the relevant statutory provisions to be treated as having been committed at any specified place for the purpose of bringing any such offence within the field of responsibility of any enforcing authority or conferring jurisdiction on any court to entertain proceedings for any such offence.

(8) Health and safety regulations may take the form of regulations applying to particular circumstances only or to a particular case only (for example, regulations applying to particular premises only).

(9) If an Order in Council is made under section 84(3) providing that this section shall apply to or in relation to persons, premises or work outside Great Britain then, notwithstanding the Order, health and safety regulations shall not apply to or in relation to aircraft in flight, vessels, hovercraft or offshore installations outside Great Britain or persons at work outside Great Britain in connection with submarine cables or submarine pipelines except in so far as the regulations expressly so provide.

(10) In this section " specified " means specified in health and safety regulations.

16.—(1) For the purpose of providing practical guidance with respect to the requirements of any provision of sections 2 to 7 or of health and safety regulations or of any of the existing statutory provisions, the Commission may, subject to the following subsection . . .

PART I
Approval of codes of practice by the Commission.

(*a*) approve and issue such codes of practice (whether prepared by it or not) as in its opinion are suitable for that purpose;

(*b*) approve such codes of practice issued or proposed to be issued otherwise than by the Commission as in its opinion are suitable for that purpose.

(2) The Commission shall not approve a code of practice under subsection (1) above without the consent of the Secretary of State, and shall, before seeking his consent, consult—

(*a*) any government department or other body that appears to the Commission to be appropriate (and, in particular, in the case of a code relating to electromagnetic radiations, the National Radiological Protection Board); and

(*b*) such government departments and other bodies, if any, as in relation to any matter dealt with in the code, the Commission is required to consult under this section by virtue of directions given to it by the Secretary of State.

(3) Where a code of practice is approved by the Commission under subsection (1) above, the Commission shall issue a notice in writing—

(*a*) identifying the code in question and stating the date on which its approval by the Commission is to take effect; and

(*b*) specifying for which of the provisions mentioned in subsection (1) above the code is approved.

(4) The Commission may—

(*a*) from time to time revise the whole or any part of any code of practice prepared by it in pursuance of this section;

(*b*) approve any revision or proposed revision of the whole or any part of any code of practice for the time being approved under this section;

and the provisions of subsections (2) and (3) above shall, with the necessary modifications, apply in relation to the approval of any revision under this subsection as they apply in relation to the approval of a code of practice under subsection (1) above.

PART I

(5) The Commission may at any time with the consent of the Secretary of State withdraw its approval from any code of practice approved under this section, but before seeking his consent shall consult the same government departments and other bodies as it would be required to consult under subsection (2) above if it were proposing to approve the code.

(6) Where under the preceding subsection the Commission withdraws its approval from a code of practice approved under this section, the Commission shall issue a notice in writing identifying the code in question and stating the date on which its approval of it is to cease to have effect.

(7) References in this Part to an approved code of practice are references to that code as it has effect for the time being by virtue of any revision of the whole or any part of it approved under this section.

(8) The power of the Commission under subsection (1)(*b*) above to approve a code of practice issued or proposed to be issued otherwise than by the Commission shall include power to approve a part of such a code of practice; and accordingly in this Part "code of practice" may be read as including a part of such a code of practice.

Use of approved codes of practice in criminal proceedings.

17.—(1) A failure on the part of any person to observe any provision of an approved code of practice shall not of itself render him liable to any civil or criminal proceedings; but where in any criminal proceedings a party is alleged to have committed an offence by reason of a contravention of any requirement or prohibition imposed by or under any such provision as is mentioned in section 16(1) being a provision for which there was an approved code of practice at the time of the alleged contravention, the following subsection shall have effect with respect to that code in relation to those proceedings.

(2) Any provision of the code of practice which appears to the court to be relevant to the requirement or prohibition alleged to have been contravened shall be admissible in evidence in the proceedings; and if it is proved that there was at any material time a failure to observe any provision of the code which appears to the court to be relevant to any matter which it is necessary for the prosecution to prove in order to establish a contravention of that requirement or prohibition, that matter shall be taken as proved unless the court is satisfied that the requirement or prohibition was in respect of that matter complied with otherwise than by way of observance of that provision of the code.

(3) In any criminal proceedings—

(*a*) a document purporting to be a notice issued by the Commission under section 16 shall be taken to be such a notice unless the contrary is proved; and (*b*) a code of practice which appears to the court to be the subject of such a notice shall be taken to be the subject of that notice unless the contrary is proved.

Enforcement

Authorities responsible for enforcement of the relevant statutory provisions.

18.—(1) It shall be the duty of the Executive to make adequate arrangements for the enforcement of the relevant statutory provisions except to the extent that some other authority or class of authorities is by any of those provisions or by regulations under subsection (2) below made responsible for their enforcement.

(2) The Secretary of State may by regulations—

(*a*) make local authorities responsible for the enforcement of the relevant statutory provisions to such extent as may be prescribed;

(*b*) make provision for enabling responsibility for enforcing any of the relevant statutory provisions to be, to such extent as may be determined under the regulations—

(i) transferred from the Executive to local authorities or from local authorities to the Executive; or

(ii) assigned to the Executive or to local authorities for the purpose of removing any uncertainty as to what are by virtue of this subsection their respective responsibilities for the enforcement of those provisions;

and any regulations made in pursuance of paragraph (*b*) above shall include provision for securing that any transfer or assignment effected under the regulations is brought to the notice of persons affected by it.

(3) Any provision made by regulations under the preceding subsection shall have effect subject to any provision made by health and safety regulations...

... in pursuance of section 15(3)(*c*).

(4) It shall be the duty of every local authority—

(*a*) to make adequate arrangements for the enforcement within their area of the relevant statutory provisions to the extent that they are by any of those provisions or by regulations under subsection (2) above made responsible for their enforcement; and

(*b*) to perform the duty imposed on them by the preceding paragraph and any other functions conferred on them by any of the relevant statutory provisions in accordance with such guidance as the Commission may give them.

Part I

(5) Where any authority other than the appropriate Agriculture Minister, the Executive or a local authority is by any of the relevant statutory provisions or by regulations under subsection (2) above made responsible for the enforcement of any of those provisions to any extent, it shall be the duty of that authority—

(*a*) to make adequate arrangements for the enforcement of those provisions to that extent; and

(*b*) to perform the duty imposed on the authority by the preceding paragraph and any other functions conferred on the authority by any of the relevant statutory provisions in accordance with such guidance as the Commission may give to the authority.

(6) Nothing in the provisions of this Act or of any regulations made thereunder charging any person in Scotland with the enforcement of any of the relevant statutory provisions shall be construed as authorising that person to institute proceedings for any offence.

(7) In this Part—

(*a*) " enforcing authority " means the Executive or any other authority which is by any of the relevant statutory provisions or by regulations under subsection (2) above made responsible for the enforcement of any of those provisions to any extent; and

(*b*) any reference to an enforcing authority's field of responsibility is a reference to the field over which that authority's responsibility for the enforcement of those provisions extends for the time being;

but where by virtue of paragraph (*a*) of section 13(1) the performance of any function of the Commission or the Executive is delegated to a government department or person, references to the Commission or the Executive (or to an enforcing authority where that authority is the Executive) in any provision of this Part which relates to that function shall, so far as may be necessary to give effect to any agreement under that paragraph, be construed as references to that department or person; and accordingly any reference to the field of responsibility of an enforcing authority shall be construed as a reference to the field over which that department or person for the time being performs such a function.

Appointment of inspectors.

19.—(1) Every enforcing authority may appoint as inspectors (under whatever title it may from time to time determine) such persons having suitable qualifications as it thinks necessary for carrying into effect the relevant statutory provisions within its field of responsibility, and may terminate any appointment made under this section.

(2) Every appointment of a person as an inspector under this section shall be made by an instrument in writing specifying which of the powers conferred on inspectors by the relevant statutory provisions are to be exercisable by the person appointed; and an inspector shall in right of his appointment under this section—

(*a*) be entitled to exercise only such of those powers as are so specified; and

(*b*) be entitled to exercise the powers so specified only within the field of responsibility of the authority which appointed him.

(3) So much of an inspector's instrument of appointment as specifies the powers which he is entitled to exercise may be varied by the enforcing authority which appointed him.

(4) An inspector shall, if so required when exercising or seeking to exercise any power conferred on him by any of the relevant statutory provisions, produced his instrument of appointment or a duly authenticated copy thereof.

Powers of inspectors.

20.—(1) Subject to the provisions of section 19 and this section, an inspector may, for the purpose of carrying into effect any of the relevant statutory provisions within the field of responsibility of the enforcing authority which appointed him, exercise the powers set out in subsection (2) below.

(2) The powers of an inspector referred to in the preceding subsection are the following, namely—

(*a*) at any reasonable time (or, in a situation which in his opinion is or may be dangerous, at any time) to enter any premises which he has reason to believe it is necessary for him to enter for the purpose mentioned in subsection (1) above;

(*b*) to take with him a constable if he has reasonable cause to apprehend any serious obstruction in the execution of his duty;

(*c*) without prejudice to the preceding paragraph, on entering any premises by virtue of paragraph (*a*) above to take with him—

(i) any other person duly authorised by his (the inspector's) enforcing authority; and

(ii) any equipment or materials required for any purpose for which the power of entry is being exercised;

(*d*) to make such examination and investigation as may in any circumstances be necessary for the purpose mentioned in subsection (1) above;

PART I

(*e*) as regards any premises which he has power to enter, to direct that those premises or any part of them, or anything therein, shall be left undisturbed (whether generally or in particular respects) for so long as is reasonably necessary for the purpose of any examination or investigation under paragraph (*d*) above;

(*f*) to take such measurements and photographs and make such recordings as he considers necessary for the purpose of any examination or investigation under paragraph (*d*) above;

(*g*) to take samples of any articles or substances found in any premises which he has power to enter, and of the atmosphere in or in the vicinity of any such premises;

(*h*) in the case of any article or substance found in any premises which he has power to enter, being an article or substance which appears to him to have caused or to be likely to cause danger to health or safety, to cause it to be dismantled or subjected to any process or test (but not so as to damage or destroy it unless this is in the circumstances necessary for the purpose mentioned in subsection (1) above);

(*i*) in the case of any such article or substance as is mentioned in the preceding paragraph, to take possession of it and detain it for so long as is necessary for all or any of the following purposes, namely—

(i) to examine it and do to it anything which he has power to do under that paragraph;

(ii) to ensure that it is not tampered with before his examination of it is completed;

(iii) to ensure that it is available for use as evidence in any proceedings for an offence under any of the relevant statutory provisions or any proceedings relating to a notice under section 21 or 22;

(*j*) to require any person whom he has reasonable cause to believe to be able to give any information relevant to any examination or investigation under paragraph (*d*) above to answer (in the absence of persons other than a person nominated by him to be present and any persons whom the inspector may allow to be present) such questions as the inspector thinks fit to ask and to sign a declaration of the truth of his answers;

(*k*) to require the production of, inspect, and take copies of or of any entry in—

(i) any books or documents which by virtue of any of the relevant statutory provisions are required to be kept; and

(ii) any other books or documents which it is necessary for him to see for the purposes of any examination or investigation under paragraph (*d*) above;

(*l*) to require any person to afford him such facilities and assistance with respect to any matters or things within that person's control or in relation to which that person has responsibilities as are necessary to enable the inspector to exercise any of the powers conferred on him by this section;

(*m*) any other power which is necessary for the purpose mentioned in subsection (1) above.

(3) The Secretary of State may by regulations make provision as to the procedure to be followed in connection with the taking of samples under subsection (2)(*g*) above (including provision as to the way in which samples that have been so taken are to be dealt with).

(4) Where an inspector proposes to exercise the power conferred by subsection (2)(*h*) above in the case of an article or substance found in any premises, he shall, if so requested by a person who at the time is present in and has responsibilities in relation to those premises, cause anything which is to be done by virtue of that power to be done in the presence of that person unless the inspector considers that its being done in that person's presence would be prejudicial to the safety of the State.

(5) Before exercising the power conferred by subsection (2)(*h*) above in the case of any article or substance, an inspector shall consult such persons as appear to him appropriate for the purpose of ascertaining what dangers, if any, there may be in doing anything which he proposes to do under that power.

(6) Where under the power conferred by subsection (2)(*i*) above an inspector takes possession of any article or substance found in any premises, he shall leave there, either with a responsible person or, if that is impracticable, fixed in a conspicuous position, a notice giving particulars of that article or substance sufficient to identify it and stating that he has taken possession of it under that power; and before taking possession of any such substance under that power an inspector shall, if it is practicable for him to do so, take a sample thereof and give to a responsible person at the premises a portion of the sample marked in a manner sufficient to identify it.

(7) No answer given by a person in pursuance of a requirement imposed under subsection (2)(*j*) above shall be admissible in evidence against that person or the husband or wife of that person in any proceedings.

PART I

(8) Nothing in this section shall be taken to compel the production by any person of a document of which he would on grounds of legal professional privilege be entitled to withhold production on an order for discovery in an action in the High Court or, as the case may be, on an order for the production of documents in an action in the Court of Session.

Improvement notices.

21. If an inspector is of the opinion that a person—

(*a*) is contravening one or more of the relevant statutory provisions ; or

(*b*) has contravened one or more of those provisions in circumstances that make it likely that the contravention will continue or be repeated,

he may serve on him a notice (in this Part referred to as " an improvement notice ") stating that he is of that opinion, specifying the provision or provisions as to which he is of that opinion, giving particulars of the reasons why he is of that opinion, and requiring that person to remedy the contravention or, as the case may be, the matters occasioning it within such period (ending not earlier than the period within which an appeal against the notice can be brought under section 24) as may be specified in the notice.

Prohibition notices.

22.—(1) This section applies to any activities which are being or are about to be carried on by or under the control of any person, being activities to or in relation to which any of the relevant statutory provisions apply or will, if the activities are so carried on, apply.

(2) If as regards any activities to which this section applies an inspector is of the opinion that, as carried on or about to be carried on by or under the control of the person in question, the activities involve or, as the case may be, will involve a risk of serious personal injury, the inspector may serve on that person a notice (in this Part referred to as " a prohibition notice ").

(3) A prohibition notice shall—

(*a*) state that the inspector is of the said opinion ;

(*b*) specify the matters which in his opinion give or, as the case may be, will give rise to the said risk ;

(*c*) where in his opinion any of those matters involves or, as the case may be, will involve a contravention of any of the relevant statutory provisions, state that he is of that opinion, specify the provision or provisions as to which he is of that opinion, and give particulars of the reasons why he is of that opinion ; and

(*d*) direct that the activities to which the notice relates shall not be carried on by or under the control of the person on whom the notice is served unless the matters specified in the notice in pursuance of paragraph (*b*) above and any associated contraventions of provisions so specified in pursuance of paragraph (*c*) above have been remedied. PART I

(4) A direction given in pursuance of subsection (3)(*d*) above shall take immediate effect if the inspector is of the opinion, and states it, that the risk of serious personal injury is or, as the case may be, will be imminent, and shall have effect at the end of a period specified in the notice in any other case.

Provisions supplementary to ss. 21 and 22.

23.—(1) In this section " a notice " means an improvement notice or a prohibition notice.

(2) A notice may (but need not) include directions as to the measures to be taken to remedy any contravention or matter to which the notice relates ; and any such directions—

(*a*) may be framed to any extent by reference to any approved code of practice ; and

(*b*) may be framed so as to afford the person on whom the notice is served a choice between different ways of remedying the contravention or matter.

(3) Where any of the relevant statutory provisions applies to a building or any matter connected with a building and an inspector proposes to serve an improvement notice relating to a contravention of that provision in connection with that building or matter, the notice shall not direct any measures to be taken to remedy the contravention of that provision which are more onerous than those necessary to secure conformity with the requirements of any building regulations for the time being in force to which that building or matter would be required to conform if the relevant building were being newly erected unless the provision in question imposes specific requirements more onerous than the requirements of any such building regulations to which the building or matter would be required to conform as aforesaid.

In this subsection " the relevant building ", in the case of a building, means that building, and, in the case of a matter connected with a building, means the building with which the matter is connected.

(4) Before an inspector serves in connection with any premises used or about to be used as a place of work a notice requiring or likely to lead to the taking of measures affecting the means of escape in case of fire with which the premises are or ought to be provided, he shall consult the fire authority.

In this subsection " fire authority " has the meaning assigned by section 43(1) of the Fire Precautions Act 1971. 1971 c. 40.

PART I

(5) Where an improvement notice or a prohibition notice which is not to take immediate effect has been served—

(*a*) the notice may be withdrawn by an inspector at any time before the end of the period specified therein in pursuance of section 21 or section 22(4) as the case may be ; and

(*b*) the period so specified may be extended or further extended by an inspector at any time when an appeal against the notice is not pending.

(6) In the application of this section to Scotland—

(*a*) in subsection (3) for the words from " with the requirements " to " aforesaid " there shall be substituted the words—

" (*a*) to any provisions of the building standards regulations to which that building or matter would be required to conform if the relevant building were being newly erected ; or

1959 c. 24.

(*b*) where the sheriff, on an appeal to him under section 16 of the Building (Scotland) Act 1959—

(i) against an order under section 10 of that Act requiring the execution of operations necessary to make the building or matter conform to the building standards regulations, or

(ii) against an order under section 11 of that Act requiring the building or matter to conform to a provision of such regulations,

has varied the order, to any provisions of the building standards regulations referred to in paragraph (*a*) above as affected by the order as so varied,

unless the relevant statutory provision imposes specific requirements more onerous than the requirements of any provisions of building standards regulations as aforesaid or, as the case may be, than the requirements of the order as varied by the sheriff." ;

(*b*) after subsection (5) there shall be inserted the following subsection—

" (5A) In subsection (3) above ' building standards regulations ' has the same meaning as in section 3 of the Building (Scotland) Act 1959.".

Appeal against improvement or prohibition notice.

24.—(1) In this section " a notice " means an improvement notice or a prohibition notice.

(2) A person on whom a notice is served may within such period from the date of its service as may be prescribed appeal to an industrial tribunal ; and on such an appeal the tribunal

PART I

may either cancel or affirm the notice and, if it affirms it, may do so either in its original form or with such modifications as the tribunal may in the circumstances think fit.

(3) Where an appeal under this section is brought against a notice within the period allowed under the preceding subsection, then—

(*a*) in the case of an improvement notice, the bringing of the appeal shall have the effect of suspending the operation of the notice until the appeal is finally disposed of or, if the appeal is withdrawn, until the withdrawal of the appeal;

(*b*) in the case of a prohibition notice, the bringing of the appeal shall have the like effect if, but only if, on the application of the appellant the tribunal so directs (and then only from the giving of the direction).

(4) One or more assessors may be appointed for the purposes of any proceedings brought before an industrial tribunal under this section.

Power to deal with cause of imminent danger.

25.—(1) Where, in the case of any article or substance found by him in any premises which he has power to enter, an inspector has reasonable cause to believe that, in the circumstances in which he finds it, the article or substance is a cause of imminent danger of serious personal injury, he may seize it and cause it to be rendered harmless (whether by destruction or otherwise).

(2) Before there is rendered harmless under this section—

(*a*) any article that forms part of a batch of similar articles; or

(*b*) any substance,

the inspector shall, if it is practicable for him to do so, take a sample thereof and give to a responsible person at the premises where the article or substance was found by him a portion of the sample marked in a manner sufficient to identify it.

(3) As soon as may be after any article or substance has been seized and rendered harmless under this section, the inspector shall prepare and sign a written report giving particulars of the circumstances in which the article or substance was seized and so dealt with by him, and shall—

(*a*) give a signed copy of the report to a responsible person at the premises where the article or substance was found by him; and

PART I

(*b*) unless that person is the owner of the article or substance, also serve a signed copy of the report on the owner;

and if, where paragraph (*b*) above applies, the inspector cannot after reasonable enquiry ascertain the name or address of the owner, the copy may be served on him by giving it to the person to whom a copy was given under the preceding paragraph.

Power of enforcing authorities to indemnify their inspectors.

26. Where an action has been brought against an inspector in respect of an act done in the execution or purported execution of any of the relevant statutory provisions and the circumstances are such that he is not legally entitled to require the enforcing authority which appointed him to indemnify him, that authority may, nevertheless, indemnify him against the whole or part of any damages and costs or expenses which he may have been ordered to pay or may have incurred, if the authority is satisfied that he honestly believed that the act complained of was within his powers and that his duty as an inspector required or entitled him to do it.

Obtaining and disclosure of information

Obtaining of information by the Commission, the Executive, enforcing authorities etc.

27.—(1) For the purpose of obtaining—

(*a*) any information which the Commission needs for the discharge of its functions; or

(*b*) any information which an enforcing authority needs for the discharge of the authority's functions,

the Commission may, with the consent of the Secretary of State, serve on any person a notice requiring that person to furnish to the Commission or, as the case may be, to the enforcing authority in question such information about such matters as may be specified in the notice, and to do so in such form and manner and within such time as may be so specified.

In this subsection " consent " includes a general consent extending to cases of any stated description.

1947 c. 39.

(2) Nothing in section 9 of the Statistics of Trade Act 1947 (which restricts the disclosure of information obtained under that Act) shall prevent or penalise—

(*a*) the disclosure by a Minister of the Crown to the Commission or the Executive of information obtained under that Act about any undertaking within the meaning of that Act, being information consisting of the names and address of the persons carrying on the undertaking, the nature of the undertaking's activities, the numbers of persons of different descriptions who work in the undertaking, the addresses or places where activities of the undertaking are or were carried on, the nature of the activities carried on there, or the numbers of persons of different descriptions who work or worked in the undertaking there ; or

(*b*) the disclosure by the Manpower Services Commission, the Employment Service Agency or the Training Services Agency to the Commission or the Executive of information so obtained which is of a kind specified in a notice in writing given to the disclosing body and the recipient of the information by the Secretary of State under this paragraph.

(3) In the preceding subsection any reference to a Minister of the Crown, the Commission, the Executive, the Manpower Services Commission or either of the said Agencies includes respectively a reference to an officer of his or of that body and also, in the case of a reference to the Commission, includes a reference to—

(*a*) a person performing any functions of the Commission or the Executive on its behalf by virtue of section 13(1)(*a*) ;

(*b*) an officer of a body which is so performing any such functions ; and

(*c*) an adviser appointed in pursuance of section 13(1)(*d*).

(4) A person to whom information is disclosed in pursuance of subsection (2) above shall not use the information for a purpose other than a purpose of the Commission or, as the case may be, of the Executive.

Restrictions on disclosure of information.

28.—(1) In this and the two following subsections—

(*a*) " relevant information " means information obtained by a person under section 27(1) or furnished to any person in pursuance of a requirement imposed by any of the relevant statutory provisions ; and

(*b*) " the recipient ", in relation to any relevant information, means the person by whom that information was so obtained or to whom that information was so furnished, as the case may be.

(2) Subject to the following subsection, no relevant information shall be disclosed without the consent of the person by whom it was furnished.

(3) The preceding subsection shall not apply to—

(*a*) disclosure of information to the Commission, the Executive, a government department or any enforcing authority ;

PART I

(*b*) without prejudice to paragraph (*a*) above, disclosure by the recipient of information to any person for the purpose of any function conferred on the recipient by or under any of the relevant statutory provisions;

(*c*) without prejudice to paragraph (*a*) above, disclosure by the recipient of information to—

(i) an officer of a local authority who is authorised by that authority to receive it,

(ii) an officer of a water authority or water development board who is authorised by that authority or board to receive it,

(iii) an officer of a river purification board who is authorised by that board to receive it, or

(iv) a constable authorised by a chief officer of police to receive it;

(*d*) disclosure by the recipient of information in a form calculated to prevent it from being identified as relating to a particular person or case;

(*e*) disclosure of information for the purposes of any legal proceedings or any investigation or inquiry held by virtue of section 14(2), or for the purposes of a report of any such proceedings or inquiry or of a special report made by virtue of section 14(2).

(4) In the preceding subsection any reference to the Commission, the Executive, a government department or an enforcing authority includes respectively a reference to an officer of that body or authority (including, in the case of an enforcing authority, any inspector appointed by it), and also, in the case of a reference to the Commission, includes a reference to—

(*a*) a person performing any functions of the Commission or the Executive on its behalf by virtue of section 13(1)(*a*);

(*b*) an officer of a body which is so performing any such functions; and

(*c*) an adviser appointed in pursuance of section 13(1)(*d*).

(5) A person to whom information is disclosed in pursuance of subsection (3) above shall not use the information for a purpose other than—

(*a*) in a case falling within paragraph (*a*) of that subsection, a purpose of the Commission or of the Executive or of the government department in question, or the purposes of the enforcing authority in question in connection with the relevant statutory provisions, as the case may be;

(*b*) in the case of information given to an officer of a local authority or of a water authority or of a river purification board or water development board, the purposes of the authority or board in connection with the relevant statutory provisions or any enactment whatsoever relating to public health, public safety or the protection of the environment;

(*c*) in the case of information given to a constable, the purposes of the police in connection with the relevant statutory provisions or any enactment whatsoever relating to public health, public safety or the safety of the State.

(6) In subsections (3)(*c*) and (5) above, before 16th May 1975, the references to a water authority in their application to Scotland shall be construed as references to a regional water board.

(7) A person shall not disclose any information obtained by him as a result of the exercise of any power conferred by section 14(4)(*a*) or 20 (including, in particular, any information with respect to any trade secret obtained by him in any premises entered by him by virtue of any such power) except—

(*a*) for the purposes of his functions; or

(*b*) for the purposes of any legal proceedings or any investigation or inquiry held by virtue of section 14(2) or for the purposes of a report of any such proceedings or inquiry or of a special report made by virtue of section 14(2); or

(*c*) with the relevant consent.

In this subsection "the relevant consent" means, in the case of information furnished in pursuance of a requirement imposed under section 20, the consent of the person who furnished it, and, in any other case, the consent of a person having responsibilities in relation to the premises where the information was obtained.

(8) Notwithstanding anything in the preceding subsection an inspector shall, in circumstances in which it is necessary to do so for the purpose of assisting in keeping persons (or the representatives of persons) employed at any premises adequately informed about matters affecting their health, safety and welfare, give to such persons or their representatives the following descriptions of information, that is to say—

(*a*) factual information obtained by him as mentioned in that subsection which relates to those premises or anything which was or is therein or was or is being done therein; and

PART I

(*b*) information with respect to any action which he has taken or proposes to take in or in connection with those premises in the performance of his functions ;

and, where an inspector does as aforesaid, he shall give the like information to the employer of the first-mentioned persons.

["(9) Notwithstanding anything in subsection (7) above, a person who has obtained such information as is referred to in that subsection may furnish to a person who appears to him to be likely to be a party to any civil proceedings arising out of any accident, occurrence, situation or other matter, a written statement of relevant facts observed by him in the course of exercising any of the powers referred to in that subsection.".]

. . .

Provisions as to offences

Offences.

33.—(1) It is an offence for a person—

(*a*) to fail to discharge a duty to which he is subject by virtue of sections 2 to 7 ;

(*b*) to contravene section 8 or 9 ;

(*c*) to contravene any health and safety regulations... ...or any requirement or prohibition imposed under any such regulations (including any requirement or prohibition to which he is subject by virtue of the terms of or any condition or restriction attached to any licence, approval, exemption or other authority issued, given or granted under the regulations) ;

(*d*) to contravene any requirement imposed by or under regulations under section 14 or intentionally to obstruct any person in the exercise of his powers under that section ;

(*e*) to contravene any requirement imposed by an inspector under section 20 or 25 ;

(*f*) to prevent or attempt to prevent any other person from appearing before an inspector or from answering any question to which an inspector may by virtue of section 20(2) require an answer ;

(*g*) to contravene any requirement or prohibition imposed by an improvement notice or a prohibition notice (including any such notice as modified on appeal) ;

(*h*) intentionally to obstruct an inspector in the exercise or performance of his powers or duties ;

(*i*) to contravene any requirement imposed by a notice under section 27(1) ;

(*j*) to use or disclose any information in contravention of section 27(4) or 28 ;

(*k*) to make a statement which he knows to be false or recklessly to make a statement which is false where the statement is made—

(i) in purported compliance with a requirement to furnish any information imposed by or under any of the relevant statutory provisions ; or

(ii) for the purpose of obtaining the issue of a document under any of the relevant statutory provisions to himself or another person ;

(*l*) intentionally to make a false entry in any register, book, notice or other document required by or under any of the relevant statutory provisions to be kept, served or given or, with intent to deceive, to make use of any such entry which he knows to be false ;

(*m*) with intent to deceive, to forge or use a document issued or authorised to be issued under any of the relevant statutory provisions or required for any purpose thereunder or to make or have in his possession a document so closely resembling any such document as to be calculated to deceive ;

(*n*) falsely to pretend to be an inspector ;

(*o*) to fail to comply with an order made by a court under section 42.

(2) A person guilty of an offence under paragraph (*d*), (*f*), (*h*) or (*n*) of subsection (1) above, or of an offence under paragraph (*e*) of that subsection consisting of contravening a requirement imposed by an inspector under section 20, shall be liable on summary conviction to a fine not exceeding £400.

(3) Subject to any provision made by virtue of section 15(6)(*d*) or by virtue of paragraph 2(2) of Schedule 3, a person guilty of an offence under any paragraph of subsection (1)

PART I

above not mentioned in the preceding subsection, or of an offence under subsection (1)(*e*) above not falling within the preceding subsection, or of an offence under any of the existing statutory provisions, being an offence for which no other penalty is specified, shall be liable—

(*a*) on summary conviction, to a fine not exceeding £400;

(*b*) on conviction on indictment—

(i) if the offence is one to which this sub-paragraph applies, to imprisonment for a term not exceeding two years, or a fine, or both;

(ii) if the offence is not one to which the preceding sub-paragraph applies, to a fine.

(4) Subsection (3)(*b*)(i) above applies to the following offences—

(*a*) an offence consisting of contravening any of the relevant statutory provisions by doing otherwise than under the authority of a licence issued by the Executive ... ... something for the doing of which such a licence is necessary under the relevant statutory provisions;

(*b*) an offence consisting of contravening a term of or a condition or restriction attached to any such licence as is mentioned in the preceding paragraph;

(*c*) an offence consisting of acquiring or attempting to acquire, possessing or using an explosive article or substance (within the meaning of any of the relevant statutory provisions) in contravention of any of the relevant statutory provisions;

(*d*) an offence under subsection (1)(*g*) above consisting of contravening a requirement or prohibition imposed by a prohibition notice;

(*e*) an offence under subsection (1)(*j*) above.

(5) Where a person is convicted of an offence under subsection (1)(*g*) or (*o*) above, then, if the contravention in respect of which he was convicted is continued after the conviction he shall (subject to section 42(3)) be guilty of a further offence and liable in respect thereof to a fine not exceeding £50 for each day on which the contravention is so continued.

1913 c. 27.

(6) In this section " forge " has, for England and Wales, the same meaning as in the Forgery Act 1913.

Extension of time for bringing summary proceedings.

34.—(1) Where—

(*a*) a special report on any matter to which section 14 of this Act applies is made by virtue of subsection (2)(*a*) of that section; or

PART I

(*b*) a report is made by the person holding an inquiry into any such matter by virtue of subsection (2)(*b*) of that section; or

(*c*) a coroner's inquest is held touching the death of any person whose death may have been caused by an accident which happened while he was at work or by a disease which he contracted or probably contracted at work or by any accident, act or omission which occurred in connection with the work of any person whatsoever; or

(*d*) a public inquiry into any death that may have been so caused is held under the Fatal Accidents Inquiry (Scotland) Act 1895 or the Fatal Accidents and Sudden Deaths Inquiry (Scotland) Act 1906, 1895 c. 36. 1906 c. 35.

and it appears from the report or, in a case falling within paragraph (*c*) or (*d*) above, from the proceedings at the inquest or inquiry, that any of the relevant statutory provisions was contravened at a time which is material in relation to the subject-matter of the report, inquest or inquiry, summary proceedings against any person liable to be proceeded against in respect of the contravention may be commenced at any time within three months of the making of the report or, in a case falling within paragraph (*c*) or (*d*) above, within three months of the conclusion of the inquest or inquiry.

(2) Where an offence under any of the relevant statutory provisions is committed by reason of a failure to do something at or within a time fixed by or under any of those provisions, the offence shall be deemed to continue until that thing is done.

(3) Summary proceedings for an offence to which this subsection applies may be commenced at any time within six months from the date on which there comes to the knowledge of a responsible enforcing authority evidence sufficient in the opinion of that authority to justify a prosecution for that offence; and for the purposes of this subsection—

(*a*) a certificate of an enforcing authority stating that such evidence came to its knowledge on a specified date shall be conclusive evidence of that fact; and

(*b*) a document purporting to be such a certificate and to be signed by or on behalf of the enforcing authority in question shall be presumed to be such a certificate unless the contrary is proved.

(4) The preceding subsection applies to any offence under any of the relevant statutory provisions which a person commits by virtue of any provision or requirement to which he is subject as the designer, manufacturer, importer or supplier of any thing;

PART I

and in that subsection " responsible enforcing authority " means an enforcing authority within whose field of responsibility the offence in question lies, whether by virtue of section 35 or otherwise.

(5) In the application of subsection (3) above to Scotland—

(*a*) for the words from " there comes " to " that offence " there shall be substituted the words " evidence, sufficient in the opinion of the enforcing authority to justify a report to the Lord Advocate with a view to consideration of the question of prosecution, comes to the knowledge of the authority " ;

(*b*) at the end of paragraph (*b*) there shall be added the words " and

(*c*) section 23(2) of the Summary Jurisdiction (Scotland) Act 1954 (date of commencement of proceedings) shall have effect as it has effect for the purposes of that section.".

1954 c. 48.

Venue.

35. An offence under any of the relevant statutory provisions committed in connection with any plant or substance may, if necessary for the purpose of bringing the offence within the field of responsibility of any enforcing authority or conferring jurisdiction on any court to entertain proceedings for the offence, be treated as having been committed at the place where that plant or substance is for the time being.

Offences due to fault of other person.

36.—(1) Where the commission by any person of an offence under any of the relevant statutory provisions is due to the act or default of some other person, that other person shall be guilty of the offence, and a person may be charged with and convicted of the offence by virtue of this subsection whether or not proceedings are taken against the first-mentioned person.

(2) Where there would be or have been the commission of an offence under section 33 by the Crown but for the circumstance that that section does not bind the Crown, and that fact is due to the act or default of a person other than the Crown, that person shall be guilty of the offence which, but for that circumstance, the Crown would be committing or would have committed, and may be charged with and convicted of that offence accordingly.

(3) The preceding provisions of this section are subject to any provision made by virtue of section 15(6).

Offences by bodies corporate.

37.—(1) Where an offence under any of the relevant statutory provisions committed by a body corporate is proved to have been committed with the consent or connivance of, or to have

PART I

been attributable to any neglect on the part of, any director, manager, secretary or other similar officer of the body corporate or a person who was purporting to act in any such capacity, he as well as the body corporate shall be guilty of that offence and shall be liable to be proceeded against and punished accordingly.

(2) Where the affairs of a body corporate are managed by its members, the preceding subsection shall apply in relation to the acts and defaults of a member in connection with his functions of management as if he were a director of the body corporate.

Restriction on institution of proceedings in England and Wales.

38. Proceedings for an offence under any of the relevant statutory provisions shall not, in England and Wales, be instituted except by an inspector or by or with the consent of the Director of Public Prosecutions.

Prosecutions by inspectors

39.—(1) An inspector, if authorised in that behalf by the enforcing authority which appointed him, may, although not of counsel or a solicitor, prosecute before a magistrates' court proceedings for an offence under any of the relevant statutory provisions.

(2) This section shall not apply to Scotland.

Onus of proving limits of what is practicable etc.

40. In any proceedings for an offence under any of the relevant statutory provisions consisting of a failure to comply with a duty or requirement to do something so far as is practicable or so far as is reasonably practicable, or to use the best practicable means to do something, it shall be for the accused to prove (as the case may be) that it was not practicable or not reasonably practicable to do more than was in fact done to satisfy the duty or requirement, or that there was no better practicable means than was in fact used to satisfy the duty or requirement.

Evidence.

41.—(1) Where an entry is required by any of the relevant statutory provisions to be made in any register or other record, the entry, if made, shall, as against the person by or on whose behalf it was made, be admissible as evidence or in Scotland sufficient evidence of the facts stated therein.

(2) Where an entry which is so required to be so made with respect to the observance of any of the relevant statutory provisions has not been made, that fact shall be admissible as evidence or in Scotland sufficient evidence that that provision has not been observed.

PART I

Power of court to order cause of offence to be remedied or, in certain cases, forfeiture.

42.—(1) Where a person is convicted of an offence under any of the relevant statutory provisions in respect of any matters which appear to the court to be matters which it is in his power to remedy, the court may, in addition to or instead of imposing any punishment, order him, within such time as may be fixed by the order, to take such steps as may be specified in the order for remedying the said matters.

(2) The time fixed by an order under subsection (1) above may be extended or further extended by order of the court on an application made before the end of that time as originally fixed or as extended under this subsection, as the case may be.

(3) Where a person is ordered under subsection (1) above to remedy any matters, that person shall not be liable under any of the relevant statutory provisions in respect of those matters in so far as they continue during the time fixed by the order or any further time allowed under subsection (2) above.

(4) Subject to the following subsection, the court by or before which a person is convicted of an offence such as is mentioned in section 33(4)(*c*) in respect of any such explosive article or substance as is there mentioned may order the article or substance in question to be forfeited and either destroyed or dealt with in such other manner as the court may order.

(5) The court shall not order anything to be forfeited under the preceding subsection where a person claiming to be the owner of or otherwise interested in it applies to be heard by the court, unless an opportunity has been given to him to show cause why the order should not be made.

Financial provisions

Financial provisions.

43.—(1) It shall be the duty of the Secretary of State to pay to the Commission such sums as are approved by the Treasury and as he considers appropriate for the purpose of enabling the Commission to perform its functions; and it shall be the duty of the Commission to pay to the Executive such sums as the Commission considers appropriate for the purpose of enabling the Executive to perform its functions.

(2) Regulations may provide for such fees as may be fixed by or determined under the regulations to be payable for or in connection with the performance by or on behalf of any authority to which this subsection applies of any function conferred on that authority by or under any of the relevant statutory provisions.

(3) Subsection (2) above applies to the following authorities, namely the Commission, the Executive, the Secretary of State,

. . . . . . every enforcing authority, and any other person on whom any function is conferred by or under any of the relevant statutory provisions. PART I

(4) Regulations under this section may specify the person by whom any fee payable under the regulations is to be paid; but no such fee shall be made payable by a person in any of the following capacities, namely an employee, a person seeking employment, a person training for employment, and a person seeking training for employment.

(5) Without prejudice to section 82(3), regulations under this section may fix or provide for the determination of different fees in relation to different functions, or in relation to the same function in different circumstances.

[" (6) The power to make regulations under this section shall be exercisable by the Secretary of State, the Minister of Agriculture, Fisheries and Food or the Secretary of State and that Minister acting jointly.".]

• • •

(8) In subsection (4) above the references to a person training for employment and a person seeking training for employment shall include respectively a person attending an industrial rehabilitation course provided by virtue of the Employment and Training Act 1973 and a person seeking to attend such a course. 1973 c. 50.

(9) For the purposes of this section the performance by an inspector of his functions shall be treated as the performance by the enforcing authority which appointed him of functions conferred on that authority by or under any of the relevant statutory provisions.

PART I

Miscellaneous and supplementary

Appeals in connection with licensing provisions in the relevant statutory provisions.

44.—(1) Any person who is aggrieved by a decision of an authority having power to issue licences (other than . . . . . . nuclear site licences) under any of the relevant statutory provisions—

(*a*) refusing to issue him a licence, to renew a licence held by him, or to transfer to him a licence held by another;

(*b*) issuing him a licence on or subject to any term, condition or restriction whereby he is aggrieved;

(*c*) varying or refusing to vary any term, condition or restriction on or subject to which a licence is held by him; or

(*d*) revoking a licence held by him,

may appeal to the Secretary of State.

(2) The Secretary of State may, in such cases as he considers it appropriate to do so, having regard to the nature of the questions which appear to him to arise, direct that an appeal under this section shall be determined on his behalf by a person appointed by him for that purpose.

(3) Before the determination of an appeal the Secretary of State shall ask the appellant and the authority against whose decision the appeal is brought whether they wish to appear and be heard on the appeal and—

(*a*) the appeal may be determined without a hearing of the parties if both of them express a wish not to appear and be heard as aforesaid;

(*b*) the Secretary of State shall, if either of the parties expresses a wish to appear and be heard, afford to both of them an opportunity of so doing.

1971 c. 62.

(4) The Tribunals and Inquiries Act 1971 shall apply to a hearing held by a person appointed in pursuance of subsection (2) above to determine an appeal as it applies to a statutory inquiry held by the Secretary of State, but as if in section 12(1) of that Act (statement of reasons for decisions) the reference to any decision taken by the Secretary of State included a reference to a decision taken on his behalf by that person.

(5) A person who determines an appeal under this section on behalf of the Secretary of State and the Secretary of State, if he determines such an appeal, may give such directions as he considers appropriate to give effect to his determination.

(6) The Secretary of State may pay to any person appointed to hear or determine an appeal under this section on his behalf such remuneration and allowances as the Secretary of State may with the approval of the Minister for the Civil Service determine.

(7) In this section— PART I

(*a*) " licence " means a licence under any of the relevant statutory provisions other than a . . .
. . . nuclear site licence ;

(*b*) " nuclear site licence " means a licence to use a site for the purpose of installing or operating a nuclear installation within the meaning of the following subsection.

(8) For the purposes of the preceding subsection " nuclear installation " means—

(*a*) a nuclear reactor (other than such a reactor comprised in a means of transport, whether by land, water or air) ; or

(*b*) any other installation of such class or description as may be prescribed for the purposes of this paragraph or section 1(1)(*b*) of the Nuclear Installations Act 1965, being an installation designed or adapted for— 1965 c. 57.

(i) the production or use of atomic energy ; or

(ii) the carrying out of any process which is preparatory or ancillary to the production or use of atomic energy and which involves or is capable of causing the emission of ionising radiations ; or

(iii) the storage, processing or disposal of nuclear fuel or of bulk quantities of other radioactive matter, being matter which has been produced or irradiated in the course of the production or use of nuclear fuel ;

and in this subsection—

" atomic energy " has the meaning assigned by the Atomic Energy Act 1946 ; 1946 c. 80.

" nuclear reactor " means any plant (including any machinery, equipment or appliance, whether affixed to land or not) designed or adapted for the production of atomic energy by a fission process in which a controlled chain reaction can be maintained without an additional source of neutrons.

Default powers.

45.—(1) Where, in the case of a local authority who are an enforcing authority, the Commission is of the opinion that an investigation should be made as to whether that local authority have failed to perform any of their enforcement functions the Commission may make a report to the Secretary of State.

(2) The Secretary of State may, after considering a report submitted to him under the preceding subsection, cause a local inquiry to be held ; and the provisions of subsections (2) to (5) of section 250 of the Local Government Act 1972 as to local inquiries shall, without prejudice to the generality of subsection (1) of that section, apply to a local inquiry so held 1972 c. 70.

Part I as they apply to a local inquiry held in pursuance of that section.

(3) If the Secretary of State is satisfied, after having caused a local inquiry to be held into the matter, that a local authority have failed to perform any of their enforcement functions, he may make an order declaring the authority to be in default.

(4) An order made by virtue of the preceding subsection which declares an authority to be in default may, for the purpose of remedying the default, direct the authority (hereafter in this section referred to as " the defaulting authority ") to perform such of their enforcement functions as are specified in the order in such manner as may be so specified and may specify the time or times within which those functions are to be performed by the authority.

(5) If the defaulting authority fail to comply with any direction contained in such an order the Secretary of State may, instead of enforcing the order by mandamus, make an order transferring to the Executive such of the enforcement functions of the defaulting authority as he thinks fit.

(6) Where any enforcement functions of the defaulting authority are transferred in pursuance of the preceding subsection, the amount of any expenses which the Executive certifies were incurred by it in performing those functions shall on demand be paid to it by the defaulting authority.

(7) Any expenses which in pursuance of the preceding subsection are required to be paid by the defaulting authority in respect of any enforcement functions transferred in pursuance of this section shall be defrayed by the authority in the like manner, and shall be debited to the like account, as if the enforcement functions had not been transferred and the expenses had been incurred by the authority in performing them.

(8) Where the defaulting authority are required to defray any such expenses the authority shall have the like powers for the purpose of raising the money for defraying those expenses as they would have had for the purpose of raising money required for defraying expenses incurred for the purpose of the enforcement functions in question.

(9) An order transferring any enforcement functions of the defaulting authority in pursuance of subsection (5) above may provide for the transfer to the Executive of such of the rights, liabilities and obligations of the authority as the Secretary of State considers appropriate ; and where such an order is revoked the Secretary of State may, by the revoking order or a

subsequent order, make such provision as he considers appropriate with respect to any rights, liabilities and obligations held by the Executive for the purposes of the transferred enforcement functions. PART I

(10) The Secretary of State may by order vary or revoke any order previously made by him in pursuance of this section.

(11) In this section "enforcement functions", in relation to a local authority, means the functions of the authority as an enforcing authority.

(12) In the application of this section to Scotland—

(*a*) in subsection (2) for the words "subsections (2) to (5) of section 250 of the Local Government Act 1972" there shall be substituted the words "subsections (2) to (8) of section 210 of the Local Government (Scotland) Act 1973", except that before 16th May 1975 for the said words there shall be substituted the words "subsections (2) to (9) of section 355 of the Local Government (Scotland) Act 1947"; 1972 c. 70. 1973 c. 65. 1947 c. 43.

(*b*) in subsection (5) the words "instead of enforcing the order by mandamus" shall be omitted.

Service of notices.

46.—(1) Any notice required or authorised by any of the relevant statutory provisions to be served on or given to an inspector may be served or given by delivering it to him or by leaving it at, or sending it by post to, his office.

(2) Any such notice required or authorised to be served on or given to a person other than an inspector may be served or given by delivering it to him, or by leaving it at his proper address, or by sending it by post to him at that address.

(3) Any such notice may—

(*a*) in the case of a body corporate, be served on or given to the secretary or clerk of that body;

(*b*) in the case of a partnership, be served on or given to a partner or a person having the control or management of the partnership business or, in Scotland, the firm.

(4) For the purposes of this section and of section 26 of the Interpretation Act 1889 (service of documents by post) in its application to this section, the proper address of any person on or to whom any such notice is to be served or given shall be his last known address, except that— 1889 c. 63.

(*a*) in the case of a body corporate or their secretary or clerk, it shall be the address of the registered or principal office of that body;

PART I

(*b*) in the case of a partnership or a person having the control or the management of the partnership business, it shall be the principal office of the partnership;

and for the purposes of this subsection the principal office of a company registered outside the United Kingdom or of a partnership carrying on business outside the United Kingdom shall be their principal office within the United Kingdom.

(5) If the person to be served with or given any such notice has specified an address within the United Kingdom other than his proper address within the meaning of subsection (4) above as the one at which he or someone on his behalf will accept notices of the same description as that notice, that address shall also be treated for the purposes of this section and section 26 of the Interpretation Act 1889 as his proper address.

1889 c. 63.

(6) Without prejudice to any other provision of this section, any such notice required or authorised to be served on or given to the owner or occupier of any premises (whether a body corporate or not) may be served or given by sending it by post to him at those premises, or by addressing it by name to the person on or to whom it is to be served or given and delivering it to some responsible person who is or appears to be resident or employed in the premises.

(7) If the name or the address of any owner or occupier of premises on or to whom any such notice as aforesaid is to be served or given cannot after reasonable inquiry be ascertained, the notice may be served or given by addressing it to the person on or to whom it is to be served or given by the description of "owner" or "occupier" of the premises (describing them) to which the notice relates, and by delivering it to some responsible person who is or appears to be resident or employed in the premises, or, if there is no such person to whom it can be delivered, by affixing it or a copy of it to some conspicuous part of the premises.

(8) The preceding provisions of this section shall apply to the sending or giving of a document as they apply to the giving of a notice.

Civil liability.

47.—(1) Nothing in this Part shall be construed—

(*a*) as conferring a right of action in any civil proceedings in respect of any failure to comply with any duty imposed by sections 2 to 7 or any contravention of section 8; or

(*b*) as affecting the extent (if any) to which breach of a duty imposed by any of the existing statutory provisions is actionable; or (*c*) as affecting the operation of section 12 of the Nuclear Installations Act 1965 (right to compensation by virtue of certain provisions of that Act). **PART I** 1965 c. 57.

(2) Breach of a duty imposed by health and safety regulations ... ... shall, so far as it causes damage, be actionable except in so far as the regulations provide otherwise.

(3) No provision made by virtue of section 15(6)(*b*) shall afford a defence in any civil proceedings, whether brought by virtue of subsection (2) above or not; but as regards any duty imposed as mentioned in subsection (2) above health and safety regulations ...

... may provide for any defence specified in the regulations to be available in any action for breach of that duty.

(4) Subsections (1)(*a*) and (2) above are without prejudice to any right of action which exists apart from the provisions of this Act, and subsection (3) above is without prejudice to any defence which may be available apart from the provisions of the regulations there mentioned.

(5) Any term of an agreement which purports to exclude or restrict the operation of subsection (2) above, or any liability arising by virtue of that subsection shall be void, except in so far as health and safety regulations...

... provide otherwise.

(6) In this section "damage" includes the death of, or injury to, any person (including any disease and any impairment of a person's physical or mental condition).

48.—(1) Subject to the provisions of this section, the provisions of this Part, except sections 21 to 25 and 33 to 42, and of regulations made under this Part shall bind the Crown. **Application to Crown.**

(2) Although they do not bind the Crown, sections 33 to 42 shall apply to persons in the public service of the Crown as they apply to other persons.

(3) For the purposes of this Part and regulations made thereunder persons in the service of the Crown shall be treated as employees of the Crown whether or not they would be so treated apart from this subsection.

(4) Without prejudice to section 15(5), the Secretary of State may, to the extent that it appears to him requisite or expedient to do so in the interests of the safety of the State or the safe custody of persons lawfully detained, by order exempt the Crown either generally or in particular respects from all or any of the provisions of this Part which would, by virtue of subsection (1) above, bind the Crown.

PART I

(5) The power to make orders under this section shall be exercisable by statutory instrument, and any such order may be varied or revoked by a subsequent order.

1947 c. 44.

(6) Nothing in this section shall authorise proceedings to be brought against Her Majesty in her private capacity, and this subsection shall be construed as if section 38(3) of the Crown Proceedings Act 1947 (interpretation of references in that Act to Her Majesty in her private capacity) were contained in this Act.

Adaptation of enactments to metric units or appropriate metric units.

49.—(1) The appropriate Minister may by regulations amend—

(*a*) any of the relevant statutory provisions; or

(*b*) any provision of an enactment which relates to any matter relevant to any of the general purposes of this Part but is not among the relevant statutory provisions; or

(*c*) any provision of an instrument made or having effect under any such enactment as is mentioned in the preceding paragraph,

by substituting an amount or quantity expressed in metric units for an amount or quantity not so expressed or by substituting an amount or quantity expressed in metric units of a description specified in the regulations for an amount or quantity expressed in metric units of a different description.

(2) The amendments shall be such as to preserve the effect of the provisions mentioned except to such extent as in the opinion of the appropriate Minister is necessary to obtain amounts expressed in convenient and suitable terms.

(3) Regulations made by the appropriate Minister under this subsection may, in the case of a provision which falls within any of paragraphs (*a*) to (*c*) of subsection (1) above and contains words which refer to units other than metric units, repeal those words if the appropriate Minister is of the opinion that those words could be omitted without altering the effect of that provision.

[15.—(1) In section 49, in subsection (1) for the words "The appropriate Minister may by regulations amend" substitute the words "Regulations made under this subsection may amend", in subsection (2) for the words "appropriate Minister" substitute the words "authority making the regulations", in subsection (3) omit the words "by the appropriate Minister" and for the words "if the appropriate Minister" substitute the words "if the authority making the regulations".]

"(4) The power to make regulations under this section shall be exercisable by the Secretary of State, the Minister of Agriculture, Fisheries and Food or the Secretary of State and that Minister acting jointly.".

50. "(1) Where any power to make regulations under any of the relevant statutory provisions is exercisable by the Secretary of State, the Minister of Agriculture, Fisheries and Food or both of them acting jointly that power may be exercised either so as to give effect (with or without modifications) to proposals submitted by the Commission under section 11(2)(*d*) or independently of any such proposals; but the authority who is to exercise the power shall not exercise it independently of proposals from the Commission unless he has consulted the Commission and such other bodies as appear to him to be appropriate.".

(2) Where the Secretary of State proposes to exercise any such power as is mentioned in the preceding subsection so as to give effect to any such proposals as are there mentioned with modifications, he shall, before making the regulations, consult the Commission.

(3) Where the Commission proposes to submit to the Secretary of State any such proposals as are mentioned in subsection (1) above except proposals for the making of regulations under section 43(2), it shall, before so submitting them, consult—

(*a*) any government department or other body that appears to the Commission to be appropriate (and, in particular, in the case of proposals for the making of regulations under section 18(2), any body representing local authorities that so appears, and, in the case of proposals for the making of regulations relating to electro-magnetic radiations, the National Radiological Protection Board);

(*b*) such government departments and other bodies, if any, as, in relation to any matter dealt with in the proposals, the Commission is required to consult under this subsection by virtue of directions given to it by the Secretary of State.

(2) In subsection (2) of that section, for the words from "Secretary of State" to "preceding subsection" substitute "authority who is to exercise any such power as is mentioned in subsection (1) above proposes to exercise that power".

(3) In subsection (3), for the words "to the Secretary of State" substitute the words "under section 11(2)(*d*)".

. . .

Exclusion of application to domestic employment.

51. Nothing in this Part shall apply in relation to a person by reason only that he employs another, or is himself employed, as a domestic servant in a private household.

Meaning of work and at work.

52.—(1) For the purposes of this Part—

(*a*) " work " means work as an employee or as a self-employed person ;

(*b*) an employee is at work throughout the time when he is in the course of his employment, but not otherwise ; and

(*c*) a self-employed person is at work throughout such time as he devotes to work as a self-employed person ;

and, subject to the following subsection, the expressions " work " and " at work ", in whatever context, shall be construed accordingly.

(2) Regulations made under this subsection may—

(*a*) extend the meaning of " work " and " at work " for the purposes of this Part ; and

(*b*) in that connection provide for any of the relevant statutory provisions to have effect subject to such adaptations as may be specified in the regulations.

[" (3) The power to make regulations under subsection (2) above shall be exercisable by the Secretary of State, the Minister of Agriculture, Fisheries and Food or the Secretary of State and that Minister acting jointly.".]

(3) The power to make regulations under subsection (2) above shall be exercisable—

(*a*) in relation to activities not relating exclusively to agricultural operations, by the Secretary of State ;

(*b*) in relation to activities relating exclusively to the relevant agricultural purposes, by the appropriate agriculture authority.

(4) Regulations under subsection (2) above in relation to activities falling within subsection (3)(*b*) above may be either regulations applying to Great Britain and made by the Minister of Agriculture, Fisheries and Food and the Secretary of State acting jointly, or regulations applying to England and Wales only and made by the said Minister, or regulations applying to Scotland only and made by the Secretary of State ; and in subsection (3)(*b*) above " the appropriate agriculture authority " shall be construed accordingly.

General interpretation of Part I.

53.—(1) In this Part, unless the context otherwise requires—

" article for use at work " means—

(*a*) any plant designed for use or operation (whether

exclusively or not) by persons at work, and

(*b*) any article designed for use as a component in any such plant;

" code of practice " (without prejudice to section 16(8)) includes a standard, a specification and any other documentary form of practical guidance;

" the Commission " has the meaning assigned by section 10(2);

" conditional sale agreement " means an agreement for the sale of goods under which the purchase price or part of it is payable by instalments, and the property in the goods is to remain in the seller (notwithstanding that the buyer is to be in possession of the goods) until such conditions as to the payment of instalments or otherwise as may be specified in the agreement are fulfilled;

" contract of employment " means a contract of employment or apprenticeship (whether express or implied and, if express, whether oral or in writing);

" credit-sale agreement " means an agreement for the sale of goods, under which the purchase price or part of it is payable by instalments, but which is not a conditional sale agreement;

" domestic premises " means premises occupied as a private dwelling (including any garden, yard, garage, outhouse or other appurtenance of such premises which is not used in common by the occupants of more than one such dwelling), and " non-domestic premises " shall be construed accordingly;

" employee " means an individual who works under a contract of employment, and related expressions shall be construed accordingly;

" enforcing authority " has the meaning assigned by section 18(7);

" the Executive " has the meaning assigned by section 10(5);

" the existing statutory provisions " means the following provisions while and to the extent that they remain in force, namely the provisions of the Acts mentioned in Schedule 1 which are specified in the third column of that Schedule and of the regulations, orders or other instruments of a legislative character made or having effect under any provision so specified;

. . .

" the general purposes of this Part " has the meaning assigned by section 1;

"health and safety regulations" has the meaning assigned by section 15(1);

"hire-purchase agreement" means an agreement other than a conditional sale agreement, under which—

(*a*) goods are bailed or (in Scotland) hired in return for periodical payments by the person to whom they are bailed or hired; and

(*b*) the property in the goods will pass to that person if the terms of the agreement are complied with and one or more of the following occurs:

(i) the exercise of an option to purchase by that person;

(ii) the doing of any other specified act by any party to the agreement;

(iii) the happening of any other event;

and "hire-purchase" shall be construed accordingly;

"improvement notice" means a notice under section 21;

"inspector" means an inspector appointed under section 19;

. . .

"local authority" means—

(*a*) in relation to England and Wales, a county council, the Greater London Council, a district council, a London borough council, the Common Council of the City of London, the Sub-Treasurer of the Inner Temple or the Under-Treasurer of the Middle Temple,

(*b*) in relation to Scotland, a regional, islands or district council except that before 16th May 1975 it means a town council or county council;

"offshore installation" means any installation which is intended for underwater exploitation of mineral resources or exploration with a view to such exploitation;

"personal injury" includes any disease and any impairment of a person's physical or mental condition;

"plant" includes any machinery, equipment or appliance;

"premises" includes any place and, in particular, includes—

(*a*) any vehicle, vessel, aircraft or hovercraft,

(*b*) any installation on land (including the foreshore and other land intermittently covered by water), any offshore installation, and any other installation (whether floating, or resting on the seabed or the subsoil thereof, or resting on other land covered with water or the subsoil thereof), and

(*c*) any tent or movable structure;

"prescribed" means prescribed by regulations made by the Secretary of State;

* * *

"prohibition notice" means a notice under section 22;

* * *

"the relevant statutory provisions" means—

(*a*) the provisions of this Part and of any health and safety regulations . . .
. . . and

(*b*) the existing statutory provisions;

"self-employed person" means an individual who works for gain or reward otherwise than under a contract of employment, whether or not he himself employs others;

"substance" means any natural or artificial substance, whether in solid or liquid form or in the form of a gas or vapour;

"substance for use at work" means any substance intended for use (whether exclusively or not) by persons at work;

"supply", where the reference is to supplying articles or substances, means supplying them by way of sale, lease, hire or hire-purchase, whether as principal or agent for another.

* * *

54. This Part, in its application to the Isles of Scilly, shall apply as if those Isles were a local government area and the Council of those Isles were a local authority. Application of Part I to Isles of Scilly.

PART II

THE EMPLOYMENT MEDICAL ADVISORY SERVICE

55.—(1) There shall continue to be an employment medical advisory service, which shall be maintained for the following purposes, that is to say— Functions of, and responsibility for maintaining, employment medical advisory service.

(*a*) securing that the Secretary of State, the Health and Safety Commission, the Manpower Services Commission and others concerned with the health of employed persons or of persons seeking or training for employment can be kept informed of, and adequately advised on, matters of which they ought respectively to take cognisance concerning the safeguarding and improvement of the health of those persons;

(*b*) giving to employed persons and persons seeking or training for employment information and advice on health in relation to employment and training for employment;

(*c*) other purposes of the Secretary of State's functions relating to employment.

(2) The authority responsible for maintaining the said service shall be the Secretary of State; but if arrangements are made by the Secretary of State for that responsibility to be discharged on his behalf by the Health and Safety Commission or some other body, then, while those arrangements operate, the body so discharging that responsibility (and not the Secretary of State) shall be the authority responsible for maintaining that service.

(3) The authority for the time being responsible for maintaining the said service may also for the purposes mentioned in subsection (1) above, and for the purpose of assisting employment medical advisers in the performance of their functions, investigate or assist in, arrange for or make payments in respect of the investigation of problems arising in connection with any such matters as are so mentioned or otherwise in connection with the functions of employment medical advisers, and for the purpose of investigating or assisting in the investigation of such problems may provide and maintain such laboratories and other services as appear to the authority to be requisite.

(4) Any arrangements made by the Secretary of State in pursuance of subsection (2) above may be terminated by him at any time, but without prejudice to the making of other arrangements at any time in pursuance of that subsection (including arrangements which are to operate from the time when any previous arrangements so made cease to operate).

(5) Without prejudice to sections 11(4)(*a*) and 12(*b*), it shall be the duty of the Health and Safety Commission, if so directed by the Secretary of State, to enter into arrangements with him for the Commission to be responsible for maintaining the said service.

(6) In subsection (1) above—

(*a*) the reference to persons training for employment shall include persons attending industrial rehabilitation courses provided by virtue of the Employment and Training Act 1973; and

1973 c. 50.

(*b*) the reference to persons (other than the Secretary of State and the Commissions there mentioned) concerned with the health of employed persons or of persons seeking or training for employment shall be taken to include organisations representing employers, employees and occupational health practitioners respectively.

56.—(1) The authority for the time being responsible for maintaining the employment medical advisory service shall for the purpose of discharging that responsibility appoint persons to be employment medical advisers, and may for that purpose appoint such other officers and servants as it may determine, subject however to the requisite approval as to numbers, that is to say— **Functions of authority responsible for maintaining the service.**

(*a*) where that authority is the Secretary of State, the approval of the Minister for the Civil Service;

(*b*) otherwise, the approval of the Secretary of State given with the consent of that Minister.

(2) A person shall not be qualified to be appointed, or to be, an employment medical adviser unless he is a fully registered medical practitioner.

(3) The authority for the time being responsible for maintaining the said service may determine the cases and circumstances in which the employment medical advisers or any of them are to perform the duties or exercise the powers conferred on employment medical advisers by or under this Act or otherwise.

(4) Where as a result of arrangements made in pursuance of section 55(2) the authority responsible for maintaining the said service changes, the change shall not invalidate any appointment previously made under subsection (1) above, and any such appointment subsisting when the change occurs shall thereafter have effect as if made by the new authority.

57.—(1) The Secretary of State may by regulations provide for such fees as may be fixed by or determined under the regulations to be payable for or in connection with the performance by the authority responsible for maintaining the employment medical advisory service of any function conferred for the purposes of that service on that authority by virtue of this Part or otherwise. Fees.

(2) For the purposes of this section, the performance by an employment medical adviser of his functions shall be treated as the performance by the authority responsible for maintaining the said service of functions conferred on that authority as mentioned in the preceding subsection.

(3) The provisions of subsections (4), (5) and (8) of section 43 shall apply in relation to regulations under this section with the modification that references to subsection (2) of that section shall be read as references to subsection (1) of this section.

(4) Where an authority other than the Secretary of State is responsible for maintaining the said service, the Secretary of State shall consult that authority before making any regulations under this section.

58.—(1) The authority for the time being responsible for maintaining the employment medical advisory service may pay— Other financial provisions.

(*a*) to employment medical advisers such salaries or such

fees and travelling or other allowances; and

(*b*) to other persons called upon to give advice in connection with the execution of the authority's functions under this Part such travelling or other allowances or compensation for loss of remunerative time; and

(*c*) to persons attending for medical examinations conducted by, or in accordance with arrangements made by, employment medical advisers (including pathological, physiological and radiological tests and similar investigations so conducted) such travelling or subsistence allowances or such compensation for loss of earnings,

as the authority may, with the requisite approval, determine.

(2) For the purposes of the preceding subsection the requisite approval is—

(*a*) where the said authority is the Secretary of State, the approval of the Minister for the Civil Service;

(*b*) otherwise, the approval of the Secretary of State given with the consent of that Minister.

(3) Where an authority other than the Secretary of State is responsible for maintaining the said service, it shall be the duty of the Secretary of State to pay to that authority such sums as are approved by the Treasury and as he considers appropriate for the purpose of enabling the authority to discharge that responsibility.

Duty of responsible authority to keep accounts and to report.

59.—(1) It shall be the duty of the authority for the time being responsible for maintaining the employment medical advisory service—

(*a*) to keep, in relation to the maintenance of that service, proper accounts and proper records in relation to the accounts;

(*b*) to prepare in respect of each accounting year a statement of accounts relating to the maintenance of that service in such form as the Secretary of State may direct with the approval of the Treasury; and

(*c*) to send copies of the statement to the Secretary of State and the Comptroller and Auditor General before the end of the month of November next following the accounting year to which the statement relates.

(2) The Comptroller and Auditor General shall examine, certify and report on each statement received by him in pursuance of subsection (1) above and shall lay copies of each statement and of his report before each House of Parliament.

(3) It shall also be the duty of the authority responsible for maintaining the employment medical advisory service to make to the Secretary of State, as soon as possible after the end of

each accounting year, a report on the discharge of its responsibilities in relation to that service during that year; and the Secretary of State shall lay before each House of Parliament a copy of each report made to him in pursuance of this subsection. **PART II**

(4) Where as a result of arrangements made in pursuance of section 55(2) the authority responsible for maintaining the employment medical advisory service changes, the change shall not affect any duty imposed by this section on the body which was responsible for maintaining that service before the change.

(5) No duty imposed on the authority for the time being responsible for maintaining the employment medical advisory service by subsection (1) or (3) above shall fall on the Commission (which is subject to corresponding duties under Schedule 2) or on the Secretary of State.

(6) In this section "accounting year" means, except so far as the Secretary of State otherwise directs, the period of twelve months ending with 31st March in any year.

60.—(1) It shall be the duty of the Secretary of State to secure that each Area Health Authority arranges for one of its officers who is a fully registered medical practitioner to furnish, on the application of an employment medical adviser, such particulars of the school medical record of a person who has not attained the age of eighteen and such other information relating to his medical history as the adviser may reasonably require for the efficient performance of his functions; but no particulars or information about any person which may be furnished to an adviser in pursuance of this subsection shall (without the consent of that person) be disclosed by the adviser otherwise than for the efficient performance of his functions. **Supplementary.**

(2) In its application to Scotland the preceding subsection shall have effect with the substitution of the words "every Health Board arrange for one of their" for the words from "each" to "its".

(3) The Secretary of State may by order made by statutory instrument subject to annulment in pursuance of a resolution of either House of Parliament modify the provisions of section 7(3) and (4) of the Employment and Training Act 1973 (which require a person's period of continuous employment by a relevant body or in the civil service of the State to be treated, for the purposes of sections 1 and 2 of the Contracts of Employment Act 1972 and of certain provisions of the Industrial Relations Act 1971 affecting the right of an employee not to be unfairly dismissed, as increased by reference to previous **1973 c. 50.** **1972 c. 53.** **1971 c. 72.**

PART II periods of continuous employment by such a body or in that service) for the purpose of securing that employment as an employment medical adviser by an authority other than the Secretary of State is similarly treated for those purposes.

An order under this subsection may be varied or revoked by a subsequent order thereunder.

(4) References to the chief employment medical adviser or a deputy chief employment medical adviser in any provision of an enactment or instrument made under an enactment shall be read as references to a person appointed for the purposes of that provision by the authority responsible for maintaining the employment medical advisory service.

1972 c. 28. (5) The following provisions of the Employment Medical Advisory Service Act 1972 (which are superseded by the preceding provisions of this Part or rendered unnecessary by provisions contained in Part I), namely sections 1 and 6 and Schedule 1, shall cease to have effect ; but—

(*a*) in so far as anything done under or by virtue of the said section 1 or Schedule 1 could have been done under or by virtue of a corresponding provision of Part I or this Part, it shall not be invalidated by the repeal of that section and Schedule by this Act but shall have effect as if done under or by virtue of that corresponding provision ; and

(*b*) any order made under the said section 6 which is in force immediately before the repeal of that section by this Act shall remain in force notwithstanding that repeal, but may be revoked or varied by regulations under section 43(2) or 57, as if it were an instrument containing regulations made under section 43(2) or 57, as the case may require.

(6) Where any Act (whether passed before, or in the same Session as, this Act) or any document refers, either expressly or by implication, to or to any enactment contained in any of the provisions of the said Act of 1972 which are mentioned in the preceding subsection, the reference shall, except where the context otherwise requires, be construed as, or as including, a reference to the corresponding provision of this Act.

1889 c. 63. (7) Nothing in subsection (5) or (6) above shall be taken as prejudicing the operation of section 38 of the Interpretation Act 1889 (which relates to the effect of repeals).

PART III

BUILDING REGULATIONS, AND AMENDMENT OF BUILDING (SCOTLAND) ACT 1959

1959 c. 24.

Amendments of enactments relating to building regulations. 1961 c. 64.

61.—(1) For sections 61 and 62 of the 1936 Act (power to make building regulations, and their application to existing buildings) there shall be substituted the following sections—

" Power to make building regulations.

61.—(1) Subject to the provisions of Part II of the Public Health Act 1961, the Secretary of State shall have power, for any of the purposes mentioned in subsection (2) below, to make regulations with respect to the design and construction of buildings and the provision of services, fittings and equipment in or in connection with buildings.

Regulations under this subsection shall be known as building regulations.

(2) The purposes referred to in the preceding subsection are the following, that is to say—

(*a*) securing the health, safety, welfare and convenience of persons in or about buildings and of others who may be affected by buildings or matters connected with buildings;

(*b*) furthering the conservation of fuel and power; and

(*c*) preventing waste, undue consumption, misuse or contamination of water.

(3) Building regulations may—

(*a*) provide for particular requirements of the regulations to be deemed to be complied with where prescribed methods of construction, prescribed types of materials or other prescribed means are used in or in connection with buildings;

(*b*) be framed to any extent by reference to a document published by or on behalf of the Secretary of State or any other person or any body, or by reference to the approval or satisfaction of any prescribed person or body.

(4) Building regulations may include provision as to—

(*a*) the giving of notices;

(*b*) the deposit of plans of proposed work or work already executed (including provision as to the number of copies to be deposited);

PART III

(*c*) the retention by local authorities of copies of plans deposited with them in accordance with the regulations;

(*d*) the inspection and testing of work;

(*e*) the taking of samples.

(5) Building regulations may exempt from all or any of the provisions of building regulations any prescribed class of buildings, services, fittings or equipment.

(6) The Secretary of State may by direction exempt from all or any of the provisions of building regulations any particular building or, as regards any particular location, buildings of any particular class thereat, and may in either case do so either unconditionally or subject to compliance with any conditions specified in the direction.

(7) A person who contravenes any condition specified in a direction given under the preceding subsection or permits any such condition to be contravened shall be liable to a fine not exceeding £400 and to a further fine not exceeding £50 for each day on which the offence continues after he is convicted.

(8) For the purposes of building regulations and of any direction given or instrument made with reference to building regulations, buildings may be classified by reference to size, description, design, purpose, location or any other characteristic whatsoever.

Application of building regulations to existing buildings etc.

62.—(1) Building regulations may be made with respect to—

(*a*) alterations and extensions of buildings and of services, fittings and equipment in or in connection with buildings;

(*b*) new services, fittings, or equipment provided in or in connection with buildings;

(*c*) buildings and services, fittings and equipment in or in connection with buildings, so far as affected by—

(i) alterations or extensions of buildings; or

(ii) new, altered or extended services, fittings or equipment in or in connection with buildings;

(*d*) the whole of any building, together with any services, fittings or equipment provided in or in connection therewith, in respect of which there are or are proposed to be carried out any operations which by virtue of section 74(1)(*c*) of the Health and Safety at Work etc. Act 1974 constitute the construction of a building for the purposes of this section ; PART III

(*e*) buildings or parts of buildings, together with any services, fittings or equipment provided in or in connection therewith, in cases where the purposes for which or the manner or circumstances in which a building or part of a building is used change or changes in a way that constitutes a material change of use of the building or part within the meaning of the expression 'material change of use' as defined for the purposes of this paragraph by building regulations.

(2) So far as they relate to matters mentioned in the preceding subsection, building regulations may be made to apply to or in connection with buildings erected before the date on which the regulations came into force but, except as aforesaid (and subject to section 65(2) of the Health and Safety at Work etc. Act 1974) shall not apply to buildings erected before that date.".

(2) Without prejudice to the generality of subsection (1) of section 61 of the 1936 Act as substituted by this section, building regulations may for any of the purposes mentioned in subsection (2) of that section make provision with respect to any of the matters mentioned in Schedule 5, may require things to be provided or done in or in connection with buildings (as well as regulating the provision or doing of things in or in connection with buildings), and may prescribe the manner in which work is to be carried out.

(3) The enactments relating to building regulations shall have effect subject to the further amendments provided for in Part I of Schedule 6.

(4) Section 65 of the 1936 Act and sections 4, 6 and 7 of the 1961 Act, as they will have effect after the coming into force of the preceding subsection, are set out in Part II of the said Schedule 6.

PART III

(5) Section 71 of the 1936 Act (exemption of certain buildings from building regulations) shall cease to have effect.

(6) Any regulations under section 4 of the 1961 Act which are in force immediately before the repeal of subsection (1) of that section by this Act shall not be invalidated by that repeal, but shall have effect as if made under section 61(1) of the 1936 Act as substituted by this section.

Further matters for which building regulations may provide.

62.—(1) Building regulations may make provision for requiring local authorities in such circumstances as may be prescribed to consult any prescribed person before taking any prescribed step in connection with any work or other matter to which building regulations are applicable.

(2) Building regulations—

(*a*) may authorise local authorities to accept, as evidence that the requirements of building regulations as to matters of any prescribed description are or would be satisfied, certificates to that effect by persons of any class or description prescribed in relation to those matters or by a person nominated in writing by the Secretary of State in any particular case ;

(*b*) may provide for the issue by local authorities of certificates to the effect that, so far as the authority concerned have been able to ascertain after taking all reasonable steps in that behalf, the requirements of building regulations as to matters of any prescribed description are satisfied in any particular case, and for such certificates to be evidence (but not conclusive evidence) of compliance with the regulations ;

(*c*) may make provision—

(i) for prohibiting, in prescribed circumstances, the carrying out of proposed work of any prescribed class involving matters of any prescribed description unless there has been deposited with the prescribed authority as regards those matters a certificate such as is mentioned in paragraph (*a*) above ;

(ii) for enabling, in cases where such a certificate is required by virtue of the preceding sub-paragraph, any dispute as to whether a certificate ought to be issued to be referred to the Secretary of State ; and

(iii) for enabling the Secretary of State, on any such reference, to give such directions as he thinks fit.

(3) Building regulations may authorise local authorities to charge prescribed fees for or in connection with the performance of prescribed functions of theirs relating to building regulations.

PART III

(4) Building regulations may make a prescribed person or class of persons responsible (instead of local authorities) for performing prescribed functions of local authorities under or in connection with building regulations, and for that purpose may provide for any prescribed enactment relating to building regulations and any prescribed provision of such regulations to apply (with any prescribed modifications) in relation to a prescribed person or a person of a prescribed class as that enactment or provision applies in relation to a local authority.

(5) Building regulations may repeal or modify any enactment to which this subsection applies if it appears to the Secretary of State that the enactment is inconsistent with, or is unnecessary or requires alteration in consequence of, any provision contained in or made under any enactment relating to building regulations.

This subsection applies to any enactment contained in this Act or in any other Act passed before or in the same Session as this Act, other than sections 61 to 71 of the 1936 Act, sections 4 to 11 of, and Schedule 1 to, the 1961 Act, and this Part.

Miscellaneous provisions as to the approval of plans.

63.—(1) A local authority with whom plans of any proposed work are deposited in accordance with building regulations may in prescribed cases pass them by stages in accordance with the regulations and, where a local authority pass any such plans to a limited extent at any stage,—

(*a*) they shall impose conditions as to the depositing of further plans in connection with the proposed work; and

(*b*) they may impose conditions for securing that, pending the deposit of such of the further plans as they may indicate, the proposed work will not be proceeded with except to such extent as they may in accordance with the regulations authorise.

(2) A person who contravenes any condition imposed by a local authority under subsection (1) above other than a condition as to the depositing of further plans, or permits any such condition to be contravened, shall be liable to a fine not exceeding £400 and to a further fine not exceeding £50 for each day on which the offence continues after he is convicted.

(3) A local authority with whom plans of any proposed work are deposited in accordance with building regulations may, notwithstanding that the plans are defective or show that the work

PART III would contravene any of the building regulations, pass the plans provisionally, that is to say, subject to any modifications which they think necessary for remedying the defect or avoiding the contravention, indicating the modifications in the notice of approval and—

(*a*) if, within a prescribed time and in a prescribed manner so indicated, the person by or on behalf of whom the plans were deposited notifies the authority that he agrees to the modifications, the plans shall be treated as having been passed subject to those modifications; and

(*b*) if not, the plans shall be treated as having been rejected.

(4) In cases where by virtue of subsection (1) or (3) above plans are passed by stages or provisionally, the provisions of section 64(1) to (3) of the 1936 Act shall have effect subject to such modifications as may be prescribed.

(5) Where plans of any proposed work have been passed under section 64 of the 1936 Act by a local authority, the person by or on behalf of whom the plans were in accordance with building regulations deposited with the authority may, and in such cases as may be prescribed shall, for the purpose of obtaining the approval of the authority to any proposed departure or deviation from the plans as passed, deposit plans of any such departure or deviation; and that section shall apply in relation to plans deposited under this subsection as it applies in relation to the plans originally deposited.

(6) Where in accordance with any existing enactment (however framed or worded) plans of a proposed building of any prescribed class are submitted to a Minister of the Crown for his approval—

(*a*) plans of the proposed building shall not be required to be deposited with the local authority for the purposes of section 64 of the 1936 Act in pursuance of building regulations;

(*b*) the Minister shall not approve the plans unless he is satisfied that, so far as applicable, the substantive requirements of building regulations will be complied with by and in connection with the proposed building;

(*c*) the approval of the plans by the Minister shall operate, for such purposes as may be prescribed, in the same way as the passing of them by the local authority would have operated;

(*d*) the Minister may exercise in connection with the proposed building the like powers of dispensing with or relaxing requirements of building regulations as are

PART III

conferred on the Secretary of State and local authorities by virtue of section 6 of the 1961 Act (other than a power excepted by subsection (7) below), subject however to the like requirements as to consultation (if any) as apply by virtue of section 62(1) in the case of a local authority (but not to the requirements in the said section 6 as to consultation with the local authority) and to the like requirements as in the case of the Secretary of State apply by virtue of section 8 of the 1961 Act (opportunity to make representations about proposal to relax building regulations).

(7) In the preceding subsection "existing enactment" means an enactment passed before the coming into force of that subsection, other than an enactment relating to town and country planning; and the power excepted from paragraph (*d*) of that subsection is one which by virtue of section 62(4) is exercisable otherwise than by a local authority.

Special provisions as to materials etc. unsuitable for permanent buildings.

64.—(1) This section applies—

(*a*) to any work consisting of a part of a building, being a part in the construction of which there is used any material or component of a type which, in relation to a part of that description, is prescribed for the purposes of this paragraph under subsection (2) below; and

(*b*) to any work provided in or in connection with a building, being work consisting of a service, fitting or item of equipment of a type so prescribed for the purposes of this paragraph.

(2) The Secretary of State may by building regulations—

(*a*) prescribe a type of material or component for the purposes of subsection (1)(*a*) above if in his opinion materials or components of that type are likely to be unsuitable for use in the construction of a particular part of a permanent building in the absence of conditions with respect to the use of the building or with respect to any material or component of that type used in the construction of a part of that description;

(*b*) prescribe a type of service, fitting or equipment for the purposes of subsection (1)(*b*) above if in his opinion services, fittings or equipment of that type are likely to be unsuitable for provision in or in connection with a permanent building in the absence of conditions with respect to the use of the building or with respect to any service, fitting or equipment of that type so provided.

PART III

(3) Where plans of any proposed work are, in accordance with building regulations, deposited with a local authority and the plans show that the proposed work would include or consist of work to which this section applies, the authority may, notwithstanding that the plans conform with the regulations—

(*a*) reject the plans ; or

(*b*) in passing the plans fix a period on the expiration of which the work to which this section applies or the relevant building (as the authority may in passing the plans direct) must be removed and, if they think fit, impose with respect to the use of the relevant building or with respect to the work to which this section applies such reasonable conditions, if any, as they consider appropriate, so however that no condition as to the use of the relevant building shall be imposed which conflicts with any condition imposed or having effect as if imposed under Part III or IV of the Town and Country Planning Act 1971.

1971 c. 78.

(4) If, in the case of any work in respect of which plans ought by virtue of building regulations to have been deposited with a local authority but have not been so deposited, the work appears to the authority to include or consist of work to which this section applies, the authority, without prejudice to their right to take proceedings in respect of any contravention of the regulations, may fix a period on the expiration of which the work to which this section applies or the relevant building (as the authority may in fixing the period direct) must be removed and, if they think fit, impose any conditions that might have been imposed under the preceding subsection in passing plans for the first-mentioned work and, where they fix such a period, shall forthwith give notice thereof, and of any conditions imposed, to the owner of the relevant building.

(5) If, in the case of any work appearing to the local authority to fall within subsection (1)(*b*) above, plans of the work were not required by building regulations to be deposited with the authority, and were not so deposited, the authority may at any time within twelve months from the date of completion of the work fix a period on the expiration of which the work must be removed and, if they think fit, impose any conditions which, if plans of the work had been required to be, and had been, so deposited, might have been imposed under subsection (3) above in passing the plans and, where they fix such a period, shall forthwith give notice thereof, and of any conditions imposed, to the owner of the relevant building.

(6) A local authority may from time to time extend any period fixed, or vary any conditions imposed, under this section, but so that, unless an application in that behalf is made to them

by the owner of the relevant building, they shall not exercise their power of varying conditions so imposed except when granting an extension or further extension of the period fixed with respect to the work or building, as the case may be.

(7) Any person aggrieved by the action of a local authority under this section in rejecting plans, or in fixing or refusing to extend any period, or in imposing or refusing to vary any conditions, may appeal to the Secretary of State within the prescribed time and in the prescribed manner.

(8) Where a period has been fixed under this section with respect to any work to which this section applies or with respect to the relevant building, the owner of that building shall on the expiration of that period or, as the case may be, of that period as extended, remove the work or building with respect to which the period was fixed ; and if he fails to do so, the local authority may remove that work or building, as the case may be, and may recover from him the expenses reasonably incurred by them in doing so.

(9) A person who—

(*a*) contravenes any condition imposed under this section or permits any such condition to be contravened ; or

(*b*) contravenes subsection (8) above ;

shall be liable to a fine not exceeding £400 and to a further fine not exceeding £50 for each day on which the offence continues or, as the case may be, on which the work or building is allowed to remain, after he is convicted ; but this subsection shall not be construed as prejudicing a local authority's rights under subsection (8) above.

(10) In this section " the relevant building " means, in any particular case, the building mentioned in paragraph (*a*) or, as the case may be, paragraph (*b*) of subsection (1) above

(11) Section 53 of the 1936 Act (which is superseded by the preceding provisions of this section) shall cease to have effect, but—

(*a*) any building regulations made, period fixed, condition imposed or other thing done by virtue of that section shall be deemed to have been made, fixed, imposed or done by virtue of this section ; and

(*b*) anything begun under that section may be continued under this Act as if begun under this section, so however that any appeal under subsection (4) of that section which is pending at the time when that section ceases to have effect, and any proceedings arising out of such appeal, shall proceed as if that section were still in force.

PART III

Continuing requirements.

65.—(1) Building regulations may impose on owners and occupiers of buildings to which building regulations are applicable such continuing requirements as the Secretary of State considers appropriate for securing, with respect to any provision of building regulations designated in the regulations as a provision to which those requirements relate, that the purposes of that provision are not frustrated; but a continuing requirement imposed by virtue of this subsection shall not apply in relation to a building unless a provision of building regulations so designated as one to which the requirement relates applies to that building.

(2) Building regulations may impose on owners and occupiers of buildings of any prescribed class (whenever erected, and whether or not any building regulations were applicable to them at the time of their erection) continuing requirements with respect to all or any of the following matters, namely—

(*a*) the conditions subject to which any services, fittings or equipment provided in or in connection with any building of that class may be used;

(*b*) the inspection and maintenance of any services, fittings or equipment so provided; and

(*c*) the making of reports to any prescribed authority on the condition of any services, fittings or equipment so provided;

and so much of section 62 of the 1936 Act as restricts the application of building regulations shall not apply to regulations made by virtue of this subsection.

(3) If a person contravenes a continuing requirement imposed by virtue of this section, the local authority, without prejudice to their right to take proceedings for a fine in respect of the contravention, may execute any work or take any other action required to remedy the contravention, and may recover from that person the expenses reasonably incurred by them in so doing.

(4) Where a local authority have power under the preceding subsection to execute any work or take any other action they may, instead of exercising that power, by notice require the owner or the occupier of the building to which the contravention referred to in that subsection relates to execute that work or take that action.

The provisions of Part XII of the 1936 Act with respect to appeals against, and the enforcement of, notices requiring the execution of works shall apply in relation to any notice given

PART III

under this section, subject however to the modification that in those provisions references to the execution of works shall be construed as references to the execution of work or the taking of other action, and references to work shall be construed accordingly.

(5) The provisions of sections 6, 7 and 8 of the 1961 Act (power to dispense with or relax requirements in building regulations, and related provisions) shall have effect in relation to continuing requirements imposed by virtue of this section subject to the following modifications, that is to say—

(*a*) a direction under the said section 6 shall, if it so provides, cease to have effect at the end of such period as may be specified in the direction; and

(*b*) in subsection (1) of the said section 7 (as amended by this Act), the reference to granting an application subject to conditions shall be read as including a reference to granting an application for a limited period.

Type relaxation of building regulations.

66.—(1) If the Secretary of State considers that the operation of any requirement of building regulations would be unreasonable in relation to any particular type of building matter, he may, either on an application made to him or of his own accord, give a direction dispensing with or relaxing that requirement generally in relation to that type of building matter, either unconditionally or subject to compliance with any conditions specified in the direction, being conditions with respect to matters directly connected with the dispensation or relaxation.

(2) A direction under subsection (1) above—

(*a*) shall, if it so provides, cease to have effect at the end of such period as may be specified in the direction;

(*b*) may be varied or revoked by a subsequent direction of the Secretary of State.

(3) Building regulations may require a person making an application under subsection (1) above to pay the Secretary of State the prescribed fee; and, without prejudice to section 4(2) of the 1961 Act, regulations made by virtue of this subsection may prescribe different fees for different cases:

Provided that the Secretary of State may in any particular case remit the whole or part of any fee payable by virtue of this subsection.

(4) Before giving a direction under this section the Secretary of State shall consult such bodies as appear to him to be representative of the interests concerned (including in particular, in the case of a direction that relates to a requirement relevant to any of their functions, the National Water Council).

Part III

(5) Where the Secretary of State gives a direction under this section, he shall publish notice of that fact in such manner as he thinks fit.

(6) A person who contravenes any condition specified in a direction given under this section or permits any such condition to be contravened shall be liable to a fine not exceeding £400 and to a further fine not exceeding £50 for each day on which the offence continues after he is convicted.

(7) If at any time a direction under subsection (1) above dispensing with or relaxing a requirement of building regulations ceases to have effect by virtue of subsection (2)(*a*) above or is varied or revoked under subsection (2)(*b*) above, that fact shall not affect the continued operation of the direction (with any conditions specified therein) in any case in which before that time—

(*a*) plans of the proposed work were, in accordance with building regulations, deposited with a local authority; or

1939 c. xcvii.

(*b*) a building notice was served on the district surveyor in pursuance of section 83 of the London Building Acts (Amendment) Act 1939.

(8) In this section and section 67 below " building matter " means any building or other matter whatsoever to which building regulations are in any circumstances applicable.

Power of Secretary of State to approve types of building etc.

67.—(1) The following provisions of this section shall have effect with a view to enabling the Secretary of State, either on an application made to him or of his own accord, to approve any particular type of building matter as complying, either generally or in any class of case, with particular requirements of building regulations.

(2) An application for the approval under this section of a type of building matter shall comply with any requirements of building regulations as to the form of such applications and the particulars to be included therein.

(3) Where under subsection (1) above the Secretary of State approves a type of building matter as complying with particular requirements of building regulations either generally or in any class of case, he may issue a certificate to that effect specifying—

(*a*) the type of building matter to which the certificate relates;

(*b*) the requirements of building regulations to which the certificate relates; and

(*c*) where applicable, the class or classes of case to which the certificate applies.

(4) A certificate under this section shall, if it so provides, cease to have effect at the end of such period as may be specified in the certificate. **Part III**

(5) If, while a certificate under this section is in force, it is found, in any particular case involving a building matter of the type to which the certificate relates, that the building matter in question is of that type and the case is one to which the certificate applies, that building matter shall in that particular case be deemed to comply with the requirements of building regulations to which the certificate relates.

(6) The Secretary of State may vary a certificate under this section either on an application made to him or of his own accord; but in the case of a certificate issued on an application made by a person under subsection (1) above, the Secretary of State, except where he varies it on the application of that person, shall before varying it give that person reasonable notice that he proposes to do so.

(7) Building regulations may require a person making an application under subsection (1) or (6) above to pay the Secretary of State the prescribed fee; and, without prejudice to section 4(2) of the 1961 Act, regulations made by virtue of this subsection may prescribe different fees for different cases:

Provided that the Secretary of State may in any particular case remit the whole or part of any fee payable by virtue of this subsection.

(8) The Secretary of State may revoke a certificate issued under this section, but before doing so in the case of a certificate issued on an application under subsection (1) above shall give the person on whose application the certificate was issued reasonable notice that he proposes to do so.

(9) Where the Secretary of State issues a certificate under this section or varies or revokes a certificate so issued, he shall publish notice of that fact in such manner as he thinks fit.

(10) If at any time a certificate under this section ceases to have effect by virtue of subsection (4) above or is varied or revoked under the preceding provisions of this section, that fact shall not affect the continued operation of subsection (5) above by virtue of that certificate in any case in which before that time—

(*a*) plans of the proposed work were, in accordance with building regulations, deposited with a local authority; or

(*b*) a building notice was served on the district surveyor in pursuance of section 83 of the London Building Acts (Amendment) Act 1939. **1939 c. xcvii.**

(11) For the purposes of subsection (3) above or any variation of a certificate under subsection (6) above, a class of case may be framed in any way that the Secretary of State thinks fit.

PART III

(12) The Secretary of State may by building regulations delegate to any person or body, to such extent and subject to such conditions as the Secretary of State may think fit, the powers of approval conferred on him by this section; and so far as those powers are for the time being so delegated to any person or body, the preceding provisions of this section, except so much of subsection (7) as precedes the proviso, and any building regulation made by virtue of that subsection shall (subject to any prescribed conditions) have effect in relation to that person or body with the substitution of references to that person or body for references to the Secretary of State.

Power to require or carry out tests for conformity with building regulations.

68.—(1) The following subsection shall have effect for the purpose of enabling a local authority to ascertain, as regards any work or proposed work to which building regulations for the enforcement of which they are responsible are applicable, whether any provision of building regulations is or would be contravened by, or by anything done or proposed to be done in connection with, that work.

(2) The local authority shall have power for that purpose—

(*a*) to require any person by whom or on whose behalf the work was, is being or is proposed to be done to carry out such reasonable tests of or in connection with the work as may be specified in the requirement; or

(*b*) themselves to carry out any reasonable tests of or in connection with the work, and to take any samples necessary to enable them to carry out any such test.

(3) Without prejudice to the generality of the preceding subsection, the matters with respect to which tests may be required or carried out under that subsection include—

(*a*) tests of the soil or subsoil of the site of any building;

(*b*) tests of any material, component or combination of components which has been, is being or is proposed to be used in the construction of a building, and tests of any service, fitting or equipment which has been, is being or is proposed to be provided in or in connection with a building.

(4) A local authority shall have power, for the purpose of ascertaining whether there is or has been, in the case of any building, any contravention of any continuing requirement that applies in relation to that building—

(*a*) to require the owner or occupier of the building to carry out such reasonable tests as may be specified in the requirement under this paragraph; or

(*b*) themselves to carry out any tests which they have power to require under the preceding paragraph, and to take any samples necessary to enable them to carry out any such test.

In this subsection " continuing requirement " means a continuing requirement imposed by building regulations made by virtue of section 65(1) or (2).

(5) The expense of carrying out any tests which a person is required to carry out under this section shall be met by that person:

Provided that the local authority, on an application made to them, may, if they think it reasonable to do so, direct that the expense of carrying out any such tests, or such part of that expense as may be specified in the direction, shall be met by the local authority.

(6) Any question arising under this section between a local authority and any person as to the reasonableness—

(*a*) of any test specified in a requirement imposed on him by the authority under this section; or

(*b*) of a refusal by the authority to give a direction under subsection (5) above on an application made by him; or

(*c*) of a direction under that subsection given on such an application,

may on the application of that person be determined by a court of summary jurisdiction; and in a case falling within paragraph (*b*) or (*c*) above the court may order the expense to which the application relates to be met by the local authority to such extent as the court thinks just.

Provisions relating to appeals etc. to the Secretary of State under certain provisions.

69.—(1) On an appeal to the Secretary of State under section 64 of the 1936 Act, section 7 of the 1961 Act or section 64 of this Act, the Secretary of State may at his discretion afford to the appellant and the local authority an opportunity of appearing before, and being heard by, a person appointed by the Secretary of State for the purpose.

(2) On determining any such appeal as is mentioned in subsection (1) above, the Secretary of State shall give such directions, if any, as he considers appropriate for giving effect to his determination.

(3) Where the Secretary of State gives a decision in proceedings—

(*a*) on any such appeal as is mentioned in subsection (1) above; or

(*b*) on a reference under section 67 of the 1936 Act; or

(*c*) on any application for a direction under section 6 of the 1961 Act where the power of giving the direction is not exercisable by the local authority,

the relevant person or the local authority may appeal to the High Court against the decision on a point of law.

Part III In this subsection " the relevant person "—

(i) as regards such an appeal as is mentioned in paragraph (*a*) above, means the appellant;

(ii) as regards a reference under the said section 67, means the person on whose application (jointly with the local authority) the reference was made;

(iii) as regards any such application as is mentioned in paragraph (*c*) above, means the applicant.

(4) At any stage of the proceedings on any such appeal, reference or application as is mentioned in the preceding subsection, the Secretary of State may state any question of law arising in the course of the proceedings in the form of a special case for the decision of the High Court; and a decision of the High Court on a case stated by virtue of this subsection shall be deemed to be a judgment of the court within the meaning of section 27 of the Supreme Court of Judicature (Consolidation) Act 1925 (jurisdiction of the Court of Appeal to hear and determine appeals from any judgment of the High Court).

1925 c. 49.

(5) In relation to any proceedings in the High Court or the Court of Appeal brought by virtue of this section the power to make rules of court shall include power to make rules—

(*a*) prescribing the powers of the High Court or the Court of Appeal with respect to the remitting of the matter with the opinion or direction of the court for re-hearing and determination by the Secretary of State; and

(*b*) providing for the Secretary of State, either generally or in such circumstances as may be prescribed by the rules, to be treated as a party to any such proceedings and to be entitled to appear and to be heard accordingly.

(6) Rules of court relating to any such proceedings as are mentioned in subsection (5) of this section may provide for excluding so much of section 63(1) of the said Act of 1925 as requires appeals to the High Court to be heard and determined by a Divisional Court; but no appeal to the Court of Appeal shall be brought by virtue of this section except with the leave of the High Court or the Court of Appeal.

(7) In this section " decision " includes a direction, and references to the giving of a decision shall be construed accordingly.

(8) Without prejudice to section 4(5) of the 1961 Act, building regulations may in connection with any such appeal as is mentioned in subsection (1) above include such supplementary provisions with respect to procedure as the Secretary of State thinks fit.

PART III

Power to make building regulations for Inner London.

70.—(1) The following enactments (which relate to the power to make, and other matters connected with, building regulations), namely sections 61, 62 and 67 of the 1936 Act and sections 4(2) and (5) to (7), 5 and 9 of the 1961 Act, shall (with this Part, except section 75 and Schedule 7) apply throughout Inner London as they apply elsewhere in England and Wales; but without prejudice to that power as extended by this subsection, this subsection shall not of itself cause any building regulations made before it comes into force to apply to Inner London.

(2) Subject to any provision made by virtue of section 62(4), it shall be the duty of the Greater London Council to enforce in Inner London any building regulations which are in force there except to the extent that other local authorities or district surveyors within the meaning of the London Building Acts 1930 to 1939 are by virtue of building regulations made responsible for their enforcement there.

(3) Where by virtue of this section or section 62(4) local authorities or any prescribed person or class of persons (other than local authorities) are made responsible for enforcing, or performing prescribed functions under or in connection with, building regulations in force in Inner London, then, without prejudice to the said section 62(4), building regulations may in that connection provide for any prescribed provision falling within section 76(1)(*a*) or (*b*) but not mentioned in subsection (1) above to apply (with any prescribed modifications, and notwithstanding paragraph 12 or 34 of Part I of Schedule 11 to the London Government Act 1963) in relation to any such authority or person, or persons of any such class, as that provision applies in relation to a local authority outside Inner London. **1963 c. 33.**

(4) Without prejudice to the generality of section 62(5) building regulations may repeal or modify any provision to which this subsection applies if it appears to the Secretary of State that the repeal or, as the case may be, the modification of that provision is expedient in consequence of the provisions of this section or in connection with any provision contained in building regulations that apply to or to any part of Inner London.

(5) The preceding subsection applies to any provision—

(*a*) of the London Building Acts 1930 to 1939;

(*b*) of any enactment contained in this Act, other than this Part, or in any other Act passed before or in the same Session as this Act, in so far as that provision—

(i) applies to or to any part of Inner London; and

PART III

(ii) relates to, or to the making of, byelaws for or for any part of Inner London with respect to any matter for or in connection with which provision can be made by building regulations;

(*c*) of any byelaws made or having effect under the said Acts or of any such byelaws as are mentioned in paragraph (*b*)(ii) above.

(6) Before making any building regulations that provide for the repeal or modification of any provision to which the preceding subsection applies, the Secretary of State shall (without prejudice to the requirements as to consultation in section 9(3) of the 1961 Act) consult the Greater London Council and any other local authority who appear to him to be concerned.

(7) In this section " Inner London " means the area comprising the Inner London boroughs, the City, and the Inner Temple and the Middle Temple.

1963 c. 33.

(8) In Part I of Schedule 11 to the London Government Act 1963 (modifications of Public Health Acts)—

(*a*) in paragraph 12, for the words " 53 to 55, and 57 to 71 " there shall be substituted the words " 54, 55, 57 to 60, 64 to 66, 69, 70 and (so far as unrepealed) 71 ";

(*b*) in paragraph 34, for the words " 4 to 11 " there shall be substituted the words " 4(3) and (4), 6 to 8 and 10 and (except in so far as it amends any enactment mentioned in section 70(1) of the Health and Safety at Work etc. Act 1974) section 11 ".

Civil liability.

71.—(1) Subject to the provisions of this section, breach of a duty imposed by building regulations shall, so far as it causes damage, be actionable except in so far as the regulations provide otherwise; and as regards any such duty building regulations may provide for any prescribed defence to be available in any action for breach of that duty brought by virtue of this subsection.

(2) Subsection (1) above and any defence provided for in regulations made by virtue thereof shall not apply in the case of a breach of such a duty in connection with a building erected before the date on which that subsection comes into force unless the regulations imposing the duty apply to or in connection with the building by virtue of section 62 of the 1936 Act or section 65(2) of this Act.

(3) Nothing in this section shall be construed as affecting the extent (if any) to which breach—

(*a*) of a duty imposed by or arising in connection with this Part or any other enactment relating to building regulations; or (*b*) of a duty imposed by building regulations in a case to which subsection (1) above does not apply, PART III

is actionable, or as prejudicing any right of action which exists apart from the enactments relating to building regulations.

(4) In this section " damage " includes the death of, or injury to, any person (including any disease and any impairment of a person's physical or mental condition).

Application to Crown.

72.—(1) Except in so far as building regulations provide otherwise, the substantive provisions of building regulations—

(*a*) shall apply in relation to work carried out or proposed to be carried out by or on behalf of a Crown authority (whether or not in relation to a Crown building) as they would apply if the person by or on behalf of whom the work was or is to be carried out were not a Crown authority; and

(*b*) so far as they consist of continuing requirements, shall apply to Crown authorities (whether or not in relation to Crown buildings) as they apply to persons who are not Crown authorities.

(2) In so far as building regulations so provide as regards any of the substantive requirements of building regulations, those requirements shall apply in relation to work carried out or proposed to be carried out as mentioned in subsection (1)(*a*) above in Inner London and, so far as they consist of continuing requirements, shall apply to Crown authorities there as mentioned in subsection (1)(*b*) above, even if those requirements do not apply there in the case of work carried out or proposed to be carried out otherwise than by or on behalf of a Crown authority or, in the case of continuing requirements, do not apply there to persons other than Crown authorities.

In this subsection " Inner London " has the same meaning as in section 70.

(3) Except in so far as building regulations provide otherwise, building regulations and the enactments relating to building regulations—

(*a*) shall apply in relation to work carried out or proposed to be carried out in relation to a Crown building otherwise than by or on behalf of a Crown authority, and, in the case of section 65 and building regulations made by virtue thereof, shall in relation to a Crown building apply to persons other than Crown authorities, as they would apply if the building were not a Crown building; and

PART III

(*b*) shall apply in relation to work carried out or proposed to be carried out by or on behalf of a government department acting for a person other than a Crown authority as they would apply if the work had been or were to be carried out by that person.

(4) Section 341 of the 1936 Act (power to apply provisions of that Act to Crown property) shall not apply to provisions relating to building regulations.

(5) Section 71 and any building regulations made by virtue of subsection (1) of that section shall apply in relation to duties imposed by building regulations in their application in accordance with the preceding provisions of this section.

(6) In the case of work carried out or proposed to be carried out by or on behalf of a Crown authority, and in any case in which a Crown authority is or (apart from any dispensation or relaxation) will be subject to any continuing requirements, that authority may exercise the like powers of dispensing with or relaxing the substantive requirements of building regulations or, as the case may be, the continuing requirements in question as are conferred on the Secretary of State and local authorities by virtue of section 6 of the 1961 Act (other than a power excepted by the following subsection), subject, however, to the like requirements as to consultation (if any) as apply by virtue of section 62(1) in the case of a local authority (but not the requirements of the said section 6 as to consultation with the local authority) and to the like requirements as in the case of the Secretary of State apply by virtue of section 8 of that Act (opportunity to make representations about proposal to relax building regulations); and no application shall be necessary for the exercise of any such powers by virtue of this subsection.

In relation to any continuing requirements references in this subsection to the said section 6 are references thereto as modified by section 65(5).

(7) The power excepted from the preceding subsection is one which by virtue of section 62(4) is exercisable otherwise than by a local authority.

(8) For the purposes of subsection (6) above work carried out or proposed to be carried out by or on behalf of a government department acting for another Crown authority shall be treated as carried out or proposed to be carried out by or on behalf of that department (and not by or on behalf of the other Crown authority).

(9) In this section—

"continuing requirement" means a continuing requirement of building regulations imposed by virtue of section 65(1) or (2)(*a*) or (*b*).

"Crown authority" means the Crown Estate Commissioners, a Minister of the Crown, a government department, any other person or body whose functions are performed on behalf of the Crown (not being a person or body whose functions are performed on behalf of Her Majesty in her private capacity), or any person acting in right of the Duchy of Lancaster or the Duchy of Cornwall;

"Crown building" means a building in which there is a Crown interest or a Duchy interest;

"Crown interest" means an interest belonging to Her Majesty in right of the Crown or belonging to a government department, or held in trust for Her Majesty for the purposes of a government department;

"Duchy interest" means an interest belonging to Her Majesty in right of the Duchy of Lancaster, or belonging to the Duchy of Cornwall.

(10) If any question arises under this section as to which Crown authority is entitled to exercise any such powers as are mentioned in subsection (6) above, that question shall be referred to the Treasury, whose decision shall be final.

(11) The preceding provisions of this section shall, with any necessary modifications, apply in relation to the making of a material change in the use of a building within the meaning of building regulations made for the purposes of section 62(1)(*e*) of the 1936 Act (as substituted by this Part) as they apply in relation to the carrying out of work.

Application to United Kingdom Atomic Energy Authority.

73.—(1) The provisions of section 72, except subsections (2) to (4), shall apply in relation to the United Kingdom Atomic Energy Authority (in this section referred to as " the Authority ") as if—

(*a*) the Authority were a Crown authority;

(*b*) any building belonging to or occupied by the Authority were a Crown building; and

(*c*) the references in subsection (1) to not being a Crown authority were references to being neither a Crown authority nor the Authority,

but so that the said provisions shall not by virtue of this subsection apply in relation to dwelling-houses or offices belonging to or occupied by the Authority.

(2) Subject to the said provisions as applied by the preceding subsection, building regulations and the enactments relating to building regulations shall not apply in relation to buildings belonging to or occupied by the Authority, being buildings other than dwelling-houses or offices.

Part III

Meaning of "building" etc. in connection with, and construction of references to, building regulations.

74.—(1) For the purposes of any enactment to which this subsection applies—

(*a*) " building " means any permanent or temporary building and, unless the context otherwise requires, includes any other structure or erection of whatever kind or nature (whether permanent or temporary), and in this paragraph, " structure or erection " shall include a vehicle, vessel, hovercraft, aircraft or other movable object of any kind in such circumstances as may be prescribed (being circumstances which in the opinion of the Secretary of State justify treating it for those purposes as a building) ;

(*b*) unless the context otherwise requires, any reference to a building includes a reference to part of a building, and any reference to the provision of services, fittings and equipment in or in connection with buildings, or to services, fittings and equipment so provided, includes a reference to the affixing of things to buildings or, as the case may be, to things so affixed ; and

(*c*) references to the construction or erection of a building shall include references to—

(i) the carrying out of such operations (whether for the reconstruction of a building, the roofing over of an open space between walls or buildings, or otherwise) as may be designated in building regulations as operations falling to be treated for those purposes as the construction or erection of a building, and

(ii) the conversion of a movable object into what is by virtue of paragraph (*a*) above a building,

and " construct " and " erect " shall be construed accordingly.

(2) The preceding subsection applies to sections 61 to 71 of the 1936 Act and to any other enactment (whether or not contained in the 1936 Act or this Act) which relates to building regulations or mentions " buildings " or " a building " in a context from which it appears that those expressions are there intended to have the same meaning as in the said sections 61 to 71.

(3) Unless the context otherwise requires, references in this Act or any other enactment (whether passed before or after this Act) to building regulations shall, in any particular case in relation to which any requirement of building regulations is for the time being dispensed with, waived, relaxed or modified by virtue of section 6 of the 1961 Act, section 66 of this Act or any other enactment, be construed as references to building regulations as they apply in that case.

PART III

Amendment of Building (Scotland) Act 1959.
1959 c. 24.

75. The Building (Scotland) Act 1959 shall have effect subject to the amendments provided for in Schedule 7.

Construction and interpretation of Part III and other provisions relating to building regulations.

76.—(1) The following provisions, namely—

(*a*) so much of Part II of the 1936 Act as relates to building regulations;

(*b*) so much of Part II of the 1961 Act as relates to building regulations; and

(*c*) this Part, except section 75 and Schedule 7;

shall be construed as one; and Part XII of the 1936 Act shall have effect as if the provisions mentioned in paragraph (*b*) and (*c*) above (as well as those mentioned in paragraph (*a*)) were contained in Part II of that Act.

(2) For the purposes of the provisions mentioned in subsection (1)(*a*) to (*c*) above—

(*a*) "local authority" means a district council, the Greater London Council, a London borough council, the Sub-Treasurer of the Inner Temple or the Under-Treasurer of the Middle Temple, and includes the Council of the Isles of Scilly; and

(*b*) the definitions of "local authority" in section 1(2) of the 1936 Act and section 2(3) of the 1961 Act shall not apply;

and in section 1(1) of the 1961 Act (Part II of that Act to be construed as one with Part II of the 1936 Act), after the words "Part II of this Act" there shall be inserted the words ", except so much of it as relates to building regulations,".

(3) In this Part—

"the 1936 Act" means the Public Health Act 1936; 1936 c. 49.

"the 1961 Act" means the Public Health Act 1961; 1961 c. 64.

"the substantive requirements of building regulations" means the requirements of building regulations with respect to the design and construction of buildings and the provision of services, fittings and equipment in or in connection with buildings (including requirements imposed by virtue of section 65(1) or (2)(*a*) or (*b*)), as distinct from procedural requirements.

(4) In this Part, in sections 61 to 71 of the 1936 Act and in sections 4 to 8 of the 1961 Act "prescribed" means prescribed by building regulations.

PART IV

MISCELLANEOUS AND GENERAL

Amendment of Radiological Protection Act 1970.
1970 c. 46.

77.—(1) Section 1 of the Radiological Protection Act 1970 (establishment and functions of the National Radiological Protection Board) shall be amended in accordance with the following provisions of this subsection—

(*a*) after subsection (6) there shall be inserted as subsection (6A)—

" (6A) In carrying out such of their functions as relate to matters to which the functions of the Health and Safety Commission relate, the Board shall (without prejudice to subsection (7) below) act in consultation with the Commission and have regard to the Commission's policies with respect to such matters." ;

(*b*) after subsection (7) there shall be inserted as subsections (7A) and (7B)—

" (7A) Without prejudice to subsection (6) or (7) above, it shall be the duty of the Board, if so directed by the Health Ministers, to enter into an agreement with the Health and Safety Commission for the Board to carry out on behalf of the Commission such of the Commission's functions relating to ionising or other radiations (including those which are not electro-magnetic) as may be determined by or in accordance with the direction; and the Board shall have power to carry out any agreement entered into in pursuance of a direction under this subsection.

(7B) The requirement as to consultation in subsection (7) above shall not apply to a direction under subsection (7A)." ;

(*c*) in subsection (8), after the words " subsection (7) " there shall be inserted the words " or (7A) ".

(2) In section 2(6) of the Radiological Protection Act 1970 (persons by whom, as regards premises occupied by the said Board, sections 1 to 51 of the Offices, Shops and Railway
1963 c. 41.
Premises Act 1963 and regulations thereunder are enforceable) for the words from " inspectors appointed " to the end of the subsection there shall be substituted the words " inspectors appointed by the Health and Safety Executive under section 19 of the Health and Safety at Work etc. Act 1974."

Amendment of Fire Precautions Act 1971.
1971 c. 40.

78.—(1) The Fire Precautions Act 1971 shall be amended in accordance with the following provisions of this section.

(2) In section 1(2) (power to designate uses of premises for which fire certificate is compulsory) at the end there shall be inserted as paragraph (*f*)—

" (*f*) use as a place of work."

PART IV

(3) In section 2 (premises exempt from section 1), paragraphs (*a*) to (*c*) (which exempt certain premises covered by the Offices, Shops and Railway Premises Act 1963, the Factories Act 1961 or the Mines and Quarries Act 1954) shall cease to have effect. 1963 c. 41. 1961 c. 34. 1954 c. 70.

(4) After section 9 there shall be inserted as section 9A—

"Duty to provide certain premises with means of escape in case of fire.

9A.—(1) All premises to which this section applies shall be provided with such means of escape in case of fire for the persons employed to work therein as may reasonably be required in the circumstances of the case.

(2) The premises to which this section applies are—

(*a*) office premises, shop premises and railway premises to which the Offices, Shops and Railway Premises Act 1963 applies; and

(*b*) premises which are deemed to be such premises for the purposes of that Act,

being (in each case) premises in which persons are employed to work.

(3) In determining, for the purposes of this section, what means of escape may reasonably be required in the case of any premises, regard shall be had (amongst other things) not only to the number of persons who may be expected to be working in the premises at any time but also to the number of persons (other than those employed to work therein) who may reasonably be expected to be resorting to the premises at that time.

(4) In the event of a contravention of subsection (1) above the occupier of the premises shall be guilty of an offence and liable on summary conviction to a fine not exceeding £400."

(5) In section 12(1) (power to make regulations about fire precautions as regards certain premises), at the end there shall be added the words " and nothing in this section shall confer on the Secretary of State power to make provision with respect to the taking or observance of special precautions in connection with the carrying on of any manufacturing process.

(6) In section 17 (duty of fire authorities to consult other authorities before requiring alterations to buildings)—

(*a*) in subsection (1), the word " and " shall be omitted where last occurring in paragraph (i) and shall be added at the end of paragraph (ii), and after paragraph

PART IV

(ii) there shall be added as paragraph (iii)—

" (iii) if the premises are used as a place of work and are within the field of responsibility of one or more enforcing authorities within the meaning of Part I of the Health and Safety at Work etc. Act 1974, consult that authority or each of those authorities." ;

(*b*) in subsection (2) (clarification of references in section 9 to persons aggrieved), for the words " or buildings authority " there shall be substituted the words " buildings authority or other authority " ;

(*c*) after subsection (2) there shall be added as subsection (3)—

" (3) Section 18(7) of the Health and Safety at Work etc. Act 1974 (meaning in Part I of that Act of ' enforcing authority ' and of such an authority's ' field of responsibility ') shall apply for the purposes of this section as it applies for the purposes of that Part."

(7) In section 18 (enforcement of Act)—

(*a*) for the word " it " there shall be substituted the words " (1) Subject to subsection (2) below, it " ;

(*b*) for the word " section " there shall be substituted the word " subsection "; and

(*c*) after the word " offence " there shall be added as subsection (2)—

" (2) A fire authority shall have power to arrange with the Health and Safety Commission for such of the authority's functions under this Act as may be specified in the arrangements to be performed on their behalf by the Health and Safety Executive (with or without payment) in relation to any particular premises so specified which are used as a place of work."

(8) In section 40 (application to Crown etc.)—

(*a*) in subsection (1)(*a*) (provisions which apply to premises occupied by the Crown), after the word " 6 " there shall be inserted the words ", 9A (except subsection (4)) " ;

(*b*) in subsection (1)(*b*) (provisions which apply to premises owned, but not occupied by, the Crown), after the word " 8 " there shall be inserted the word " 9A " ;

(*c*) in subsection (10) (application of Act to hospital premises in Scotland), for the words from " Regional " to " hospitals " there shall be substituted the words " Health Board " ;

PART IV

(*d*) after subsection (10) there shall be inserted the following subsection—

" (10A) This Act shall apply to premises in England occupied by a Board of Governors of a teaching hospital (being a body for the time being specified in an order under section 15(1) of the National Health Service Reorganisation Act 1973) as if they were premises occupied by the Crown.". 1973 c. 12.

(9) In section 43(1) (interpretation) there shall be added at the end the following definition—

" work " has the same meaning as it has for the purposes of Part I of the Health and Safety at Work etc. Act 1974 ".

(10) Schedule 8 (transitional provisions with respect to fire certificates under the Factories Act 1961 or the Offices, Shops and Railway Premises Act 1963) shall have effect. 1961 c. 34. 1963 c. 41.

Amendment of Companies Acts as to directors' reports.

1967 c. 81.

79.—(1) The Companies Act 1967 shall be amended in accordance with the following provisions of this section.

(2) In section 16 (additional general matters to be dealt with in directors' reports) in subsection (1) there shall be added after paragraph (*f*)—

" (*g*) in the case of companies of such classes as may be prescribed by regulations made by the Secretary of State, contain such information as may be so prescribed about the arrangements in force in that year for securing the health, safety and welfare at work of employees of the company and its subsidiaries and for protecting other persons against risks to health or safety arising out of or in connection with the activities at work of those employees."

(3) After subsection (4) of the said section 16 there shall be added—

" (5) Regulations made under paragraph (*g*) of subsection (1) above may—

(*a*) make different provision in relation to companies of different classes ;

(*b*) enable any requirements of the regulations to be dispensed with or modified in particular cases by any specified person or by any person authorised in that behalf by a specified authority ;

(*c*) contain such transitional provisions as the Secretary of State thinks necessary or expedient in connection with any provision made by the regulations.

PART IV

(6) The power to make regulations under the said paragraph (*g*) shall be exercisable by statutory instrument which shall be subject to annulment in pursuance of a resolution of either House of Parliament.

(7) Any expression used in the said paragraph (*g*) and in Part I of the Health and Safety at Work etc. Act 1974 shall have the same meaning in that paragraph as it has in that Part of that Act and section 1(3) of that Act shall apply for interpreting that paragraph as it applies for interpreting that Part of that Act; and in subsection (5) above "specified" means specified in regulations made under that paragraph.".

General power to repeal or modify Acts and instruments.

80.—(1) Regulations made under this subsection may repeal or modify any provision to which this subsection applies if it appears to the authority making the regulations that the repeal or, as the case may be, the modification of that provision is expedient in consequence of or in connection with any provision made by or under Part I.

(2) Subsection (1) above applies to any provision, not being among the relevant statutory provisions, which—

(*a*) is contained in this Act or in any other Act passed before or in the same Session as this Act; or

(*b*) is contained in any regulations, order or other instrument of a legislative character which was made under an Act before the passing of this Act; or

(*c*) applies, excludes or for any other purpose refers to any of the relevant statutory provisions and is contained in any Act not falling within paragraph (*a*) above or in any regulations, order or other instrument of a legislative character which is made under an Act but does not fall within paragraph (*b*) above.

(3) Without prejudice to the generality of subsection (1) above, the modifications which may be made by regulations thereunder include modifications relating to the enforcement of provisions to which this section applies (including the appointment of persons for the purpose of such enforcement, and the powers of persons so appointed).

. . .

"(4) The power to make regulations under subsection (1) above shall be exercisable by the Secretary of State, the Minister of Agriculture, Fisheries and Food or the Secretary of State and that Minister acting jointly; but the authority who is to exercise the power shall, before exercising it, consult such bodies as appear to him to be appropriate.

(5) In this section 'the relevant statutory provisions' has the same meaning as in Part I.".

. . .

Expenses and receipts.

81. There shall be paid out of money provided by Parliament—

(*a*) any expenses incurred by a Minister of the Crown or government department for the purposes of this Act; and

(*b*) any increase attributable to the provisions of this Act in the sums payable under any other Act out of money so provided;

and any sums received by a Minister of the Crown or government department by virtue of this Act shall be paid into the Consolidated Fund.

General provisions as to interpretation and regulations.

82.—(1) In this Act—

(*a*) "Act" includes a provisional order confirmed by an Act;

(*b*) "contravention" includes failure to comply, and "contravene" has a corresponding meaning;

(*c*) "modifications" includes additions, omissions and amendments, and related expressions shall be construed accordingly;

(*d*) any reference to a Part, section or Schedule not otherwise identified is a reference to that Part or section of, or Schedule to, this Act.

(2) Except in so far as the context otherwise requires, any reference in this Act to an enactment is a reference to it as amended, and includes a reference to it as applied, by or under any other enactment, including this Act.

Part IV

(3) Any power conferred by Part I or II or this Part to make regulations—

(*a*) includes power to make different provision by the regulations for different circumstances or cases and to include in the regulations such incidental, supplemental and transitional provisions as the authority making the regulations considers appropriate in connection with the regulations ; and

(*b*) shall be exercisable by statutory instrument, which shall be subject to annulment in pursuance of a resolution of either House of Parliament.

Minor and consequential amendments, and repeals.

83.—(1) The enactments mentioned in Schedule 9 shall have effect subject to the amendments specified in that Schedule (being minor amendments or amendments consequential upon the provisions of this Act).

(2) The enactments mentioned in Schedule 10 are hereby repealed to the extent specified in the third column of that Schedule.

Extent, and application of Act.

84.—(1) This Act, except—

(*a*) Part I and this Part so far as may be necessary to enable regulations under section 15 to be made and operate for the purpose mentioned in paragraph 2 of Schedule 3 ; and

(*b*) paragraphs 2 and 3 of Schedule 9,

does not extend to Northern Ireland.

(2) Part III, except section 75 and Schedule 7, does not extend to Scotland.

(3) Her Majesty may by Order in Council provide that the provisions of Parts I and II and this Part shall, to such extent and for such purposes as may be specified in the Order, apply (with or without modification) to or in relation to persons, premises, work, articles, substances and other matters (of whatever kind) outside Great Britain as those provisions apply within Great Britain or within a part of Great Britain so specified.

For the purposes of this subsection " premises ", " work " and " substance " have the same meaning as they have for the purposes of Part I.

(4) An Order in Council under subsection (3) above—

(*a*) may make different provision for different circumstances or cases ;

(*b*) may (notwithstanding that this may affect individuals or bodies corporate outside the United Kingdom) provide for any of the provisions mentioned in that subsection, as applied by such an Order, to apply to individuals whether or not they are British subjects and to bodies corporate whether or not they are incorporated under the law of any part of the United Kingdom; — PART IV

(c) may make provision for conferring jurisdiction on any court or class of courts specified in the Order with respect to offences under Part I committed outside Great Britain or with respect to causes of action arising by virtue of section 47(2) in respect of acts or omissions taking place outside Great Britain, and for the determination, in accordance with the law in force in such part of Great Britain as may be specified in the Order, of questions arising out of such acts or omissions;

(d) may exclude from the operation of section 3 of the Territorial Waters Jurisdiction Act 1878 (consents required for prosecutions) proceedings for offences under any provision of Part I committed outside Great Britain; — 1878 c. 73.

(e) may be varied or revoked by a subsequent Order in Council under this section;

and any such Order shall be subject to annulment in pursuance of a resolution of either House of Parliament.

(5) In relation to proceedings for an offence under Part I committed outside Great Britain by virtue of an Order in Council under subsection (3) above, section 38 shall have effect as if the words " by an inspector, or " were omitted.

(6) Any jurisdiction conferred on any court under this section shall be without prejudice to any jurisdiction exercisable apart from this section by that or any other court.

85.—(1) This Act may be cited as the Health and Safety at Work etc. Act 1974. — Short title and commencement.

(2) This Act shall come into operation on such day as the Secretary of State may by order made by statutory instrument appoint, and different days may be appointed under this subsection for different purposes.

(3) An order under this section may contain such transitional provisions and savings as appear to the Secretary of State to be necessary or expedient in connection with the provisions thereby brought into force, including such adaptations of those provisions or any provision of this Act then in force as appear to him to be necessary or expedient in consequence of the partial operation of this Act (whether before or after the day appointed by the order).

SCHEDULES

Sections 1 and 53.

SCHEDULE 1

Existing Enactments which are Relevant Statutory Provisions

Chapter	Short title	Provisions which are relevant statutory provisions
1875 c. 17.	The Explosives Act 1875.	The whole Act except sections 30 to 32, 80 and 116 to 121.
1882 c. 22.	The Boiler Explosions Act 1882.	The whole Act.
1890 c. 35.	The Boiler Explosions Act 1890.	The whole Act.
1906 c. 14.	The Alkali, &c. Works Regulation Act 1906.	The whole Act.
1909 c. 43.	The Revenue Act 1909.	Section 11.
1919 c. 23.	The Anthrax Prevention Act 1919.	The whole Act.
1920 c. 65.	The Employment of Women, Young Persons and Children Act 1920.	The whole Act.
1922 c. 35.	The Celluloid and Cinematograph Film Act 1922.	The whole Act.
1923 c. 17.	The Explosives Act 1923.	The whole Act.
1926 c. 43.	The Public Health (Smoke Abatement) Act 1926.	The whole Act.
1928 c. 32.	The Petroleum (Consolidation) Act 1928.	The whole Act.
1936 c. 22.	The Hours of Employment (Conventions) Act 1936.	The whole Act except section 5.
1936 c. 27.	The Petroleum (Transfer of Licences) Act 1936.	The whole Act.
1937 c. 45.	The Hydrogen Cyanide (Fumigation) Act 1937.	The whole Act.
1945 c. 19.	The Ministry of Fuel and Power Act 1945.	Section 1(1) so far as it relates to maintaining and improving the safety, health and welfare of persons employed in or about mines and quarries in Great Britain.
1946 c. 59.	The Coal Industry Nationalisation Act 1946.	Section 42(1) and (2).
1948 c. 37.	The Radioactive Substances Act 1948.	Section 5(1)(*a*).

• • •

Chapter	Short title	Provisions which are relevant statutory provisions
1951 c. 58.	The Fireworks Act 1951.	Sections 4 and 7.
1952 c. 60.	The Agriculture (Poisonous Substances) Act 1952.	The whole Act.

SCH. 1

Chapter	Short title	Provisions which are relevant statutory provisions
1953 c. 47.	The Emergency Laws (Miscellaneous Provisions) Act 1953.	Section 3.
[1954 c. 57	The Baking Industry (Hours of Work) Act 1954	The whole Act.]
1954 c. 70.	The Mines and Quarries Act 1954.	The whole Act except section 151.
1956 c. 49.	The Agriculture (Safety, Health and Welfare Provisions) Act 1956.	The whole Act.
1961 c. 34.	The Factories Act 1961.	The whole Act except section 135.
1961 c. 64.	The Public Health Act 1961.	Section 73.
1962 c. 58.	The Pipe-lines Act 1962.	Sections 20 to 26, 33, 34 and 42, Schedule 5.
1963 c. 41.	The Offices, Shops and Railway Premises Act 1963.	The whole Act.
1965 c. 57.	The Nuclear Installations Act 1965.	Sections 1, 3 to 6, 22 and 24, Schedule 2.
1969 c. 10.	The Mines and Quarries (Tips) Act 1969.	Sections 1 to 10.
1971 c. 20.	The Mines Management Act 1971.	The whole Act.
1972 c. 28.	The Employment Medical Advisory Service Act 1972.	The whole Act except sections 1 and 6 and Schedule 1.

SCHEDULE 2

Section 10.

ADDITIONAL PROVISIONS RELATING TO CONSTITUTION ETC. OF THE COMMISSION AND EXECUTIVE

Tenure of office

1. Subject to paragraphs 2 to 4 below, a person shall hold and vacate office as a member or as chairman or deputy chairman in accordance with the terms of the instrument appointing him to that office.

2. A person may at any time resign his office as a member or as chairman or deputy chairman by giving the Secretary of State a notice in writing signed by that person and stating that he resigns that office.

3.—(1) If a member becomes or ceases to be the chairman or deputy chairman, the Secretary of State may vary the terms of the instrument appointing him to be a member so as to alter the date on which he is to vacate office as a member.

(2) If the chairman or deputy chairman ceases to be a member he shall cease to be chairman or deputy chairman, as the case may be.

SCH. 2

4.—(1) If the Secretary of State is satisfied that a member—

(*a*) has been absent from meetings of the Commission for a period longer than six consecutive months without the permission of the Commission ; or

(*b*) has become bankrupt or made an arrangement with his creditors ; or

(*c*) is incapacitated by physical or mental illness ; or

(*d*) is otherwise unable or unfit to discharge the functions of a member,

the Secretary of State may declare his office as a member to be vacant and shall notify the declaration in such manner as the Secretary of State thinks fit ; and thereupon the office shall become vacant.

(2) In the application of the preceding sub-paragraph to Scotland for the references in paragraph (*b*) to a member's having become bankrupt and to a member's having made an arrangement with his creditors there shall be substituted respectively references to sequestration of a member's estate having been awarded and to a member's having made a trust deed for behoof of his creditors or a composition contract.

Remuneration etc. of members

5. The Commission may pay to each member such remuneration and allowances as the Secretary of State may determine.

6. The Commission may pay or make provision for paying, to or in respect of any member, such sums by way of pension, superannuation allowances and gratuities as the Secretary of State may determine.

7. Where a person ceases to be a member otherwise than on the expiry of his term of office and it appears to the Secretary of State that there are special circumstances which make it right for him to receive compensation, the Commission may make to him a payment of such amount as the Secretary of State may determine.

Proceedings

8. The quorum of the Commission and the arrangements relating to meetings of the Commission shall be such as the Commission may determine.

9. The validity of any proceedings of the Commission shall not be affected by any vacancy among the members or by any defect in the appointment of a member.

Staff

10. It shall be the duty of the Executive to provide for the Commission such officers and servants as are requisite for the proper discharge of the Commission's functions ; and any reference in this Act to an officer or servant of the Commission is a reference to an officer or servant provided for the Commission in pursuance of this paragraph.

11. The Executive may appoint such officers and servants as it may determine with the consent of the Secretary of State as to numbers and terms and conditions of service. **Sch. 2**

12. The Commission shall pay to the Minister for the Civil Service, at such times in each accounting year as may be determined by that Minister subject to any directions of the Treasury, sums of such amounts as he may so determine for the purposes of this paragraph as being equivalent to the increase during that year of such liabilities of his as are attributable to the provision of pensions, allowances or gratuities to or in respect of persons who are or have been in the service of the Executive in so far as that increase results from the service of those persons during that accounting year and to the expense to be incurred in administering those pensions, allowances or gratuities.

Performance of functions

13. The Commission may authorise any member of the Commission or any officer or servant of the Commission or of the Executive to perform on behalf of the Commission such of the Commission's functions (including the function conferred on the Commission by this paragraph) as are specified in the authorisation.

Accounts and reports

14.—(1) It shall be the duty of the Commission—

(*a*) to keep proper accounts and proper records in relation to the accounts ;

(*b*) to prepare in respect of each accounting year a statement of accounts in such form as the Secretary of State may direct with the approval of the Treasury ; and

(*c*) to send copies of the statement to the Secretary of State and the Comptroller and Auditor General before the end of the month of November next following the accounting year to which the statement relates.

(2) The Comptroller and Auditor General shall examine, certify and report on each statement received by him in pursuance of this Schedule and shall lay copies of each statement and of his report before each House of Parliament.

15. It shall be the duty of the Commission to make to the Secretary of State, as soon as possible after the end of each accounting year, a report on the performance of its functions during that year ; and the Secretary of State shall lay before each House of Parliament a copy of each report made to him in pursuance of this paragraph.

Supplemental

16. The Secretary of State shall not make a determination or give his consent in pursuance of paragraph 5, 6, 7 or 11 of this Schedule except with the approval of the Minister for the Civil Service.

17. The fixing of the common seal of the Commission shall be authenticated by the signature of the secretary of the Commission or some other person authorised by the Commission to act for that purpose.

18. A document purporting to be duly executed under the seal of the Commission shall be received in evidence and shall, unless the contrary is proved, be deemed to be so executed.

19. In the preceding provisions of this Schedule—

(*a*) " accounting year " means the period of twelve months ending with 31st March in any year except that the first accounting year of the Commission shall, if the Secretary of State so directs, be such period shorter or longer than twelve months (but not longer than two years) as is specified in the direction ; and

(*b*) " the chairman ", " a deputy chairman " and " a member " mean respectively the chairman, a deputy chairman and a member of the Commission.

20.—(1) The preceding provisions of this Schedule (except paragraphs 10 to 12 and 15) shall have effect in relation to the Executive as if—

(*a*) for any reference to the Commission there were substituted a reference to the Executive ;

(*b*) for any reference to the Secretary of State in paragraphs 2 to 4 and 19 and the first such reference in paragraph 7 there were substituted a reference to the Commission ;

(*c*) for any reference to the Secretary of State in paragraphs 5 to 7 (except the first such reference in paragraph 7) there were substituted a reference to the Commission acting with the consent of the Secretary of State ;

(*d*) for any reference to the chairman there were substituted a reference to the director, and any reference to the deputy chairman were omitted ;

(*e*) in paragraph 14(1)(*c*) for the words from " Secretary " to " following " there were substituted the words " Commission by such date as the Commission may direct after the end of ".

(2) It shall be the duty of the Commission to include in or send with the copies of the statement sent by it as required by paragraph 14(1)(*c*) of this Schedule copies of the statement sent to it by the Executive in pursuance of the said paragraph 14(1)(*c*) as adapted by the preceding sub-paragraph.

(3) The terms of an instrument appointing a person to be a member of the Executive shall be such as the Commission may determine with the approval of the Secretary of State and the Minister for the Civil Service.

SCHEDULE 3

Section 15.

Subject-Matter of Health and Safety Regulations

1.—(1) Regulating or prohibiting—

(*a*) the manufacture, supply or use of any plant ;

(*b*) the manufacture, supply, keeping or use of any substance ;

(*c*) the carrying on of any process or the carrying out of any operation.

(2) Imposing requirements with respect to the design, construction, guarding, siting, installation, commissioning, examination, repair, maintenance, alteration, adjustment, dismantling, testing or inspection of any plant.

(3) Imposing requirements with respect to the marking of any plant or of any articles used or designed for use as components in any plant, and in that connection regulating or restricting the use of specified markings.

(4) Imposing requirements with respect to the testing, labelling or examination of any substance.

(5) Imposing requirements with respect to the carrying out of research in connection with any activity mentioned in sub-paragraphs (1) to (4) above.

2.—(1) Prohibiting the importation into the United Kingdom or the landing or unloading there of articles or substances of any specified description, whether absolutely or unless conditions imposed by or under the regulations are complied with.

(2) Specifying, in a case where an act or omission in relation to such an importation, landing or unloading as is mentioned in the preceding sub-paragraph constitutes an offence under a provision of this Act and of the Customs and Excise Act 1952, the Act under which the offence is to be punished. 1952 c. 44.

3.—(1) Prohibiting or regulating the transport of articles or substances of any specified description.

(2) Imposing requirements with respect to the manner and means of transporting articles or substances of any specified description, including requirements with respect to the construction, testing and marking of containers and means of transport and the packaging and labelling of articles or substances in connection with their transport.

4.—(1) Prohibiting the carrying on of any specified activity or the doing of any specified thing except under the authority and in accordance with the terms and conditions of a licence, or except with the consent or approval of a specified authority.

(2) Providing for the grant, renewal, variation, transfer and revocation of licences (including the variation and revocation of conditions attached to licences).

SCH. 3

5. Requiring any person, premises or thing to be registered in any specified circumstances or as a condition of the carrying on of any specified activity or the doing of any specified thing.

6.—(1) Requiring, in specified circumstances, the appointment (whether in a specified capacity or not) of persons (or persons with specified qualifications or experience, or both) to perform specified functions, and imposing duties or conferring powers on persons appointed (whether in pursuance of the regulations or not) to perform specified functions.

(2) Restricting the performance of specified functions to persons possessing specified qualifications or experience.

7. Regulating or prohibiting the employment in specified circumstances of all persons or any class of persons.

8.—(1) Requiring the making of arrangements for securing the health of persons at work or other persons, including arrangements for medical examinations and health surveys.

(2) Requiring the making of arrangements for monitoring the atmospheric or other conditions in which persons work.

9. Imposing requirements with respect to any matter affecting the conditions in which persons work, including in particular such matters as the structural condition and stability of premises, the means of access to and egress from premises, cleanliness, temperature, lighting, ventilation, overcrowding, noise, vibrations, ionising and other radiations, dust and fumes.

10. Securing the provision of specified welfare facilities for persons at work, including in particular such things as an adequate water supply, sanitary conveniences, washing and bathing facilities, ambulance and first-aid arrangements, cloakroom accommodation, sitting facilities and refreshment facilities.

11. Imposing requirements with respect to the provision and use in specified circumstances of protective clothing or equipment, including clothing affording protection against the weather.

12. Requiring in specified circumstances the taking of specified precautions in connection with the risk of fire.

13.—(1) Prohibiting or imposing requirements in connection with the emission into the atmosphere of any specified gas, smoke or dust or any other specified substance whatsoever.

(2) Prohibiting or imposing requirements in connection with the emission of noise, vibrations or any ionising or other radiations.

(3) Imposing requirements with respect to the monitoring of any such emission as is mentioned in the preceding sub-paragraphs.

14. Imposing requirements with respect to the instruction, training and supervision of persons at work.

15.—(1) Requiring, in specified circumstances, specified matters to be notified in a specified manner to specified persons.

(2) Empowering inspectors in specified circumstances to require persons to submit written particulars of measures proposed to be taken to achieve compliance with any of the relevant statutory provisions.

16. Imposing requirements with respect to the keeping and preservation of records and other documents, including plans and maps.

17. Imposing requirements with respect to the management of animals.

18. The following purposes as regards premises of any specified description where persons work, namely—

(*a*) requiring precautions to be taken against dangers to which the premises or persons therein are or may be exposed by reason of conditions (including natural conditions) existing in the vicinity;

(*b*) securing that persons in the premises leave them in specified circumstances.

19. Conferring, in specified circumstances involving a risk of fire or explosion, power to search a person or any article which a person has with him for the purpose of ascertaining whether he has in his possession any article of a specified kind likely in those circumstances to cause a fire or explosion, and power to seize and dispose of any article of that kind found on such a search.

20. Restricting, prohibiting or requiring the doing of any specified thing where any accident or other occurrence of a specified kind has occurred.

21. As regards cases of any specified class, being a class such that the variety in the circumstances of particular cases within it calls for the making of special provision for particular cases, any of the following purposes, namely—

(*a*) conferring on employers or other persons power to make rules or give directions with respect to matters affecting health or safety;

(*b*) requiring employers or other persons to make rules with respect to any such matters;

(*c*) empowering specified persons to require employers or other persons either to make rules with respect to any such matters or to modify any such rules previously made by virtue of this paragraph; and

SCH. 3

(*d*) making admissible in evidence without further proof, in such circumstances and subject to such conditions as may be specified, documents which purport to be copies of rules or rules of any specified class made under this paragraph.

22. Conferring on any local or public authority power to make byelaws with respect to any specified matter, specifying the authority or person by whom any byelaws made in the exercise of that power need to be confirmed, and generally providing for the procedure to be followed in connection with the making of any such byelaws.

Interpretation

23.—(1) In this Schedule "specified" means specified in health and safety regulations.

(2) It is hereby declared that the mention in this Schedule of a purpose that falls within any more general purpose mentioned therein is without prejudice to the generality of the more general purpose.

• • •

Section 61.

SCHEDULE 5

SUBJECT-MATTER OF BUILDING REGULATIONS

1. Preparation of sites.

2. Suitability, durability and use of materials and components (including surface finishes).

3. Structural strength and stability, including—

(*a*) precautions against overloading, impact and explosion;

(*b*) measures to safeguard adjacent buildings and services;

(*c*) underpinning.

4. Fire precautions, including—

(*a*) structural measures to resist the outbreak and spread of fire and to mitigate its effects;

(*b*) services, fittings and equipment designed to mitigate the effects of fire or to facilitate fire-fighting;

(*c*) means of escape in case of fire and means for securing that such means of escape can be safely and effectively used at all material times.

5. Resistance to moisture and decay. SCH. 5

6. Measures affecting the transmission of heat.

7. Measures affecting the transmission of sound.

8. Measures to prevent infestation.

9. Measures affecting the emission of smoke, gases, fumes, grit or dust or other noxious or offensive substances.

10. Drainage (including waste disposal units).

11. Cesspools and other means for the reception, treatment or disposal of foul matter.

12. Storage, treatment and removal of waste.

13. Installations utilising solid fuel, oil, gas, electricity or any other fuel or power (including appliances, storage tanks, heat exchangers, ducts, fans and other equipment).

14. Water services (including wells and bore-holes for the supply of water) and fittings and fixed equipment associated therewith.

15. Telecommunications services (including telephones and radio and television wiring installations).

16. Lifts, escalators, hoists, conveyors and moving footways.

17. Plant providing air under pressure.

18. Standards of heating, artificial lighting, mechanical ventilation and air-conditioning and provision of power outlets.

19. Open space about buildings and the natural lighting and ventilation of buildings.

20. Accommodation for specific purposes in or in connection with buildings, and the dimensions of rooms and other spaces within buildings.

21. Means of access to and egress from buildings and parts of buildings.

22. Prevention of danger and obstruction to persons in and about buildings (including passers-by).

23. Matters connected with or ancillary to any of the matters mentioned in the preceding provisions of this Schedule.

SCHEDULE 6

Section 61.

AMENDMENTS OF ENACTMENTS RELATING TO BUILDING REGULATIONS

PART I

AMENDMENTS

Amendments of Public Health Act 1936

1936 c. 49.

1. In section 64 of the 1936 Act (passing or rejection of plans)—

(*a*) for subsection (3) substitute—

"(3) Where plans of any proposed work deposited with a local authority are rejected in pursuance of the preceding provisions of this section, the person by whom or

SCH. 6

on whose behalf they were deposited may appeal against the rejection to the Secretary of State within the prescribed time and in the prescribed manner; and where the rejection results wholly or partly from the fact that a person or body whose approval or satisfaction in any respect is required by the regulations has withheld approval or not been satisfied, an appeal under this subsection may be brought on (or on grounds which include) the ground that the person or body in question ought in the circumstances to have approved or been satisfied in that respect." ; and

(*b*) subsection (4) shall cease to have effect.

2. In section 65 of the 1936 Act (power to require removal or alteration of work not in conformity with building regulations etc.)—

(*a*) in subsection (1), after " therein " insert " and additions thereto and to execute such additional work in connection therewith " ;

(*b*) after subsection (2) insert as subsection (2A)—

" (2A) Where a local authority have power to serve a notice under subsection (1) or (2) above on the owner of any work, they may in addition or instead serve such a notice on one or more of the following persons, namely the occupier and any builder or other person appearing to the authority to have control over the work." ;

(*c*) in subsection (3), after " therein " insert " and additions thereto and execute such additional work in connection therewith ", and at the end add as a proviso—

" Provided that where a notice under subsection (1) or (2) above is given to two or more persons in pursuance of subsection (2A) above, then—

(*a*) if they are given the notices on different dates, the said period of twenty-eight days shall for each of them run from the later or latest of those dates ; and

(*b*) if the notice is not complied with before the expiration of the said period or such longer period as a court of summary jurisdiction may on the application of any of them allow, any expenses recoverable as aforesaid may be recovered from any of them." ; and

(*d*) in subsection (4), for " or subsection (2) " substitute " , (2) or (2A) ", and at the end add as a proviso—

" Provided that, in a case where plans were deposited nothing in this subsection shall be taken to prevent such a notice from being given (before the expiration of twelve months from the completion of the work in question) in respect of anything of which particulars were not required to be shown in the plans.".

3. In section 90 of the 1936 Act (interpretation of Part II of that Act)— **Sch. 6**

(*a*) in subsection (2) (extended meaning, in that Part and building regulations, of references to the erection of a building), for the words from "and, so far" to "those regulations" substitute "except sections 61 to 71 and any other enactment to which section 74(1) of the Health and Safety at Work etc. Act 1974 applies"; and

(*b*) for subsection (3) (meaning of references to deposited plans) substitute—

"(3) In this Part of this Act, unless the context otherwise requires,—

(*a*) any reference to the deposit of plans in accordance with building regulations shall be construed as a reference to the deposit of plans in accordance with those regulations for the purposes of section 64 of this Act; and

(*b*) "plans" includes drawings of any other description and also specifications or other information in any form, and any reference to the deposit of plans shall be construed accordingly."

Amendments of Public Health Act 1961 **1961 c. 64.**

4. In section 4 of the 1961 Act (power to make building regulations)—

(*a*) in subsection (2) (power to make different provision for different areas) at the end add "and generally different provision for different circumstances or cases"; and

(*b*) in subsection (6) (penalties for contravening building regulations) after "building regulations" insert "other than a provision designated in the regulations as one to which this subsection does not apply,", and for "one hundred pounds" and "ten pounds" substitute respectively "£400" and "£50".

5. In section 6 of the 1961 Act (power to dispense with or relax requirements of building regulations)—

(*a*) in subsection (1), add at the end the words "either unconditionally or subject to compliance with any conditions specified in the direction, being conditions with respect to matters directly connected with the dispensation or relaxation.";

(*b*) in the proviso to subsection (2), for the words from "shall" onwards substitute "may except applications of any description";

(*c*) for subsection (6) substitute—

"(6) An application by a local authority in connection with a building or proposed building in the area of that authority shall be made to the Secretary of State except where the power of giving the direction is exercisable by that authority.";

Sch. 6

(*d*) after subsection (7), there shall be inserted as subsections (7A) and (7B)—

"(7A) If, on an application to the Secretary of State for a direction under this section, the Secretary of State considers that any requirement of building regulations to which the application relates is not applicable or is not or would not be contravened in the case of the work or proposed work to which the application relates, he may so determine and may give any directions that he considers necessary in the circumstances.

(7B) A person who contravenes any condition specified in a direction given under this section or permits any such condition to be contravened shall be liable to a fine not exceeding £400 and to a further fine not exceeding £50 for each day on which the offence continues after he is convicted."; and

(*e*) subsection (8) shall be omitted.

6. In section 7 of the 1961 Act (appeal against local authority's refusal to dispense with or relax requirements of building regulations)—

(*a*) in subsection (1), after second "relax" insert "or grant such an application subject to conditions", for "by notice in writing" substitute "in the prescribed manner", for "one month" substitute "the prescribed period" and for "refusal" substitute "decision on the application";

(*b*) in subsection (2), for the words from "a period" to "and the local authority" substitute "the prescribed period";

(*c*) subsections (3) to (6) shall be omitted; and

(*d*) at the end there shall be added the following subsection:—

"(7) Section 6(7A) of this Act shall apply in relation to an appeal to the Secretary of State under this section as it applies in relation to an application to him for a direction under section 6.".

7. For section 8 of the 1961 Act (advertisement of proposal to relax building regulations) substitute—

"Opportunity to make representations about proposal to relax building regulations.

8.—(1) Before the Secretary of State or a local authority give a direction under section 6 of this Act the prescribed steps shall be taken for affording to persons likely to be affected by the direction an opportunity to make representations about it; and before giving the direction the Secretary of State or, as the case may be, the local authority shall consider any representations duly made in accordance with the regulations.

(2) Building regulations—

(*a*) may make provision as to the time to be allowed for making representations under the preceding subsection;

(*b*) may require an applicant for such a direction, as a condition that his application shall be entertained, to pay or undertake to pay the cost of publishing any notice which is required by the regulations to be published in connection with the application ; and SCH. 6

(*c*) may exclude the requirements of the preceding subsection in prescribed cases.".

8. In section 9(3) of the 1961 Act (consultation with Building Regulations Advisory Committee and other bodies before making building regulations), at the end add "(including in particular, as regards regulations relevant to any of their functions, the National Water Council).".

PART II

PUBLIC HEALTH ACT 1936 SECTION 65 AND PUBLIC HEALTH ACT 1961 SECTIONS 4, 6 AND 7 AS AMENDED

1936 c. 49.
1961 c. 64.

The Public Health Act 1936

65.—(1) If any work to which building regulations are applicable contravenes any of those regulations, the authority, without prejudice to their right to take proceedings for a fine in respect of the contravention, may by notice require the owner either to pull down or remove the work or, if he so elects, to effect such alterations therein and additions thereto and to execute such additional work in connection therewith as may be necessary to make it comply with the regulations.

(2) If, in a case where the local authority are by any section of this Act other than the last preceding section expressly required or authorised to reject plans, any work to which building regulations are applicable is executed either without plans having been deposited, or notwithstanding the rejection of the plans, or otherwise than in accordance with any requirements subject to which the authority passed the plans, the authority may by notice to the owner either require him to pull down or remove the work, or require him either to pull down or remove the work or, if he so elects, to comply with any other requirements specified in the notice, being requirements which they might have made under the section in question as a condition of passing plans.

(2A) Where a local authority have power to serve a notice under subsection (1) or (2) above on the owner of any work, they may in addition or instead serve such a notice on one or more of the following persons, namely the occupier and any builder or other person appearing to the authority to have control over the work.

(3) If a person to whom a notice has been given under the foregoing provisions of this section fails to comply with the notice before the expiration of twenty-eight days, or such longer period as a court

SCH. 6 of summary jurisdiction may on his application allow, the local authority may pull down or remove the work in question, or effect such alterations therein and additions thereto and execute such additional work in connection therewith as they deem necessary, and may recover from him the expenses reasonably incurred by them in so doing:

Provided that where a notice under subsection (1) or (2) above is given to two or more persons in pursuance of subsection (2A) above, then—

(*a*) if they are given the notices on different dates, the said period of twenty-eight days shall for each of them run from the later or latest of those dates ; and

(*b*) if the notice is not complied with before the expiration of the said period or such longer period as a court of summary jurisdiction may on the application of any of them allow, any expenses recoverable as aforesaid may be recovered from any of them.

(4) No such notice as is mentioned in subsection (1), (2) or (2A) of this section shall be given after the expiration of twelve months from the date of the completion of the work in question, and, in any case where plans were deposited, it shall not be open to the authority to give such a notice on the ground that the work contravenes any building regulation or, as the case may be, does not comply with their requirements under any such section of this Act as aforesaid, if either the plans were passed by the authority, or notice of their rejection was not given within the prescribed period from the deposit thereof, and if the work has been executed in accordance with the plans and of any requirement made by the local authority as a condition of passing the plans:

Provided that, in a case where plans were deposited, nothing in this subsection shall be taken to prevent such a notice from being given (before the expiration of twelve months from the completion of the work in question) in respect of anything of which particulars were not required to be shown in the plans.

(5) Nothing in this section shall affect the right of a local authority, or of the Attorney-General, or any other person, to apply for an injunction for the removal or alteration of any work on the ground that it contravenes any regulation or any enactment in this Act, but if the work is one in respect of which plans were deposited and the plans were passed by the local authority, or notice of their rejection was not given within the prescribed period after the deposit thereof, and if the work has been executed in accordance with the plans, the court on granting an injunction shall have power to order the local authority to pay to the owner of the work such compensation as the court thinks just, but before making any such order the court shall in accordance with rules of court cause the local authority, if not a party to the proceedings, to be joined as a party thereto.

1961 c. 64. *The Public Health Act* 1961

4. (1) . . . .

(2) Any provision contained in building regulations may be made so as to apply generally, or in an area specified in the regulations, and the regulations may make different provision for different areas and generally different provision for different circumstances or cases. **Sch. 6**

(3) It shall be the function of every local authority to enforce building regulations in their district.

(4) Local authorities shall, in relation to building regulations, have all such functions under sections 64 and 65 of the Public Health Act 1936 (which confer power to pass plans, and to enforce building byelaws) as they have in relation to building byelaws. . . . **1936 c. 49.**

(5) Building regulations may include such supplemental and incidental provisions as appear to the Secretary of State to be expedient.

(6) If a person contravenes or fails to comply with any provision contained in building regulations, other than a provision designated in the regulations as one to which this subsection does not apply, he shall be liable to a fine not exceeding £400 and to a further fine not exceeding £50 for each day on which the default continues after he is convicted.

(7) The power of making building regulations shall be exercisable by statutory instrument which shall be subject to annulment in pursuance of a resolution of either House of Parliament.

6.—(1) Subject to the provisions of this section, if the Secretary of State, on an application made in accordance with the provisions of this Act, considers that the operation of any requirement in building regulations would be unreasonable in relation to the particular case to which the application relates, he may after consultation with the local authority, give a direction dispensing with or relaxing that requirement either unconditionally or subject to compliance with any conditions specified in the direction, being conditions with respect to matters directly connected with the dispensation or relaxation.

(2) If building regulations so provide as regards any requirement contained in the regulations, the power to dispense with or relax that requirement under subsection (1) of this section shall be exercisable by the local authority (instead of by the Secretary of State after consultation with the local authority):

Provided that any building regulations made by virtue of this subsection may except applications of any description.

(3) Building regulations may provide as regards any requirement contained in the regulations that the foregoing subsections of this section shall not apply.

(4) An application under this section shall be in such form . . . . . . and shall contain such particulars as may be . . . . . . prescribed.

(5) The application shall be made to the local authority and, except where the power of giving the direction is exercisable by the

SCH. 6 local authority, the local authority shall at once transmit the application to the Secretary of State and give notice to the applicant that it has been so transmitted.

(6) An application by a local authority in connection with a building or proposed building in the area of that authority shall be made to the Secretary of State except where the power of giving the direction is exercisable by that authority.

(7) The provisions of Part I of the First Schedule to this Act shall have effect as regards any application made under this section for a direction which will affect the application of building regulations to work which has been carried out before the making of the application.

(7A) If, on an application to the Secretary of State for a direction under this section, the Secretary of State considers that any requirement of building regulations to which the application relates is not applicable or is not or would not be contravened in the case of the work or proposed work to which the application relates he may so determine and may give any directions that he considers necessary in the circumstances.

(7B) A person who contravenes any condition specified in a direction given under this section or permits any such condition to be contravened shall be liable to a fine not exceeding £400 and to a further fine not exceeding £50 for each day on which the offence continues after he is convicted.

. . . . .

7.—(1) If a local authority refuse an application to dispense with or relax any requirement in building regulations which they have power to dispense with or relax, or grant such an applicatiion subject to conditions, the applicant may in the prescribed manner appeal to the Secretary of State within the prescribed period from the date on which the local authority notify the applicant of their decision on the application.

(2) If within the prescribed period the local authority do not notify the applicant of their decision on the application, subsection (1) of this section shall appply in relation to the application as if the local authority had refused the application and notified the applicant of their decision at the end of the said period.

. . . .

(7) Section 6(7A) of this Act shall apply in relation to an appeal to the Secretary of State under this section as it applies in relation to an application to him for a direction under section 6.

Section 75.

SCHEDULE 7

1959 c. 24.

AMENDMENTS OF BUILDING (SCOTLAND) ACT 1959

1. In section 3 (building standards regulations)—

(*a*) in subsection (2), after the words "health, safety" there shall be inserted the word "welfare", and at the end there shall be added the words "and for furthering the conservation of fuel and power";

(*b*) in subsection (3), there shall be added the words— Sch. 7

"(*d*) be framed to any extent by reference to a document published by or on behalf of the Secretary of State or any other person.";

(*c*) at the end of the section there shall be added the following subsection—

"(7) The Secretary of State may by order made by statutory instrument repeal or modify any enactment to which this subsection applies if it appears to him that the enactment is inconsistent with, or is unnecessary or requires alteration in consequence of, any provision contained in the building standards regulations.

This subsection applies to any enactment contained in any Act passed before or in the same Session as the Health and Safety at Work etc. Act 1974 other than an enactment contained in the Building (Scotland) Act 1959."

2. In section 4 (relaxation of building standards regulations)—

(*a*) for subsection (5) there shall be substituted the following subsections—

"(5) A direction under subsection (1)(*b*) above—

(*a*) shall, if it so provides, cease to have effect at the end of such period as may be specified in the direction;

(*b*) may be varied or revoked by a subsequent direction of the Secretary of State.

(5A) If at any time a direction under subsection (1)(*b*) above ceases to have effect by virtue of subsection (5)(*a*) above or is varied or revoked under subsection (5)(*b*) above, that fact shall not affect the continued operation of the direction (with any conditions specified therein) in any case in which before that time an application for a warrant in connection with the construction or change of use of a building, part or all of which is of the class to which the direction relates, was, in accordance with regulations made under section 2 of this Act, lodged with a buildings authority.";

(*b*) in subsections (6) and (7), after the words "subsection (1)(*b*)" there shall be inserted the words "or (5)(*b*)";

(*c*) after subsection (7) there shall be inserted the following subsection:—

"(7A) A person making an application under subsection (1)(*b*) above shall pay to the Secretary of State such fee as may be prescribed; and regulations made by virtue of this subsection may prescribe different fees for different cases:

Provided that the Secretary of State may in any particular case remit the whole or part of any fee payable by virtue of this subsection.".

SCH. 7

3. After section 4A, there shall be inserted the following section—

"Power of Secretary of State to approve types of building, etc.

4B.—(1) The following provisions of this section shall have effect with a view to enabling the Secretary of State, either on an application made to him in that behalf or of his own accord, to approve any particular type of building as conforming, either generally or in any class of case, to particular provisions of the building standards regulations.

(2) An application for the approval under this section of a type of building shall be made in the prescribed manner.

(3) Where under subsection (1) above the Secretary of State approves a type of building as conforming to particular provisions of the building standards regulations either generally or in any class of case, he may issue a certificate to that effect specifying—

(*a*) the type of building to which the certificate relates ;

(*b*) the provisions of the building standards regulations to which the certificate relates ; and

(*c*) where applicable, the class or classes of case to which the certificate applies.

(4) A certificate under this section shall, if it so provides, cease to have effect at the end of such period as may be specified in the certificate.

(5) If, while a certificate under this section is in force, it is found, in any particular case involving a building of the type to which the certificate relates, that the building in question is of that type and the case is one to which the certificate applies, that building shall in that particular case be deemed to conform to the provisions of the building standards regulations to which the certificate relates.

(6) The Secretary of State may from time to time vary a certificate under this section either on an application made to him in that behalf or of his own accord ; but in the case of a certificate issued on an application made by a person under subsection (1) above, the Secretary of State, except where he varies it on the application of that person, shall before varying it give that person reasonable notice that he proposes to do so.

(7) A person making an application under subsection (1) or (6) above shall pay to the Secretary of State such fee as may be prescribed ; and regulations made by virtue of this subsection may prescribe different fees for different cases:

Provided that the Secretary of State may in any particular case remit the whole or part of any fee payable by virtue of this subsection.

(8) The Secretary of State may at any time revoke a certificate issued under this section, but before doing so shall give the person, if any, on whose application the certificate was issued reasonable notice that he proposes to do so.

(9) Where the Secretary of State issues a certificate under this section or varies or revokes a certificate so issued, he shall publish notice of that fact in such manner as he thinks fit.

(10) If at any time a certificate under this section ceases to have effect by virtue of subsection (4) above or is varied or revoked under the preceding provisions of this section, that fact shall not affect the continued operation of subsection (5) above by virtue of that certificate in any case in which before that time an application for a warrant in connection with the construction of a type of building to which the certificate relates was, in accordance with regulations made under section 2 of this Act, lodged with a buildings authority.

(11) For the purposes of subsection (3) above or any variation of a certificate under subsection (6) above, a class of case may be framed in any way that the Secretary of State thinks fit."

4. In section 6 (application of building standards regulations and building operations regulations to construction or demolition, and to change of use, of buildings)—

(*a*) after subsection (3) there shall be inserted the following subsection—

"(3A) Notwithstanding that a buildings authority are not satisfied that the information submitted to them with an application for a warrant for the construction of a building is sufficient in respect of such stage in the construction as may be prescribed to show that the building when constructed will not fail to conform to the building standards regulations, they may grant a warrant for the construction of the building but subject to the condition that work on such prescribed stage shall not be proceeded with until such further information relating to that stage as they may require is submitted to them and until they have made an amendment to the terms of the warrant authorising such work to proceed:

Provided that they shall, subject to subsection (8) of this section, make such an amendment on application being made therefor in the prescribed manner only if they are satisfied that nothing in the information submitted to them in respect of the prescribed stage shows that that stage when constructed will fail to conform to the building standards regulations.";

(*b*) in subsection (10), after the words "any such" there shall be inserted the words "prescribed stage as is mentioned in subsection (3A) of tbis section and any such".

SCH. 7

5. In section 9 (certificates of completion)—

(*a*) in subsection (2), for the words " but only if, they are satisfied that " there shall be substituted the words " , so far as they are able to ascertain after taking all reasonable steps in that behalf, " ;

(*b*) in subsection (3), for the words, " be satisfied as mentioned in the last foregoing subsection " there shall be substituted the words " grant a certificate of completion " ;

(*c*) after subsection (3) there shall be inserted the following subsection—

" (3A) In respect of so much of a building as consists of such an installation as may be prescribed, not being an electrical installation, a buildings authority shall not grant a certificate of completion unless there is produced to them a certificate granted by a person of such class as may be prescribed certifying that the installation complies with such of the said conditions as relate to it:

Provided that this subsection shall not apply in a case where it is shown to the satisfaction of the buildings authority that for some reasonable cause such a certificate cannot be produced." ;

(*d*) in subsection (4) for the words " the last foregoing subsection " there shall be substituted the words " subsection (3) or (3A) above ".

6. In section 11(1)(*b*) (power of local authorities to require buildings to conform to building standards regulations), after the words " health, safety " there shall be inserted the word " welfare ", and after the word " generally " there shall be inserted the words " and for furthering the conservation of fuel and power ".

7. In section 19 (penalties), for the words " ten pounds " and " one hundred pounds ", wherever they occur, there shall be substituted respectively the words " £50 " and " £400 ".

8. After section 19 there shall be inserted the following section—

" Civil liability

19A.—(1) Subject to the provisions of this section, a breach to which this section applies shall, so far as it causes damage, be actionable except in so far as may be otherwise prescribed ; and in any action brought by virtue of this subsection such defence as may be prescribed shall be available.

(2) This section applies to the following breaches—

(*a*) failure to comply with the terms or conditions of a warrant for the construction, demolition or change of use of a building or with any order under this Act relating to the construction of a building ;

(*b*) contravention of any provision of the building operations regulations ;

(*c*) constructing a building without a warrant otherwise than in accordance with the building standards regulations ; SCH. 7

(*d*) changing the use of a building without a warrant where after the change of use the building does not conform to so much of the building standards regulations as become applicable, or apply more onerously, to the building by reason of the change of use.

(3) Subsection (1) above and any defence provided for in regulations made by virtue thereof shall not apply in the case of a breach to which this section applies in connection with a building erected before the date on which that subsection comes into force unless the breach arises in relation to the change of use, extension, alteration, demolition, repair, maintenance or fitting of such a building.

(4) Nothing in this section shall be construed as affecting the extent (if any) to which a breach to which this section applies is actionable in a case to which subsection (1) above does not apply, or as prejudicing any right of action which exists apart from the provisions of this section.

(5) In this section " damage " includes the death of, or injury to, any person (including any disease and any impairment of a person's physical or mental condition)."

9. In section 26 (Crown rights)—

(*a*) in subsection (1) after the words " Crown and " there shall be inserted the words " subject to the provisions of this section " ;

(*b*) after subsection (2) there shall be inserted the following subsections—

" (2A) The building standards regulations shall, except in so far as they otherwise prescribe, apply to a Crown building as they would apply if the building were not a Crown building.

(2B) A Crown building to which the building standards regulations apply shall be constructed in accordance with those regulations.

(2C) Any extension to or alteration of a Crown building to which the building standards regulations apply or would apply on the extension or alteration of the building shall not cause the building as extended or altered, as a direct result of the extension or, as the case may be, the alteration—

(*a*) if it conformed to the building standards regulations immediately before the date of commencement of the operations, to fail to conform to them ; or

SCH. 7

(*b*) if it failed to conform to the building standards regulations immediately before that date, to fail to conform to them to a greater degree than that to which it failed to conform immediately before that date ;

and any change of use of a Crown building shall not cause the building after the change of use to fail to conform to so much of the building standards regulations as will become applicable, or will apply more onerously, to the building by reason of the change of use.

(2D) Section 19A of this Act shall apply to a Crown building as it applies to a building other than a Crown building, but as if for subsection (2) there were substituted the following subsection:—

"(2) A breach to which this section applies is a failure to comply with subsection (2B) or (2C) of section 26 of this Act or a contravention of any provision of the building operations regulations ".

(2E) Without prejudice to any case to which proviso (*a*) to subsection (1) above is applicable, the Secretary of State shall have the like powers of dispensing with or relaxing the provisions of the building standards regulations in relation to a Crown building as he has under section 4(1) of this Act in relation to a building other than a Crown building ; and subsections (3), (4), (5), (5A) and (9) of the said section 4 shall apply for the purposes of this section as if—

(*a*) in subsection (4), the words " or, as the case may be, the buildings authority " were omitted ;

(*b*) in subsection (5A), for the words from " an application " to the end there were substituted the words " the construction or change of use of a building, part or all of which is of the class to which the direction relates, was begun " ;

(*c*) in subsection (9), the words " or section 4A(3) of this Act " were omitted.

(2F) Without prejudice to any case to which the said proviso is applicable, in the application of section 4B of this Act to a Crown building, subsection (10) shall have effect as if for the words from " an application " to the end there were substituted the words " the construction of a building, part or all of which is of the type to which the certificate relates, was begun ". "

Section 78.

SCHEDULE 8

1961 c. 34.
1963 c. 41.

TRANSITIONAL PROVISIONS WITH RESPECT TO FIRE CERTIFICATES UNDER FACTORIES ACT 1961 OR OFFICES, SHOPS AND RAILWAY PREMISES ACT 1963

1. In this Schedule—

1971 c. 40.

" the 1971 Act " means the Fire Precautions Act 1971 ;

" 1971 Act certificate " means a fire certificate within the meaning of the 1971 Act ;

“ Factories Act certificate ” means a certificate under section 40 of the Factories Act 1961 (means of escape in case of fire-certification by fire authority) ; SCH. 8 1961 c. 34.

“ Offices Act certificate ” means a fire certificate under section 29 of the Offices, Shops and Railway Premises Act 1963. 1963 c. 41.

2.—(1) Where by virtue of an order under section 1 of the 1971 Act a 1971 Act certificate becomes required in respect of any premises at a time when there is in force in respect of those premises a Factories Act certificate or an Offices Act certificate (“ the existing certificate ”), the following provisions of this paragraph shall apply.

(2) The existing certificate shall continue in force (irrespective of whether the section under which it was issued remains in force) and—

(*a*) shall as from the said time be deemed to be a 1971 Act certificate validly issued with respect to the premises with respect to which it was issued and to cover the use or uses to which those premises were being put at that time ; and

(*b*) may (in particular) be amended, replaced or revoked in accordance with the 1971 Act accordingly.

(3) Without prejudice to sub-paragraph (2)(*b*) above, the existing certificate, as it has effect by virtue of sub-paragraph (2) above, shall as from the said time be treated as imposing in relation to the premises the like requirements as were previously imposed in relation thereto by the following provisions, that is to say—

(*a*) if the existing certificate is a Factories Act certificate, the following provisions of the Factories Act 1961, namely sections 41(1), 48 (except subsections (5), (8) and (9)), 49(1), 51(1) and 52(1) and (4) and, so far as it relates to a proposed increase in the number of persons employed in any premises, section 41(3) ;

(*b*) if the existing certificate is an Offices Act certificate the following provisions of the Offices, Shops and Railway Premises Act 1963, namely sections 30(1), 33, 34(1) and (2), 36(1) and 38(1) and, so far as it relates to a proposed increase in the number of persons employed to work in any premises at any one time, section 30(3).

3. Any application for a Factories Act certificate or an Offices Act certificate with respect to any premises which is pending at the time when by virtue of an order under section 1 of the 1971 Act a 1971 Act certificate becomes required in respect of those premises shall be deemed to be an application for a 1971 Act certificate in respect of them duly made in accordance with the 1971 Act and may be proceeded with accordingly ; but (without prejudice to section 5(2) of the 1971 Act) the fire authority may, as a condition of proceeding with such an application, require the applicant to specify any matter or give them any information which would ordinarily have been required by section 5(1) of that Act.

Section 83.

SCHEDULE 9

Minor and Consequential Amendments

1926 c. 59.

The Coroners (Amendment) Act 1926

1. In section 13(2)(*c*) of the Coroners (Amendment) Act 1926 (by virtue of which an inquest must be held with a jury in cases of death from certain causes of which notice is required to be given to any inspector or other officer of a government department), after the words "of a government department" there shall be inserted the words "or to an inspector appointed under section 19 of the Health and Safety at Work etc. Act 1974,".

1957 c. 20.

The House of Commons Disqualification Act 1957

2. In Part II of Schedule 1 to the House of Commons Disqualification Act 1957 (which specifies bodies of which all members are disqualified under that Act), as it applies to the House of Commons of the Parliament of the United Kingdom, there shall be inserted at the appropriate place in alphabetical order the words "The Health and Safety Commission".

1967 c. 13.

The Parliamentary Commissioner Act 1967

3. In Schedule 2 to the Parliamentary Commissioner Act 1967 (which lists the authorities subject to investigation under that Act) there shall be inserted in the appropriate places in alphabetical order the words "Health and Safety Commission" and "Health and Safety Executive".

Section 83.

SCHEDULE 10

Repeals

Chapter	Short Title	Extent of repeal
26 Geo. 5 & 1 Edw. 8. c. 49.	The Public Health Act 1936.	Section 53. Section 64(4) and (5). In section 67, the words from "and the Secretary of State's decision" to the end of the section. Section 71. In section 343(1), the definition of "building regulations".
7 & 8 Geo. 6. c. 31.	The Education Act 1944.	Section 63(1).
10 & 11 Geo. 6. c. 51.	The Town and Country Planning Act 1947.	In Schedule 8, the amendment of section 53 of the Public Health Act 1936.
2 & 3 Eliz. 2. c. 32.	The Atomic Energy Authority Act 1954.	Section 5(5).
4 & 5 Eliz. 2. c. 52.	The Clean Air Act 1956.	Section 24.

Chapter	Short Title	Extent of Repeal
9 & 10 Eliz. 2. c. 64.	The Public Health Act 1961.	In section 4, subsection (1) and, in subsection (4), the words from " and building " to the end of the subsection. In section 6, in subection (4), the words " as may be prescribed by building regulations " and the word " so ", and subsection (8). Section 7(3) to (6). Section 10(1) and (2). In Schedule 1, in Part III, the amendments of sections 53, 61, 62 and 71 of the Public Health Act 1936 and, in the amendments of the Clean Air Act 1956, the amendment of section 24 and the word " twenty-four " in the last paragraph.
1965 c. 16.	The Airports Authority Act 1965.	In section 19(3), the words from " and section 71 " to " regulations) " and the words " and the proviso to the said section 71 ".
1971 c. 40.	The Fire Precautions Act 1971.	In section 2, paragraphs (*a*) to (*c*). Section 11. In section 17(1)(i), the word " and " where last occurring. In section 43(1), the definition of " building regulations ".
1971 c. 75.	The Civil Aviation Act 1971.	In Schedule 5, in paragraph 2(1), the words from " and section 71 " to " regulations)" and the words " and the proviso to the said section 71 ".
1972 c. 28.	The Employment Medical Advisory Service Act 1972.	Sections 1 and 6. Schedule 1.
1972 c. 58.	The National Health Service (Scotland) Act 1972.	In Schedule 6, paragraph 157.
1972 c. 70.	The Local Government Act 1972.	In Schedule 14, paragraph 43.
1973 c. 32.	The National Health Service Reorganisation Act 1973.	In Schedule 4, paragraph 137.
1973 c. 50.	The Employment and Training Act 1973.	In Schedule 3, paragraph 14.
1973 c. 64.	The Maplin Development Act 1973.	In Schedule 2, in paragraph 2(1), the words from " and section 71 " to " regulations) ".

Appendix 2

Committees and Representatives: the Regulations, Code and Guidance Notes

SAFETY REPRESENTATIVES AND SAFETY COMMITTEES REGULATIONS 1976

Citation and commencement

1. These Regulations may be cited as the Safety Representatives and Safety Committees Regulations 1976 and shall come into operation on a date to be decided by the Secretary of State for Employment.

Interpretation

2. (1) In these Regulations, unless the context otherwise requires:

"the 1974 Act" means the Health and Safety at Work etc. Act 1974;

"the 1975 Act" means the Employment Protection Act 1975;

"employee" has the meaning assigned by section 53 (1) of the 1974 Act and "employer" shall be construed accordingly.

"recognised trade union" means an independent trade union as defined in section 30 (1) of the Trade Union and Labour Relations Act 1974 which the employer concerned recognises for the purpose of negotiations relating to or connected with one of more of the matters specified in section 29 (1) of that Act in relation to persons employed by him or as to which the Advisory, Conciliation and Arbitration Service has made a recommendation for recognition under the Employment Protection Act 1975 which is operative within the meaning of section 15 of that Act;

"safety representative" means a person appointed under Regulation 3 (1) of these Regulations to be a safety representative;

"welfare at work" means those aspects of welfare at work which are the subject of health and safety regulations or of any of the existing statutory provisions within the meaning of section 53 (1) of the 1974 Act;

"workplace" in relation to a safety representative means any place or places where the group or groups of employees he is appointed to represent are likely to work or which they are likely to frequent in the course of their employment or incidentally to it.

(2) The Interpretation Act 1889 shall apply to the interpretation of these Regulations as it applies to the interpretation of an Act of Parliament.

(3) These Regulations shall not be construed as giving any person a right to inspect any place, article, substance or document which is the subject of restrictions on the grounds of national security unless he satisfies any test or requirement imposed on those grounds by or on behalf of the Crown.

Appointment of safety representatives

3. (1) For the purposes of section 2 (4) of the 1974 Act, a recognised trade union may appoint safety representatives from amongst the employees in all cases where one or more employees are employed by an employer by whom it is recognised, except in the case of employees employed in a mine within the meaning of section 180 of the Mines and Quarries Act 1954 which is a coal mine

(2) Where the employer has been notified in writing by or on behalf of a trade union of the names of the persons appointed as safety representatives under this Regulation and the group or groups of employees they represent, each such safety representative shall have the functions set out in Regulation 4 below.

(3) A person shall cease to be a safety representative for the purposes of these Regulations when:

(*a*) the trade union which appointed him notifies the employer in writing that his appointment has been terminated; or

(*b*) he ceases to be employed at the workplace but if he was appointed to represent employees at more than one workplace he shall not cease by virtue of this sub-paragraph to be a safety representative so long as he continues to be employed at any one of them; or

(*c*) he resigns.

(4) A person appointed under paragraph (1) above as a safety representative shall so far as is reasonably practicable either have been employed by his employer throughout the preceding two years or have had at least two years' experience in similar employment.

Functions of safety representatives

4. (1) In addition to his function under section 2 (4) of the 1974 Act to represent the employees in consultation with the employer under section 2 (6) of the 1974 Act (which requires every employer to consult safety representatives with a view to the making and maintenance of arrangements which will enable him and his employees to cooperate effectively in promoting and developlng measures to ensure the health and safety at work of the employees and in checking the effectiveness of such measures), each safety representative shall have the following functions:

(*a*) to investigate potential hazards and dangerous occurrences at the workplace (whether or not they are drawn to his attention by the employees he represents) and to examine the causes of accidents at the workplace;
(*b*) to investigate complaints by any employee he represents relating to that employee's health, safety or welfare at work;
(*c*) to make representations to the employer on matters arising out of sub-paragraphs (*a*) and (*b*) above;
(*d*) to make representations to the employer on general matters affecting the health, safety or welfare at work of the employees at the workplace;
(*e*) to carry out inspections in accordance with Regulation 5, 6 and 7 below;
(*f*) to represent the employees he was appointed to represent in consultations at the workplace with inspectors of the Health and Safety Executive and of any other enforcing authority;
(*g*) to receive information from inspectors in accordance with section 28 (8) of the 1974 Act; and
(*h*) to attend meetings of safety committees where he attends in his capacity as a safety representative in connection with any of the above functions;

but, without prejudice to sections 7 and 8 of the 1974 Act, no function given to a safety representative by this paragraph shall be construed as imposing any duty on him.

(2) An employer shall permit a safety representative to take such time off with pay during the employee's working hours as shall be necessary for the purposes of:

(*a*) performing his functions under section 2 (4) of the 1974 Act and paragraph (1) (*a*) to (*h*) above;
(*b*) undergoing such training in aspects of those functions as may be reasonable in all the circumstances having regard to any relevant provisions of a code of practice relating to time off for training approved for the time being by the Health and Safety Commission under section 16 of the 1974 Act.

In this paragraph "with pay" means with pay in accordance with the Schedule to these Regulations.

Inspections of the workplace

5. (1) Safety representatives shall be entitled to inspect the workplace or a part of it if they have given the employer or his representative reasonable notice in writing of their intention to do so and have not inspected it or that part of it, as the case may be, in the previous three months; and may carry out more frequent inspections by agreement with the employer.

(2) Where there has been a substantial change in the conditions of work (whether because of the introduction of new machinery or otherwise) or new information has been published by the Health and Safety Commission or the Health and Safety Executive relevant to the hazards of the workplace since the last inspection under this regulation the safety representatives after consultation with the employer shall be entitled to carry out a further inspection of the part of the workplace concerned notwithstanding that three months have not elapsed since the last inspection.

(3) The employer shall provide such facilities and assistance as the safety representatives may reasonably require (including facilities for independent investigation by them and private discussion with the employees) for the purpose of carrying out an inspection under this Regulation but nothing in this paragraph shall preclude the employer or his representative from being present in the workplace during the inspection.

(4) An inspection carried out under section 123 of the Mines and Quarries Act 1954 shall count as an inspection under this Regulation.

Inspections following notifiable accidents, occurrences and diseases

6. (1) Where there has been a notifiable accident or dangerous occurrence in a workplace or a notifiable disease has been contracted there and:

(*a*) it is safe for an inspection to be carried out, and
(*b*) the interests of employees in the group or groups which safety representatives are appointed to represent might be involved.

those safety representatives may carry out an inspection of the part of the workplace concerned and so far as is necessary for the purpose of determining the cause they may inspect any other part of the workplace; where it is reasonably practicable to do so they shall notify the employer or his representative of their intention to carry out the inspection.

(2) The employer shall provide such facilities and assistance as the safety representatives may reasonably require (including facilities for independent investigation by them and private discussion with the employees) for the purpose of carrying out an inspection under this Regulation; but nothing in this paragraph shall preclude the employer or his representative from being present in the workplace during the inspection.

(3) In this Regulation "notifiable accident or dangerous occurrence" and "notifiable disease" mean any accident, dangerous occurrence or disease, as the case may be, notice of which is required to be given by virtue of any of the relevant statutory provisions within the meaning of section 53 (1) of the 1974 Act.

Inspection of documents and provision of information

7. (1) Safety representatives shall for the performance of their functions under section 2 (4) of the 1974 Act and under these Regulations, if they have given the employer reasonable notice, be entitled to inspect and take copies of any document relevant to the workplace or to the employees the safety representatives represent which the employer is required to keep by virtue of any relevant statutory provision within the meaning of section 53 (1) of the 1974 Act except a document consisting of or relating to any health record of an identifiable individual.

(2) An employer shall make available to safety representatives the information within the employer's knowledge, necessary to enable them to fulfil their functions except:

(*a*) any information the disclosure of which would be against the interests of national security, or

(*b*) any information which he could not disclose without contravening a prohibition imposed by or under an enactment, or

(*c*) any information relating specifically to an individual, unless he has consented to its being disclosed, or

(*d*) any information the disclosure of which would, for reasons other than its effect on health, safety or welfare at work, cause substantial injury to the employer's undertaking or, where the information was supplied to him by some other person, to the undertaking of that other person, or

(*e*) any information obtained by the employer for the purpose of bringing, prosecuting or defending any legal proceedings.

(3) Paragraph (2) above does not require an employer to produce or allow inspection of any document or part of a document which is not related to health, safety or welfare.

Cases where safety representatives need not be employees

8. (1) In the cases mentioned in paragraph (2) below safety representatives appointed under Regulation 3 (1) of these Regulations need not be employees of the employer concerned; and section 2 (4) of the 1974 Act shall be modified accordingly.

(2) The said cases are those in which the employees in the group or groups the safety representatives are appointed to represent are members of the British Actors' Equity Association or of the Musicians' Union.

(3) Regulations 3 (3) (*b*) and (4) and 4 (2) of these Regulations shall not apply to safety representatives appointed by virtue of this Regulation and in the case of safety representatives to be so appointed Regulation 3 (1) shall have effect as if the words "from amongst the employees" were omitted.

Safety committees

9. (1) For the purposes of section 2 (7) of the 1974 Act (which requires an employer in prescribed cases to establish a safety committee if requested to do so by safety representatives), the prescribed cases shall be any cases in which at least two safety representatives request the employer in writing to establish a safety committee.

(2) Where an employer is requested to establish a safety committee in a case prescribed in paragraph (1) above, he shall establish it in accordance with the following provisions:

(*a*) he shall consult with the safety representatives who made the request and with the representatives of recognised trade unions whose members work in any workplace in respect of which he proposes that the committee should function;

(*b*) the employer shall post a notice stating the composition of the committee and the workplace or workplaces to be covered by it in a place where it may be easily read by the employees;

(*c*) the committee shall be established not later than three months after the request for it.

Power of Health and Safety Commission to grant exemptions

10. The Health and Safety Commission may grant exemptions from any requirement imposed by these Regulations and any such exemption may be unconditional or subject to such conditions as the Commission may impose and may be with or without a limit of time.

Provisions as to industrial tribunals

11. (1) A safety representative may, in accordance with the jurisdiction conferred on industrial tribunals by paragraph 16 (2) of Schedule 1 to the Trade Union and Labour Relations Act 1974, present a complaint to an industrial tribunal that:

(*a*) the employer has failed to permit him to take time off in accordance with Regulation 4 (2) of these Regulations; or

(*b*) the employer has failed to pay him in accordance with Regulation 4 (2) of and the Schedule to these Regulations.

(2) An industrial tribunal shall not consider a complaint under paragraph (1) above unless it is presented within three months of the date when the failure occurred or within such further period as the tribunal considers reasonable in a case where it is satisfied that it was not reasonably practicable for the complaint to be presented within the period of three months.

(3) Where an industrial tribunal finds a complaint under paragraph (1) (*a*) above well-founded the tribunal shall make a declaration to that effect and may make an award of compensation to be paid by the employer to the employee which shall be of such amount as the tribunal considers just and equitable in all the circumstances having regard to the employer's default in failing to permit time off to be taken by the employee and to any loss sustained by the employee which is attributable to the matters complained of.

(4) Where on a complaint under paragraph (1) (*b*) above an industrial tribunal finds that the employer has failed to pay the employee the whole or part of the amount required to be paid under paragraph (1) (*b*), the tribunal shall order the employer to pay the employee the amount which it finds due to him.

(5) Paragraph 16 of Schedule 1 to the Trade Union and Labour Relations Act 1974 (jurisdiction of industrial tribunals) shall be modified by adding the following sub-paragraph:

"(2) An industrial tribunal shall have jurisdiction to determine complaints relating to time off with pay for safety representatives appointed under regulations made under the Health and Safety at Work etc. Act 1974".

THE SCHEDULE

Reg. 4 (2)

Pay for time off allowed to safety representatives for performing their functions

1. Subject to paragraph 3 below, where a safety representative is permitted to take time off in accordance with Regulation 4 (2) of these Regulations, his employer shall pay him:

(*a*) where the safety representative's remuneration for the work he would ordinarily have been doing during that time does not vary with the amount of work done, as if he had worked at that work for the whole of that time;
(*b*) where the safety representative's remuneration for that work varies with the amount of work done, an amount calculated by reference to the average hourly earnings for that work (ascertained in accordance with paragraph 2 below)

2. The average hourly earnings referred to in paragraph 1 (*b*) above are the average hourly earnings of the safety representative concerned or, if no fair estimate can be made of those earnings, the average hourly earnings for work of that description of persons in comparable employment with the same employer or, if there are no such persons, a figure of average hourly earnings which is reasonable in the circumstances.

3. Any payment to a safety representative by an employer in respect of a period of time off:

(*a*) if it is a payment which discharges any liability which the employer may have under section 57 of the Employment Protection Act 1975 in respect of that period, shall also discharge his liability in respect of the same period under Regulation 4 (2) of these Regulations;
(*b*) if it is a payment under any contractual obligation, shall go towards discharging the employer's liability in respect of the same period under Regulation 4 (2) of these Regulations;
(*c*) if it is a payment under Regulation 4 (2) of these Regulations shall go towards discharging any liability of the employer to pay contractual remuneration in respect of the same period.

CODE OF PRACTICE: REPRESENTATIVES AND SAFETY COMMITTEES

1. The Safety Representatives and Safety Committees Regulations 1976 concern safety representatives appointed in accordance with Section 2 (4) of the Act and cover:

(*a*) prescribed cases in which recognised trade unions may appoint safety representatives from amongst the employees;
(*b*) prescribed functions of safety representatives.

Section 2 (6) of the Act requires employers to consult with safety representatives with a view to the making and maintenance of arrangements which will enable him and his employees to cooperate effectively in promoting and developing measures to ensure the health and safety at work of the employees, and in checking the effectiveness of such measures. Under section 2 (4) safety representatives are required to represent the employees in those consultations.

2. This Code of Practice has been approved by the Health and Safety Commission with the consent of the Secretary of State. It relates to the requirements placed on safety representatives by section 2 (4) of the Act and on employers by the Regulations and takes effect on the date the Regulations come into operation.

3. The employer, the recognised trade unions concerned and safety representatives should make full and proper use of the existing agreed industrial relations machinery to reach the degree of agreement necessary to achieve the purpose of the Regulations and in order to resolve any differences.

Interpretation

4. (*a*) In this Code, "the 1974 Act" means the Health and Safety at Work etc. Act 1974 and "the Regulations" mean the Safety Representatives and Safety Committees Regulations 1976;
(*b*) words and expressions which are defined in the Act or in the Regulations have the same meaning in this Code unless the context requires otherwise.

Functions of safety representatives

5. In order to fulfil their functions under section 2 (4) of the Act safety representatives should:

(*a*) take all reasonably practical steps to keep themselves informed of:
  (i) the legal requirements relating to the health and safety of persons at work, particularly the group or groups of persons they directly represent,
  (ii) the particular hazards of the workplace and the measures deemed necessary to eliminate or minimise the risk deriving from these hazards, and
  (iii) the health and safety policy of their employer and the organisation and arrangements for fulfilling that policy;
(*b*) encourage cooperation between their employer and his employees in promoting and developing essential measures to ensure the health and safety of employees and in checking the effectiveness of these measures;
(*c*) bring to the employer's notice normally in writing any unsafe or unhealthy conditions or working practices or unsatisfactory arrangements for welfare at work which come to their attention whether on an inspection or day to day observation. The report does not imply that all other conditions and working practices are safe and healthy or that the welfare arrangements are satisfactory in all other respects.

Making a written report does not preclude the bringing of such matters to the attention of the employer or his representative by a direct oral approach in the first instance, particularly in situations where speedy remedial action is necessary. It will also be appropriate for minor matters to be the subject of direct oral discussion without the need for a formal written approach.

Information to be provided by employers

6. The Regulations require employers to make information within their knowledge available to safety representatives necessary to enable them to fulfil their functions. Such information should include:

(*a*) information about the plans and performance of their undertaking and any changes proposed insofar as they affect the health and safety at work of their employees;

(*b*) information of a technical nature about hazards to health and safety and precautions deemed necessary to eliminate or minimise them, in respect of machinery, plant, equipment, processes, systems of work and substances in use at work, including any relevant information provided by consultants or designers or by the manufacturer, importer or supplier of any article or substance used, or proposed to be used, at work by their employees;

(*c*) information which the employer keeps relating to the occurrence of any accident, dangerous occurrence or notifiable industrial disease and any statistical records relating to such accidents, dangerous occurrences or cases of notifiable industrial disease;

(*d*) any other information specifically related to matters affecting the health and safety at work of his employees, including the results of any measurements taken by the employer or persons acting on his behalf in the course of checking the effectiveness of his health and safety arrangements;

(*e*) information on articles or substances which an employer issues to homeworkers.

GUIDANCE NOTES

1 *The Safety Representatives and Safety Committees Regulations, 1976,* made under section 2(4) of *The Health and Safety at Work etc. Act, 1974,* prescribe the cases in which recognised trade unions may appoint safety representatives, specify the functions of such safety representatives, and set out the obligations of employers towards them.

2 The Code of Practice, approved by the Commission under Section 16 of the Act and issued in amplification of those Regulations, gives guidance on how safety representatives should fulfil their statutory functions, and guidance to employers regarding the information which they should make available to safety representatives to enable them to fulfil their functions.

3 The Commission have decided that it would be wrong to try and make regulations which cater in detail for the wide variety of circumstances in which they will have to be applied. Accordingly, the purpose of the Regulations and the Code of Practice is to provide a framework within which each undertaking can develop effective working arrangements. To supplement this statutory framework these guidance notes are being issued which the Commission hope will be of help to employers, to trade unions, to safety representatives and to members of safety committees.

4 This part of the guidance notes offers advice to all who are concerned with the appointment and functioning of safety representatives. Advice regarding safety committees is given below.

Appointment of safety representatives

5 The Regulations provide that recognised trade unions may appoint safety representatives to represent the employees. The Commission have decided that recognition for this purpose must be on the same basis as in *The Trade Union and Labour Relations Act, 1974* and *The Employment Protection Act, 1975.* Any disputes between employers and trade unions about this matter should be dealt with under the provisions of the Employment Protection Act.

6 The Commission expect that such unions would normally appoint representatives to represent a group or groups of workers of a class for which the union has negotiating rights. The limitation of representation to a particular group or groups should not, however, be regarded as a hindrance to the raising by that representative of general matters affecting the health and safety of employees as a whole.

7 Equally, these general principles do not preclude the possibility of a safety representative representing, by mutual agreement between the appropriate unions, more than one group or groups of employees, e.g. in a small workplace or within the organisation of a small employer when the number of recognised trade unions is high relative to the total numbers employed.

8 When consideration is being given to the numbers of safety representatives to be appointed in a particular case the guidance given by the Commission in paragraph three of the Code of Practice should be borne in mind. Appropriate criteria would include:

a the total numbers employed;
b the variety of different occupations;

c the size of the workplace and the variety of workplace locations;
d the operation of shift systems;
e the type of work activity and the degree and character of the inherent dangers.

9 At certain undertakings there will be a particular need for flexibility of approach both to the question of the group or groups of the employees the safety representative represents and to the numbers of safety representatives which might be appropriate in particular circumstances. Examples of such circumstances might include:

a workplaces with rapidly changing situations and conditions as the work develops and where there might be rapid changes in the level of manpower, e.g. building and construction sites, shipbuilding and ship repairing docks.
b workplaces from which the majority of employees go out to their actual place of work and subsequently report back, e.g. goods and freight depots, builders' yards, service depots of all kinds.
c workplaces where there is a wide variety of different work activities going on within a particular location.
d workplaces with a specially high process risk, e.g. construction sites at particular stages – demolition, excavations, steel erection, etc., and some chemical works and research establishments.
e workplaces where the majority of employees are employed in low risk activities, but where one or two processes or activities or items of plant have special risks connected with them.

10 The Regulations require that appointed safety representatives normally have either worked for their present employer throughout the preceding two years or have had at least two years experience in similar employment. This is to ensure that those who are appointed have the kind of experience and knowledge of their particular type of employment necessary to enable them to make a responsible and practical contribution to health and safety in their employment. Circumstances may, however, arise where it will not be reasonably practicable that the appointed safety representative shall possess such experience, e.g. where the employer or workplace location is newly established, or where work is of short duration, or where there is a high labour turnover.

Functions of safety representatives

11 It is provided in the Regulations that no function given to a safety representative shall be construed as imposing any duty on him other than duties he may have as an employee under Sections 7 and 8 of the

Act. For example, a safety representative, by accepting, agreeing with or not objecting to a course of action taken by the employer to deal with a health or safety hazard, does not take upon himself any legal responsibility for that course of action. In addition, the Commission have directed that the Health and Safety Executive shall not institute criminal proceedings against any safety representative for any act or omission by him in respect of the performance of functions assigned to him by the Regulations or indicated by the Code of Practice. Similar arrangements have been made with the other enforcing authorities.

12 Recognised trade unions will have well established methods of communication within a workplace, or within a particular employer's undertaking. These will be the appropriate channels by which the appointed safety representatives can keep the members of the group or groups which they represent informed on all matters of consequence affecting their health, safety and welfare at work. Appointed safety representatives will also need to establish close relationships with the other appointed safety representatives, including those appointed by trade unions other than their own, for example, in order to look at hazardous situations, develop a common approach, and responsibility complementary to their responsibility for the group or groups they represent directly.

13 It is important that safety representatives should be able to take matters up with management without delay. They must therefore have ready access to the employer or his representatives; who those should be will be determined in the light of local circumstances. It may not be desirable to specify one individual for all contacts, bearing in mind that hazards could involve differing degrees of urgency and importance. The need is to ensure that safety representatives have a clear idea as to who is authorised to act as the employer's representative for the purpose of these Regulations.

14 Safety representatives should record when they have made an inspection. Specimens of the kinds of *pro forma* which might be adopted by safety representatives both to record that an inspection has been made and to draw the employer's attention to an unsafe or unhealthy condition, etc., are given below. A copy of each completed form should be given to the employer. For those who wish, stocks of these forms may be purchased from offices of the Health and Safety Executive.

15 Section 28(8) of the HSW Act requires inspectors to give certain types of information to employees and employers. Where safety representatives have been appointed under the Regulations, they are the appropriate persons to receive this information on behalf of the employees.

Examples of suggested pro-forma

A Sample of suggested form to be used for recording that an inspection by a safety representative(s) has taken place.

Date of inspection	Area or Workplace inspected	Name(s) of safety representative(s) taking part in inspection

[This record does not imply that the conditions are safe and healthy or that the arrangements for welfare at work are satisfactory.]

Signature(s) of safety representative(s) . . . .

Date . . . .

B Sample of suggested form to be used for notifying to the employer, or his representative, unsafe and unhealthy conditions and working practices and unsatisfactory arrangements for welfare at work.

Date of inspection or matter observed	Particulars of matter(s) notified to employer or his representative (include location where appropriate)	Name(s) of safety representative notifying matter(s) to employer (or his representative)	Remedial action taken (with date) or explanation if not taken.

[This report does not imply that the conditions are safe and healthy or that the arrangements for welfare at work are satisfactory in all other respects.]

Signature(s) of safety representative(s) . . . .

Date . . . .

Signature of employer . . . .
(or his representative)

Date . . . .

Inspections by safety representatives

16 The Regulations deal with the frequency of formal inspections by the appointed safety representatives. In some circumstances where a high risk activity or rapidly changing circumstances are confined to a

particular area of a workplace or sector of an employee's activities it may be appropriate for more frequent inspections of that area or sector to be agreed.

17 In providing for formal inspection of the workplace by the appointed safety representatives the Regulations require that they shall give reasonable notice to the employer of their intention to do so. In the Commission's view it is desirable that the employer and the safety representatives should plan a programme of formal inspections in advance, which will itself fulfil the conditions as to notice. Variations in this planned programme should of course be subject to agreement.

18 The Commission see advantages in formal inspections being jointly carried out by the employer or his representatives and safety representatives, but this should not prevent safety representatives from carrying out independent investigations or private discussion with employees. The safety representatives should co-ordinate their work to avoid unnecessary duplication. It will often be appropriate for the safety officer or specialist advisers to be available to give technical advice on health and safety matters which may arise during the course of the inspection.

19 There are various forms which the formal inspection may take and it will be for the appointed safety representatives to agree with their employer about this, but the Commission consider that the following types of inspection, or a combination of any or all of them over a period of time, may be appropriate in the fulfilment of this function:

a *Safety tours* – general inspections of the workplace.

b *Safety sampling* – systematic sampling of particular dangerous activities, processes or areas.

c *Safety surveys* – general inspections of the particular dangerous activities, processes or area.

The numbers of safety representatives taking part in any one formal inspection should be a matter for agreement between the appointed safety representatives and their employer in the light of their own particular circumstances and the nature of the inspection.

20 At large workplaces it may be impracticable to conduct a formal inspection of the entire workplace at a single session or for the complete inspection to be carried out by the same group of safety representatives. In these circumstances arrangements may be agreed between the employer (or his representative) and the appointed safety representatives for the inspection to be carried out by breaking it up into manageable units, e.g. on a departmental basis. It may also be appropriate, as part of the planned programme, for different groups of safety representatives to carry out inspections in different parts of the workplace either

simultaneously or at different times but in such a manner as to ensure complete coverage before the next round of formal inspections becomes due. There may be special circumstances in which appointed safety representatives and their employer will wish to agree a different frequency of inspections for different parts of the same workplace e.g. where there are areas or activities of especially high risk.

21 Where safety representatives have made a written report to the employer in accordance with paragraph 5(c) of the Code of Practice, appropriate remedial action will normally be taken by the employer. Where remedial action is not considered appropriate or cannot be taken within a reasonable period of time, or the form of remedial action is not acceptable to the safety representatives, then the employer or his representative should explain the reasons and give them in writing to the safety representatives. A suggested method for this is to record it in Form B. Where remedial action has been taken, the safety representatives who notified the matter(s) should be given the opportunity to make any necessary reinspection in order to satisfy themselves that the matter(s) notified have received appropriate attention and they should also be afforded the opportunity to record their views on this aspect.

22 Such action should be publicised throughout the workplace and to other appropriate parts of the employer's organisation – if necessary the whole – by the normal channels of communication. It may also be appropriate that they should be brought to the specific attention of the safety committee, if one exists.

23 For the purpose of ascertaining the circumstances of a notifiable accident, dangerous occurrence or notifiable disease, it will be necessary for the representatives to examine any relevant machinery, plant, equipment or substance in the workplace. It is the Commission's view that the main purpose of the examination should be to determine the causes so that the possibility of action to prevent a recurrence can be considered. For this reason it is important that the approach to the problem should be a joint one by the employer and the safety representatives.

It may be necessary, following an accident or dangerous occurrence for the employer to take urgent steps to safeguard against further hazards. If he does this he should notify the safety representatives of the action he has taken and confirm this in writing.

24 Such examinations may include visual inspection, and discussions with persons who are likely to be in the possession of relevant information and knowledge regarding the circumstances of the accident or occurrence. The examination must not, however, include interference

with any evidence or the testing of any machinery, plant, equipment or substance which could disturb or destroy the factual evidence before any inspector from the appropriate enforcing authority has had the opportunity to investigate as thoroughly as is necessary the circumstances of the accident or occurrence.

25 In the course of the performance of their functions, in particular concerning formal inspections of the workplace and examinations, following notifiable accidents, dangerous occurrences, or notifiable diseases, safety representatives have rights under the Regulations to inspect and take copies of relevant documents which the employer is required to keep in accordance with the Act and other relevant statutory provisions.

Safety representatives should in exercising this right have regard to the reasonableness of time as well as any other circumstances with which the employer may be faced in producing such documents.

26 Where technical matters are involved the appointed safety representatives may find that the necessary expertise is available within the undertaking. The employer and the safety representatives may wish to seek advice from outside the undertaking, for example from appropriate universities or polytechnics. The Commission considers that arrangements should be agreed as to the persons from such institutions who may be called upon. If the representatives wish to have advice from their own technical advisers, such advisers may be called in where this has been agreed in advance with the employer. A copy of any report specifically relating to health or safety matters made to the safety representatives should also be available to the employer.

Obligations of employers

27 Employers have a duty under section 2(2)(c) of the 1974 Act to provide such information, instruction and training as is reasonably practicable, to ensure the health and safety at work of all their employees. Appointed safety representatives will need to be given information and knowledge over and above that nevessary for employees generally to enable them to play an informed part in promoting health and safety at work. The recognised trade unions responsible for appointing safety representatives will make their own arrangements for the information and guidance of their appointed safety representatives as to how they will carry out their functions.

* * *

1 *The Safety Representatives and Safety Committees Regulations, 1976,* prescribe the cases in which an employer shall establish a safety committee. These guidance notes are concerned with such committees.

2 The Commission believe that the detailed arrangements necessary to fulfil this particular requirement of the Act should evolve from discussion and negotiation between employers and the appointed safety representatives who are best able to interpret the needs of the particular workplace or places with which the committee is to concern itself. These guidance notes are, however, issued by the Commission to provide background advice to those involved in the setting up and functioning of such committees. Although the title 'Safety Committees' might suggest functions limited to purely safety matters, the opening words of the Act refer to 'health, safety and welfare of persons at work': and safety committees should therefore be concerned with all relevant aspects of these matters in the working environment.

3 Circumstances will vary greatly between one workplace and another. Now that the Act covers virtually all persons at work, safety committees will be set up to deal with work situations as varied as that between a foundry and a forest or a construction site and a general hospital. Each situation must be looked at carefully by those involved in it and systems for safety, including safety committees, will need to be developed to take full account of all the relevant circumstances.

4 Although the relationship of the safety committee to other works committees is a matter for local organisation, it is necessary to ensure that the work of the safety committee has a separate identity, and that safety matters do not become interposed in the agenda for other meetings.

5 Safety committees are most likely to prove effective where their work is related to a single establishment rather than to a collection of geographically distinct places. There may be a place for safety committees at group or company level for larger organisations; this will apply where relevant decisions are taken at a higher level than the establishment. In general, it should be unnecessary for an employer to appoint duplicate committees for the same workplace, e.g. representing different levels of staff. In large workplaces, however, a single committee may either be too large, or if kept small, may become too remote. In these circumstances, it may be necessary to set up several committees with adequate arrangements for coordination between them.

Objectives and functions of safety committees

6 Under Section 2(7) of the HSW Act, safety committees have the function of keeping under review the measures taken to ensure the health and safety at work of the employees. In carrying out this function safety committees ought to consider the drawing up of agreed objectives or terms of reference.

An objective should be the promotion of cooperation between employers and employees in instigating, developing and carrying out measures to ensure the health and safety at work of the employees.

7 Within the agreed basic objectives certain specific functions are likely to become defined. These might include:

a The study of accident and notifiable diseases statistics and trends, so that reports can be made to management on unsafe and unhealthy conditions and practices, together with recommendations for corrective actions.

b Examination of safety audit reports on a similar basis.

c Consideration of reports and factual information provided by inspectors of the enforcing authority appointed under the HSW Act.

d Consideration of reports which safety representatives may wish to submit.

e Assistance in the development of works safety rules and safe systems of work.

f A watch on the effectiveness of the safety content of employee training.

g A watch on the adequacy of safety and health communication and publicity in the workplace.

h The provision of a link with the appropriate inspectorates of the enforcing authority.

8 In certain instances safety committees may consider it useful to carry out an inspection by the committee itself. But it is management's responsibility to take executive action and to have adequate arrangements for regular and effective checking for health and safety precautions and for ensuring that the declared health and safety policy is being fulfilled. The work of the safety committees should supplement these arrangements; it cannot be a substitute for them.

Membership of safety committees

9 The membership and structure of safety committees should be settled in consultation between management and the trade union

representatives concerned through the use of the normal machinery. The aim should be to keep the total size as reasonably compact as possible and compatible with the adequate representation of the interests of management and all the employees, including safety representatives. The number of management representatives should not exceed the number of employee's representatives.

10 Management representatives should not only include those from line management but such others as works engineers and personnel managers. The supervisory level should also be represented. Management representation should be aimed at ensuring:

a adequate authority to give proper consideration to views and recommendations;

b the necessary knowledge and expertise to provide accurate information to the committee on company policy, production needs and on technical matters in relation to premises, processes, plant machinery and equipment.

11 In undertakings where a company doctor, industrial hygienist or safety officer/adviser is employed, they should be ex-officio members of the safety committee. Other company specialists, such as project engineers, chemists, organisation and methods staff and training officers might be co-opted for particular meetings when subjects on which they have expertise are to be discussed.

12 It should be fully understood that a safety representative is not appointed by the safety committee or vice versa, but the relationship between safety representatives and the safety committee should be a flexible but intimate one. Neither is responsible to, or for, the other. The aim should be to form the most effective organisation appropriate to the particular undertaking, and in particular effective co-ordination between the work of the committee and the safety representatives.

13 It should be the practice for membership of safety committees to be regarded as part of an individual's normal work. As a consequence he or she should suffer no loss of pay through attendance at meetings of safety committees or at other agreed activities such as inspections undertaken by, or on behalf of, such committees.

14 The purpose of studying accidents is to stop them happening again; it is not the committees' business to allocate blame, its job should be:

a To look at the facts in an impartial way.

b To consider what sort of precautions might be taken.

c To make appropriate recommendations.

15 There are advantages in looking at not only legally notifiable cases but also at selected groups or minor injuries. The records for such injuries can yield valuable information if it is extracted and analysed.

16 The committee may well be able to:
a Advise on the appropriateness and adequacy of the rules for safety and health proposed by management and/or
b Draw attention to the needs to establish rules for a particular hazardous work activity or class of operations.
Adherence to these rules will also be secured more easily if employees appreciate the reasons for having them and know that their representatives have been consulted in the making of them.

17 Where written reports have been made by safety representatives following inspections, they may be brought to the attention of the safety committee. In such cases the committee may suggest suitable publicity.

18 An essential condition to the effective working of a safety committee is good communications between management and the committee and between the committee and the employees. In addition, there must be a genuine desire on the part of management to tap the knowledge and experience of its employees and an equally genuine desire on the part of the employees to improve the standards of health and safety at the workplace.

19 The effectiveness of a joint safety committee will depend on the pressure and influence it is able to maintain on all concerned. The following activities could assist in maintaining the impetus of the committee's work:
a Regular meetings with effective publicity of the committee's discussions and recommendations.
b Speedy decisions by management on the committee's recommendations, where necessary promptly translated into action and effective publicity.
c Participation by members of the safety committee in periodical joint inspection.
d Development of ways of involving more employees.

The conduct of safety committees

20 Safety committees should meet as often as necessary. The frequency of meetings will depend on the volume of business, which in turn is likely to depend on local conditions, the size of the workplace, numbers

employed, the kind of work carried out and the degree of risk inherent. Sufficient time should be allowed during each meeting to ensure full discussion of all business.

21 Meetings should not be cancelled ot postponed except in very exceptional circumstances. Where postponement is absolutely necessary an agreed date for the next meeting should be made and announced as soon as possible.

22 The dates of the meetings should as far as possible be arranged well in advance, even to the extent of planning a programme six months or a year ahead. In these circumstances all members of the committee should be sent a personal copy of the programme giving the dates of the meetings. Notices of the dates of meetings should also be published where all employees can see them. A copy of the agenda and any accompanying papers should be sent to all committee members at least one week before each meeting.

23 Committees may wish to draw up additional rules for the conduct of meetings. These might include procedures by which committees might reach decisions.

24 In certain undertakings it might be useful for the safety committee to appoint sub-committees to study particular health and safety problems.

25 Agreed minutes of each meeting should be kept and a personal copy supplied to each member of the committee as soon as possible after the meeting to which they relate and a copy sent to each safety representative appointed for workplaces covered by the committee. A copy of the minutes should be sent to the most senior executive responsible for health and safety; and arrangements should be made to ensure that the Board of Directors is kept informed generally of the work of the committee. An adequate number of copies of the minutes should be displayed, or made available by other means, along with any other information which the employer provides whether required by statute or not.

Appendix 3

The Guidance Notes on Statements of Safety Policy, Organisation and Arrangements

These preliminary guidance notes are given in two parts: Part 1 answers some basic questions on the statutory duty of employers under Section 2(3) of The Health and Safety at Work etc. Act, 1974, *which came into operation on 1 April 1975; Part 2 gives general guidelines to the preparation of a written statement.*

The written policy statement – blueprint for greater safety and better health at work.

The Health and Safety Commission attaches the greatest importance to this requirement of the Act. For each employer it is the blueprint on which his entire health and safety at work policy, organisation and activity are based. It should therefore be drafted clearly so that the entire labour force, management and employed, understands it and knows what its responsibilities are.

The Commission issues this pamphlet to give employers preliminary guidance on the preparation of their written policy statements. In the light of experience the Commission will decide what additional guidance is necessary, and whether at any time codes of practice on written policy statements should be prepared to cover particular industries or circumstances.

Part 1: Some basic questions

What is the law?

Section 2(3) of *The Health and Safety at Work etc. Act, 1974,* says: 'Except in such cases as may be prescribed, it shall be the duty of every employer to prepare and as often as may be appropriate revise a written statement of his general policy with respect to the health and safety at work of his employees and the organisation and arrangements for the time being in force for carrying out that policy, and to bring that statement and any revision of it to the notice of all his employees.'

The Act places on employers the ststutory duty to ensure so far as is reasonably practicable the safety and health and welfare of their employees at work. Section 2(3) of the Act requires every employer (except those prescribed in regulations) to prepare, revise and bring to the notice of his employees, a written statement covering two distinct aspects:

1 His general policy with respect to the health and safety at work of his employees;
2 The organisation and arrangements for carrying out that policy.

Note: In the larger companies or undertakings it might be necessary to deal separately with matters of organisation and with the arrangements for carrying out the general policy.

What is meant by 'employee' and 'employer'?

The Act defines 'employee' as an individual who works under a contract of employment and adds that related expressions shall be construed accordingly. Although the Act does not specifically define an 'employer', it can be taken to mean that an employer is any person, partnership, corporate body or unincorporated association which employs one or more individuals under a contract of employment. All such employers (with the exception of those prescribed in regulations) are to have written policy statements. Where the structure of an enterprise or service, is such that a number of subsidiaries, e.g. in a local authority, under its overall policy of financial control are themselves employers, it may be possible for a common policy statement to be applied, but in such cases each individual employer would need to promulgate it under his own authority as part of his written statement.

Can the employer pass on his responsibility to employees, their appointed/elected safety representatives or to safety committees?

No. The employer cannot pass on his responsibility to his employees or their representatives. It will be sensible for an employer to consult his employees, through their safety representatives and to heed to the advice of the safety committees, where these exist, in order to ensure that the best arrangements and organisations for safety and health are evolved and maintained. Such consultation does not diminish his responsibility; it is clearly part of his greater responsibility under the Health and Safety at Work etc. Act. The Commission will issue separate guidance and draw up the necessary codes of practice concerning safety representatives and safety committees.

Will all written policy statements look alike?

No. The length and content of each written policy statement, like any blueprint, must be specifically prepared to meet the situation of the particular employer. He must thoroughly assess the possible hazards to the health and safety of his employees which might arise in connection with the activities on which they are employed and in the premises or other working area in which they are required to work.

Cannot the Health and Safety Commission draw up a model policy statement?

Although it might be possible to produce some sample statements, it is unlikely that these would suit any individual employer. To provide a model might cause some employers to overlook important health and safety measures which their particular activities and premises demanded. Nevertheless, the Commission feel that certain general guidelines might be helpful and these are set out and discussed in Part 2 of this leaflet. In addition, the Executive and its staff will be prepared to advise individual employers on the compilation of written policy statements. Some employers' organisations, industry associations, professional bodies and similar groups have already issued their own guidance directly related to the activities with which they are concerned, and others may wish to do so.

What needs to be done about existing written policy statements?

They should be examined against the requirements of Section 2(3) of the Act and considered in the light of the advice given in this leaflet as well as that issued by the employer organisations, etc. Some existing written policy statements might be found to meet all these requirements, others might need some adjustment. The re-writing of policy statements should do nothing to disturb satisfactory arrangements already existing between the employer and employees.

Will the written policy statement be all that is required to be communicated to employees?

No. Under Section 2(2)(c) of the Act there is an obligation on every employer to provide such information, instruction, training and supervision as is necessary to ensure, so far as is reasonably practicable, the health and safety at work of his employees. This means, particularly where there are large labour forces and the more complex and potentially dangerous industrial processes, that there is an additional need to publish detailed rules and regulations for particular activities. The written policy statement is not, for instance, the appropriate way of covering detailed rules for the handling of toxic substances, although it would be appropriate for it to refer to the fact that such additional detailed rules were to be maintained and followed. The Commission will issue separate guidance or codes of practice on these additional responsibilities.

How should the written policy statement be brought to the notice of employees?

There may already be adequate methods of written communication between the employer and all individual employees. Otherwise the way in which the statement is brought to their notice might be a suitable point for discussion with workers' representatives. A suitable channel for ensuring adequate communication might be the joint safety committee or any other existing joint consultative arrangement in the firm. Nevertheless the employer must ensure that it is brought to the notice of every employee.

How should the statement be kept up-to-date?

Every employer must recognise his statutory obligation for keeping up-to-date both parts of the written statement. Where, for instance, those named in the second part as responsible for the various aspects of health and safety are replaced, amendments must be published without delay and brought to the notice of all employees. Then as joint safety committees are developed, these should provide the impetus for improving the existing arrangements and such improvements must then be incorporated into the written policy statements. Other improvements will stem from new regulations, codes of practice, guidance issued by the Commission, research into health and safety at work, from accident analysis and investigation, and from developments in the design and safeguarding of machinery. Wherever such improvements or changes affect the written policy of an employer, they should be reflected in its periodic revision.

Part 2: Guidelines to drafting

Structure of written statement

1 Although no model layout could possibly suit all situations, all written policy statements should cover both the essential parts referred to in Section 2(3) of the Act, i.e.

a The General policy.

b The organisation and arrangements for carrying it out. (In larger undertakings these two subjects may best be dealt with in separate sections.)
In some larger or more complex undertakings it may also be better to produce the policy statement in the form of two documents:

a A concise statement of the general policy, organisation and arrangements in a single document which could be distributed to all employees and which would make reference to

b A more detailed document or collection of documents, e.g. including manuals of rules and procedures, which could be held in a central position in each location for all to see on request, or posted where it could be seen by all employees.

Detailing the levels of responsibility

2 The general policy statement should be a declaration of the employer's intent to seek to provide the safest and healthiest working conditions possible and to enlist the support of his employees towards achieving these ends.

3 In the case of employers engaged in a number of different activities or where the operations are geographically widespread, the policy may require formulation at more than one level. The highest management level should lay down in writing the principles of the policy whilst the sub-groups or operational units interpret that policy in a realistic written form to suit the identified needs at the lower levels.

4 The policy statement should give the name and where necessary business address of the Director, Secretary, Manager, or Senior Executive who is responsible for fulfilling the policy, or designate the appointment wherein that responsibility lies. In the case of mines and quarries, reference should be made to the holders of statutory appointments.

5 Whilst the overall policy responsibility for health and safety rests at the highest management level, all individuals at every level will have to accept degrees of responsibility for carrying out that policy. Wherever appropriate key individuals or their appointments should be named and their responsibilities defined. In addition there should be adequate arrangements to cover the absence of personnel with key safety functions.

6 Where functional expertise exists to advise line management, then the relationship of these functions, e.g. safety adviser, chemist, etc. should be made clear and the extent of their functions defined in relation to safety and health.

7 The policy statement should make it clear that the final level of responsibility is that of each and every individual employee.

Safety representatives and joint safety committees

8 Where appropriate, the organisation for joint consultation on health and safety (e.g. joint safety committees) should be described and should be accompanied by a list of persons responsible within the safety organisation, including employees' safety representatives or inspectors (which must be kept up-to-date).

The employer's policy on training and supervision

9 The written statement should ensure that all who are at risk are well aware of the hazards, the reasons for control in working practices and the part that they as individuals have to play in maintaining a safe and healthy working environment.

10 However adequate these written statements, etc. are in themselves the aim will not be achieved without good training and thorough supervision. Employers' policy statements should reflect their determination in these areas. It is, for instance, vital to spell out the supervisor's key role as he is the person on the spot who knows how the job is done. It is equally important for management to consider, and then set down,

the positive steps which are to be taken to train and equip supervisors for this responsibility.

Detailing the hazards

11 Many accidents occur because workpeople do not understand the hazards involved and the precautions that have to be taken. The main hazards should be identified and reference made in the statement to additional rules and regulations which must be observed. It should be quite specific about the employer's policy in respect of certain fairly common hazards, such as the dangers of untidy working areas, the failure to use guards or wear protective clothing, the introduction of new machinery or substances, maintainence work, etc.

12 Procedure should be laid down for accidents, particularly those involving any personal injury, to be systematically recorded by an employer. Also any information, based on expert analyses of accidents or dangerous occurrences, published by employers' federations, safety organisations or the HSC itself, should be monitored by the employer and relevant extracts made pertaining to his particular activity. The employer should regularly present such records and information to all management levels and his safety committee with a view to identifying and providing against new, or hitherto unidentified, hazards and checking on the frequency of occurrence of known hazards.

Further information

13 Additional copies of this document and further information on specific queries are available from local offices of the Health and Safety Executive, or from the Health and Safety Executive Baynards House, 1, Chepstow Place, London W2 4TF. Tel: 01-229 3456, Ext. 688.

Index